Everyday Morality

AN INTRODUCTION TO APPLIED ETHICS

Mike W. Martin

CHAPMAN COLLEGE

Wadsworth Publishing Company

BELMONT, CALIFORNIA
A DIVISION OF WADSWORTH, INC.

PHILOSOPHY EDITOR: *Kenneth King*
EDITORIAL ASSISTANT: *Cheri Peterson*
PRODUCTION EDITOR: *Deborah Cogan*
MANAGING DESIGNER: *Stephen Rapley*
PRINT BUYER: *Barbara Britton*
TEXT AND COVER DESIGNER: *Luba Yudovich*
COPY EDITOR: *Thomas Briggs*
COMPOSITOR: *G&S Typesetters, Inc.*
SIGNING REPRESENTATIVE: *Joann Ludovici*
COVER ART: *"Differing Views," by James Valerio, 1980–81.*
© *Frumkin/Adams Gallery, New York.*

Printed in the United States of America   49

1 2 3 4 5 6 7 8 9 10———93 92 91 90 89

Library of Congress Cataloging-in-Publication Data

Martin, Mike W., 1946–
  Everyday morality.

  Bibliography: p.
  Includes index.
  1. Ethics.   I. Title.
BJ1012.M365   1988   170   88-17432
ISBN 0-534-09738-3

Dedicated to Sonia Renée Martin and Nicole Marie Martin

Contents

Preface   xv

PART ONE   *Character, Conduct, and Relationships*   2

1   Moral Reasoning and Applied Ethics   5

A Student's Dilemma   5
Sartre on Authenticity   6
Is Authenticity Enough?   7
Choosing Moralities   9
Morality and Moral Concern   10
"Ethics"   12
Philosophical Ethics: General and Applied   13
Summary   14
Discussion Topics   15
Suggested Readings   16

2   Creativity, Autonomy, and Moral Growth   18

Moral Creativity   19
Socrates: Intellectual Humility and Honesty   19
King: Love and Justice Through Nonviolence   21
Stanton: Women's Dignity and Self-Development   22
Gilligan and Kohlberg: Caring Versus Justice   24

Two Theories of Moral Development   26
Moral Growth and Aims in Studying Ethics   30
Summary   32
Discussion Topics   33
Suggested Readings   34

3   Theories of Virtue   35

Virtues as Character Traits   35
Human Nature and Virtue Theories   37
Plato: Good Character as Moral Health   37
   Division of the Mind into Three Parts   38
   Plato and Freud   39
Aristotle: Rational Emotions and Desires   40
   The Doctrine of the Mean   40
   Moral Prudence   43
Difficulties with Greek Ethics   44
Aquinas: Religious Virtues   45
Hume: Benevolence and Sympathy   46
From Theory to Practice   47
MacIntyre: Self-Knowledge and Social Goods   47
   Life as a Narrative Quest   48
Pincoffs: Choices Among Persons   49
   Instrumental and Noninstrumental Virtues   50
Summary   52
Discussion Topics   53
Suggested Readings   54

4   Theories of Right Action   56

   Lying   56
Duty Ethics: Kant and Respect for Persons   57
Duty Ethics: Ross and Prima Facie Duties   59
Rights Ethics: Locke and Liberty Rights   61
Rights Ethics: Melden and Welfare Rights   62
Utilitarianism: Mill and Act-Utilitarianism   63
Utilitarianism: Brandt and Rule-Utilitarianism   66
Which Theory Is Best?   67
Summary   69

Discussion Topics   70
Suggested Readings   71

PART TWO   *Self-Respect and Integrity*   74

5 Harming Oneself   79

Duties Not to Harm Oneself   79
Masochism   81
Servility   83
Irrational Shame and Guilt   84
Drug Abuse   87
Summary   89
Discussion Topics   90
Suggested Readings   92

6 Self-Deception   93

Definitions and Tactics   94
Paradoxes   95
Responsibility   97
Self-Respect, Self-Esteem, and Immorality   99
Summary   103
Discussion Topics   104
Suggested Readings   105

7 Weakness of Will   107

Loss of Self-Control: Occasional Versus Habitual   107
Paradoxes   109
   Value Judgments as Knowledge or Beliefs   109
   Value Judgments as Commitments ² 110
   Value Judgments as Entailing Wants   111
Inner Conflict and Self-Respect   113
Excuses   115
Summary   118
Discussion Topics   119
Suggested Readings   121

8   Courage   122

Acts and Patterns of Action   122
Courage, Cowardice, and Fear   124
A Definition of Courageous Actions   125
The Good of Courage   127
Integrity, Fanaticism, and Hypocrisy   129
Summary   130
Discussion Topics   131
Suggested Readings   131

PART THREE   *Respect for Others*   134

9   Rape and Sexual Harassment   139

Coercion and the Right to Personal Autonomy   139
Cruelty   141
Motivations to Rape   142
What Is Wrong with Rape?   143
Date Rape Versus Consent   143
Sexual Harassment   145
   The Workplace   146
   Academia   146
Summary   148
Discussion Topics   149
Suggested Readings   150

10   Prejudice   152

Overt Versus Covert Prejudice   152
Stereotypes   153
Language   155
Gender Roles   157
Summary   160
Discussion Topics   160
Suggested Readings   162

11 Ridicule, Rudeness, and Snobbery 163

Ridicule Through Bigoted Humor 163
The Ethics of Humor 164
Definitions of Humor 166
Rudeness 167
Snobbery 168
Summary 170
Discussion Topics 170
Suggested Readings 171

12 Envy and Jealousy 173

Envy as a Vice 173
Particular Envy 174
General Envy 175
"Ressentiment" and Self-Deceiving Envy 177
Creative Responses to Envy 179
Jealousy 180
Evaluating Jealousy 181
Summary 182
Discussion Topics 183
Suggested Readings 184

PART FOUR *Sexual Morality* 186

13 Sex and Love 189

Definitions of Love 190
Arguments for Sex Without Love 192
Arguments for Sex with Love 193
True Love: Obligations or Ideals? 195
Summary 196
Discussion Topics 197
Suggested Readings 199

14 Marriage and Adultery   200

Is Marriage a Moral Issue?   200
Potential Drawbacks to Marriage   201
    Outside Control   201
    Sexual Confinement   202
    Sexual Ownership   203
    Psychological Constriction   203
Extramarital Affairs: Two Cases   205
A Defense of Extramarital Affairs   206
Summary   208
Discussion Topics   209
Suggested Readings   210

15 Homosexuality and Homophobia   212

Closets and Coming Out   213
The Reproductive Purpose of Sex   214
Other Senses of "Unnatural"   216
Promiscuity   218
Homophobia and Sexual Tastes   219
Summary   220
Discussion Topics   221
Suggested Readings   222

16 Pornography and Fantasy   223

A Definition of Pornography   224
Examples of Pornography   225
Fantasy   227
    Fantasy as Morally Neutral   228
    Fantasy as Sometimes Immoral   228
    A Synthesis of Opposing Views   230
Obscenity   231
Summary   233
Discussion Topics   234
Suggested Readings   235

PART FIVE *Caring Relationships* 238

17 Parents and Children 241

An Example of a Parent-Child Relationship 241
Parental Responsibility: Respect Versus Abuse 243
Definition of Child Abuse 244
Filial Duties and Gratitude 247
　Duties 247
　Gratitude 248
Love 250
Summary 251
Discussion Topics 251
Suggested Readings 252

18 Friendship 254

An Example of Friendship 254
Definition of Friendship 256
The Value of Friendship 257
Moral Limits on Friendship 258
Summary 260
Discussion Topics 260
Suggested Readings 261

19 Work 263

Examples of Two Workers 263
Alienation and Work Ethics 265
Collegiality 267
Loyalty 268
Altruism and Career Choice 270
Summary 272
Discussion Topics 273
Suggested Readings 274

20 Community   276

An Example of Community Service   277
Individualism and Community   278
How Much Should We Give?   279
Generosity and Supererogation   281
To Whom Should We Give?   283
Summary   284
Discussion Topics   284
Suggested Readings   285

21 Animals   287

Animals as Companions   287
Attitudes Toward Animals   289
Do Animals Have Rights?   291
Extreme and Moderate Views of the Moral Status of Animals   292
Caring for Pets   294
Summary   295
Discussion Topics   296
Suggested Readings   297

Notes   299
Index   312

Preface

This book is an introduction to applied ethics, that is, to the philosophy of morality as it applies to practical moral needs. It focuses on the moral concerns of everyday life rather than on general social issues. Moral character is explored in all its dimensions: virtues, vices, attitudes, emotions, commitments, and personal relationships, in addition to right and wrong conduct.

Applied moral philosophy, as approached here, seeks to clarify, organize, and enrich our grasp of practical moral interests. It seeks to sharpen the ideas that we use as tools in coping responsibly with our daily lives. And it explores contrasting moral perspectives that increase moral understanding.

I have tried to maintain contact with the wellspring of common moral experience, or at least overlapping moral understanding, that enables us to discuss moral issues with one another. I have also attempted to heed Molière's injunction to "humanize your talk, and speak to be understood" (the counsel he offers to writers in *The Critique of the School for Wives*). The aim is to stimulate personal reflection and group dialogue rather than to offer solutions. This remains true even in places where I set forth my own views instead of merely summarizing those of others.

The book contains twenty-one chapters organized by unifying themes into five parts. Discussion topics and suggested readings are provided at the end of each chapter. Some of the readings discussed and recommended are works of literature and social science, reflecting the interdisciplinary approach present in much of the book.

In writing this book I received financial support in 1984 and 1985 from an Arnold L. and Lois S. Graves Award from Pomona College, administered under the auspices of the American Council of Learned Societies. Chapman College gave me a sabbatical leave and a reduced teaching load to allow me to work on the manuscript.

Shannon Snow Martin shaped the book in many ways, suggesting topics and illustrations, discussing arguments and approaches, and providing insights. My students provided a valuable stimulus, as did my colleagues Virginia Warren and Joseph Runzo. Anita Storck displayed an array of virtues in helping with the typing and in contributing to a supportive work environment.

I am deeply grateful to Wadsworth editor Ken King for his guidance and encouragement. I would also like to acknowledge the reviewers who provided comments that proved enormously helpful in improving the manuscript: Shane Andre, California State University, Long Beach; John Arthur, Harvard University Law School; Joseph Des Jardins, Villanova University; Ronald Duska, Rosemont College; Thomas K. Flint, North Idaho College; Ruth B. Heizer, Georgetown College; Craig Ihara, California State University, Fullerton; Tom Moody, California State College, San Bernardino; Ellen Suckiel, University of California, Santa Cruz; and Joel Zimbelman, California State University, Chico.

I especially wish to thank my wife, Shannon Snow Martin, and my mother, Ruth Lochhead Martin, for their support and for their love.

Everyday Morality

AN INTRODUCTION
TO APPLIED ETHICS

PART ONE

Character, Conduct, and Relationships

What is a good man like? How can we make ourselves morally better? Can we make ourselves morally better? These are questions the philosopher should try to answer.[1]

Iris Murdoch

We are often more at ease discussing the global moral issues affecting society at large than we are exploring the moral texture of everyday life. Why is that? Larger social issues such as euthanasia, capital punishment, world hunger, genetic engineering, and nuclear deterrence evoke our genuine concern, and sometimes they require our immediate action. Because we lack the authority to settle these issues, however, we can maintain a comfortable distance between us and them.

In contrast, personal responsibility for the moral aspects of day-to-day living is more direct, persistent, and urgent. Each day, fundamental moral considerations affect our lives in commonplace ways. Perhaps today we told or laughed at a joke expressing sexist attitudes we would eagerly disavow. Or maybe we were sufficiently angry at a friend to harbor sweet fantasies of revenge that, if implemented, would inflict extraordinarily cruel retribution. Possibly we were envious of a co-worker and expressed the envy in a way that undermined mutual respect. We may have failed to respond to an act of kindness with the gratitude dictated by common decency. Perhaps we abused alcohol, drugs, or food with a compulsiveness that made us wonder if we respected ourselves anymore.

Social morality concerns global issues about the kinds of social policies and institutions that are desirable. *Everyday morality,* by contrast, concerns the kinds of persons we aspire to be in our daily relationships with others.

Are we grateful and generous, or envious and filled with spite? Are we conscientious and concerned with helping others, or weak of will and readily self-deceived about the good we can do? Are we trying to become more sensitive to the suffering of other people and animals, or gradually hardening ourselves through indifference and vanity? Do we strive to be honest and open, or to avoid hurting others' feelings, especially when we cannot do both? Do we genuinely respect ourselves and other people?

Words like *generous, conscientious,* and *honest* refer to morally good character traits—*virtues.* Words like *envious, insensitive,* and *vain* refer to morally bad character traits—*vices.** *Character* is simply the pattern of virtues and vices revealed in the life and relationships of an individual.

Some dictionaries define morality in terms of right and wrong actions, emphasizing conduct over character. Until recently, philosophers also tended to focus on conduct in their attempts to define morality. This book seeks to give balanced attention to character and conduct, as well as to the relationships in which they are embedded. Accordingly, our first task is to understand the connections between good persons, right action, and meaningful relationships.

Chapter 1 introduces some of the complexities of moral reasoning about character, conduct, and personal relationships. Morality is defined and distinguished from ethics, which is the philosophical study of morality. Chapter 2 explores the role of moral creativity and autonomy in shaping character and resolving dilemmas. Being morally autonomous means reasoning and acting on the basis of moral concern, sometimes in creative ways. The study of ethics strengthens moral autonomy, given a background of earlier moral development. Chapter 3 introduces several major theories about virtue, and Chapter 4 sketches the main theories about right action. These key concepts and theories will be used throughout the book.

---

* In some contexts the words *virtue* and *vice* have an old-fashioned ring, perhaps reminding us of a preoccupation with chastity and certain stuffy or priggish forms of behavior. In other contexts *vice* brings to mind vice squads fighting drug addiction and prostitution. We shall ignore these connotations.

CHAPTER 1

*Moral Reasoning
and Applied Ethics*

Morality is complex. It involves many different reasons for being a certain kind of person, maintaining certain kinds of relationships with others, and acting in particular ways. These reasons on occasion come into conflict with each other. *Moral dilemmas* are situations where two or more moral reasons come into conflict and point to different courses of action.

We will begin by discussing one moral dilemma in detail in order to illustrate not only the complexity of morality but also the possibility of reasoning in the midst of that complexity. In addition, the dilemma illustrates how conduct both shapes and expresses character. The discussion of the dilemma is then used as a springboard from which to offer preliminary definitions of morality and ethics (the philosophical study of morality).

A Student's Dilemma

During World War II the French philosopher Jean-Paul Sartre (1905–1980) lived in Nazi-occupied Paris. One of his students came to him seeking advice about whether to leave France in order to join the Free French Forces fighting Hitler from their headquarters in England.

> His father was quarrelling with his mother and was also inclined to be a "collaborator"; his elder brother had been killed in the German offensive of 1940 and this young man, with a sentiment somewhat primitive but generous, burned to avenge him. His mother was living alone with him,

deeply afflicted by the semi-treason of his father and by the death of her eldest son, and her one consolation was in this young man. But he, at this moment, had the choice between going to England to join the Free French Forces or of staying near his mother and helping her to live. He fully realized that this woman lived only for him and that his disappearance—or perhaps his death—would plunge her into despair. He also realized that, concretely and in fact, every action he performed on his mother's behalf would be sure of effect in the sense of aiding her to live, whereas anything he did in order to go and fight would be an ambiguous action which might vanish like water into sand and serve no purpose. For instance, to set out for England he would have to wait indefinitely in a Spanish camp on the way through Spain; or, on arriving in England or in Algiers he might be put into an office to fill up forms.[1]*

Sartre on Authenticity

What should the student do? As Sartre points out, familiar maxims fail to provide ready-made answers to his dilemma. The injunction to love one's neighbor, for example, does not tell us whether the greater love is in staying with the mother or in fighting the humanitarian cause against fascism. The Golden Rule does not help either. It requires that we impartially do unto others as we would have them do unto us or, conversely, not do unto others as we would not have them do unto us. But impartiality provides no resolution to the dilemma. Also, the principle that we should respect people does not point in one direction more than the other.

Should the student simply trust his feelings? This view is reflected in popular slogans such as "Go with your feelings" and "It's right if it feels right." But the student has strong feelings drawing him in different directions. Moreover, Sartre asks, how can the mere strength of a feeling justify an action? To use an extreme example, rapists have strong feelings that are hardly self-justifying. Another problem is that a primary way of measuring the strength of feelings is how we end up acting. Our question, however, is not how the student will act but how he ought to act.

Sartre suggests that, even though there is not just one right decision in this case, there is a right way to go about making the decision. That is, morality cannot tell the student *what* act is right, but it can tell him *how* he ought to proceed in making his decision. Simply stated, the decision should be made in an *authentic* way, in a way that will make the student an authentic person on that occasion.

---

*Reprinted by permission of Methuen & Co.

Authenticity is the only virtue that Sartre endorses, but it embraces several more specific and familiar virtues. It requires being *autonomous* in the sense of exercising one's own reasoning rather than passively letting events or other people direct one's life. It requires *intellectual honesty* in facing all the facts squarely, including the fact that one is free to make the decision autonomously. It requires *courage* in resisting the temptation to deceive oneself by ignoring the painful implications of one's decision or the anguish involved in making it. Finally, it requires being *responsible* in the sense of accepting the consequences of the decision. Because responsibility may require responding to criticisms by other people, one should act in a way that one believes is permissible for anyone confronting a similar dilemma.

Is Authenticity Enough?

Sartre's discussion of authenticity is insightful. It encourages us to take more seriously the virtues of intellectual honesty and courage in dealing with facts. It enriches our sense of freedom and responsibility in conducting our lives and maintaining our relationships. And it suggests that creativity is important in shaping our character and personal ideals (this idea will be explored more fully in Chapter 2). But should authenticity be the sole value used in making a decision? Authenticity is important, but it is not enough. In fact, we can only make sense of the student's dilemma by reference to further moral values.

Sartre has described two options, but surely the student has many more choices. Why not take the pressure off himself by going on a month's vacation to Australia? Why not, after anguished reflection, head for California to become a beachcomber? If he is depressed, why not kill himself, and perhaps put his mother out of her agony as well? It seems quite possible that such decisions could be made authentically. But they would be wrong—objectively wrong in the sense that good moral reasons forbid them.

You may be wondering about Sartre's final advice to the student: "You are free, therefore choose—that is to say, invent."[2] Sartre saw no objectively binding moral reasons that the student had to weigh in making his decision.* Justifiable reasons are possible, he thought, only if there is a God to provide them: "Dostoevsky once wrote 'If God did not exist, everything would be permitted.' . . . Everything is indeed permitted if God does not exist."[3] And Sartre did not believe in the existence of God. The student must simply make a choice; that choice will create the values he will live by. Hence, for Sartre,

---

*Although Sartre favors authenticity, he denies that even it can be objectively justified. In *Being and Nothingness* he claims "that nothing, absolutely nothing, justifies me in adopting this or that particular value, this or that particular scale of values."[4]

values are created through actions, rather than actions being guided in advance by objectively justifiable values.

This is backwards! Notice that the student had a problem only because there were moral reasons making objective claims on him. His anguish, uncertainty, and need for advice all arise because these reasons point to opposite paths.

The good reasons for staying with his mother are clear: to help her in a time of vulnerability and dependence, and to do so as an expression of the love, compassion, and gratitude emerging from a lifetime relationship with her. The valid reasons for leaving his mother to go to war are equally clear: to oppose fascism, to avenge his brother's unjust killing, to make reparation on behalf of his family for his father's collaboration with the Nazis. The student need not "invent" moral reasons to live by; he already recognizes (or should recognize) the moral reasons that create his dilemma.

What other advice might we offer to help the student in weighing the conflicting reasons? Let us first acknowledge that Sartre may be correct in suggesting there is no *one* right solution to the dilemma that every reasonable person would have to choose. That is not because all authentic acts are permissible, however; our claim here is that some are not. Rather, it is because there are two sets of compelling moral reasons and there may be no single permissible way of assigning priorities to them. Thus, staying with the mother and going to war may both be morally permissible acts.

Nevertheless, a good moral counselor might have helped the student to think through all the morally relevant aspects of the situation. For example, had he explored the possibility that friends or neighbors could support his mother while he was away? Had he fully discussed the matter with his mother to be sure how she felt and to see if her feelings might be modified as they explored the problem together? Had he talked with someone who could provide reliable information about his likely contribution to the Free French Forces?

Keeping in mind Sartre's own emphasis on avoiding self-deception, we can ask whether the student was fully honest in thinking about the situation and his motives. To what extent was he motivated simply by a desire for revenge, and could that desire, by itself, justify the suffering he would cause his mother? Were there nobler reasons for fighting that could unite him with his mother's own deepest commitments and so bring her solace? (Recall that the mother was "deeply afflicted by the semi-treason" of her husband.)

Perhaps answers to some of these questions might identify one course of action as preferable for this student, all things considered. In any case, despite what Sartre recommends, we need more than just intellectual honesty in confronting facts; we also need sensitivity in identifying and weighing relevant moral reasons.

Choosing Moralities

The student's dilemma is a momentous one. It evokes our interest in part because it brings to mind other decisions that dramatically shape our lives: decisions about love relationships, about colleges, about careers. Sartre suggests the dilemma also involves picking one type of morality over another. The student, he writes, was "hesitating between two kinds of morality; on the one side the morality of sympathy, or personal devotion and, on the other side, a morality of wider scope but of more debatable validity" centered on broader commitments to his nation.

This is an intriguing suggestion. It raises the possibility of shaping one's life around selected virtues and commitments that are emphasized over others. We shall explore this possibility in the next section; but first let us note a few cautions.

Sartre implies that the student must make an exclusive, either-or selection between two radically different moral outlooks: a morality of personal devotion based on sympathy and a morality of wider social commitments. In picking the one he must give up the other. Keep in mind, however, that considerations of personal devotion impinge on both sides of the student's dilemma. Loyalty to his mother dictates that he stay home, but loyalty to his brother and to his family's honor (betrayed by his father) dictates that he go to war. As we noted earlier, the anguish he feels over the choice between staying with his mother and fighting fascism reveals his deep commitment to a morality encompassing both personal devotion *and* wider social loyalties. Only such a dual devotion could explain why he experiences conflicting moral obligations.

Furthermore, whichever way he decides to act, these dual loyalties can and should remain strong. If he goes to war, he must not betray his mother by freezing his heart toward her as he seeks his revenge. And if he stays with her, he must not rationalize away his responsibility to oppose fascism, nor must he rule out the possibility that some form of opposition will be available to him at home. Even his hopes both for his mother's well-being and for the success of the war effort will be crucial in shaping his character. Thus, giving priority to one loyalty on this occasion does not require removing the other from his moral outlook.

Nor is the student even forced to decide that one loyalty is always more important than the other. Perhaps the next time these loyalties come into conflict, in a different situation at a different time, there may be good reasons for assigning a different priority to them. Morality is complex because it involves many kinds of reasons, because the reasons can conflict, *and* because the reasons often cannot be assigned any absolute hierarchy of importance.

Morality and Moral Concern

As the breadth of the previous discussion has tried to show, morality deals with the kinds of persons we should be and become, with the kinds of relationships we should have, and with the way we should act. Morality encompasses, but is hardly reducible to, such familiar rules as respect your parents, be fair, don't lie, don't steal, don't cheat, keep your promises, and so on.

As we saw in discussing the student's dilemma, the point of moral reasoning is not simply to act correctly but to live through the dilemma with moral concern. Moral concern involves *appreciating* certain aspects of the situation. It requires *sensitivity* to people as morally significant creatures who sometimes deserve esteem, compassion, and support and who experience guilt, shame, vulnerability, and despair. It requires *understanding* our emotions and commitments in a way that reveals their moral significance and that is *responsive* to the worth of others. This appreciation, sensitivity, understanding, and responsiveness are not mere means to "doing the right thing." Instead they constitute our *character*—the moral substance of who we are and how we relate to others.

Morality concerns what we morally should become, how we morally should relate to others, how we morally should act. It is not concerned with other kinds of "shoulds," such as what should be done in order to start a car, to write a computer program, to become a famous lawyer, or to gain power in relationships with other people. Our definition is circular and somewhat empty, however, because in defining morality using the term *morally should,* we have not really defined it at all.

Providing a comprehensive definition of morality turns out to be a complicated task. The theories about virtue and right action that we examine later in this chapter attempt to provide such a comprehensive definition. For now, we offer only a rough preliminary characterization.

"Morally should" refers to what is required or recommended by moral reasons, and we have suggested that moral reasons derive from both virtues and principles of conduct. Thus, we can define morality through the use of examples. How do we determine how the student should act? By determining what is required by such virtues as honesty, courage, authenticity, benevolence, compassion, gratitude, integrity, and justice. Moral reasons also have to do with principles of conduct such as respecting people (including oneself) and sympathetically caring about the needs of other conscious creatures.

According to this characterization, selfishness or excessive preoccupation with ourselves is incompatible with morality. Selfishness is different from legitimate self-interest, that is, morally permissible concern for our own interests. Selfish people pursue their own interests at the expense of others or in callous indifference to them. Thus, a decision to ignore both the mother and the fight against fascism by becoming a beachcomber in California would have been selfish because it violated moral limits to the pursuit of self-interest.

In addition to placing limits on the pursuit of self-interest, moral reasons also place limits on laws and customs. Sartre and his student, who both lived under Nazi rule during World War II, were justified by morality in resisting that rule. Indeed, moral reasons obligated them to help overthrow Hitler's patently unjust system of laws. Similar statements could be made about South African apartheid laws and about nineteenth-century American laws that institutionalized racism.

This explains what is wrong with saying that morality is "relative" to given societies, even though there is also some truth in this familiar assertion. Certainly, laws and customs are often morally *relevant* factors in deciding how we should act. For example, in England we ought to drive on the left side of the road in order not to kill people, and when entering a traditional Japanese home, we should take off our shoes as a sign of respect. It is important to understand, however, that morality is not reducible to laws and customs. We might even say that laws and customs are relative to morality in that they are evaluated in light of moral reasons, and they are often relevant to deciding how to apply moral reasons to our dealings with foreign cultures.

Clarifying the relationship between morality and religion will round out this brief characterization of morality. Moral reasons are not reducible to religious reasons. In discussing the student's dilemma, we dealt with moral reasons that were compelling independent of any particular religious beliefs. Such virtues as personal loyalty, gratitude, compassion, honesty, courage, justice, and other moral factors made claims on the student in their own right, regardless of whether or not they were embedded in a religious view of the world.

For many people religious beliefs provide additional supportive motives for responding to moral reasons. Some of these motives are admirable, such as the love for and emulation of a morally perfect being in whom one has faith. Some religious motives are of more debatable quality, such as a preoccupation with damnation or a desire to outshine other people in God's eyes. But the essential point here is that moral reasons make their own distinctive appeal to us—or they should!

In fact, it makes good sense to say that moral reasons would also be appreciated by a morally perfect being. This point was made by Socrates (470–399 B.C.) as recorded by his student Plato (428–348 B.C.). Socrates posed the question, "Is what is holy holy because the gods approve it, or do they approve it because it is holy?"[5] Let us rephrase the question, replacing the allusion to many gods (polytheism) with a reference to one god (monotheism), and assuming that God exists: "What makes right acts right? Are they right simply because God commands them, and for no other reason? Or does God command them because God (as a morally perfect being) sees they are morally right?" For example, is rape immoral only because God forbids it, so that if there were no God, it would not be immoral? Or does God forbid rape precisely because God (like you and I) sees that it is wrong?

Socrates thought it obvious that moral reasons are not created by God, but that instead God would recognize and appreciate moral reasons as warranting divine commands. (It's just that God would have perfect recognition and appreciation of them, unlike fallible humans.) Thus, Socrates would reject Sartre's claim that only God could make possible objective moral reasoning.

"Ethics"

When scientists study morality, they seek to describe the beliefs and conduct of individuals and cultures, as well as to explain why these beliefs and conduct arise. The tasks of describing and causally explaining are part of psychology, sociology, anthropology, and sociobiology (the study of genetic origins of social behavior and attitudes). Although we will distinguish between the philosophical and the scientific study of morality, note that these fields are interrelated and mutually enriching. In fact, from time to time we will draw upon psychology, as, for example, when we discuss moral development in the next chapter.

Ethics, as we shall use the term, is the philosophical study of morality; it is also called moral philosophy. Before explaining what is meant by philosophical ethics, we should take note of other senses of the word *ethics* in everyday language.

Sometimes the word is used to classify moral issues, experiences, judgments, and so on, identifying them as a category of human interest distinct from law, religion, art, science, economics, or sports. In this sense, for example, an ethical controversy is one involving moral reasons, and an ethical judgment is one using moral concepts or backed by moral reasons.

In another sense *ethics* refers to the particular moral outlook of a group or an individual. Thus, we speak of the Protestant work ethic, the ethics of Albert Schweitzer, and the ethics of Victorian England. This usage relates to the Greek work *ethos,* which means customs or characteristic habits (just as the Latin root of *morals* is *mores,* meaning customs).

In yet another sense *ethical* has strongly positive connotations, referring to admirable character and morally correct judgments and acts. This honorific or praising meaning applies when we say that a friend acted ethically or when we call Abraham Lincoln an ethical person. The intended contrast is with unethical conduct or immoral character.

Philosophical Ethics: General and Applied

As a study of morality, philosophical ethics embraces four main goals or interests: (1) *clarification* of important moral ideas and issues by defining and investigating their implications; (2) a *comprehensive vision* of ideas and insights by uncovering the connections that place them in proper perspective; (3) *critical assessment* of moral claims by testing their truth, justification, and adequacy through argument; and (4) *moral guidance,* sometimes via simple principles, but more often through improved practical judgment about what we should aspire to be, what forms of relationships are desirable, and how we should seek those ends.

Philosophical ethics has two main branches: general ethics and applied ethics. (See Figure 1.1.) *General ethics* deals with the more abstract theoretical issues. For example, it seeks to develop comprehensive theories about virtues and right action of the sort we shall examine in Chapters 3 and 4, respectively. *Applied ethics* focuses on the practical considerations of morally concerned people. Wherever helpful, applied ethics integrates the comprehensive theories of general ethics, but its aim is practical clarity and guidance rather than the development and testing of general theories.

The distinction between general and applied ethics is a rough one. Sometimes it is more a matter of style and approach based on the applied ethicist's goal to communicate effectively with a particular audience, such as the members of a profession. This orientation to the concerns and needs of specific audiences has led to entire new specializations in applied ethics in such diverse fields as medicine, business, law, engineering, environmental policies, and the media and journalism.

Finally, we can introduce one additional broad distinction within applied ethics itself. *Applied social ethics* focuses on moral issues related to social practices, professions, and institutions (including political institutions). *Applied everyday ethics* represents philosophy's response to the practical needs of individuals in shaping their characters, maintaining desirable forms of relationships, and exercising responsible conduct in daily activities.

As presented in this book, applied everyday ethics is a very practical matter indeed. It is the activity of clarifying, organizing, and occasionally refining moral ideas with the goal of enriching everyday moral experience and judgment. Hopefully that enrichment will have a significant effect on our lives. But the relationship between studying ethics and moral growth is complicated, and we will discuss it further in the next chapter. For now, let us conclude with a metaphor that reflects much of our approach in this book.

Each of us, in applying ethics to our lives, can be compared to a caretaker in charge of a collection of tools.[6] Most of our tools are moral concepts and insights drawn from our culture and our previous moral experience, although new ones occasionally have to be created for special tasks. The job of the care-

FIGURE 1.1 *Branches of Philosophical Ethics*

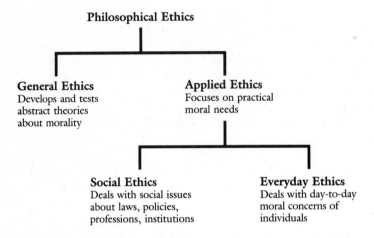

taker is to keep the tools in good repair by cleaning and sharpening and to arrange them for a variety of practical purposes. Some of the more complicated tools will require explanations about their proper use. The caretaker, however, must also use the tools effectively in a variety of settings and for a variety of practical purposes.

Some of us may be adept at keeping the tools clean, in good repair, and properly ordered in relation to the other tools yet have difficulty in applying the tools to practical tasks. Others of us may be less conscientious in caring for the tools but more effective in applying them. The study of ethics can improve our ability to apply these moral tools, although that ability needs to be exercised on the basis of moral commitment beyond what classroom studies have to offer.

Summary

Morality concerns desirable forms of character, relationships, and conduct. Moral reasons derive from the worth of people (and other conscious beings) that makes them worthy of respect and consideration. These reasons are not reducible to matters of narrow self-interest, law and custom, or religion. They are linked closely with virtues, that is, with good character traits like honesty, compassion, and justice. As such, they require more than being authentic (which is a combination of thinking for oneself, intellectual honesty and courage, and responsibly acknowledging one's freedom).

Applying moral reasoning to everyday living becomes complex because moral reasons (1) are numerous; (2) can conflict, thereby creating moral dilemmas; (3) cannot be placed in a simple hierarchy of relative importance; and (4) may or may not evoke action, even when they are understood and appreciated.

In studying morality, philosophical ethics has four aims: clarity, comprehensive perspective, critical assessment, and guidance. The main branches of philosophical ethics are general ethics and applied ethics, and branching off from applied ethics are social ethics and everyday ethics.

DISCUSSION TOPICS

1. Imagine that the student in Sartre's example had chosen to go away to college in order to become a scientist, hoping to aid both his mother and his country after the war. Describe variations on this decision that portray the student as (a) inauthentic, (b) authentic, (c) selfish, (d) fully sensitive morally.

2. Can moral reasons correctly be defined as those reasons that are always most important and that should override all other kinds of reasons, such as those concerning art, science, and self-interest? In answering this question, imagine several situations in which moral reasons come into conflict with other kinds of reasons. For example, consider a person at the scene of an accident who refuses to help in order to stand back and observe the "aesthetic" spectacle of movements, colors, and sounds. Also consider the artist who decides that his art is more important than his responsibilities to his family. Such is the popular (though not entirely accurate) image of the Post-Impressionist painter Paul Gauguin (1848–1903), who left his family in Paris to devote himself to the study of art. Could Gauguin's very important contributions to art outweigh his neglect of his family?

3. According to the book of Genesis, Abraham was convinced that he heard God command him to kill his son Isaac as a sacrifice. Without asking any questions, Abraham proceeded to obey the command.

   > God did tempt Abraham, and said unto him. . . . Take now thy son, thine only son Isaac, whom thou lovest, and get thee into the land of Moriah; and offer him there for a burnt offering upon one of the mountains which I will tell thee of. . . . And they came to the place which God had told him of; and Abraham built an altar there, and laid the wood in order and bound Isaac his son, and laid him on the altar upon the wood. And Abraham stretched forth his hand, and took the knife to slay his son.[7]

   Hitchcock never set a more chilling scene. Fortunately, an angel intervenes, telling Abraham to replace Isaac with a sacrificial ram.

   Sartre suggests that Abraham should have been more self-critical about interpreting the initial voice he believed was from God telling him to sacrifice Isaac.[8] We might also suggest that a morally perfect being would not command such a thing, not even to test Abraham's faith. But the philosopher Søren Kierkegaard

(1813–1855) held a different view.[9] He thought that God might well override human morality for some higher, divine purpose. Kierkegaard called this the "teleological suspension of the ethical," that is, the transcending of morality for some higher *telos*, which in Greek means purpose. How do you interpret and respond to the Abraham–Isaac story?

4. Religious people sometimes speak of God as the source of values, but scripture dealing with the world's creation does not usually speak of God as inventing values. For example, in the Genesis account of creation, after God creates the universe, he *sees* that it is good: "God saw everything that he had made, and behold it was very good."[10] Relate this quotation to Socrates' question, "Is what is holy holy because the gods approve it, or do they approve it because it is holy?"

5. Evaluate the following arguments:
   a. Beliefs about morality differ from culture to culture. Therefore, what is right in one culture is wrong in another culture. (Be sure to distinguish "what is right/wrong" from "what is believed to be right/wrong.")
   b. Beliefs about morality differ from society to society. Therefore, what is right for one society may not be right for another society. (In your answer distinguish between two senses of "right for a society": meaning morally justified in the society or believed to be justified in the society.)
   c. Some Eskimos and American Indians once practiced the custom of leaving their elders to die when they could no longer travel with the tribe to fresh hunting grounds. Because this was the accepted custom, their conduct was morally permissible.
   d. Sometimes what is morally right (permissible or obligatory) in one society may be wrong in another society. This is not merely because customs differ, but because the customs may be morally justified in one situation and not in another. For example, economic conditions are sometimes relevant in evaluating the customs of a society. When the Eskimos and American Indians lived under conditions of extreme scarcity, they may have been justified in leaving their elderly to die if they became unable to travel with the tribe to find new hunting territories, even though comparable neglect of our elderly would be immoral in our society or in contemporary Eskimo and Indian societies.

SUGGESTED READINGS

Brandt, Richard B. *Ethical Theory.* Englewood Cliffs, NJ: Prentice-Hall, 1959.

Frankena, William K. *Ethics.* 2nd ed. Englewood Cliffs, NJ: Prentice-Hall, 1973.

Gowans, Christopher W. (ed.). *Moral Dilemmas.* New York: Oxford University Press, 1987.

Halberstam, Joshua (ed.). *Virtues and Values.* Englewood Cliffs, NJ: Prentice-Hall, 1988.

Kekes, John. "Moral Sensitivity." *Philosophy,* vol. 59 (1984).

Kruschwitz, Robert B., and Robert C. Roberts (eds.). *The Virtues: Contemporary Essays on Moral Character.* Belmont, CA: Wadsworth, 1987.

Laird, John. "Act-Ethics and Agent-Ethics." *Mind,* vol. 55 (1946).

Martin, Mike W. "Applied and General Ethics." In Michael Bradie, Thomas W. Attig, and Nicholas Rescher (eds.), *The Applied Turn in Contemporary Philosophy.* Bowling Green, OH: Bowling Green State University, Department of Philosophy, 1983.

Murdoch, Iris. *The Sovereignty of Good.* Boston: Ark Paperbacks, 1985.

Rachels, James. *The Elements of Moral Philosophy.* New York: Random House, 1986.

Sartre, Jean-Paul. "Existentialism Is a Humanism." Trans. Philip Mairet. In Walter Kaufmann (ed.), *Existentialism from Dostoevsky to Sartre,* rev. ed. New York: New American Library, 1975.

Sher, George (ed.). *Moral Philosophy: Selected Readings.* New York: Harcourt Brace Jovanovich, 1987.

Sommers, Christina Hoff (ed.). *Vice and Virtue in Everyday Life: Introductory Readings in Ethics.* New York: Harcourt Brace Jovanovich, 1985.

Williams, Bernard. *Morality: An Introduction to Ethics.* New York: Harper and Row, 1972.

CHAPTER 2

Creativity, Autonomy, and Moral Growth

The development of moral responsibility is a complex process that culminates in creative, autonomous reasoning. Autonomous reasoning, which is exercising one's own reasoning (as Sartre said) on the basis of moral concern (going beyond Sartre), develops gradually over a period of years. The study of ethics plays a role in that development, as do other studies in the liberal arts. Moral creativity and moral growth, and their connection with the study of ethics and the liberal arts, are the main themes explored in this chapter.

Sartre focused attention on moral creativity in the sense of inventing moral reasons. Yet his student did not invent the reasons for helping his mother and for fighting Hitler. Instead, he was confronted with objectively valid reasons that made conflicting claims on him. His anguish and need for advice arose because reasons not of his invention came into conflict, thereby causing a moral dilemma. The need for creativity arose not in inventing moral reasons, but instead in attempting to resolve the dilemma by balancing the valid moral claims on him.

Moral creativity can also shape an entire life by emphasizing some particular moral ideals and virtues. This creative self-shaping is exemplified by moral leaders. Not only do moral leaders identify certain values as especially significant for their time and place, but they also inspire a similar recognition in others. In this chapter we will consider three examples of moral leaders: Socrates, Martin Luther King, Jr., and Elizabeth Cady Stanton. We will also consider the intriguing possibility that men and women tend to emphasize different moral ideals and virtues.

Moral Creativity

Moral creativity consists of innovative autonomous reasoning and living. But what specifically does that mean?

Creativity implies newness, but newness with respect to what? Newness can be identified by reference to one's past. Newness can mean going beyond one's previously narrow or biased ways of thinking, or one's rigid and juvenile patterns of conduct, emotions, and attitude. Other reference points lie outside oneself. Newness can mean surmounting stifling views inherited from parents, peers, culture, or religion. But it may also mean seeing more deeply than is customary into inherited views and attitudes so as to appreciate their importance. All these forms of creative moral development play a significant role in our lives.

Newness alone is not creative, however. Merely novel responses to moral problems may be as uncreative as doodling on paper. If Sartre's student had decided to devote all his time to beachcombing in California, his decision would have been novel but not creative. In all forms of creativity something *valuably new* is achieved. Moral creativity thus represents the discovery or accomplishment of something new and morally desirable. As such it both requires and exemplifies moral autonomy: reasoning for oneself in trying to live a morally good life.

Morally valuable newness can be revealed in several ways. Individuals who respond in new and morally valuable ways are creative in (1) identifying moral problems, issues, and needs, (2) identifying moral reasons and facts relevant to moral concerns, (3) effectively reasoning in resolving moral problems and guiding lives (both one's own and others'), and (4) shaping lives with a focus on particular ideals and virtues. All these areas of creativity, but especially the final one, are illustrated in the lives of moral leaders.

Socrates: Intellectual Humility and Honesty

Socrates centered his life on a creative search for moral understanding. As the story is told in Plato's *Apology,* one of Socrates' friends asked the oracle of Apollo at Delphi whether anyone was wiser than Socrates. The priestess replied that no one was. This astonished Socrates, for he was certain he knew very little. To disprove the oracle's pronouncement, he began searching for someone wiser than himself by talking with politicians, poets, craftsmen, and anyone else having a reputation for wisdom. In each case he uncovered only ignorance, dogmatism, and intellectual complacency, which led him to conclude that what set him apart from others was his knowledge of his own ignorance. "What is probable," he explained, is in fact that god is wise and that his oracular response meant that human wisdom is worth little or nothing, and that when he says this man, Socrates, he is using my name as an example, as if he said: "This man among you, mortals, is wisest who, like Socrates, understands that his wisdom is worthless." So even now I continue this investigation as the gods bade me—and I go around seeking out anyone, citizen or stranger, whom I think wise. Then if I do not think he is, I come to the assistance of the god and show him that he is not wise.[1]*

There is a positive goal in this Socratic enterprise of showing ignorant people that they lack the moral understanding they claim to have. Individuals who think they are wise see no reason to search for increased wisdom. By showing them that they were not wise, Socrates encouraged the intellectual humility and self-critical attitude with which moral inquiry must begin. And according to Socrates, moral inquiry is the prerequisite for meaningful life: "It is the greatest good for a man to discuss virtue every day . . . for the unexamined life is not worth living."[2]† People do not attain the capacity for moral inquiry and the self-understanding once and for all, but rather must maintain an ongoing effort as part of everyday life.

Here is an example of the importance of self-understanding based on intellectual humility and honesty. According to Plato's dialogue *Euthyphro,* Socrates encounters a man named Euthyphro who has just filed murder charges against his own father. Apparently one of Euthyphro's employees, in a drunken frenzy, had killed a family slave. Uncertain what to do, Euthyphro's father tied up the murderer and threw him in a ditch, then sent a messenger to the local priest for advice. While the father awaited the messenger's return, the bound man died from hunger and exposure, so Euthyphro prosecuted his father for murder—the same crime that the employee had committed.

Socrates is shocked by Euthyphro's assertion that the father is as guilty as the employee. He is even more astonished when Euthyphro argues that the virtue of justice requires him to prosecute his father despite their special relationship. In Socrates' view the moral situation was murky, and Euthyphro's self-righteous pronouncements threatened to compound the harm already done. Socrates proceeds to deflate Euthyphro's conceit, showing that he really knows nothing about virtue.‡ He also implies that Euthyphro is motivated by hatred of and rivalry with his father, rather than by a virtuous concern for justice, and that his lack of self-understanding distorts his sense of justice.

---

*Reprinted by permission of Hackett Publishing Company, Inc.

†Reprinted by permission of Hackett Publishing Company, Inc.

‡Upon questioning, Euthyphro defined virtue as what the gods command. Recall, however, in Chapter 1 where Socrates asserted that virtue is not created by the gods but rather that the gods would recognize valid moral reasons as worthy of their commandments.

Socrates' commitment to truth was uncompromising. During a lifetime of exposing and debunking ignorance he offended many people. Part of that offending was inevitable given the nature of his mission, but part of it also resulted from Socrates' lack of compassion in dealing with people, as suggested by his famous epigram, "The unexamined life is not worth living." If self-examination requires the kind of philosophical scrutiny he engaged in, then most lives lack worth! It would be more compassionate, if less inspirational, to say that the unexamined life is *less* worth living (other things being equal) than is the life based on self-understanding.

Despite his excesses, or perhaps in part because of them, Socrates offers an inspiring paradigm of a life devoted to the virtues of honesty and intellectual humility. His death solemnized his commitment to truth and the virtues it demands of us. He was convicted and sentenced to death on the basis of false charges trumped up by some of the ignorant men he had offended. During his trial he was offered acquittal if he would abandon his mission on behalf of truth, the mission that had made him an annoying "gadfly of Athens." He replied,

> As long as I draw breath and am able, I shall not cease to practise philosophy, to exhort you and to point out to anyone of you whom I happen to meet: Good Sir, you are an Athenian, a citizen of the greatest city with the greatest reputation for both wisdom and power; are you not ashamed of your eagerness to possess as much wealth, reputation and honours as possible, while you do not care for nor give thought to wisdom or truth, or the best possible state of your soul?[3]*

King: Love and Justice Through Nonviolence

The central moral commitment of Martin Luther King, Jr. (1929–1968), was to achieve racial justice. In 1955 he was working in Montgomery, Alabama, as a Baptist minister, having that year completed a Ph.D. at Boston University. Largely because he was too new to Montgomery to be compromised by political debts, he was asked to lead the Montgomery bus boycott in protest of the arrest of Mrs. Rosa Parks. Mrs. Parks, a black woman, had refused to give up her bus seat to a white man, thereby violating a Montgomery city ordinance (which also required blacks to sit at the back of the bus). King knew there were enormous risks in using this untried form of economic protest, yet he also saw the opportunity to draw national attention to the Jim Crow laws of segregation.

The boycott lasted one year until the Supreme Court ruled that Mrs.

---

*Reprinted by permission of Hackett Publishing Company, Inc.

Parks's rights had indeed been violated and that bus segregation laws were unconstitutional. Beginning that year King's life was repeatedly threatened by hate mail and phone calls. His home was bombed. He was arrested and harassed. And this pattern intensified throughout the next dozen years until he was assassinated.

While leading the Montgomery boycott, King articulated his philosophy of nonviolence based on agape, the Christian version of benevolence or love toward all humans. It enjoins, "Love your enemies, bless them that curse you, do good to them that hate you, and pray for them which despitefully use you, and persecute you."[4] According to King, agape is not an emotional form of love, unlike romantic love and friendship; nevertheless, it requires more than mere respect for others. Agape is a positive attitude of goodwill toward all people as children of God who are capable of redemption.

Agape also requires forgiving enemies who have terribly wronged us. Forgiveness, however, is not simply overlooking harm done. Rather, it entails the free gift of releasing an enemy from having to pay for that wrong, the refusal to hate in response to hate, and the willingness to be reconciled to those who have wronged us.

Finally, in King's interpretation, agape requires confronting unjust institutions and practices in a nonviolent way. He knew that verbal confrontation alone was ineffective in dealing with institutionalized racism. Even economic boycott was not enough. What was necessary was civil disobedience: nonviolent, public, conscientiously motivated law-breaking with a willingness to accept legal penalties. This form of protest was consistent with agape and could appeal to the consciences of the masses of Americans.

King did not invent civil disobedience as a tactic of social protest. He was directly influenced by Henry David Thoreau (1817–1862), who had refused to pay his Massachusetts taxes as a protest against both the Mexican-American War and slavery. He was also influenced by Mohandas Gandhi (1869–1948), who had led the successful fight against British control of India by encouraging civil disobedience on a mass scale. King's moral creativity was not in inventing the tactic, but in Christianizing it and adapting it to the American civil rights movement. King's genius lay in part in his belief that, in the face of violent opposition, nonviolent civil disobedience could bring an end to a century of segregation. It was also his continuing dream that people "no longer be judged by the color of their skin but by the content of their character."[5]

Stanton: Women's Dignity and Self-Development

Elizabeth Cady Stanton (1815–1902) is widely regarded as the foremost intellectual of the early American feminist movement. She conceived and helped organize the first convention on women's rights in 1848 at Seneca Falls, New

York. That convention, together with its statement of grievances, ignited the organized struggle for women's rights in the United States.

Stanton was the primary author of the statement of grievances entitled the "Declaration of Sentiments," modeled on the language of the *Declaration of Independence*. In an early paragraph she states:

> We hold these truths to be self-evident: that all men and women are created equal; that they are endowed by their Creator with certain inalienable rights; that among these are life, liberty, and the pursuit of happiness. . . . The history of mankind is a history of repeated injuries and usurpations on the part of man toward woman, having in direct object the establishment of an absolute tyranny over her. To prove this, let facts be submitted to a candid world.[6]

The document asserted that fundamental rights were being denied to women, including the right to vote, to own property (including their earned wages), to initiate divorce, to retain custody of their children when a husband initiated a divorce, to attend college (except for Oberlin College, which had become coeducational, all American colleges and universities refused to admit women students), and to guide daily business activities without supervision by their husbands.

Defining these actions as rights, and demanding their exercise, was an explosive act. Even the right to vote was regarded by many convention members as too radical to assert at that time. (Indeed, it was another seventy years before women's voting rights were recognized in the Nineteenth Amendment to the Constitution.) And pursuing marriage and divorce rights was viewed as even more unrealistic and harmful. Only Stanton's enormous persistence, energy, and forceful arguments finally won endorsement of the Declaration at the convention.

Like King, Stanton did not invent the moral concepts and ideals she pressed to the center of public debate. She drew not only upon the *Declaration of Independence* but also upon earlier feminist writing such as *A Vindication of the Rights of Woman* by Mary Wollstonecraft (1759–1797). Stanton's creative moral leadership stemmed from her insight that the concept of human rights could serve as the rallying point against men who avowed principles of equality for all humans while denying equality to women.

Stanton knew from her own experience, which included raising seven children, how women were suppressed and exploited. Her husband, an activist in the antislavery movement, was largely indifferent to her efforts. And her father disowned her because of her activities (even though on his deathbed he sought a reconciliation with her).

Stanton also knew that the roots of patriarchy—that is, male dominance—ran deeper even than the roots of racial oppression. She traced them in part to religious thought. In the 1880s she published the *Woman's Bible* in which she and others commented on scriptures concerning the relationship between men and women. For example, she cited Mark 12 : 43–44, where Jesus praises a poor widow for giving her last farthing to the church. Although Stanton agreed with Jesus that the widow's gift showed greater generosity than did the much larger gifts of the rich, she also pointed out that praise of women's self-sacrifice had been used by organized religion throughout history to perpetuate women's second-class status.

> This woman, belonging to an impoverished class, was trained to self-abnegation; but when women learn the higher duty of self-development, they will not so readily expend all their forces in serving others. Paul says that a husband who does not provide for his own household is worse than an infidel. So a woman, who spends all her time in churches, with priests, in charities, neglects to cultivate her own natural gifts, to make the most of herself as an individual in the scale of being, a responsible soul whose place no other can fill, is worse than an infidel. "Self-development is a higher duty than self-sacrifice," should be woman's motto henceforward.[7]

Stanton called into question the conventional expectation that women be more self-sacrificing, helpful, and caring than men. How far this expectation is generated by society's stereotypes of women, and whether it has any biological basis, is a "nurture-nature" dispute of considerable importance. Of more immediate interest here, however, is the question of whether women and men do tend to emphasize different virtues, whatever the origin of those differences may be.

Gilligan and Kohlberg: Caring Versus Justice

Do men and women, as groups, differ in the kinds of virtues they emphasize? Studies by some contemporary experimental psychologists suggest they do. We will look in particular at the works of Carol Gilligan and of Lawrence Kohlberg (1927–1987).

Gilligan distinguishes between two general outlooks on morality: the justice perspective and the care perspective. According to the results of her experiments, these outlooks are roughly linked to gender. That is, men and women employ both perspectives, but on average men emphasize the justice perspective and women emphasize the care perspective.*

---

*In the essay "Moral Orientation and Development" Gilligan summarizes the results of one study as follows:

> When asked to describe a moral conflict they had faced, 55 out of 80 (69 percent) educationally advantaged North American adolescents and adults raised considerations of both justice and care. Two-thirds (54 out of 80), however, focused their attention on one set of

The *justice perspective* stresses abstract rules, which deal primarily with the (liberty) right to be left alone and not interfered with by other people. Within this perspective moral dilemmas are interpreted as conflicts among rights that are resolved by identifying which right has the highest priority in general. Morality, in short, is viewed as rules about rights ordered within a hierarchy of relative importance. The moral identity of people is defined primarily in terms of their rights: asserting the right to pursue their lives freely while respecting the freedom of others. The aim of autonomous moral reasoning is to determine how to balance rights fairly or justly.

"Heinz's Dilemma" illustrates the kind of reasoning used within the justice perspective. This story, which poses a moral dilemma, was written by Kohlberg but used by Gilligan as well.

In Europe, a woman was near death from a very bad disease, a special kind of cancer. There was one drug that the doctors thought might save her. It was a form of radium that a druggist in the same town had recently discovered. The drug was expensive to make, but the druggist was charging ten times what the drug cost him to make. He paid $200 for the radium and charged $2,000 for a small dose of the drug. The sick woman's husband, Heinz, went to everyone he knew to borrow the money, but he could get together only about $1,000, which was half of what it cost. He told the druggist that his wife was dying and asked him to sell it cheaper or let him pay later. But the druggist said, "No, I discovered the drug and I'm going to make money from it." Heinz got desperate and broke into the man's store to steal the drug for his wife.[9]

The question is, Was the husband's act justified (permissible, obligatory)?

According to Kohlberg, morally mature individuals resolve this dilemma by contrasting the pharmacist's property rights with the wife's right to life and then deciding which right should have priority. Typically, they argue that the right to life is more important than the right to property, and hence that the husband should steal the drug. They might also reason that the general principle of respect for life has priority over the principle of respect for property.

---

concerns, with focus defined as 75 percent or more of the considerations raised pertaining either to justice or to care. Thus the person who presented, say, two care considerations in discussing a moral conflict was more likely to give a third, fourth, and fifth than to balance care and justice concerns—a finding consonant with the assumption that justice and care constitute organizing frameworks for moral decision. The men and women involved in this study (high school students, college students, medical students, and adult professionals) were equally likely to demonstrate the focus phenomenon (two-thirds of both sexes fell into the focus categories). There were, however, sex differences in the direction of focus. With one exception, all of the men who focused, focused on justice. The women divided, with roughly one third focusing on justice and one third on care.[8]

Gilligan does not attempt to determine whether such differences are genetically inherited or socially induced.

Gilligan contrasts this justice-oriented approach with the *care perspective* in which priority is placed on kindness, giving, and caring about the needs of others. The aim is to avoid hurting others and to maintain relationships without hurting oneself. Moral dilemmas thus revolve around competing needs and incompatible ways of caring. They are resolved through communicating and maintaining sensitivity to context rather than by imposing general rules and priorities among rules. Moral reasons are defined through a web of caring relationships rather than through the interplay of rights to be left alone. In this view autonomous moral reasoning seeks a proper balance between the needs of others and of oneself.

"Heinz's Dilemma" also illustrates the use of reasoning within the care perspective. Perhaps surprisingly, Kohlberg's studies suggested that fewer females than males endorsed Heinz's theft of the drug. Kohlberg interpreted this as a sign of moral immaturity, saying that women were bound by social conventions about respecting property and obeying laws. In applying the care perspective, however, Gilligan offered a very different interpretation. Gilligan suggests that the reluctance to steal the drug reveals sensitivity to the personal relationships. Not only will Heinz probably end up in jail where he can no longer help his wife, but also the relationship with the pharmacist will be severed altogether. In Gilligan's studies women frequently recommended further discussions with the pharmacist in hopes of changing his mind or proposed innovative ways of raising money to pay for the drug.

In sum, according to Gilligan, women more than men use a care-oriented moral perspective. They seek innovative ways to sustain all relationships and to meet all needs. They are more context-focused than men and less preoccupied with abstract rules ranked in order of importance.

Two Theories of Moral Development

Kohlberg's emphasis on the justice perspective and Gilligan's emphasis on the care perspective underlie their differing theories about the stages of moral growth or development toward moral maturity. In his highly influential schema of moral development, Kohlberg lists three levels, each with a characteristic view of right action:

1. Preconventional Level: Right action is defined in terms of what brings pleasure or reward to oneself.
2. Conventional Level: Right action is interpreted as loyalty to others and respect for law and custom.
3. Postconventional Level: Right action is identified in terms of general principles discerned with one's autonomous judgment.

Each level is further divided into two stages, as summarized in Table 2.1.

TABLE 2.1   *Kohlberg's Schema of Moral Development*

Level of Moral Development	Stage or Orientation	View of Right Action
1. Preconventional	1. Punishment and obedience	Avoid punishment and submit to power
	2. Egoistic	Satisfy one's own needs
2. Conventional	3. Good-boy, nice-girl	Please and help others
	4. Society-maintaining	Respect authority and social rules
3. Postconventional	5. Social contract or legalistic	Obey useful, albeit arbitrary, social rules
	6. Conscience and universal principles	Autonomously recognize universal rules such as the Golden Rule

Kohlberg claimed that these stages represent the appropriate steps of moral growth for all people in all cultures. People reach advanced stages only after progressing through earlier ones, and only a few rare individuals like Socrates reach the highest stage. In addition, fewer women than men move beyond the conventional level to the postconventional level.

Gilligan charges that these conclusions, and indeed Kohlberg's schema of moral development, are biased. She points out that Kohlberg studied only males in creating his schema and then simply assumed that it was equally valid for both sexes. Moreover, in structuring the stages of moral progression, Kohlberg also assumed that reasoning based on abstract rules reflects greater moral maturity. As a result, caring-based reasoning focused on specific contexts is condemned in advance as "conventional" in a pejorative sense. Thus, Kohlberg's emphasis on general rules about justice and rights may express his own bias as a male.

Gilligan offers an alternative schema, based on several studies, of the levels of development:

1. Preconventional Level: Rightness is viewed exclusively as what is good for oneself.
2. Conventional Level: Right action is viewed as self-sacrifice in always placing the interests of others before one's own—the socially favored view of how women in particular should behave.
3. Postconventional Level: The ethic of caring in which both the interests of oneself and of others are valued and balanced with the aim of maintaining attachments to all people involved in specific situations.

Gilligan's study of women making abortion decisions was especially valuable in her redefinition of levels of moral development. That study examined how women reason about an important moral issue they are forced to act on, unlike Kohlberg's study of Heinz's Dilemma, which concerns hypothetical problems. Gilligan's subjects were women referred to her by a counseling service, indicating they had experienced conflict in making the abortion decision. They were first interviewed while they were making their decisions and again a year later. Gilligan identified their levels of reasoning in terms of patterns of reasoning rather than the conclusions they reached.

The women who were solely or primarily concerned about what was best for themselves were at the preconventional (self-centered) level. Sometimes this meant having an abortion in order to avoid harm or social stigma, without considering anyone else involved; other times it meant deciding to have a baby to bring them social recognition. The women who were preoccupied with what was socially expected or with what helped others without regard to their own well-being were at the conventional (self-sacrificing) level. For some women this meant having a baby, even at enormous self-sacrifice, out of a concern for the developing fetus; for others it meant having an abortion in order to please a spouse or lover. Finally, those women who struggled to balance their own needs with the needs of others involved in order to sustain relationships, including in some cases the relationship with the fetus, were at the postconventional (mature, caring) level. For these women the decision to have an abortion was perhaps motivated by the impossibility of properly caring for a baby while maintaining a relationship with a lover and pursuing a college education. Likewise, the decision to have a baby was perhaps prompted by the desire to develop a new relationship with the child that would complement other relationships.

The women in Gilligan's study frequently used the concepts of selfishness, self-sacrifice, caring, needs, and relationships. They seldom mentioned, however, the concepts used in public debates over abortion: the rights of women (to their bodies, to make their own decisions) versus the (possible) rights to life of fetuses. Moreover, when Gilligan interviewed the women a second time, she frequently saw patterns of growth in terms of her schema of devel-

FIGURE 2.1 *Duck-Rabbit*

TABLE 2.2 *Kohlberg and Gilligan's Schemas of Moral Development*

Levels of Moral Development	Kohlberg's Justice Perspective	Gilligan's Care Perspective
1. Preconventional	Self-centered, with concern for (1) avoiding punishment and (2) satisfying one's own needs	Self-centered: viewing one's own needs as all that matters
2. Conventional	Expectation-meeting, with concern for (3) pleasing others and (4) meeting society's expectations	Self-sacrificing: viewing others' needs as more important
3. Postconventional	Autonomous recognition of (5) social agreements and (6) universal rules	Mature care ethic: able to reason toward a balance of one's own and others' needs.

opment: Many of the women had moved from preconventional and conventional levels to the postconventional level. Evidently, making the decision about abortion had encouraged maturation. By choosing autonomously between the lesser of two evils, they were forced to move beyond the conventional self-sacrificing level that emphasized never harming others.

Gilligan's criticisms of Kohlberg led him to modify his claims about the universal applicability of the six stages of development. He came to acknowledge that they merely represent growth within a justice perspective and that a care-oriented perspective may be equally valid. For her part, Gilligan has emphasized that both the care and the justice perspectives express important aspects of most moral situations. In a recent essay she draws an analogy with alternative ways of perceiving in which visual data are organized according to different interpretations. Just as the image in Figure 2.1 can be seen as a duck or as a rabbit, many moral situations can be viewed in terms of rights or of caring.

According to Gilligan, the richest and most adequate moral outlook would integrate both moral perspectives. Men can benefit from integrating elements of the care perspective more fully into their moral outlook, and women can benefit from appreciating the justice perspective. In fact, the justice perspective can aid women in advancing from the conventional self-sacrificing level to the postconventional level, which balances the needs of others and oneself. (Table 2.2 summarizes the similarities and differences between Kohlberg's and Gilligan's views.)

In this connection Gilligan refers to Elizabeth Cady Stanton's appeal to rights as a way of raising women's awareness of their needs and their legitimate self-development. Gilligan might thus rephrase Stanton's slogan, "Self-development is a higher duty than self-sacrifice," to read, "Self-development is as high a duty as caring for others." At the same time, she is aware that on some occasions there are good reasons to emphasize one's own rights and needs. This is consistent with the sensitivity to context, rather than abstract rules, which is integral to her ethic of caring. It is also compatible with the theme of this chapter that morality allows room for emphasis on selected virtues and values.

Moral Growth and Aims in Studying Ethics

Moral autonomy sometimes leads creative thinkers to emphasize certain commitments and virtues over others, as we saw with Socrates, King, and Stanton. Similar emphasis of selected virtues might be roughly linked with gender. Both Gilligan and Kohlberg agree that the capacity for moral autonomy and creative decision making develops gradually, although they trace different paths of development. Do liberal education and ethics courses contribute to this moral growth? And should they try or be expected to make people more morally responsible?

Let us consider these questions one at a time, bearing in mind that the study of morality is an aspect of much of liberal education, not just ethics courses. Liberal education is the study of the humanities, arts, and sciences with the overall aim of deepening understanding and broadening appreciation of values. It has three practical goals as well.

First, liberal education prepares one for significant work by strengthening abilities to reason, research, and communicate. Significant work contributes to self-fulfillment and to the social good in such areas as public health (the goal of the health professions), justice (the goal of law), and education (the goal of teaching).

Second, liberal education embodies an array of inherently worthwhile activities. These diverse activities include understanding cultures and computer systems, appreciating modern painting and physics, and mastering theories of ethics and economics.

Third, liberal education seeks to liberate us from ignorance and prejudice by fostering certain skills, attitudes, emotions, and virtues. Which skills? Those that enable clear thinking, cogent reasoning, and effective communication—the same skills that contribute to significant work. Which attitudes? Respect for truth and evidence, commitment to consistency and nonarbitrariness, and appreciation of beauty and understanding. Which emotions?

Enjoyment of significant ideas, delight in creative endeavors, respect for honest reflection, and contempt for shoddy thinking. Which virtues? The ones that combine the preceding skills, attitudes, and emotions into settled patterns. Most central are the virtues of intellectual honesty, integrity, and courage; truthful communication; wisdom and passionate concern for truth; sensitivity to beauty and discernment in taste; and moral sensitivity, understanding, responsibility, and tolerance.

Studies in ethics form an essential part of liberal education and contribute to all of these practical aims, sometimes directly and sometimes indirectly. They contribute to preparation for significant work because professions are forms of work devoted to the public good and guided by moral norms (as well as based on advanced education). Ethics courses enrich moral understanding in inherently valuable ways. And ethics courses contribute more directly to moral development by strengthening capacities for moral autonomy.

Moral autonomy requires many specific skills: the ability to identify moral problems and reasons; creative vision in imagining moral possibilities; skill in reasonably weighing conflicting moral reasons; adeptness in clarifying concepts that otherwise might cause vagueness or ambiguity; knowledge about people and the world relevant to making wise decisions. All these capacities mature through liberal learning and studies in ethics.

But should colleges seek to make people more responsible morally? On the one hand ethics courses in college ought to continue the development of moral understanding already underway when students enter college. On the other hand it is inappropriate to expect college professors to make their students more responsible morally. That would require professors to invade their students' personal lives to ensure that they practice the discipline and sensitivity necessary for moral responsibility. Not only do professors lack the right to invade students' privacy, they also lack certification as moral counsellors and trainers.

These views can be reconciled by distinguishing between the direct aims of college courses and the underlying hopes concerning them. Certainly one direct aim of studies in ethics and the liberal arts is very practical: to strengthen the ability to reason autonomously about morality. By strengthening moral autonomy educators can hope to contribute indirectly to the development of morally responsible conduct and character. College courses cannot be expected to shape character directly. Increasing virtue directly cannot be a gradable classroom exercise because it involves aspects of character development beyond autonomous reasoning. Moral responsibility remains a personal achievement, whether for students or teachers.

One qualification needs to be added. Moral responsibility and classroom goals in studying ethics are at some points more closely connected. Some character traits and patterns of conduct enter as prerequisites for effective education. Tolerance, for example, is a prerequisite for conducting any class, for without it dialogue based on mutual respect is impossible. Honesty is equally essential, because cheating erodes the trust among students and professors that helps facilitate learning.

Summary

Moral creativity means discovering or achieving new and valuable solutions to moral dilemmas and ways of living. It involves responding to the objective claims of values already present in human culture rather than inventing new values. This response to values, however, leaves much room for creativity, allowing individuals to emphasize some virtues over others, as Socrates, Martin Luther King, Jr., and Elizabeth Cady Stanton all did.

Psychologists who study moral development are exploring the possibility that there may be gender-linked differences in how virtues are emphasized. Lawrence Kohlberg identified patterns of moral development that he thought were universal, although he later accepted Carol Gilligan's criticisms that these patterns represented only development of a sense of justice. Kohlberg defined morally mature reasoning as the autonomous recognition of universal moral rules, especially rules about rights not to be interfered with by others, and their order of priority. Gilligan argued that this justice perspective is favored by males and that females often emphasize a care perspective based on sensitivity to needs and personal relationships within particular contexts.

Kohlberg and Gilligan agree that moral autonomy, in the sense of the ability to reason for oneself without passive adherence to social conventions, emerges from earlier stages of moral development. Both of them also distinguish three basic levels of moral development—preconventional, conventional, and postconventional—and agree that the preconventional level is characterized by a self-centered preoccupation with satisfying one's own needs. Kohlberg describes reasoning at the conventional level as primarily based on a concern to please others or to meet society's expectations, whereas the postconventional level reflects autonomous recognition of social conventions as morally justified or (at the highest stage) autonomous acceptance of universal moral rules. Gilligan, in contrast, describes the conventional level as reasoning based on the self-sacrificing attitude that other people's needs are more important than one's own, and the postconventional level as autonomous reasoning in balancing one's own needs with the needs of others.

Moral autonomy is strengthened through studies in ethics and the liberal arts. It is also linked to all three practical goals of these studies: to prepare for significant work, to engage in inherently valuable activities, and to liberate from ignorance and prejudice.

DISCUSSION TOPICS

1. Euthyphro and Socrates disagreed about whether one's relationship with parents is relevant to how one pursues general principles of justice. Do you agree with what Euthyphro says in the following passage? Apply the issue raised to the controversy over whether children should report their parents to the police for using drugs (and vice versa). Also, relate the disagreement between Socrates and Euthyphro to the differences between Kohlberg's and Gilligan's views of moral autonomy.

   SOCRATES: Is then the man your father killed one of your relatives? Or is that obvious, for you would not prosecute your father for the murder of a stranger.

   EUTHYPHRO: It is ridiculous, Socrates, for you to think that it makes any difference whether the victim is a stranger or a relative. One should only watch whether the killer acted justly or not; if he acted justly, let him go, but if not, one should prosecute, even if the killer shares your hearth and table. The pollution is the same if you knowingly keep company with such a man and do not cleanse yourself and him by bringing him to justice.[10]*

2. Carol Gilligan believes that the justice and care perspectives are complementary and ideally should be integrated. Do you see such an integration in the life and thought of Martin Luther King, Jr.?

3. Gilligan suggests that most moral situations can be interpreted in terms of both the justice and care perspectives. Yet, is the justice perspective perhaps better suited to social and political contexts and the care perspective better suited to more personal relationships among people (and perhaps animals)? In answering this question, compare and contrast public debates over abortion laws with making personal decisions about abortions. Are different moral concepts emphasized in these two contexts? Should they be?

4. Interpret the dilemma faced by Sartre's student (cited in Chapter 1) in terms of the justice and the care perspectives. Does one of the perspectives seem more helpful? Do they point in similar directions for resolving the dilemma?

5. Return to the biblical story of Abraham and Isaac cited as a discussion topic in Chapter 1. In her book *In a Different Voice,* Gilligan links Abraham's willingness to sacrifice his son to a male, justice-oriented way of thinking. Do you agree? Is it less likely that a woman would do what Abraham did, as Gilligan also suggests?

6. Apply both Kohlberg's and Gilligan's schemas of moral development to classroom cheating, both plagiarism and cribbing during tests. Describe the kinds of reasoning that would be used at the preconventional, conventional, and postconventional levels of development within each schema.

7. Compare and contrast moral creativity with creativity in science and in art. In each case, is creativity best thought of as making a discovery or as inventing something?

8. We suggested that moral creativity consists of emphasizing particular virtues or sensitively applying them to situations, but not of inventing values as Sartre had

---

*Reprinted by permission of Hackett Publishing Company, Inc.

suggested. Does anyone ever invent an entirely new virtue? In answering this question, consider the following passage written by philosopher Mary Midgley:

> If there had been no such thing as mercy before, the first merciful man would have been an innovator of a quite dramatic kind. . . . But in fact . . . mercy is, and has to be, an extremely ancient and gradual development, something *evolved* as a precondition of social life by any social species, not a sudden invention to transform it. And the same is true of the other virtues. Slow, painful evolution, not sudden cleverness nor divine fiat, puts them in our repertoire.[11]

SUGGESTED READINGS

Blanshard, Brand. *The Uses of a Liberal Education*. La Salle, IL: Open Court, 1973.

Cua, A. S. *Dimensions of Moral Creativity*. University Park, PA: Pennsylvania State University, 1978.

Deutsch, Eliot. *Personhood, Creativity and Freedom*. Honolulu, HI: University of Hawaii Press, 1982.

Gilligan, Carol. *In a Different Voice: Psychological Theory and Women's Development*. Cambridge, MA: Harvard University Press, 1982.

Gilligan, Carol. "Moral Orientation and Moral Development." In Eva Feder Kittay and Diana T. Meyers (eds.), *Women and Moral Theory*. Totowa, NJ: Rowman & Littlefield, 1987.

Griffith, Elisabeth. *In Her Own Right: The Life of Elizabeth Cady Stanton*. New York: Oxford University Press, 1984.

Jaspers, Karl. *Socrates, Buddha, Confucius, Jesus: The Paradigmatic Individuals*. Trans. Ralph Mannheim. New York: Harcourt Brace Jovanovich, 1962.

King, Martin Luther, Jr. *Strength to Love*. Philadelphia, PA: Fortress Press, 1981.

Kittay, Eva Feder, and Diana T. Meyers (eds.). *Women and Moral Theory*. Totowa, NJ: Rowman & Littlefield, 1987.

Kohlberg, Lawrence. *The Philosophy of Moral Development*. San Francisco: Harper & Row, 1981.

Midgley, Mary. "Creation and Originality." In *Heart and Mind: The Varieties of Moral Experience*. New York: St. Martin's Press, 1981.

Noddings, Nel. *Caring: A Feminine Approach to Ethics and Moral Education*. Berkeley: University of California Press, 1984.

Norton, David L. *Personal Destinies: A Philosophy of Ethical Individualism*. Princeton, NJ: Princeton University Press, 1976.

Oates, Stephen B. *Let the Trumpet Sound: The Life of Martin Luther King, Jr*. New York: New American Library, 1982.

Perry, William G., Jr. *Forms of Intellectual and Ethical Development in the College Years*. New York: Holt, Rinehart & Winston, 1970.

Peters, R. S. "The Justification of Education." In R. S. Peters (ed.), *The Philosophy of Education*. New York: Oxford University Press, 1973.

Plato. *Apology* and *Euthyphro* in *The Trial and Death of Socrates*, trans. G. M. A. Grube. Indianapolis, IN: Hackett, 1975.

Stanton, Elizabeth Cady, and Susan B. Anthony, *Correspondence, Writings, Speeches*. Ellen Carol Du Bois (ed.). New York: Shocken Books, 1981.

CHAPTER 3

Theories of Virtue

Character is both revealed and shaped by how we respond to moral dilemmas such as the one Sartre's student confronted, as well as by special commitments to ideals and virtues such as those of Socrates, Martin Luther King, Jr., and Elizabeth Cady Stanton. Yet everyday patterns of conduct and response are equally important in manifesting and molding character. In exploring these everyday patterns in subsequent chapters, we will often draw upon insights from philosophical theories about good character and right conduct.

This chapter introduces key ideas of some influential virtue ethicists: Plato, Aristotle, Aquinas, Hume, MacIntyre, and Pincoffs. According to these philosophers, the moral aim of life is to be a good person—to have a virtuous character and to relate to other people in desirable ways. Right conduct is important, but morally secondary; its role is to support and to express good character. (Chapter 4 will discuss ethicists who regard right actions, duties, or rights as more fundamental to understanding morality than is good character.)

Virtues as Character Traits

Virtue ethicists each develop their own detailed definitions of virtues. For our purposes, however, it will be helpful to provide a concise definition of virtues that is not tied to any one theory. This definition will also draw together what has already been said about virtues as traits of character—that is, as features of persons rather than of institutions, groups, or social practices.

What is a virtue? It is a trait of character that is desirable because it contributes to the good of humans (and sometimes of animals). Usually the human good includes both the good of the person who has the trait and the good affected by that person. In contrast, a vice is an undesirable trait of character that causes harm to people (or animals, as we shall discuss in Chapter 21).

What is a trait of character? It is a general feature of a person that is manifested in patterns of actions, intentions, emotions, desires, attitudes, and reasoning. Virtues thus involve, but are not reducible to, actions.* Virtues involve tendencies to act *in the right spirit*—that is, for the right reasons, with the right intentions, motivated by appropriate emotions, desires, and attitudes. Moreover, character traits can be revealed not only through actions but also in feelings, wants, intentions, hopes, interests, attitudes, thoughts, reasoning, and speech.

In order to illustrate how character traits involve more than acts, consider the virtue of benevolence. Imagine a wealthy man making a very large donation to a charity that distributes food and shelter to the needy, helping many people enormously. Considered by itself the act can be called a beneficent one. Does it necessarily follow that the man is benevolent, at least on this occasion? Clearly not.

Suppose the government had just passed a law allowing large tax deductions for contributions to this charity. Suppose also that the sole reason the man made the donation was to gain the deduction, based on the strong recommendation of his financial advisor. In fact, suppose that the man felt revulsion for the needy people helped by his money, regarding them as weak failures who would be better off dead. The man even feels guilty about the donation, wishing he did not have to make it for the sake of his personal finances. Perhaps he takes some consolation from the public recognition he receives after he makes sure others learn about the donation. Considered by itself, in abstraction from his character, perhaps the *act* can still be called beneficent. But the man is not a benevolent *person* when he makes the donation!

Benevolent people, such as Martin Luther King, Jr., Socrates, and Elizabeth Cady Stanton, are kindhearted. Their actions spring from concern for the well-being of others. They are motivated to give something they value because they see it will benefit someone else, whether the gift is their money, energy, time, or talent. They experience satisfaction in seeing someone helped and in being the one who helps. They hope, wish, desire, intend, and act with the aim of benefiting others.

In general, virtues require approaching actions with appropriate attitudes and commitments. They require being motivated by a perception of the moral good to be achieved rather than by ulterior motives alone. And virtues

---

*This definition implies a rejection of behaviorism, which is the theory that all mental states and psychological traits reduce to actions, and which defines actions as outwardly visible behavior.

involve patterns of emotion, desire, attitude, preference, and reasoning that define us just as much as do our actions.

Human Nature and Virtue Theories

Theories of virtue are grounded in theories about human nature, that is, theories about what it means to be a human being. Human nature is described in terms of the capacities, problems, possibilities, and aspirations of people. Virtues are then defined as character traits that enable people to achieve the good that is possible for them. Virtue theories also offer systematic frameworks revealing the connections among the various virtues and explaining which are most fundamental.

Theories of virtue, then, seek to do three things: (1) Provide a theory of human nature that identifies morally relevant facts about human possibilities; (2) using that theory of human nature, define those character traits, or virtues, that enable people to achieve the good made possible by their nature; and (3) present a schema for understanding the interrelationships among the virtues.

Plato and Aristotle, the two great Greek ethicists inspired by Socrates, base their theories of human nature on a key assumption. They assume that reasoning is the primary purpose or function that sets humans apart from other creatures. In their view, virtues are the excellences that enable humans to exercise their powers of reasoning and live in accordance with their conclusions. Hence, in living the virtuous life, one lives well that distinctive form of life possible for humans.

Plato: Good Character as Moral Health

According to Plato, the function of something is the task that it is best or uniquely suited to perform. As an example he noted that many objects can be used to trim vines: a carving knife, a chisel, fingernails, or a sharp rock. Only a pruning knife, however, is perfectly suited to the task. Hence, pruning is the function of pruning knives but not of the other objects. As another example Plato noted that parts of the body have functions to which they are especially well suited: eyes for seeing, ears for hearing, and lungs for breathing. And workers also have professional functions defined by their social roles: for physicians, promoting health; for soldiers, defending the country; for teachers, instructing. By analogy he concluded that humans have a distinctive function to which their lives as a whole are best suited: to exercise and live by reason.

Division of the Mind into Three Parts

Plato developed this thesis by distinguishing three main parts of the mind (or soul)—Reason, the Spirited Element, and the Appetites—each of which has a characteristic function to perform. Reason coordinates and directs the diverse activities of the individual. The Spirited Element, which we might call a sense of honor or pride, has the task of supporting reason in controlling the Appetites. Even though Reason has its own motives for self-control, the Spirited Element is needed to strengthen Reason's ability to maintain control and to avoid shameful conduct. The Appetites maintain the body by satisfying physical cravings for food, drink, exercise, and sex. But the Appetites also include undesirable urges.

Why did Plato divide the mind into three parts? These divisions seemed to him to explain psychological conflict. For example, a person has a desire to eat too much and also a directly opposed desire not to overeat. These conflicting desires suggest that one part of the person, Reason, is at war with another part, the Appetites. Or consider the person who has an overpowering urge to do something morbid and shameful, such as (to use Plato's example) to gaze with pleasure at corpses, but an inner struggle ensues. In resisting the strong impulse to view the corpses, Reason needs the help of the Spirited Element (a sense of honor).

Wrongdoing occurs when Reason and the Spirited Element are unable to control the Appetites. Immoral action is thus a symptom of a disordered personality whose proper functions are out of balance. In contrast, morally right action is a sign of inner harmony with each part of the mind performing its function well. Virtues make this possible.

Each mental part has its own distinctive virtue that enables it to perform its function with excellence.* *Wisdom* is the virtue that enables Reason to effectively guide both the Appetites and the Spirited Element. *Courage* makes it possible for the Spirited Element to forcibly aid Reason in controlling troublesome Appetites. *Temperance* or moderation enables the Appetites to be satisfied to a healthy degree and without overindulgence. *Justice* is simply a summary label indicating that the other virtues are present. The just (or moral) person is someone whose Reason wisely supervises the Appetites in a temperate manner with the help of a courageous Spirited Element. The four classical Greek virtues, then, are wisdom, courage, temperance, and justice.†

Just as Reason is the most important aspect of humans, wisdom is the most important virtue. In fact, wisdom makes possible all the other virtues.

---

*The Greek word for "excellence," *aretē*, also translates as "virtue."

†In the *Republic* Plato develops an elaborate analogy between good character as inner harmony and morally just countries (or city-states). He divides countries into three main parts—Rulers, Guardians (police and military), and Producers (farmers and businesspeople)—each with a corresponding virtue: wisdom, courage and temperance.

The insight it provides guides the Spirited Element and determines how far the Appetites should be restrained or indulged. Thus, genuine courage and temperance are expressions of wisdom. Plato also believed that complete wisdom would automatically lead to courage and temperance (and hence to justice). This controversial belief is called the Doctrine of the Unity of the Virtues: to fully have any one of the main virtues implies having them all.

Plato also applied the idea of virtue as inner harmony in defending another controversial doctrine: the life of virtue as the happy life. Today we think of virtue and happiness as having no necessary connection. By happiness, however, Plato did not mean emotional contentment or satisfaction with one's life but rather the life that fulfills us. And he was convinced that such a life was guided by the virtues, which bring inner harmony. Moreover, he argued, because wisdom makes inner harmony possible, and because people gain wisdom through philosophical reflection, the most happy life was that of the philosopher!

Plato and Freud

It is interesting to note some similarities between the ideas of Plato and the theories of Sigmund Freud (1856–1939), similarities that are especially striking in view of the fact that their lives were separated by 2,200 years.[1]

Like Plato, Freud divided the mind into three main parts: the ego, the id, and the superego, each with its special function. The *ego,* which corresponds roughly with Plato's Reason, integrates activities and deals with problems. The *id* is something like the unconscious parts of the Appetites, especially in relation to sexual and aggressive desires. The *superego* is composed of the values instilled by parents and society. Although the superego differs from the Spirited Element (sense of honor), both can be viewed as aspects of conscience (the sense of right and wrong). To carry the analogy one step further, note that Freud's superego pressures the ego to control the id, much as the Spirited Element helps Reason control the Appetites.

Furthermore, both Freud and Plato hypothesized that this three-part framework could be used to explain mental conflicts and to understand mental health. Freud regarded human life as best when the ego is in full control in dealing with the pressures from the id, the superego, and everyday reality. Neuroses and other forms of mental illness arise when the ego is overwhelmed by an out-of-control id or superego or by a traumatic experience. Mental health involves inner harmony, or at least a healthy balancing of tensions, which we achieve when we are able to confront internal and external dangers courageously based on self-understanding. According to Freud, self-understanding made possible meaningful life through healthy forms of pleasure and work, even though it did not guarantee happiness and self-fulfillment as Plato thought.

These similarities are remarkable, but one major difference concerning the nature of wisdom needs to be stressed. Plato viewed wisdom as insight into what he called the Form of the Good through pure rational thought, and it was through that vision that insight into all other virtues could be gained. Freud, however, would entirely reject Plato's Form of the Good. From Freud's secular and scientific world view Plato's attempt to ground the virtues in a vision of the Form of the Good was an illusion. In these respects Freud is closer to Aristotle than to Plato.

Aristotle: Rational Emotions and Desires

Aristotle (like Freud) rejected Plato's doctrine of a supernatural Form of the Good not accessible to the senses. Even if there were such a Form, he asserted, it would have no relevance to morality, which is concerned with practical understanding within this world of experience. Goodness is known through practical endeavors and relationships rather than through semi-mystical encounters with supernatural entities.

Nevertheless, Aristotle accepts virtually all of Plato's other main ethical doctrines. He agrees that the distinctive function of humans is to exercise reason. Good character entails reasoning in accord with wisdom, which brings with it happiness understood as well-being and self-fulfillment. And the highest form of happiness is the life of philosophical reflection.

The Doctrine of the Mean

Aristotle, the most influential virtue ethicist of all time, developed these themes in rich detail, the intricacies of which defy brief summarizing. Here we will focus only on his central doctrine concerning the virtues: the Doctrine of the Mean, or the Doctrine of the Golden Mean, as it has since been called.

The Doctrine of the Mean is intended to apply only to moral virtues such as courage, temperance, justice, and generosity, which Aristotle distinguished from intellectual virtues such as wisdom, intelligence, and prudence. Although the two groups of virtues are intimately connected in that intellectual virtues are necessary for complete moral virtue (just as Plato stated that wisdom makes the other virtues possible), they differ in two respects. First, intellectual virtues represent excellences in reasoning skills that can be taught through inquiry and study. Moral virtues, by contrast, are products of habits that begin in childhood and are strengthened in adult life. For example, intellectual understanding of the virtues can be taught in an ethics course, but prudence and courage in confronting danger must evolve from habitual acts of facing risks with discipline and self-control. Second, there are no limits on the skills and desires involved in exercising intellectual virtues. When it comes to insight, careful reasoning, and the desire to reflect and inquire, more is indeed better. The moral virtues, by contrast, are defined precisely by limits.

Moral virtues are tendencies (or habits) to identify and to seek an intermediate point, or mean, between two extremes on various ranges of desire, emotion, and action. At one extreme in the range is excess (too much), while at the other extreme is deficiency or defect (too little). Aristotle regards this idea of the mean between excess and deficiency as the key to understanding moral virtues: "Moral virtue is . . . a mean between two vices, one of excess and the other of deficiency, and . . . it aims at hitting the mean point in feelings and actions."[2] That is, moral virtues involve regularly discerning and acting on the appropriate middle ground between extremes (of feeling and action), unless prevented by external obstacles. In this sense moral virtues are dispositions or habits.

Each virtue is directed toward a specific range or spectrum of emotions, desires, and actions. For example, courage comprises excellence in responding to danger and pertains to the emotions of fear and confidence. Cowards feel fear on inappropriate occasions or respond to fear and danger without confidence and self-control—that is, they are deficient in self-confidence or self-control. At the other end of the spectrum are foolhardy or rash people, who increase the chances of harm from dangers by being excessively confident. Because courage involves appropriate confidence and self-control in confronting dangers, thereby minimizing the likelihood of harm, it represents the mean between too little daring and confidence (the defect of cowardice) and too much (the excess of foolhardiness).

Other virtues that were especially important for Aristotle and classical Greek society include temperance, proper pride, and friendliness. Temperance is the tendency to hit the mean between unrestrained indulgence of the appetites (the excess of gluttony) and too little enthusiasm for the pleasures of the appetites (the equally undesirable defect of lacking lively tastes and, as we say today, being inhibited). Proper pride is the mean between self-glorification (the excess of vanity) and insufficient self-affirmation (the defect of "poor-spiritedness," or of having an inferiority complex). Friendliness is the mean between phony flattering of others (the excess of obsequiousness) and aloofness or surliness (the defect of rudeness).

Table 3.1 summarizes these and other virtues Aristotle discussed; note, however, that in places we update his terminology.[3]

It may come as a surprise to see wittiness included in the table—we do not generally think of wit and a sense of humor as moral virtues. For Aristotle, however, *all* desirable qualities of persons were virtues. Wit, friendliness, good manners, and social decorum all counted as moral virtues.

Aristotle intended his Doctrine of the Mean to apply to emotions and desires as well as to the actions they motivate. The Doctrine of the Mean is a

TABLE 3.1 *Summary of the Virtues As Discussed by Aristotle*

Sphere of Action; Kind of Situation	Type of Emotion, Desire, Attitude	Vice of Too Much (Excess)	Virtue (Mean)	Vice of Too Little (Deficiency or Defect)
Responses to danger	Fear, confidence	Foolhardiness	Courage	Cowardice
Satisfying appetites	Physical pleasure	Overindulgence	Temperance	Inhibition
Giving gifts	Desire to help	Extravagance	Generosity	Miserliness
Pursuing accomplishments	Desire to succeed	Vaulting ambition	Proper ambition	Unambitiousness
Appraising oneself	Self-affirmation	Vanity	Proper pride	Sense of inferiority
Self-expression	Desire to be recognized	Boastfulness	Truthfulness	False modesty
Responding to insults	Anger	Irascibility	Patience	Apathy
Social conduct	Attitudes to others	Obsequiousness	Friendliness	Rudeness
Indignation at others' undeserved good fortune*	Distress	Envy	Righteous indignation	Malicious enjoyment
Awareness of one's flaws	Shame	Shyness	Modesty	Shamelessness
Conversation, humor	Amusement	Buffoonery	Wittiness	Boorishness

*This entry may seem puzzling. Aristotle writes: "Righteous Indignation is a mean between Envy and Spite [or malicious enjoyment], and they are all concerned with feelings of pain or pleasure at the experiences of our neighbors. The man who feels righteous indignation is distressed at instances of undeserved good fortune, but the envious man goes further and is distressed at *any* good fortune, while the spiteful man is so far from feeling distress that he actually rejoices [at others' misfortune]."[4]

theory about rational desires and morally desirable emotions. This may seem problematic. We tend to think of morality as concerned with what is under our immediate control, which appears to rule out emotions from a discussion of morality. Recall, however, that Aristotle regarded moral virtues as the product of years of training in proper habits and modes of response, and emotions and desires can be shaped through habit.

Moral Prudence

Virtue consists in "hitting the mean" of emotions and desires as well as the actions they motivate. But how is this mean determined? Is it simply moderation in the sense of always feeling and desiring in lukewarm ways, never having very strong or very weak responses? Definitely not! Very strong emotions—even distressing emotions like anger or very exciting emotions like joy, love, and political enthusiasm—often are precisely the mean. (Hence, the maxim "moderation in all things" does not accurately express Aristotle's view.) Furthermore, if mere emotional calm were the goal, virtue would be relatively easy to identify. As Aristotle emphasizes, this is not the case.

> It is a difficult business to be good; because in any given case it is difficult to find the midpoint—for instance, not everyone can find the center of a circle; only the man who knows how. So too it is easy to get angry—anyone can do that—or to give and spend money; but to feel or act towards the right person to the right extent at the right time for the right reason in the right way—that is not easy, and it is not everyone that can do it. Hence to do these things well is a rare, laudable and fine achievement.[5]

The mean is not the lukewarm, but instead the morally reasonable. Reasonable emotions and desires are those directed toward the appropriate person or object, on the suitable occasion, for the correct reason, and with fitting intensity. Unfortunately, this is not very informative. Aristotle seems to move in a circle that does not advance understanding. Virtue may indeed be the mean between extremes, and the mean may indeed be the virtuous middle ground between two nonvirtuous extremes. But how are the virtuous middle ground and the nonvirtuous extremes determined?

Aristotle offers two ways out of the circle. First, he analyzes in detail the many occasions and motives appropriate to each virtue and its characteristic sphere of action, emotion, and desire. Many of these analyses remain illuminating, or at least helpful, starting points for more precise contemporary discussions of virtues. Second, Aristotle insists there is a limit to how far such analyses can go. Morality is too complex and too imprecise to be captured in simple rules. It requires the finely tuned sensitivity of wise and prudent individuals. Indeed, Aristotle completes his definition of virtue by alluding to such individuals: "So virtue is a purposive disposition, lying in a mean that is relative to us and determined by a rational principle, and by that which a prudent man would use to determine it."[6] By "rational principle" Aristotle does not mean an abstract rule, but instead exercising sound practical judgment on that occasion.

Critics of Aristotle charge that this ultimate appeal to moral prudence is as much a dead-end as Plato's fruitless appeal to the Form of the Good. Lawrence Kohlberg, for example, dismissed Aristotle's ethics as the "bag of virtues" approach to morality. Most of the act-oriented ethicists discussed in Chapter 4 also reject Aristotle for failing to look hard enough for general rules about right action.

Yet perhaps Aristotle is simply being true to the moral facts! Even though rational emotions and desires are an essential aspect of the moral life, they defy formulation in abstract rules, which cannot express the intricacies of context. Moreover, the subtleties of moral insight and sensitivity that develop through the years of experience, study, struggle, and habit formation cannot be formulated in generalizations. Carol Gilligan would find this aspect of Aristotle's context-oriented moral reasoning to be on the right track, as do many contemporary virtue ethicists.

Difficulties with Greek Ethics

Much of classical Greek ethics has contemporary relevance, such as Plato's idea of virtue as moral health and Aristotle's insights into practical reasoning. Yet Greek ethics rests on three questionable claims: (1) human beings have one distinctive function, (2) that function is reasoning, and (3) because this function is distinctively human, it defines human good (as life in accord with reason). Most contemporary ethicists would reject all these claims.

To begin with the third questionable claim, is it obvious why the distinctiveness of a function should define goodness? How do we move from "is distinctive of" to "is the basis of goodness"? No doubt it is also distinctive of humans that they display more cruelty than any other earthly creature, but obviously that capacity does not define the good. Perhaps human good lies instead in developing capacities that are shared with other mammals, for example, the capacity to care for members of one's species, or even for members of other species. (One thinks of Koko, the gorilla who lovingly raised a kitten.)

Concerning the second questionable claim, is it true that reasoning is distinctive of human beings? It is now known that some mammals, such as gorillas, chimpanzees, and dolphins, have remarkable reasoning capacities. Admittedly there are great differences of degree between their reasoning capacities and ours. But that is true of many other shared capacities, such as caring for others, forming social ties, or even enjoying sophisticated physical pleasures—capacities that Plato and Aristotle refused to regard as distinctively human.

Turning to the first questionable claim, is it true that humans have just one distinctive function? *Homo sapiens* does many things better than members of other species. Perhaps most of them involve reasoning in the very wide sense of making inferences and thinking cogently. However, this wide sense of reason is too broad to define human good. Such reasoning is used in pursuing ingenious forms of evil and sophisticated forms of play, work, and inquiry.

Moreover, what about capacities that are not reducible to reason, such as living by religious faith or being altruistic?

Aquinas: Religious Virtues

Emphasis on other human capacities has formed the basis for alternative theories about human nature and virtue. Let us briefly consider two of these theories, which stress religious faith and altruism.

In discussing the Reverend Martin Luther King, Jr., we alluded to the Christian tradition of virtue ethics. Like other religious traditions, it defines human nature by reference to faith in God. Saint Thomas Aquinas (1224–1274) is of special interest because he developed his virtue ethics as a synthesis of the Greeks' four cardinal virtues—wisdom, courage, temperance, and justice—and the key Christian virtues—faith, hope, and charity (love).

Aquinas agreed with Plato and Aristotle that the one purpose of human beings is to live by reason and that pursuing this purpose results in human well-being or happiness. Aquinas, however, saw the primary role of reason as proving that God exists and discerning the "natural law" that God built into our very nature. Hence, for Aquinas, the natural purpose in living by reason became a supernatural purpose: supreme happiness through communion with God, a happiness imperfectly realizable in this world and perfected only in life after death.

Aquinas thought that wisdom (the paramount Greek virtue) implies the theological virtues of faith, hope and love. He also thought he could use wise reasoning to give several proofs that God exists. Then, because God is loving and commands that we love, Aquinas derived the virtue of love for Him and charity (benevolence) toward humans. Faith became fidelity to God's commandments with the hope of salvation. The other Greek virtues were also reinterpreted along Christian lines. Courage became the virtue that enables us to endure the dangers of this world, in particular the temptations of sin on the journey toward salvation. Temperance was expanded to include patience and humility, fasting and chastity.

Aquinas's approach to the virtues differs greatly from Aristotle's. For example, Aristotle would view the Christian virtue of humility as resembling the vice of failing to have proper pride. Christian discipline of the body through chastity and fasting hardly gibe with the Greek exuberance in the physical. And the idea of charity as the virtue of loving all humankind would be alien to Aristotle, who valued only outstanding humans who achieved high degrees of virtue.

Even more foreign to Aristotle and Plato would be the Christian idea of sin as betrayal of God. For Aquinas and other orthodox Christians, pride in the sense of setting oneself above God by refusing to live by God's commandments is the worst sin or vice. By contrast, Aristotle did not view pride in this sense as a vice at all. Earlier than Aquinas, the monastic movement had stressed Seven Deadly Sins: Pride, Envy (coveting), Anger, Sloth, Avarice, Gluttony, and Lust. Aristotle would not have regarded at least two of these— anger and lust—as vices, nor would he have singled out the others as the worst failures of virtue.

Hume: Benevolence and Sympathy

Now consider a very different kind of virtue ethics, the one offered by David Hume (1711–1776). Hume was a skeptic who incisively criticized Aquinas's attempts to offer proofs of God's existence. His view of human nature was based neither on religious faith nor on praise of reason, but rather on the psychology of his day combined with his own attempts to explain the origin of virtue. Yet there is an important overlap between Hume and Aquinas: Both view benevolence or altruism as a central virtue. Hume makes it the supreme virtue, and of all virtue ethicists Hume most deserves to be called the philosopher of benevolence.*

Hume divided the human mind into the domains of reason and sentiment. Unlike Plato, Aristotle, and Aquinas, Hume argued that reason does not provide the moral ends of human life but merely identifies facts and logical relationships among ideas. Moral purposes in human life derive from sentiment—our emotional capacities and attitudes. One sentiment in particular is crucial: sympathy, which is the capacity and tendency to feel distress when we see others in distress, and to be pleased when we see them happy. Sympathy is not a virtue, but it enables us to identify and appreciate virtues. It makes us naturally inclined to approve of benevolence in all its forms.

> It may be esteemed, perhaps, a superfluous task to prove, that the benevolent or softer affections are estimable; and wherever they appear, engage the approbation and good-will of mankind. The epithets *sociable, good-natured, humane, merciful, grateful, friendly, generous, beneficent,* or their equivalents, are known in all languages, and universally express the highest merit, which *human nature* is capable of attaining.[8]

Accordingly, for Hume the worst vice is cruelty, not ignorance (as Plato and Aristotle thought) or pride (as Aquinas thought).

In Hume's view reason does play an important role in morality by providing information about how to act virtuously and by enabling us to adopt an impartial point of view that counteracts bias and ensures consistency. Reason

---

*Carol Gilligan's ethic of caring is clearly foreshadowed by Hume.[7]

also aids in developing useful social conventions about how best to distribute property. Because societies differ so greatly, Hume recognizes as legitimate variations in the social conventions defining justice. He also refers to justice as an "artificial virtue," that is, one defined by social conventions, in contrast with the "natural virtue" of benevolence, which recommends certain responses independently of laws and customs.

From Theory to Practice

Our four classical theories of virtue all attempt to identify distinctive human capacities and use them to show the direction of human good and self-fulfillment. Yet these theories are founded on ideas of human nature that differ greatly, some stressing reason, others faith, and still others sympathy. Which theory of human nature is correct or best? Whereas theoretical ethics has the luxury of engaging in subtle disputes over these theories, as it has done for several millenia, applied ethics must proceed with the urgent task of addressing practical moral needs. Because applied ethicists cannot hope to resolve theoretical disputes before proceeding, it may seem that the theories are irrelevant for our purposes. Or should each of us simply choose a theory we find personally appealing and apply it to practical issues?

The view advanced in this book is that the applied ethicists—you and I—are justified in bypassing abstract disputes about human nature and the ultimate theoretical foundations for the virtues. We are free to borrow from any and all theories that offer insights into practical concerns. Notice that we have begun to do just that by emphasizing Plato's notion of inner harmony, an idea of both interest and contemporary relevance. We have also focused on Aristotle's Doctrine of the Mean independently of his theoretical contentions about the function of humans. Continuing in this way does not lead to methodological chaos. It simply indicates a desire to benefit from the practical wisdom of great thinkers, a wisdom that can be disentangled from their more debatable speculations.

MacIntyre: Self-Knowledge and Social Goods

This approach to the rich legacy of philosophical theory is in tune with the works of two recent virtue ethicists: Alasdair MacIntyre in *After Virtue* and Edmund L. Pincoffs in *Quandaries and Virtues*. Both MacIntyre and Pincoffs retrieve and develop central concepts from the tradition of virtue ethics while at the same time freeing them from any narrow view of human nature.

MacIntyre retains the hope of grounding the virtues in a theory of human nature, perhaps one emerging from contemporary social science. In this and other respects he can lay claim to an Aristotelian perspective. Yet, unlike Aristotle, he stresses that individuals can find their good in an enormous variety of ways. He is sensitive to the great range of settings and legitimate emphases on particular virtues that we referred to in our discussions of Socrates, King, and Stanton. Above all, he emphasizes that the good for an individual cannot be spelled out all at once in advance using abstract notions like "reason." Instead it must be uncovered piecemeal by each of us through a continuing search for self-knowledge.

Life as a Narrative Quest

MacIntyre views each human life as a "narrative quest": a search through time, with intricate threads connecting past, present, and hoped-for future. The quest is a search for self-fulfillment while maintaining unity among activities and relationships. At every step there is uncertainty, unpredictability, and confusion. Hence, we have a recurring need to reexamine our purposes and our grasp of the good. In this sense a human life "is always an [ongoing] education both as to the character of that which is sought and in self-knowledge."[9]

Virtues represent qualities that support us in this pursuit of our good rather than a complete vision of what that good is. MacIntyre writes: "The good life for man is the life spent in seeking for the good life for man, and the virtues necessary for the seeking are those which will enable us to understand what more and what else the good life for man is."[10] This aspect of MacIntyre's theory reminds us more of Socrates' ongoing search for a meaningful life, with the virtues as aids in that search, than of Plato's and Aristotle's belief that the virtues fully define the good and happy life.

Yet the quest for our good and its supporting virtues is not conducted in a vacuum. Nor is it entirely the product of personal autonomy and authenticity, as Sartre asserted. Many of its key ingredients derive from social practices, a practice being any complex form of cooperative human activity directed toward "internal goods," such as professions, academic disciplines in science and the humanities, the fine arts, political institutions, families, and even games like chess. In this context internal goods are desirable ends that partially define the practice itself: The profession of medicine aims at health, law aims at social justice, and family life aims at intimate and supportive personal relationships. Achieving these internal goods is largely made possible by the practice itself. In contrast, "external goods" like money and fame do not define the nature of the practice. They can be achieved in many other ways besides engaging in the practice.

Virtues are traits that enable individuals effectively to pursue these internal goods and thereby to enrich their lives. As it pertains to practices, MacIntyre defines a virtue as *"an acquired human quality the possession and exercise of which tends to enable us to achieve those goods which are internal to practices and the lack of which effectively prevents us from achieving any such goods."*[11] For example, conscientiousness, trustworthiness, loyalty, benevolent concern for the public good, and respect for colleagues are virtues that contribute to the successful pursuit of the internal goods of most professions.

Virtues also help make practices prosper. Unless many individuals displayed virtues, the practices could not survive or advance. For example, courage in undertaking risks and challenges makes possible the advancement of professional knowledge. Honesty in being careful about facts is essential to all professional practices. And justice plays a role in recognizing proper authority and respecting others' contributions to the profession.

Each of us participates in many practices, and those forms of participation can come into conflict. Familiar examples involve professional versus private life, college studies versus parental demands, one friendship versus another. The virtues, especially practical wisdom, enable us to integrate the numerous roles we play in various practices and keep them in proper perspective. MacIntyre's most complete characterization of the virtues as aiding us in achieving unity and self-fulfillment is in the following passage:

> The virtues . . . are to be understood as those dispositions which will not only sustain practices and enable us to achieve the goods internal to practices, but which will also sustain us in the relevant kind of quest for the good, by enabling us to overcome the harms, dangers, temptations and situations which we encounter, and which will furnish us with increasing self-knowledge and increasing knowledge of the good.[12]

In addition to practices, the virtues are exercised within particular moral traditions that individuals inherit. The good for members of particular families, religions, nations, and cultures is not altogether the same as for others.[13] We are free to modify but not altogether remove the influence of the traditions within which we conduct our personal quest for the good. Sometimes, in fact, denying its influence and relevance is immoral, as with those Americans who deny any responsibility for dealing with racism on the grounds that they never owned slaves or shot Indians.

Pincoffs: Choices Among Persons

Edmund L. Pincoffs is another contemporary virtue theorist who frees virtue ethics from any narrow theory of human nature. Pincoffs, however, criticizes MacIntyre for focusing so much on practices. In Pincoffs's view the primary focus in understanding the virtues is not social practices but choices among persons: "The natural home of the language of virtue and vice is in that region of our lives in which we must choose between, not acts, lines of acting, or policies, but persons."[14] Choosing among persons has many dimensions: picking people for a job or public office; choosing to pursue personal relationships with individuals such as friends, lovers, or a spouse; choosing a lawyer, physician, or other professional for some service. It also includes making nuanced adjustments in relationships.

Instrumental and Noninstrumental Virtues

Although Pincoffs is critical of all attempts to confine the virtues within a theory of human nature, he sees it as a legitimate task to organize and clarify connections among the virtues. His classification scheme is depicted in Figure 3.1.[15] As the figure indicates, Pincoffs, like Aristotle, includes as virtues (which are special instances of personality traits) all excellences of the personality, not just moral excellences. Unlike Aristotle, however, he tries to distinguish between moral virtues and nonmoral good traits like wit, social decorum, and noble bearing. Let us briefly explain the terms he uses as headings in the figure.

Instrumental virtues are traits that enable people to pursue their goals effectively or to perform tasks well, whether as individuals (*agent instrumental virtues* like persistence) or as part of a group (*group instrumental virtues* like cooperativeness). *Noninstrumental virtues* are traits inherently desirable for their own sake, whether or not they serve as means to further ends. Some noninstrumental virtues, such as nobility and charm, are *aesthetic*, that is, aspects of beauty. Others are *meliorating;* they make life with other people more tolerable. These include the virtues of tolerance, tact, and other qualities of peacemakers and negotiators (*mediating virtues*), and virtues like gentleness and cheerfulness, which make individuals more pleasant to live with (*temperamental virtues*). They also include traits like politeness and decency, which make interactions more pleasant (*formal virtues*).

Finally we arrive at the specifically *moral virtues*. According to Pincoffs, moral

> virtues and vices have the common characteristic that they are forms of regard or lack of regard for the interests of others. They are, roughly, of two closely related classes: those that have to do with direct concern or lack of concern for the interests of other persons, on the one hand, and those that have to do with the unfair advantage that one accords to one's own interests over the interests of others.[16]

Avoiding unfair advantages to ourselves is the minimal requirement of morality, and it is a firm requirement. The *mandatory virtues* pertain to this area of morality. Honesty, truthfulness, and nonrecklessness, for example, are always required. The *nonmandatory virtues*, by contrast, indicate desirable

FIGURE 3.1 *Pincoffs's Classification of Virtues*

PERSONALITY TRAITS

|

VIRTUES

| Noninstrumental | | | Instrumental |

Aesthetic

NOBLE	CHARMING
dignity	gracefulness
virility	wittiness
magnanimity	vivaciousness
serenity	imaginativeness
nobility	whimsicality
	liveliness

Meliorating

MEDIATING	TEMPERAMENTAL	FORMAL
tolerance	gentleness	civility
reasonableness	humorousness	politeness
tactfulness	amiability	decency
	cheerfulness	modesty
	warmth	hospitableness
	appreciativeness	unpretentiousness
	openness	
	even-temperedness	
	noncomplainingness	
	nonvindictiveness	

Agent Instrumental

persistence
courage
alertness
carefulness
resourcefulness
prudence
energy
strength
cool-headedness
determination

Moral

MANDATORY	NONMANDATORY
honesty	benevolence
sincerity	altruism
truthfulness	selflessness
loyalty	sensitivity
consistency	forgivingness
reliability	helpfulness
dependability	understandingness
trustworthiness	super honesty
nonrecklessness	super conscientiousness
nonnegligence	super reliability
nonvengefulness	
nonbelligerence	
nonfanaticism	

Group Instrumental

cooperativeness
"practical wisdom"
the virtues of leaders
and followers

though not obligatory traits. Their presence in a person is good, but their absence need not indicate a vice. This is true of benevolence, altruism, forgivingness, and exceptional ("super") degrees of honesty and conscientiousness.

It is possible to accept Pincoffs's main distinctions while objecting to his classification of specific virtues. For example, some of the virtues he lists as nonmoral, such as tolerance, appreciativeness, and decency, might better be regarded as moral virtues, because they are forms of direct regard, however minimal, for the interests of other people.

Another objection concerns his characterization of the "natural home" of the virtues as choosing among persons, thereby oddly centering virtue ethics on acts (acts of choosing among people). It might be closer to the truth to say that virtues guide our *evaluations* of and *attitudes* toward persons, as well as our *relationships* with them. Moreover, choosing among persons, even in Pincoffs's wide sense of "choosing," represents only one dimension of evaluating them. Other dimensions include understanding, encouraging, being inspired by, pitying, and criticizing them.

Even evaluating persons, however, is too restrictive a label. The virtues are just as important in shaping and fulfilling our own lives and in evaluating practices, as MacIntyre argued. Moreover, the virtues serve as guides for all our actions, not just those of choosing among persons. Very often moral reasoning and guidance come in the form of asking what is the honest, decent, considerate, or courageous thing to do. Admittedly, this guidance is rough, as Aristotle acknowledged. But virtues play multiple "natural" roles in our lives: guiding individual acts, lines of action, participation in practices, and relationships, as well as guiding choices among persons.

Beyond noting these criticisms, we need not choose between MacIntyre's and Pincoffs's theories. Each offers enriching theoretical frameworks for doing applied ethics without entering into disputes over theories of human nature.

Summary

Virtues are desirable character traits consisting of patterns of emotions, desires, attitudes, intentions, and reasoning as well as actions. Classical virtue theories sought to link the virtues to particular theories about human nature, that is, about the distinctive or most significant human capacities and possibilities. Virtues were then defined as excellences that enable people to achieve their good by fulfilling their human nature. Virtue theories also identified the virtues most important for self-fulfillment. Table 3.2 summarizes some key concepts discussed in four classical theories of virtue.

Applied ethics bypasses theoretical disputes over which aspects of human nature are most significant for understanding morality and over which virtues

TABLE 3.2 *Four Classical Theories of Virtue*

Theorist	View of Human Nature	Main Concepts	Paramount Virtue	Worst Vice
Plato	Exercise reason to achieve happiness	Moral health as inner harmony	Wisdom, courage, temperance, justice	Ignorance
Aristotle	Exercise reason to achieve happiness	Golden mean	Wisdom, courage, temperance, justice	Ignorance
Aquinas	God's plan leading to happiness after death	Faith; sin	Faith, hope, charity	Pride
Hume	Sentiment vs. reason	Sympathy	Benevolence	Cruelty

are paramount. Applied ethicists are free to draw on insights from all virtue theories whenever they are helpful in dealing with practical concerns. Recently, MacIntyre and Pincoffs provided theories of virtue that offer frameworks for doing applied ethics of this sort. MacIntyre defined the virtues as desirable traits that bring unity to the lives of people whose specific good is constantly being reshaped through participation in practices, moral traditions, and personal relationships. Pincoffs defined the virtues as excellences used in choosing among persons. For our purposes the virtues are best viewed as desirable traits that guide our attitudes toward other people and provide ideals for shaping our own lives and relationships. Pincoffs also offers a classification of the virtues and distinguishes the moral virtues as forms of regard for others' interests.

DISCUSSION TOPICS

1. Discuss Plato's Doctrine of the Unity of the Virtues, which says that to have any one of the main virtues implies having them all. This doctrine contradicts common sense, which tells us that people can be courageous but not benevolent, or honest but not temperate. Is Plato's doctrine more plausible if it is interpreted to apply only to perfect achievement of the four main virtues he discusses?

2. Both Plato and Freud divided the mind into three parts in order to explain inner conflict and to understand mental health. Discuss whether their distinctions are plausible and helpful. Compare and contrast them with Hume's distinction between the sentiments and reason.

3. Plato described the relationship between good character and right conduct in the following passage.

> Justice [i.e., morality] . . . is not a matter of external behavior, but of the inward self and of attending to all that is, in the fullest sense, a man's proper concern. The just man does not allow the several elements in his soul to usurp one another's functions; he is indeed one who sets his house in order, by self-mastery and discipline coming to be at peace with himself. . . . When he speaks of just and honorable conduct, he will mean the behavior that helps to produce and to preserve this habit of mind; and by wisdom he will mean the knowledge which presides over such conduct. Any action which tends to break down this habit will be for him unjust; and the notions governing it he will call ignorance and folly.[17]

This passage seems to suggest that right conduct is determined by looking within our personalities and characters. Do you agree? What would Aristotle say about this, given his Doctrine of the Mean?

4. Discuss the similarities and differences between Carol Gilligan's ethics of care (discussed in Chapter 2) and the theories of virtue of Hume and Aristotle.

5. In this chapter we focused on virtues while alluding to vices. Based on what was said, compare and contrast the views of Plato, Aristotle, Aquinas, and Hume about which vices are worst. In doing so, explain their views by reference to their theories of human nature. Which view do you find most insightful?

6. Using Pincoffs's definition of a moral virtue, is faith in God a moral virtue? How about faith in the prospects for sustaining human community and for avoiding nuclear holocaust?

7. Apply MacIntyre's distinction between the internal and the external goods of practices to education, from both a student's and a teacher's viewpoint. Relate it to what was said in Chapter 2 about the aims of liberal education.

8. Select four of the moral virtues listed in Figure 3.1, two mandatory ones and two nonmandatory ones. For each, try to identify what Aristotle would call their corresponding vices (excess and deficiency), their characteristic spheres of action, and their types of emotions and desires.

SUGGESTED READINGS

Aquinas, Saint Thomas. *Introduction to St. Thomas Aquinas.* Anton C. Pegis (ed.). New York: Modern Library, 1948.

Aristotle. *Ethics.* Trans. J. A. K. Thomson and Hugh Tredennick. New York: Penguin, 1976.

Baier, Annette C. "Hume, the Women's Moral Theorist?" In Eva Feder Kittay and Diana T. Meyers (eds.), *Women and Moral Theory.* Totowa, NJ: Rowman & Littlefield, 1987.

Brandt, Richard B. "Traits of Character: A Conceptual Analysis." *American Philosophical Quarterly,* vol. 7 (1970): 23–37.

Fairlie, Henry. *The Seven Deadly Sins Today.* Notre Dame, IN: University of Notre Dame Press, 1979.

Foot, Philippa. *Virtues and Vices.* Berkeley, CA: University of California Press, 1978.

Hudson, Stephen D. *Human Character and Morality.* Boston: Routledge & Kegan Paul, 1986.

Hume, David. *Hume's Ethical Writings.* Alasdair MacIntyre (ed.). New York: Macmillan, 1965.

MacIntyre, Alasdair. *After Virtue.* Notre Dame, IN: University of Notre Dame Press, 1981.

Meilaender, Gilbert C. *The Theory and Practice of Virtue.* Notre Dame, IN: University of Notre Dame Press, 1984.

Norman, Richard. *The Moral Philosophers.* New York: Clarendon Press, 1983.

Pieper, Josef. *The Four Cardinal Virtues.* Notre Dame, IN: University of Notre Dame Press, 1966.

Pincoffs, Edmund L. *Quandaries and Virtues.* Lawrence, KS: University Press of Kansas, 1986.

Plato. *The Republic of Plato.* Trans. Francis MacDonald Cornford. New York: Oxford University Press, 1945.

Stevenson, Leslie. *Seven Theories of Human Nature.* 2nd ed. New York: Oxford University Press, 1987.

Wallace, James D. *Virtues and Vices.* Ithaca, NY: Cornell University Press, 1978.

CHAPTER 4

Theories of Right Action

Character and conduct are distinguishable but inseparable. Character is displayed primarily through patterns of conduct, and conduct shapes and modifies character. The kinds of persons we are and how we act are intimately connected dimensions of relationships. Up to this point we have emphasized character. Now we focus on right actions and the philosophical theories about what makes acts right or wrong.

These theories fall into three major categories: duty ethics, rights ethics, and utilitarianism. Duty ethics regards duty as the fundamental moral concept, rights ethics sees human rights as essential, and utilitarianism views overall good consequences as basic. For each type of theory we will discuss an early classical thinker and a more recent defender.

Lying

Although we will also use other illustrations, we will return throughout this discussion to one common example: the moral status of lying. Lying is a useful point for comparing and contrasting the various theories of right action because it is a simple and familiar act that all of us have engaged in and have all been hurt by. A lie is any act of communicating something false, knowing it is false, with the intention of deceiving.

Keep in mind, however, that although lying is an instance of trying to deceive, it is not synonymous with deceiving. For one thing, to deceive is to succeed in misleading someone, whereas lying merely represents trying to do so. Lies sometimes fail to achieve their intended purpose of deceiving, such as when the hearer knows the truth or has reason to suspect that a lie is being told. Furthermore, deception takes forms other than lying, including pretense, withholding information, and purposefully giving so much information that a hearer is overwhelmed, confused, or misled. For the sake of simplicity we shall focus on lies, even though most of what we will say applies to other forms of deception as well.

Duty Ethics: Kant and Respect for Persons

Most of us believe that some lies are morally justified, whether permissible (allowable) or obligatory (required), but that most lies are not. Philosophers have generally shared this commonsense view, with one dramatic exception. Immanuel Kant (1724–1804), one of the greatest of the ethicists, argued that lying is never morally permissible. Kant was a duty ethicist, that is, someone who defines right acts as those required by duty. Unlike most of his followers, he believed there is an *absolute*—exceptionless—duty never to lie. His reasons for this belief will become clear as we discuss the more influential elements of his moral theory.

Kant endorsed as valid a long list of duties, such as to be honest, to keep promises, to be fair, to help others, to show gratitude for favors, to develop our talents, and not to hurt others or ourselves. For Kant, morality consisted of always trying to do our duty because we see it is our duty. His importance as a moral philosopher rests in his account of what makes something our duty. He suggested that three abstract duties underlie all others: (1) respect persons, (2) act on universal principles, and (3) act autonomously. Let us consider each of these duties.

First, Kant saw our most fundamental duty as respect for persons. To respect persons is to recognize them as being rational or autonomous in ways that should restrict our own actions. Rationality or autonomy is the capacity to make decisions for oneself in the pursuit of reasonable purposes, such as seeking happiness, developing talents, and obeying universal principles of duty that apply to all rational beings. Kant expressed this idea of respect by saying that people are "ends-in-themselves," as opposed to mere means to be used for our own purposes or ends. To put it another way, people have their own rational purposes, which place moral constraints on how we may treat them. Their rationality or autonomy gives them a worth and dignity beyond any price.

For example, to murder, rape, or torture other people is to flagrantly treat them as objects to be used for our purposes, in disregard of their own rational desires not to be treated in these ways. Kant also thought that by lying to and deceiving other people we are using them as objects. Lying manipulates people's beliefs, as well as their actions based on those beliefs, thus striking disrespectfully at the heart of their rationality as they attempt to live truthful lives. Lying represents a kind of coercion by which we distort other people's minds.*

Second, all duties have in common that they are universal—that is, they apply to all rational beings, both human beings and divine beings (if any). To determine how we ought to act, we must formulate principles that we can envision everyone acting on. For example, we can easily imagine everyone acting on the principle "Do not lie," but we cannot imagine everyone acting on the principle "Lie when it suits your own purposes." If everyone followed the latter principle, communication would break down. People could no longer take one another's statements seriously, so both sincere and deceitful statements would become impossible. In trying to conceive of everyone acting on the principle "Lie when it suits your own purposes," a contradiction arises: Everyone does tell lies (which is the hypothesis we begin with) and no one can tell lies (which is the implication of the hypothesis).

Third, the duty to respect persons entails the duty to respect oneself. That duty involves appreciating our own autonomy as we recognize and respond to specific duties. It is not enough just to do what is required by universal duties; we must also act out a sense of duty, what Kant calls a *good will* (or good intentions). This sense of duty is the only thing he praises as intrinsically good—good in and of itself, independently of its consequences.

Our real nobility lies in this capacity to do what is right because we see it is right and not solely from ulterior motives such as to make our parents or peers or ourselves happy, advance in careers, or gain religious rewards. Because this good will is a personal expression of our own rational nature, we can be said to "give ourselves the moral law" we live by. And because the moral law consists of universal principles applicable to everyone, we can also regard our own rational nature as the source of moral principles.

To sum up, Kant thought there were three principles underlying all the more specific principles of duty or, as he called them, "maxims" and "moral laws." In his words these principles are as follows:

1. *Respect persons:* "Act so that you treat humanity, whether in your own person or in that of another, always as an end and never as a means only."[1]
2. *Universalize principles:* "Act only according to that maxim by which you can at the same time will that it should become a universal law."[2]
3. *Be autonomous:* "Act only so that the will through its maxims could regard itself at the same time as universally lawgiving."[3]

Kant spoke of his three fundamental duties as three versions of *the categorical imperative.* He also referred to specific duties like "Don't lie" as cate-

---

*Kant also thought that in lying to ourselves we undermine our own purposes as rational beings. In Chapter 6 we will take up the topic of self-deception and self-directed lies.

gorical imperatives. An imperative is simply a command, and a categorical command is one without conditions or qualifications attached. Morality requires that we do our duty simply because it is our duty and not because any special conditions are attached. For example, a slogan like "Honesty pays" says, in effect, that *if* (on the condition that) you want to be successful in business, then you ought to be honest. Such "iffy" commands are *hypothetical imperatives,* to which a condition or hypothesis is attached. Categorical moral commands, by contrast, prescribe "Be honest" and "Don't lie"—period.

Duty Ethics: Ross and Prima Facie Duties

More recent ethicists who share Kant's duty orientation reject his belief that everyday principles like "Don't lie" are absolute. To take an extreme case (borrowed from James Rachels), consider the Dutch fishermen who during World War II helped Jewish refugees escape to England by hiding them in their boats. Nazi patrol boats would periodically stop the fishermen and ask them if they had any passengers on board. This created a moral dilemma in which two duties came into conflict: the duty to protect innocent life versus the duty not to lie. One duty had to give way in order that the other duty could be met. Virtually all duty ethicists agree that the duty to protect innocent life should have priority. In fact, even Kant's own fundamental principle to respect persons supports this judgment. Respecting the Jews' autonomy required lying; and not to lie would have supported the Nazis' attempt to violate that autonomy.

David Ross (1877–1971) was a duty ethicist who was especially sensitive to conflicts among duties. In order to underscore the frequency of these conflicts, he introduced a technical term now widely used. He said that duties that can be superseded when they conflict with other duties are *prima facie duties.* All, or almost all, familiar moral maxims, such as "Tell the truth," "Keep your promises," and "Do not kill," express prima facie duties in that they all have the potential to conflict with and be overridden by other duties. Even the duty not to kill may be overridden by the duty to defend innocent life, as in a war, or to defend oneself or others against a murderer. Prima facie duties, then, contrast with absolute or exceptionless duties, if such there are. They also contrast with what Ross called one's *actual duty*—what we should do in a specific situation, all things considered, and all conflicting duties weighed reasonably.

What does it mean to weigh prima facie duties reasonably so as to determine our actual duty? How should we decide which duty has priority on a particular occasion? There is no infallible test. According to Ross, Kant's guidelines of universalizing the principle we act on, respecting other persons, and being autonomous are insufficient for resolving all practical dilemmas. Rather, one simply has to think through all relevant aspects of the situation and exercise one's most careful judgment.

> When I am in a situation, as perhaps I always am, in which more than one of these *prima facie* duties is incumbent on me, what I have to do is to study the situation as fully as I can until I form the considered opinion (it is never more) that in the circumstances one of them is more incumbent than any other.[4]

This context-bound reasoning, which is reminiscent in some ways of both Carol Gilligan and Aristotle, can be illustrated by reference to the dilemma faced by Sartre's student (discussed in Chapter 1). In Ross's terms the student had a prima facie duty to help his mother and a prima facie duty to oppose fascism. Determining his actual duty was a matter of patiently bringing to mind and attending closely to all facts made relevant by these two duties. No general ranking of the duties exists to indicate that the student should always give preference to the one duty over the other. Critics of Ross find this approach too imprecise to be helpful, but Ross believed that moral reasoning involves this kind of imprecision.

When are we allowed to make exceptions to the duty not to lie? Sometimes in order to conform to the duty of benevolence, as when the Dutch fishermen lied to protect the Jews they were helping. But should we lie out of benevolence to a close relative who is dying from cancer and does not know it? It depends perhaps on whether the person would want to know the truth in order to make final decisions about his or her affairs or whether the person would want a few peaceful final hours.

Unlike Kant, Ross saw no need to search beneath the numerous prima facie duties for underlying fundamental moral principles. He does, however, organize prima facie duties into clusters that highlight certain connections among them, yielding the following organizational scheme, which he admitted might be incomplete.[5]

1. Duties deriving from my previous acts
   a. Duties of fidelity: those arising from my promises and commitments
   b. Duties of reparation: those arising from my previous harm to others
2. Duties deriving from other people's acts
   a. Duties of gratitude: duties to return favors or unearned services
3. Duties of justice: to support fair distribution, and oppose unfair distribution, of benefits and burdens in accord with merit
4. Duties of beneficence: duties to help other people
5. Duties of self-improvement: duties to improve our own virtue, intelligence, and talents
6. Duties of non-maleficence: duties not to injure others

Ross contended that it is intuitively obvious, at least to morally mature adults, that each of these is our duty (our prima facie duty), without the need to base them on more fundamental duties. This intuitive obviousness vanishes, however, when duties come into conflict with each other, creating moral dilemmas. Then we must simply exercise our best moral judgment, realizing, we might add, that others can sometimes aid our reflections.

Rights Ethics: Locke and Liberty Rights

Duty ethicists regard duties as basic, but for every duty they acknowledge a corresponding or correlated right. For example, if I have a duty to you to tell the truth, then you have a right to be told the truth; if I have a duty not to kill you, then you have a right not to be killed by me. Rights ethicists contend that this is backwards. Rights and duties are correlated, but rights rather than duties are morally fundamental. Duties arise because people (and perhaps animals) have moral rights.

The most basic rights of people are *human rights*—rights that exist because we are human beings. We are familiar with this idea from the American *Declaration of Independence*:* "We hold these truths to be self-evident; that all men are created equal; that they are endowed by their creator with inherent and inalienable rights; that among these are life, liberty, and the pursuit of happiness." John Locke (1632–1704), who was a major influence on Thomas Jefferson as he drafted the *Declaration of Independence,* listed the three fundamental rights as life, liberty, and property. Other rights ethicists offer different lists, but the key idea remains constant: All people have rights simply because they are people.

Human rights are "inalienable"; they cannot be given or taken away. We may, of course, decide to not exercise them on certain occasions or to allow someone else to exercise them on our behalf. For example, we may sign a "living will" that authorizes our selected guardian to exercise our rights in deciding how we should be treated by physicians if our capacity to think is irreversibly damaged by accident or disease. Even in a coma, however, we retain rights; we merely transfer their exercise to our guardian.

The rights mentioned in the *Declaration of Independence* are human rights; as such they are recognized but not created by that document. Note that human rights and political rights are distinct, even when their content is the same. Political rights are simply those accepted by governments, whereas human rights exist even when governments do not recognize them. Black South Africans, for example, have human rights that their government violates.

---

*We also mentioned human rights in Chapter 2 while discussing Elizabeth Cady Stanton.

Similarly, the human rights of women and minorities, especially black people and Indians, have been continually violated in the United States.*

Locke was especially interested in *liberty rights,* that is, the rights to be left alone by governments and by the majority of citizens, who sometimes persecute individuals. Because liberty rights are rights *not* to be interfered with, they are also called *negative rights.* This emphasis on liberty (or negative) rights is represented in contemporary politics by libertarians, who emphasize the rights to property and to privacy, that is, the general right to live as we choose without interference from others.

Privacy rights play an important role in everyday life and justify some lies, for example, lies to strangers who ask prying questions. Intrusive callers have no right to know certain information, and if a lie is the only way to protect our privacy, so be it. Parents may prudently exercise rights to security when they teach their children to tell certain lies to strangers who call when the children are at home alone.

People have a right, however, to be told the truth in certain situations. In the political context citizens within a democracy have a right to be informed of important governmental actions (except when national security requires secrecy—a much-abused exception). In the context of professions clients and consumers have the right to be warned of the risks in using products and services, a right that derives from the fundamental right to life. And in the context of personal relationships a spouse or close friend may have the right to be told many things that a stranger has no right to know.

Rights Ethics: Melden and Welfare Rights

Just as duty ethicists try to identify some hierarchy among the various duties, so rights ethicists try to distinguish between more and less fundamental rights. Unlike Locke and Jefferson, who singled out just three rights as basic (although not exactly the same three), A. I. Melden, a contemporary rights ethicist, suggests there is just one ultimate right from which others can be derived and justified: the right to pursue one's legitimate interests. Legitimate interests are those interests that do not violate other people's similar and equal rights.

The right to pursue one's interest underlies even the right to life, because we cannot pursue our interests unless other people allow us to live. This basic

---

*How is that possible given the statement endorsing human rights in the *Declaration of Independence?* Clearly, blacks and women were not regarded by the "founding fathers" as being full and complete people who therefore had human rights. They were treated, in varying degrees, as property rather than persons.

right can also be applied to show why lying is usually wrong. Lies give misleading information that interferes with the pursuit of our interests in large or small ways. Lying subverts, or at least shows a willingness to subvert, the agency (i.e., ability to act) of the person lied to, thereby infringing on that person's right to pursue her or his interests. Justified lies involve situations in which more pressing considerations enter, such as the right to life (as in the Dutch fishermen example) or the rights to privacy and security (as in the example of telephone lies).

Going well beyond Locke, Melden suggests that the basic right to pursue our interests entails rights to be helped in some situations. These are *welfare rights* or *positive rights* to receive certain goods, as opposed to liberty or negative rights not to be interfered with. Melden argues that contemporary societies ought to institutionalize welfare systems (contrary to the libertarian political ideology) to support the needy—who, under certain circumstances, could be any of us. The basic right to pursue our affairs entails a right to the minimal necessities for a decent existence within societies that can readily provide them. This right is limited, however, in that we have no right, for example, to bankrupt society by demanding millions of dollars of medical care each year.

What are the precise limits of welfare rights to be helped and of liberty rights to pursue our interests? At what point do others' rights restrict our own? No possible answer can be both general and specific enough to resolve all practical disagreements. The extent of rights, and the reasonable exercise of rights, must be understood within given communities of people living together, making certain claims on one another, and sometimes able to help one another. Melden views the interplay of rights within a community of shared moral concern to be as complex as Ross's account of how duties are interrelated.

Utilitarianism: Mill and Act-Utilitarianism

Utilitarianism is the view that there is a single moral requirement: to produce the most good for the most people, giving equal consideration to each person potentially affected, and defining "good" without mentioning moral notions. All duties and all rights arise because of this requirement.

Notice first that utilitarianism is entirely forward-looking—it defines right conduct strictly in terms of future consequences. This contrasts sharply with both duty ethics and rights ethics. Consider the question of why promises should be kept. Both duty ethicists and rights ethicists would look first to the past: to the promise itself. The promise is an act of committing oneself to do something, and that commitment, according to the duty ethicist, generates a duty. Or the promise is an act of giving someone else the right to have something done by the promiser, and that right, according to the rights ethicist, provides the reason to keep the promise. By contrast, according to the utilitarian, promises should be kept only because of the good effects of keeping them and the bad effects of not keeping them.

What about lies? According to John Stuart Mill (1806–1873), the greatest of the utilitarians, lies are usually wrong because they lead to more bad than good effects. Yet there are exceptions to the rule against lying,

> the chief of which is when the withholding of some fact (as of information from a malefactor, or of bad news from a person dangerously ill) would save an individual (especially an individual other than oneself) from great and unmerited evil, and when the withholding can only be effected by denial. . . . It is not the fault of any creed, but of the complicated nature of human affairs, that rules of conduct cannot be so framed as to require no exceptions, and that hardly any kind of action can safely be laid down as either always obligatory or always condemnable.[6]

With the exception of Kant all the philosophers we have discussed would agree that some lies are justified. Mill, however, offers a different account of what is usually wrong but occasionally right about telling lies. Instead of referring to duties of veracity (to tell the truth) or respect for persons, and instead of appealing to rights to privacy or to pursue our interests, he appeals solely to the good and bad effects of telling lies. Mill says that we should examine each individual action to assess its consequences compared with other options in the situation. That option that produces the greatest balance of good over bad is the right action. This view is called *act-utilitarianism* (to distinguish it from rule-utilitarianism, which we shall examine later).*

What is the status of everyday rules like "Do not lie" and "Keep your promises"? Mill believed they are very important rules of thumb that express what should usually be done in a given situation. They accurately summarize shared human experience that usually more bad than good results from lies and broken promises. The rules do, however, have valid exceptions when breaking them is likely to produce more good than bad.

For all utilitarians, rightness is defined in terms of goodness. But what is goodness? Although utilitarians do not agree on the answer to that question, Mill's answer has been influential. Only happiness, according to Mill, is intrinsically good, that is, good in and of itself, independent of any further good effects it may have. All other good things are either components of happiness or means to attaining it ("instrumental goods"). Likewise, unhappiness is intrinsically bad.

What is happiness? Mill often confused it with pleasure. In his more care-

---

*In some passages, however, Mill seems closer to the rule-utilitarian view we will discuss later.

ful moments, however, he distinguished between pleasures, which are short-term emotions, and happiness, which is a long-term state that involves many pleasures, in great variety, mixed with some inevitable pains.* Moreover, Mill stated that the happy life is rich in "higher pleasures," which are *better in kind* than lower pleasures. The higher pleasures are those of the mind: pleasures of the intellect, of friendship, of love of art and beauty. The lower pleasures are those of the body: pleasures of eating, drinking, sex, and napping on a sunny afternoon.

Utilitarianism is attractive in part because it seems to provide a way of avoiding the reliance on intuitive judgments about how to weigh conflicting duties or competing rights. One simply tallies up the happiness and unhappiness likely to be produced by various options and picks the option that maximizes overall happiness or minimizes overall unhappiness (considering everyone affected). Unfortunately, Mill's distinction between higher and lower pleasures, as well as between kinds of happiness, greatly complicates matters. Instead of considering quantities of pleasures and pains, as measured by their intensity and duration, one must factor in elusive quality as well. How, in any case, can we be sure that Mill was correct in his judgments about quality?

Mill proposes to measure quality by taking a poll of qualified judges, that is, people who have experienced and appreciated both of the pleasures being compared. A large majority is decisive.

> Of two pleasures, if there be one to which all or almost all who have experience of both give a decided preference, irrespective of a feeling of moral obligation to prefer it, that is the more desirable pleasure. . . . Now it is an unquestionable fact that those who are equally acquainted with and equally capable of appreciating and enjoying both, do give a marked preference to the manner of existence which employs their higher faculties. Few human creatures would consent to be changed into any of the lower animals for a promise of the fullest allowance of a beast's pleasures.[7]

In a famous sentence he adds, "It is better to be a human being dissatisfied than a pig satisfied; better to be Socrates dissatisfied than a fool satisfied."[8]

Something puzzling occurs in the passage quoted. Mill begins by comparing the quality of kinds of pleasures, but ends up talking about "manners of existence" or ways of life involving various kinds of pleasures. It is true that few humans would choose to change places with pigs, but how does that fact prove that physical pleasures are inferior in quality to mental pleasures? Even if philosophers and artists did the voting, would the pleasures of eating and sex (at their best) be voted inferior to those of philosophy and art? The happy

---

* Perhaps happiness is better viewed as a positive attitude toward our lives when they consist of a satisfying mixture of pleasures, pains, activities, and relationships.

life does not banish or minimize physical pleasures but involves lots of both physical and mental pleasures, or so it would seem.

Nevertheless, Mill's attempt to distinguish among qualities of pleasures is instructive. Without some such distinctions the utilitarian would be forced to sympathetically take into account the pleasures that rapists, sadists, and murderers derive from their grisly deeds. Common sense, however, sees no value or intrinsic goodness in the pleasures of cruelty. How can such pleasures be ruled out without assuming we already know what is right or wrong independently of the utilitarian standard?

Utilitarianism: Brandt and Rule-Utilitarianism

Richard B. Brandt is a contemporary utilitarian who places restrictions on which pleasures are intrinsically good. He suggests that only rational desires, rational preferences based on those desires, and rational pleasures derived from satisfying those desires should be counted in calculating good and bad consequences. Intrinsic good thus becomes the satisfaction of rational desires.

Rational desires are those that survive after intensive and persistent scrutiny in light of all facts relevant to them and on the basis of clear and logical thinking. Desires to overeat, to smoke, to use harmful drugs, or to hurt ourselves in other ways would not survive this scrutiny. Nor, Brandt hopes, would cruel desires such as those of the rapist and the sadist. This process of making ourselves vividly aware of the full implications of our desires is "cognitive psychotherapy" in that it involves the same kind of dramatic transformations brought about by therapeutic psychology.

An act-utilitarian who accepted this view of intrinsic goodness would define right acts as those that maximize satisfaction of the rational desires of all people affected. Brandt, however, does not proceed in this direction. Like all the ethicists discussed in this chapter except for Mill, Brandt thinks that morality must give more weight to principles or rules than to individual actions. He suggests that calculating the consequences of each act individually encourages biased reasoning rather than impartial concern for all people's interests. It also means we are less able to count on how others will behave. For example, it is more impartial, as well as more publicly reliable, to have all people obey the rule "Pay your taxes as required by law" than to encourage each person to calculate the good and bad effects of reporting all their taxable income. Similarly, it is better for people simply to obey the rule "Don't lie" except in certain exceptional instances (such as to protect innocent life) than to encourage people to calculate the good and bad effects of each contemplated lie.

Brandt also points out that, with respect to other moral considerations, act-utilitarianism requires far too much of us. It would have us constantly striving to be benevolent so that each of our actions would bring about maximum good. Such moral pressure is better suited to saints than to humans. A realistic morality would require only limited benevolence, such as helping other people in desperate need. Nevertheless, Brandt agrees with Mill that good consequences are all that matter in deciding what is right and wrong. This, together with his emphasis on rules rather than individual acts, led him to develop rule-utilitarianism.

Rule-utilitarianism is the view that an act is right when (and only when) it falls under a set of rules that, if accepted by the society in which one lives, would produce the most good for the most people. The set of rules is called a moral code. Acts are right, then, when they conform to that moral code that would produce more overall good than would other possible moral codes.

Justifiable moral codes must be workable within a given society. They are not ideal principles for angels, but rules that the vast majority of people in a given society can grasp and use to guide their conduct. A satisfactory moral code must also be comprehensive and specific enough to apply to most of the moral decisions we confront. Brandt objects, for example, that some of Ross's rules are too abstract. He prefers rules like "Tell the truth except when great harm would result."

Which Theory Is Best?

Each of the theories we have examined has many defenders, and philosophical debates over them are subtle and centuries-old. What does this controversy imply for applied ethics? Does it mean that we should disregard all theories until disputes about them are resolved? Or should the applied ethicist simply pick the one that seems most reasonable?

Let us first ask what it means to say that one theory is as reasonable or more reasonable than another. Several criteria are widely used in evaluating theories about right action. The theory must be clear, logically coherent rather than self-contradictory, widely applicable to moral problems, and not contradicted by any facts. The most important criterion, however, is that the theory be consistent with our most carefully considered moral convictions about what ought to be done in practical situations. If, for example, a theory implied that it is all right to torture babies or lie just to hurt others for fun, we would know something was wrong with the theory!

Most of the arguments about theories turn on whether the theories do have unacceptable implications in specific instances. One problem is that tracing the precise implications of an abstract theory for a specific example can be an intricate procedure. Another problem is that different people have different judgments about what is right or wrong in given examples! For example, people are notorious for having different opinions about whether early fetuses are persons, which handicaps the testing of theories with respect to abortion questions.

So should we then just pick a theory, somewhat arbitrarily or on the basis of debatable intuitions? Or should we jettison all the theories while doing applied ethics? We would suggest here that one need not pick a particular theory but rather feel free to employ all the theories (as we suggested in connection with theories about virtues).

There are three reasons for this. First, for the most part all the theories are compatible; they usually agree with each other in their practical implications. For example, duty ethics, rights ethics, and utilitarianism all condemn lies that wantonly hurt people. With the exception of Kant's absolutistic versions of duty ethics, all the theories also agree that lies to protect innocent life, as with the Dutch fishermen's lie to the Nazis, are justified.

Such a wide agreement in applications should not be surprising, because all the theories arise from our overlapping moral experience. All are designed to express that experience, and all are roughly consistent with it. These wide areas of overlap suffice for many purposes of the applied ethicist.

Second, besides being largely compatible, the theories are also complementary. Each points to important moral considerations but highlights them in different ways. Suppose, for example, we ask whether it is permissible to lie to our parents to protect a friend whom the parents unfairly condemn because of his or her ethnic origin. The duty ethicist emphasizes the relationships of trust with both the parents and the friend, as well as the duties that arise from those relationships. The rights ethicist emphasizes the rights of parents to know certain things about their children, and also the rights of children to their own lives. The utilitarian points to the effects of lying on both relationships. Although the three theories have different emphases, each appreciates the importance of the relationships involved.

Third, and perhaps most important, relatively little of import turns on whether one is a duty ethicist, a rights ethicist, or a utilitarian. Theories are best viewed as general frameworks for organizing moral reflection and for developing moral arguments. The precise practical implications of those arguments depend on the specific version of the theory employed. Notice the remarkable differences between the two versions of each theory that we mentioned. Kant's absolute duties (which, for example, condemn all lies) are dramatically different from Ross's prima facie duties that must be weighed against one another on the basis of contextual judgments. Locke's emphasis on liberty rights has vastly different practical implications from Melden's acceptance of welfare rights. Mill's act-utilitarianism, which also stresses certain kinds of pleasures, is considerably different from Brandt's rule-utilitarianism, which stresses rational desires.

In fact, for practical purposes it seems that Brandt's rule-utilitarianism has more in common with Ross's duty ethics than it does with Mill's act-utilitarianism. Act-utilitarianism might allow occasional cheating on taxes when good effects for oneself outweigh minimal good effects to others. Brandt is as stern as Ross, however, in urging obedience to rules that sustain social trust.

Again, a libertarian who, like Locke, emphasizes liberty rights (not to be interfered with by others) would find many taxes immoral because they are used to support welfare systems. Hence, he or she may feel justified in not reporting some taxable income. In contrast, a rights ethicist who shares Melden's appreciation of welfare rights would stress the importance of paying taxes to benefit those in need.

In short, the applied ethicist should feel free to employ all three types of ethical theories when they aid practical reflection. The concepts of duties, rights, and utility are all of practical use in doing applied ethics, without the need to decide which is more fundamental than the other.

Summary

There are three main types of ethical theories about right action, each of which can be further subdivided based on individual philosopher's viewpoints. Duty ethicists define right acts as those required by duties. Kant views duties as absolute (having no exceptions); however, Ross believes that duties are typically prima facie (possibly having exceptions when they conflict with other duties). One's actual duty is thus determined by context-bound reasoning about which prima facie duty is most important on a specific occasion.

Rights ethicists define right acts as those that respect rights. Locke sees the basic human right as liberty, or the negative right not to be interfered with by others; however, Melden theorizes that the basic human right is to pursue one's legitimate interests, which sometimes include welfare or positive rights to be helped by other members of a community.

Utilitarians reduce all obligations to one moral requirement: Produce the most good for the most people, giving equal consideration to each person affected. Mill asserts that act-utilitarianism requires each act to produce the most happiness for the most people, where happiness involves both quantity and quality of pleasures. In contrast, Brandt favors rule-utilitarianism, which classifies right acts as those falling under a moral code that, if adopted in a specific society, would produce the greatest satisfaction of rational desires (those desires that survive persistent scrutiny in light of all relevant facts).

DISCUSSION TOPICS

1. Is it permissible (all right), obligatory (required), or impermissible (wrong) to lie in each of the following instances? If you cannot answer, what more information do you need to know? Which moral considerations are relevant to each case according to duty ethics, rights ethics, act-utilitarianism, and rule-utilitarianism?

   a. You are invited to a party that you do not wish to attend. So as not to hurt the feelings of the host, you lie, saying you have to go somewhere else that night.

   b. Persistent insomnia and nervousness send you to your doctor seeking tranquilizers. Your doctor discerns that the problem is psychosomatic, caused by temporary problems at home. When she cannot convince you of this, she says she will give you only one month's supply of tranquilizers. Unbeknownst to you she writes a prescription for a placebo—a sugar pill—that actually calms you down because you believe it is a tranquilizer.

   c. You know your car needs major repairs, but you also need to sell it for more than it is worth in order to pay an overdue college tuition bill. When a potential buyer asks if anything is wrong with it, you state emphatically that it is in great shape.

   d. Like 20 million other Americans, you have genital herpes—a viral disease, usually transmitted through sexual contact, whose symptoms range from painless blisters to extremely painful sores, shooting muscle pains, and fever. You have been celibate for fifteen months when the partner you are dating offers to change that. You very much desire to consent and do not think that the affair would be immoral. At the time you have good reason to believe that the herpes is not contagious because you have no open sores or incipient sores. In a half-joking tone your partner asks, "You don't have any medical problems, do you?" With similar playfulness you shake your head no.

   e. You are in a situation similar to the previous one, except this time your partner lies to you to conceal the fact that he or she has AIDS, the deadly, sexually transmitted Acquired Immune Deficiency Syndrome.

2. In an essay entitled "On a Supposed Right to Lie from Altruistic Motives," Kant argued that if we lie in an attempt to prevent a murder, we are legally and morally blameworthy for any ill effects of the lie:

   > If by telling a lie you have prevented murder, you have made yourself legally responsible for all the consequences; but if you have held rigorously to the truth, public justice can lay no hand on you, whatever the unforeseen consequences may be. After you have honestly answered the murderer's question as to whether this intended victim is at home, it may be that he has slipped out so that he does not come in the way of the murderer, and thus that the murder may not be committed. But if you had lied and said he was not at home when he had really gone out without your knowing it, and if the murderer had then met him as he went away and murdered him, you might justly be accused as the cause of his death. For if you had told the truth as far as you knew it, perhaps the murderer might have been apprehended by the neighbors while he searched the house and thus the deed might have been prevented. Therefore, whoever tells a lie, however well intentioned it might be, must answer for the consequences, however unforeseeable they were.[9]

Do you agree with Kant?

In commenting on Kant's view, also consider a lie told in Sartre's short story, "The Wall." A soldier tries to deceive enemy interrogators by saying his compatriot is hidden at a cemetery. The soldier believes he is lying because he is confident that his compatriot is staying at a cousin's house, not at the cemetery. Unbeknownst to the soldier, the compatriot sneaks to the cemetery, where he is captured and shot by the enemy soldiers. Is the soldier guilty for the death of the compatriot?

3. List all the absolute moral duties for which you believe there are no permissible exceptions. Is it a long list?

4. The protagonist in Dostoevsky's novel *Crime and Punishment* plans and carries out the murder of a very wealthy pawnbroker. He does so with the intention of stealing her money and distributing it to poor people who desperately need it. The idea was inspired by the following remarks about the pawnbroker he overheard in a restaurant.

> On one side we have a stupid, senseless, worthless, spiteful, ailing, horrid old woman, not simply useless but doing actual mischief, who has not an idea what she is living for herself, and who will die in a day or two in any case. . . . On the other side, fresh young lives thrown away for want of help and by thousands, on every side! A hundred thousand good deeds could be done and helped, on that old woman's money. . . . Hundreds, thousands perhaps, might be set on the right path; dozens of families saved from destitution, from ruin, from vice. . . . Kill her, take her money and with the help of it devote oneself to the service of humanity and the good of all. What do you think, would not one tiny crime be wiped out by thousands of good deeds?[10]

How would a duty ethicist, a rights ethicist, an act-utilitarian, and a rule-utilitarian respond to this question?

5. In discussing Locke and Melden we drew a distinction between liberty (negative) and welfare (positive) rights. Apply that distinction to Carol Gilligan's conception of rights (Chapter 2): Which of the two kinds of rights did she have in mind in her "ethics of justice"? How might her "ethic of care" accommodate what Melden says about positive rights?

6. Lawrence Kohlberg, discussed in Chapter 2, was directly inspired by the work of Kant. What connections do you see between the ideas of Kant and Kohlberg?

SUGGESTED READINGS

Bok, Sissela. *Lying*. New York: Vintage Books, 1979.

Bok, Sissela. *Secrets*. New York: Pantheon Books, 1982.

Brandt, Richard B. *A Theory of the Good and the Right*. Oxford: Clarendon Press, 1979.

Kant, Immanuel. *Foundations of the Metaphysics of Morals*. Trans. L. W. Beck. New York: Liberal Arts Press, 1959.

Kant, Immanuel. "On a Supposed Right to Lie from Altruistic Motives." In L. W. Beck (trans. and ed.), In *Critique of Practical Reason and Other Writings in Moral Philosophy*. Chicago: University of Chicago Press, 1949.

Locke, John. *Two Treatises of Government*. Cambridge: Cambridge University Press, 1960.

Melden, A. I. "Are There Welfare Rights?" In Peter G. Brown, Conrad Johnson, and Paul Vernier (eds.), *Income Support: Conceptual Policy Issues*. Totowa, NJ: Rowman & Littlefield, 1981.

Melden, A. I. (ed.). *Ethical Theories: A Book of Readings*. 2nd ed. Englewood Cliffs, NJ: Prentice-Hall, 1967.

Mill, John Stuart. *Utilitarianism*. Indianapolis, IN: Hackett, 1979.

Norman, Richard. *The Moral Philosophers: An Introduction to Ethics*. Oxford: Clarendon Press, 1983.

Rachels, James. *The Elements of Moral Philosophy*. New York: Random House, 1986.

Rawls, John. *A Theory of Justice*. Cambridge, MA: Harvard University Press, 1971.

Ross, David. *The Right and the Good*. Oxford: Clarendon Press, 1930.

Sartre, Jean-Paul. "The Wall." In Walter Kaufmann (ed.), *Existentialism from Dostoevsky to Sartre*. New York: New American Library, 1975.

PART TWO

Self-Respect and Integrity

Humility, on the one hand, and true, noble pride on the other, are elements of proper self-respect. . . . In the light of the law of morality, which is holy and perfect, our defects stand out with glaring distinctness and on comparing ourselves with this standard of perfection we have sufficient cause to feel humble. But if we compare ourselves with others, there is no reason to have a low opinion of ourselves; we have a right to consider ourselves as valuable as another. This self-respect in comparison with others constitutes noble pride.[1]

Immanuel Kant

By "proper self-respect" Kant meant appreciating our own moral worth and showing that appreciation by treating ourselves with respect. To treat ourselves with respect requires acting in ways that express our self-worth as moral agents, having moral capacities and concerns. In turn, this means striving to be moral by treating ourselves and other people as having moral worth. This connection between self-respect and moral striving makes sense of the above quotation. Self-respect entails moral humility, that is, awareness of our moral flaws. Yet self-respect also entails having a sense of our moral worth and dignity—"noble pride"—as beings who strive to be moral.

Self-respect is closely tied to moral integrity—integrity of moral concern. In Kant's terms it requires (1) committing ourselves to live by correct moral principles and (2) struggling to live up to those commitments in our actions and relationships. This effort to live a morally unified life is the basis for proper self-respect.

Self-respect is different from *self-esteem*. Whereas self-esteem refers to valuing or approving of oneself, self-respect means doing so for the right reasons, on the basis of moral integrity. Self-esteem and self-respect are often confused. For example, John Rawls, an influential contemporary Kantian philosopher, did not clearly distinguish them:

> We may define self-respect (or self-esteem) as having two aspects. First of all . . . it includes a person's sense of his own value, his secure conviction that his conception of his good, his plan of life, is worth carrying out. And second, self-respect implies a confidence in one's ability, so far as it is within one's power, to fulfill one's intentions. When we feel that our plans are of little value, we cannot pursue them with pleasure or take delight in their execution. Nor plagued by failure and self-doubt can we continue in our endeavors. It is clear then why self-respect is a primary good [i.e., a good that every rational person desires]. Without it nothing may seem worth doing, or if some things have value for us, we lack the will to strive for them. All desire and activity becomes empty and vain, and we sink into apathy and cynicism.[2]

Here Rawls seems to equate self-respect and self-esteem, defining them in terms of two positive attitudes about oneself: (1) that one's life is worthwhile (valuing oneself) and (2) that one has the ability to meet one's goals given the opportunity (self-confidence). Apparently, these two attitudes could be held by sadists like Adolf Hitler or by entirely selfish people. Such people might value their lives and be self-confident. They would then have self-esteem but not self-respect, in Kant's sense, for they would lack moral integrity, which requires striving to unify one's life around moral commitments.

Despite this difference Kant might agree with Rawls's insight into the psychological importance of self-esteem, and he might extend it to emphasize the importance of proper self-respect. Both self-esteem and self-respect are essential if we are to pursue a life of moral integrity. Self-respect brings a sense of moral significance to our endeavors and evokes a certain vigor in how we pursue them. Without self-respect we easily become cynical about the moral contribution we have to offer, and cynicism affects our relationships with other people; hence, self-respect is a prerequisite for respecting other people.

As we will apply the term, *self-respect* is what Kant called proper self-respect: appreciating one's moral worth based on moral integrity and showing that appreciation by treating oneself with respect. Part Two explores some of the ways in which self-respect is undermined or supported.

At the very least, treating ourselves with respect requires caring about ourselves, valuing our talents and aspirations, and seeking our self-fulfillment. In Chapter 5 it is argued that self-destructiveness violates our moral duty to treat ourselves with respect.

Self-understanding is needed in order to appreciate our moral worth and to assess our character in light of moral standards. We can become aware of our character flaws and wrongdoing only by being honest with ourselves. This honesty requires avoiding self-deception about immorality, as Chapter 6 discusses.

Self-respect is based on moral integrity, which requires a genuine effort to live up to our moral convictions and commitments. Moral weakness is the failure to make such an effort. Chapter 7 shows how moral weakness undermines integrity and erodes self-respect.

Finally, sustaining moral commitments sometimes requires confronting risks and dangers. Whereas cowardice consists of turning away from dangers because of fear, courage entails confronting dangers and hardships with self-control and insight. This is the topic of Chapter 8.

CHAPTER 5

Harming Oneself

The most blatant way to show disrespect for other people is to inflict undeserved harm on them. (Another way is to ignore them.) Similarly, the most obvious way to demonstrate a lack of self-respect is to inflict undeserved harm on oneself. This chapter examines four examples of harming oneself: masochism, servility, irrational shame and guilt, and drug abuse. There are certainly other ways to harm oneself (such as neglecting one's talents), but these four examples provide an interesting range: intentionally causing suffering, passively submitting to degradation, irrationally responding emotionally, and risking one's life imprudently.

Duties Not to Harm Oneself

The examples to be discussed provide an argument for Kant's belief that there are duties to ourselves. This is a controversial thesis that has been denied by philosophers who draw a sharp distinction between morality and prudence. Prudence, they assert, means promoting one's own good (self-interest), whereas morality is concerned with promoting others' good. The only moral duties concerning self-interest are negative ones: duties not to pursue self-interest when it hurts other people.

This separation of morality and prudence seems tempting if we are preoccupied with the strong human tendency toward selfishness, that is, toward excessive pursuit of self-interest at the expense of other people. Thinking along these lines, it is easy to assume that people are naturally inclined to seek their own good and that morality essentially represents a set of restrictions on that pursuit. Yet, as the examples in this chapter will make clear, people do not always pursue their own good. Rather, they frequently engage in conduct that undermines their self-interest.

Another source of the separation between morality and prudence is a narrow conception of rights. If morality is regarded essentially as respecting others' rights while exercising one's own rights, then harming oneself does not seem immoral. If we choose to harm ourselves, that is our right and our business as long as we do not infringe on other people's rights. Yet some human rights ethicists have rejected this line of thought. They emphasize that we ought to appreciate our own moral rights and assert them responsibly so that we do not allow other people to enslave or degrade us. Implicit in this argument is the idea that we ought to have a sense of dignity because we possess human rights.

If rights ethics leaves room for duties not to harm ourselves, so too do the other major ethical theories. Utilitarians stress that we ought to produce the most good for the most people, counting each person equally—including ourselves. To inflict harm on ourselves without justification is as wrong as wantonly harming other people, and for exactly the same reason. Moreover, utilitarians emphasize that many of our actions bear primarily on ourselves. Because we have direct control over our own actions, we have more chances to avoid harming, as well as to increase good for, ourselves.

Virtue ethicists stress that good character traits are often as beneficial to ourselves as to others. This is certainly true of the virtues of courage and self-discipline, which enable us to pursue both our own good and the good of other people. Similarly, through our vices we harm not only others but also ourselves. For example, cruelty is bad whether it is directed toward other people or toward oneself, and weakness of will damages our own interests as frequently as it does those of other people.

Of all the ethicists, Kant placed the greatest emphasis on moral duties to ourselves. He insisted that these duties arise because we have the same moral worth as other people. Consider his fundamental principle to "act so that you treat humanity, whether in your own person or in that of another, always as an end and never as a means only."[1] The basic duty to treat ourselves with respect is not a mere "hypothetical imperative" that states, "If you want to be happy, then don't harm yourself." Instead, it is a categorical imperative that commands without conditions attached: "Respect yourself!" In his more practical writings on ethics Kant illustrated this assertion with the same kinds of examples used in this chapter.

We might add that Kant thought that duties to ourselves were even more fundamental than duties to other people: "Far from ranking lowest in the scale of precedence, our duties towards ourselves are of primary importance and should have pride of place. . . . The prior condition of our duty to others is our duty to ourselves; we can fulfill the former only in so far as we first fulfill the latter."[2] In particular, failing to meet our duties to ourselves to maintain our rational capacities erodes our ability to meet our duties to other people. An extreme example is unjustifiable suicide in which we end our capacity to act. Abuse of drugs and alcohol can in varying degrees undermine our resources to meet our duties to other people.

Masochism

Let us begin with a clear-cut example of self-destructiveness. Lise, in *The Brothers Karamazov*, breaks her engagement to Alyosha. She explains to him that he is too gentle and forgiving for her taste:

> I was just thinking for the thirtieth time what a good thing it is that I broke off our engagement and decided not to become your wife. You wouldn't be much of a husband, you know. . . . I want someone to marry me, tear me to pieces, betray me, and then desert me. I don't want to be happy.[3]

After Alyosha leaves, Lise

> unlocked the door, opened it a little, put her finger in the crack, and slammed the door as hard as she could. Ten seconds later she released her hand, went slowly to her chair, sat down, and looked intently at her blackened, swollen finger and the blood that was oozing out from under the nail. Her lips quivered.
>   "I'm a vile, vile, vile, despicable creature," she whispered.[4]

As this example suggests, we should distinguish between pain and emotional responses to pain, and between suffering and the attitudes adopted toward suffering. Pain cannot be defined as something inherently unenjoyable, or suffering as something that a person dislikes. Lise both seeks and causes her pain and suffering. To that extent she enjoys it and has an affirmative attitude toward it. This partially explains why she inflicts it on herself (with the deeper explanation lying in her upbringing and cultural conditioning).

Lise is a masochist. She causes and enjoys her own pain, without justification. Many a saint and marathon runner have inflicted worse harm to their bodies and found value in doing so. Indeed, all of us have enjoyed "toying" with the mild pain of a loose and slightly irritating tooth. People are masochists when, like Lise, they enjoy or seek *severe* pain, subjugation, or degradation because of *irrational* motives. As with Lise, the suffering of masochists is not redeemed by some reasonable goal for which the masochistic act is the necessary means.

But why can't the enjoyment of suffering for its own sake be all right, or at least not irrational? There are many acceptable diversions that need not serve some overarching reasonable goal. Why isn't enjoyed pain just an entertaining, albeit bizarre, form of diversion?

Perhaps occasionally it is, depending on what motivates it and on what role it plays in one's life. Most often, however, it constitutes an attempt to damage oneself, if not to hurt others as well. The causes of masochism, such as parental influences that instill low self-esteem, are a matter for psychology to explore. But whatever the explanation, masochists usually undermine their own capacities for enriching relationships as equals among other equals. They cut themselves off from the enjoyment of more fulfilling activities. And they are typically in conflict with themselves in ways that prevent a more meaningful life. Lise's actions for example are compulsive, anxiety-ridden, and damaging to her relationships with other people.

Many of us, however, display masochistic tendencies that are not related to neuroses. In addition, we frequently fail to perceive (or are self-deceiving about) our self-destructive tendencies, which may be more vague and ambiguous than Lise's. For example, we begin to eat smaller quantities of food. Are we undertaking a healthy diet, fasting for some spiritual goal, beginning a hunger strike to childishly "punish" our parents, or showing symptoms of anorexia nervosa? We may not know for sure, and we may have hidden motives for hurting ourselves and find satisfaction in self-denial for its own sake.

To pursue this example, how should we characterize Simone Weil, the French mystic and religious thinker who starved herself to death? At the time, in 1943, she was thirty-four years old and in a sanitorium being treated for tuberculosis. Although her prospects for recovery were judged to be good, she nevertheless refused to eat what her doctors ordered and eventually refused medical treatment as well. She insisted on receiving no more than the meager rations given to her compatriots in Nazi-occupied France. The coroner ruled that her death was a suicide. Was it an act of masochism as well? Or was it an act of admirable self-sacrifice?

Examining the wider context of her life is only somewhat helpful in answering this question. At age five she had refused to eat sugar because soldiers fighting in World War I were not allowed to eat it either. As a young adult she denied herself a professional career that her well-to-do parents made possible, choosing instead to work in factories alongside workers whose plight deeply affected her. Eventually her health broke, forcing her to quit. Later she volunteered to fight against Franco's fascism during the Spanish Civil War, and still later took a job as a farm worker. Throughout her life there is a striking pattern of self-denial and identification with oppressed groups and the poor. Surely there are grounds, then, for interpreting her self-starvation as an act of moral and religious devotion. At the same time there seems to be a deep thread of seemingly masochistic suffering that makes her actions morally ambiguous.

Servility

Servility is the attitude that one lacks moral worth, or at least lacks moral worth equal to that of others. Though distinguishable from masochism, servility is also closely related to it. Servile people do not always enjoy or seek suffering, nor do they always suffer from their servility. Often, however, they do, and as such are masochists.

The servile attitude should be distinguished from the attitudes of the humble person. Humility is the honest recognition of one's lesser abilities and talents, and the moral virtue of humility reflects genuine acknowledgment of one's moral imperfections. Servility, by contrast, reflects an attitude of undervaluing the worth of one's genuine achievements, of one's worthwhile interests and activities, of one's highest aspirations and capacities. One form of servility is an excessively deferential or submissive attitude, known as obsequiousness. One type of obsequiousness is exemplified by the flatterer or sycophant. Another is the fawning attempt always to please others and never to make waves. Still another is the willingness to do whatever one is told by people in power, no matter what the circumstances.

What repels us about these examples is not just the groveling behavior itself, but the frame of mind it expresses. Often it is the motive that is distressing, as in the attempt to gain money or power, while losing one's dignity, or in the attempt to create a basis for self-worth in the shadowy reflection of others. Yet we are also disturbed by the failure of the servile person to appreciate and honor his or her own worth.

Another form of servility is an anxiety-ridden sense of inferiority, or what Alfred Adler (1870–1937) called an inferiority complex. This means more than the occasional feelings of inadequacy we all experience. It involves experiencing these feelings in excess and on inappropriate occasions, and accompanied by crippling anxiety and depression. The person with an inferiority complex is overwhelmed by these feelings and by being unable to cope with them. Or the person develops irrational coping devices, such as the tendency toward self-deprecation and toward expecting mistreatment, as if this helps to maintain a stable self-identity as a failure.

Yet another form of servility is more ambiguous morally. This is the servility of the excessive altruist, who carries doing good to the point of self-degradation. A familiar example is the woman who, pressured by cultural stereotypes, zealously devotes herself to her husband and children to the point where she betrays her own talents and interests. The psychiatrist Theodore Isaac Rubin captures the ambivalence we feel about such a person. Reflecting on his mother, who was overflowing with "love, esteem of me, devotion and care," he remarks:

> She was never exploitative and despite deep concern for me had never been manipulative, overprotective, or in any way stifling.

So I describe the perfect mother? NO: she was exasperating in her compliance to my father. . . . I suppose she exasperated him, too, in her complete abandonment of herself in favor of him. This was certainly a form of glorious martyrdom for her.[5]

There is a fine line between admirable and self-fulfilling sacrifice of one's own interests for the good of others and self-destructive forms of servility. Rubin suggests that his mother displayed both, sometimes in inextricable combinations. And although he deeply admires her and is grateful for her sacrifices, he also sees her as falling into society's trap of glorifying the altruistic wife-mother even when it leads to self-harm. Where we draw the line between admirable altruism and degrading servility may depend primarily on the motives of the person in question: a genuine care for others versus an ulterior desire for gain (such as social approval); or the need to protect oneself and one's children from a violent husband versus the fear of asserting oneself and taking risks in order to develop one's talents. In Rubin's case he saw an element of timidity in his mother's relationship with her husband. Yet the line between altruism and servility can also be crossed when one habitually underappreciates one's worth.

In addition, there is a fine line between self-deprecation and genuine humility. Humility is the virtue of not being arrogant or, more positively, of maintaining perspective on one's accomplishments and possibilities. Truly humble people avoid the excess of arrogance (conceit or excessive self-regard) without falling into the defect of undervaluing themselves or failing to appreciate their achievements. Genuinely humble individuals do not "put themselves down." Instead, they put their lives into appropriate perspective, typically on the basis of a deeper value perspective than conventional society, with its preoccupation with prestige and reputation, has to offer. Their concern is for truth and accurate evaluation, not with self-disparagement and devaluation.

Irrational Shame and Guilt

Shame and guilt are painful, self-critical emotions that represent responses to what we believe are our failures to live by our values.* As such they are inevitable aspects of being committed to values. To never feel shame would imply a brazen—a "shameless"—apathy toward ideals and standards. To never feel guilt would imply that one holds a very low set of moral standards, or that

---

*The words *shame* and *guilt* are ambiguous. In the sense intended here they refer to emotions, to *feeling* guilty or ashamed. They can also refer, however, to actions and to the moral status of persons who commit the actions: *being* guilty for wrongdoing or acting in shameful

one psychotically believes oneself to be morally perfect, or even that one is a callous sociopath who, by definition, has no sense of moral right and wrong. We *ought* to experience shame and guilt insofar as we are blameworthy— "ought" in the sense that these emotions comprise appropriate responses to many of our failures. Yet, as we all know from personal experience, shame and guilt can be enormously self-destructive when they are excessive or when we adopt irrational responses to them.

Shame and guilt are distinguishable from each other, even when they are felt simultaneously toward the same object, and even when they have similar physiological manifestations (such as tightened muscles, constricted breathing, and lowered energy level). Whereas shame is focused on personal shortcomings—falling short of standards—guilt is focused on harm done to people. Shame is the experience of feeling lowered self-esteem because we believe we have betrayed our ideals, standards, or sense of propriety. *Nonmoral shame* pertains to nonmoral standards, as in feeling ashamed of one's social awkwardness, poor athletic ability, bowed legs, or crooked teeth. *Moral shame* entails feeling lowered self-respect for failing to meet our moral ideals.

By contrast, *moral guilt* is the pain felt because we think we have morally wronged someone, whether by insulting them, physically hurting them, violating their rights to privacy, or breaking a promise to them.* It is also possible to feel guilt for morally wronging oneself, as through masochism or gluttony. In this case, moral guilt and moral shame are very similar, even though there remains a technical distinction between shame for falling below one's standards and guilt for wronging oneself.

Irrational shame and guilt are usually based on unreasonable beliefs about one's wrongdoing or vices. The beliefs are false, unsupported by evidence, or persistent even when the facts indicate otherwise. Such beliefs reflect unwarranted evaluations of our conduct or character traits. Shame and guilt can also be irrational because of their excessive intensity or because of our unreasonable reactions to them.

A vivid example of irrational shame is given by Virginia Woolf in her short story "The New Dress." Her main character, Mabel Waring, is a forty-year-old woman who displays the emotional flip-flops characteristic of adolescence. She had spent hours with her dressmaker helping to fashion a new yellow dress that will be perfect for a party, but upon arriving at the party she collapses in self-doubt:

---

ways. *Feeling* guilty or ashamed does not imply that we actually *are* guilty or shameful, because we may be entirely mistaken in believing we are at fault or have failed. Conversely, we are frequently guilty or deserving of shame for faults to which we are blind or indifferent and concerning which we do not feel guilt or shame.

*In addition to moral guilt, there is *religious* guilt in which a theist feels guilt for violating what are believed to be God's standards. The theist presumably harms him- or herself, not God.

> Mabel had her first serious suspicion that something was wrong as she
> took her cloak off. . . . No! It was not *right*. And at once the misery
> which she always tried to hide, the profound dissatisfaction—the sense
> she had had, ever since she was a child, of being inferior to other
> people—set upon her, relentlessly, remorselessly, with an intensity which
> she could not beat off . . . for oh these men, oh these women, all were
> thinking—"What's Mabel wearing? What a fright she looks! What a hid-
> eous new dress!"[6]

Mabel's spiraling shame quickly extends to include her own cowardice in
being so ashamed about such a trivial matter and her pettiness in devoting so
much time to the dress in the first place. Her shame revives a long-standing
sense of failure for choosing a safe, dull marriage, for being a mediocre mother
and wife, and for leading a "creeping, crawling life" that she compares to a fly
struggling to escape a saucer while its wings are stuck together by milk. The
story ends with her fantasies about becoming a nun so as not to have to
worry about clothes and about discovering an astonishing book at the library
that will radically transform her life.

As this example suggests, intense experiences of inappropriate shame (as
well as guilt) provide clues to understanding what most matters to us. Shame
and guilt, like most emotions, are largely involuntary and spontaneous responses. As such, they have singular importance in revealing our values, because by definition they are painful experiences of having failed to live by
those values.

Thus, for example, when parents and children catch themselves being
ashamed of one another's physique or clothing, they may be shocked into
awareness of how self-centered their concern for one another has become.
Similarly, writers who feel deep shame over negative reviews of their work
may be forced to admit how dependent they have grown on praise from critics. And young adults who continue to feel guilty about their sexual desires
may be helped to see that they are not free from the inhibitions of a puritanical upbringing.

Irrational guilt can be as self-destructive as irrational shame, but with
added complications arising from the sense of having wronged someone. Appropriate responses to warranted feelings of guilt include making amends
(where possible) for the wrong done. Perhaps all that is required is a sincere
apology. Other times one must try to recompense for the damage done.
When guilt is irrational, however, matters can become painfully complex.

Let us consider an example of guilt that initially represents a rational or
warranted emotion and later moves in an irrational direction. In *The Scarlet
Letter* Nathaniel Hawthorne tells the story of the adultery of Reverend Dimmesdale and Hester Prynne that leads to Hester's pregnancy. From their perspective a serious moral wrong has occurred, and given that perspective, their
feelings of guilt are fully warranted. Although from our perspective their

judgments may seem unduly harsh, we nevertheless see a deep moral wrong in Dimmesdale's cowardly refusal to assume responsibility for his adultery. He does not marry Hester, but rather conceals his role and allows her to bear the public shame by herself.

After failing to act responsibly in making amends for his wrongdoing, Dimmesdale's guilt quickly takes an irrational turn. He tortures himself with self-loathing and physical self-flagellation. By the end of his life he is left without self-respect or even a clear sense of his own identity. Hawthorne writes about his self-destructive guilt and hypocrisy that

> it is the unspeakable misery of a life so false as his, that it steals the pith and substance out of whatever realities there are around us, and which were meant by Heaven to be the spirit's joy and nutriment. To the untrue man, the whole universe is false—it is impalpable—it shrinks to nothing within his grasp. And he himself, in so far as he shows himself in a false light, becomes a shadow, or, indeed ceases to exist.[7]

Only near death does Dimmesdale attain a moment of peace by seeking Hester's forgiveness.

Hester's guilt and responses to her guilt stand in sharp contrast with Dimmesdale's. In caring for their daughter under the cruel gaze of a puritan society, she finds a way to make amends for any wrongdoing and thereby release her feelings of guilt. Whereas Dimmesdale's suffering is pathetic and tragic, Hester's is noble. Dimmesdale cowardly refuses to admit his guilt openly; Hester courageously refuses to betray her love by revealing Dimmesdale as her lover. Dimmesdale spurns responsibility for his daughter; Hester lovingly raises her. Dimmesdale shows how the self-condemnation inherent in guilt becomes sick when indulged in masochistically; Hester reminds us of the creative growth that comes with acting responsibly concerning our feelings of guilt.

Drug Abuse

Our last example of harming oneself is drug abuse. We focus on consciousness-altering drugs because of their curious seductiveness and because of the dangers involved in using them.

There are many forms of drug abuse: addiction, dependence, long-term abuse, and periodic misuse. Addiction, such as to nicotine in tobacco, is defined by a compulsion to use a drug, whether because of a physiological process or because of a deeply entrenched habit. The compulsion may or may not be resistible without help from others, but (by definition) it entails a strong desire that can be resisted only with extreme effort. Dependence involves a desire that is more easily resisted than a full-blown compulsion, as with caffeine addiction. Periodic misuse entails the occasional use of a drug in a manner that generates problems, such as disrupting a party after becoming stoned on marijuana or driving a car while drunk. Long-term drug abuse involves a pattern of drug use that disrupts reasonable coping patterns over an extended period of time.

Use of consciousness-altering drugs is tempting for many reasons. Peer pressure, a desire for social interaction, curiosity, and a desire to experiment are frequent motives for drug use. In addition, many drugs are charged with symbolic meanings. For example, marijuana may convey a sense of rebellion against parents and conventional society. Cocaine seems to add glamour to life, if not a charming element of danger. Peyote and mescaline enter into religious celebrations designed to evoke mystical experiences (as celebrated in Aldous Huxley's *Doors of Perception*).

Of special interest here, however, is a curious double-mindedness we have about drugs that invites us to use them without intending to harm ourselves and that adds to the devastation they wreak. Drugs appear to offer greater control over our immediate consciousness and hence over our lives. They charm us with a sense of power by stimulating our energies (amphetamines), reducing stress (barbiturates, alcohol), or inducing euphoria (cocaine, heroin). Yet when they do not satisfy our expectations, they offer excuses for the problems they cause. We readily dismiss irresponsible conduct under their influence as the fault of the drug: "I wasn't myself last night: that last drink made me do things I couldn't help." Drugs, then, have a double seductiveness. They promise greater self-control and simultaneously offer excuses for misconduct deriving from their influence.

This double-mindedness about the power of drugs is reflected in two general perspectives about drug use that are conflated or embraced selectively, as convenient. From a medical perspective drug abusers are regarded as sick and unfortunate victims who need medical attention. Witness the proliferation of "rehabilitation programs" at drug "clinics" for "treating" drug abuse. Also, the medical profession has taught us to speak of the "disease of alcoholism." From an agency perspective, by contrast, drug abusers are chastised as immoral lawbreakers who ought to be punished.

The difficulty is that these two perspectives can in fact be appropriate with respect to different aspects of drug use. Perhaps the initial decision to use a dangerous drug was fully voluntary, and thus blameworthy, but subsequent addiction removed it from the person's control, turning it into a sickness. Conversely, perhaps the original use was partially excusable as a product of intense peer pressure, but at present it is within one's power to stop abusing the drug. Even when full-blown addiction has developed, individuals have the power to ask for help. We respect and admire people who seek help, and this presupposes that we do not view them as completely helpless invalids.

The invitation to use dangerous drugs is seductive, we have stated, because of our double-mindedness about the power we think we have over them and our eagerness to use them as ready-made excuses for our conduct when they exert their power over us. Our double-mindedness is reflected in the ambivalence shown by the medical and agency perspectives on drug use. One further seduction is most obvious of all: not everyone gets hurt using dangerous drugs, and it is impossible to be sure who will.

We are all familiar with how all forms of drug abuse can have devastating effects. Heroin addiction can lead to prostitution and a life of stealing to support the habit. Cocaine dependence can lead to suicide. Misuse of alcohol on just one occasion can lead to a car accident that kills someone. Long-term abuse of marijuana can destroy a college education or end a promising career. Yet none of this always or even usually occurs and, despite the somber tone of this discussion, even dangerous drugs occasionally have beneficial effects. This makes it easy to believe we will be exempt from harm in using drugs.

Two general attitudes about and strategies toward drug use and abuse are worth exploring. The first might be called a conservative version of rule-utilitarian thinking. The risks of consciousness-altering drugs, at least the most dangerous ones, are so great and so amply illustrated in our society that we ought to adopt the rule not to use them (for the sake of both our own good and the good of others).

The second attitude is closer to an act-utilitarian perspective that focuses on the good and bad consequences of individual acts rather than on general rules. This attitude concerns specific decisions whether to use a given drug, in a given quantity, at a given time, and in a given context. It then urges us to ask and responsibly answer a cluster of crucial questions: What direct or indirect harm to others might be caused? What is the threat to our own health, indeed to our lifespan? Is it worth the risk, given the likely benefits? Are we becoming so preoccupied with the drug that our attention, energy, money, and time are diverted from more worthwhile activities? Is the drug causing a dependency that lessens our sense of self-control, autonomy, and self-respect? Does the drug threaten to distort our capacity to process information rationally and to conduct a meaningful life?

Summary

Morality has to do with our relationship to ourselves as well as to others. As morally concerned persons, we have the same moral worth as other people and we owe ourselves self-respect. Self-respect differs from self-esteem: Self-esteem simply entails feeling good about oneself (for whatever reason), whereas self-respect entails appreciating one's moral worth. This appreciation is shown by trying to live up to duties to oneself, such as the duty not to harm oneself without justification.

Four forms of harming oneself are masochism, servility, irrational guilt and shame, and drug abuse. Masochism involves causing one's own suffering prompted by irrational motives. Servility is having the attitude that one lacks full moral worth and then acting on this attitude by becoming subservient to others at the expense of one's own rights and talents. Irrational guilt is feeling that one has wronged another person in a situation where one has not done so, and irrational shame is feeling, without justification, that one has failed to live up to appropriate standards of personal excellence. Drug abuse includes addiction, dependencies, long-term abuses, and periodic misuses of harmful drugs.

DISCUSSION TOPICS

1. This chapter concluded by sketching how a rule-utilitarian and an act-utilitarian might approach the question of whether to use dangerous drugs. Do you agree with what was said about how those two theories might be applied to the topic of drug abuse? That is, are there alternative ways of applying those theories so as to reach different conclusions about drug use? Present and defend your view of when and why the use of potentially harmful drugs is justified, drawing on an ethical theory.

2. Emotions and moods usually have some rough correspondence to our beliefs about events. For example, when we are cheerful, it is usually because our lives seem to us to be going well, and when we are sad, it is because of a loss of something or someone valuable to us. What would you say about people who repeatedly use drugs to alter the emotions appropriate to situations? For example, they use drugs to make themselves feel cheerful at the funeral of a friend or parent, to feel amused while reading a book about Nazi atrocities, to feel exhilarated after failing exams, or to feel affection for people who insult them.

3. Does the presence of peer pressure constitute coercion to use drugs, such that people are not able to make a voluntary decision based on their own wishes? Consider several examples, possibly from your own experience with friends and peers. Is the antidrug campaign initiated by Nancy Reagan realistic when it urges young people to "Just Say No"? Is it more effective when it encourages the formation of "Just Say No Clubs" in which young people create peer groups that pressure people not to use drugs? Are such groups coercive in a way that removes people's ability to make their own decisions or supportive of autonomous efforts to act reasonably?

4. Masochism is not just causing or enjoying one's pain. There must also be an irrational motive in doing so. Often, however, there are disagreements about which motives are irrational. For example, do the following situations constitute examples of masochism, at least sometimes? (1) Enjoying pain during sex; (2) Hurting oneself while engaging in dangerous sports like hang-gliding or auto racing; (3) Risking one's health through engaging in excessive amounts of work.

5. Is it masochistic to use drugs that enhance one's short-term ability to perform at the cost of one's long-term well-being? For example, both amateur Olympic sports and professional sports are intensely competitive. When athletes use steroids or other drugs in order to gain a competitive edge (or to avoid being put at a disadvantage in situations where others are using the drugs), are they being masochistic?

6. What responses to our feelings of guilt are morally appropriate? Consider the following examples.

   a. In *The Scarlet Letter,* Dimmesdale was able to find peace from the guilt that tortured him only when he sought Hester's forgiveness. Seeking forgiveness is an act of humbling oneself by placing oneself at the mercy of another person. Why is seeking forgiveness, as in Dimmesdale's case, often a morally appropriate response to guilt? Why isn't it enough just to resolve not to commit similar wrongdoing in the future? How does seeking forgiveness differ from being servile?

   b. We saw that prior to seeking Hester's forgiveness, Dimmesdale punished himself in ways that were masochistic. Is self-punishment always an unhealthy response to guilt, or can you think of instances in which some kinds of self-punishment are appropriate?

   c. Sometimes we seek to relieve guilt for hurting one person by engaging in a project to help other people, perhaps at some sacrifice to ourselves. Describe situations in which this is not an appropriate response to guilt (such as Dimmesdale ministering to others while disregarding Hester, or a thief trying to make amends by giving a token donation to charity but not returning the rest of the money to its owner). Describe other situations in which helping others *is* an appropriate response to guilt (as might be the case for a drunk driver who killed someone and cannot seek forgiveness). What is the moral difference between the two cases?

7. Depression has been called one of the worst afflictions of our century. It is the emotional state in which we experience a sweeping loss of our responsiveness to values, and also a loss of self-confidence and self-esteem, making our lives seem dull, boring, and hopeless. Is depression an emotional form of masochism? Consider both the tendency to frequent depression and individual episodes of depression. In doing so, respond to Robert Solomon's apparently positive view of (at least some) episodes of depression as expressed in the following passage:

   > Our depression is our way of wrenching ourselves from the established values of our world, the tasks in which we have been unquestioningly immersed, the opinions we have uncritically nursed, the relationships we have accepted without challenge and often without meaning. A depression is a self-imposed purge. It is the beginning of self-realization, unless it is simply ignored, or drugged away, or allows itself to give in to the demands for its own avoidance—the most extreme of which is suicide.[8]

SUGGESTED READINGS

Adler, Alfred. *The Individual Psychology of Alfred Adler.* Heinz L. Ansbacher and Rowena R. Ansbacher (eds.). New York: Harper Torchbooks, 1964.

Bach, Julie S. (ed.). *Drug Abuse: Opposing Viewpoints.* St. Paul, MN: Greenhaven, 1988.

Deigh, John. "Shame and Self-Esteem: A Critique." *Ethics,* vol. 93 (1983).

Fingarette, Herbert. "Alcoholism and Self-Deception." In Mike W. Martin (ed.), *Self-Deception and Self-Understanding.* Lawrence, KS: University Press of Kansas, 1985.

Fingarette, Herbert. *Heavy Drinking: The Myth of Alcoholism as a Disease.* Berkeley: University of California Press, 1988.

Goldstein, Irwin. "Pain and Masochism." *Journal of Value Inquiry,* vol. 17 (1983).

Hill, Thomas. "Servility and Self-Respect." *The Monist,* vol. 57 (1973).

Horney, Karen. *Neurosis and Human Growth.* New York: Norton, 1950.

Huxley, Aldous. *The Doors of Perception* and *Heaven and Hell.* New York: Harper, 1963.

Jones, Hardy. "Treating Oneself Wrongly." *Journal of Value Inquiry,* vol. 17 (1983).

Kant, Immanuel. "Proper Self-Respect" and "Duties to Oneself." In *Lectures on Ethics,* trans. Louis Infield. New York: Harper & Row, 1963.

Lynd, Helen Merrill. *On Shame and the Search for Identity.* New York: Harcourt, Brace & World, 1958.

Massey, Stephen J. "Is Self-Respect a Moral or a Psychological Concept?" *Ethics,* vol. 93 (1983).

Massey, Stephen J. "Kant on Self-Respect." *Journal of the History of Philosophy,* vol. 21 (1983).

Morris, Herbert (ed.). *Guilt and Shame.* Belmont, CA: Wadsworth, 1971.

Petrement, Simone. *Simone Weil: A Life.* Trans. Raymond Rosenthal. New York: Pantheon, 1976.

Rawls, John. *A Theory of Justice.* Cambridge, MA: Harvard University Press, 1971.

Ray, Oakley. *Drugs, Society, and Human Behavior.* 4th ed. St. Louis: Mosby, 1987.

Solomon, Robert. *The Passions.* Notre Dame, IN: University of Notre Dame Press, 1983.

Taylor, Gabriele. *Pride, Shame, and Guilt: Emotions of Self-Assessment.* Oxford: Clarendon Press, 1985.

Warren, Virginia. "Explaining Masochism." *Journal for the Theory of Social Behavior* (1985).

CHAPTER 6

Self-Deception

Self-respect entails valuing oneself as a moral self, that is, as someone who is responsive to moral reasons and ideals. Recall that self-respect is not simply having self-esteem in the sense of feeling good about oneself: Mere self-esteem can be, and often is, based on illusions and self-deceptions. Self-respect, by contrast, demands a high degree of honesty about oneself. There must be a truthful recognition of one's moral concern and moral relationships. This honesty with oneself, in turn, requires avoiding or overcoming self-deception about wrongdoing and character faults.

Self-deception was alluded to earlier. In Chapter 1 we noted that Jean-Paul Sartre viewed the overcoming of self-deception as central to authenticity—to being genuine and to assuming responsibility for one's life. In the previous chapter we implied that self-deception can conceal the harm we do to ourselves and others through drug abuse and other forms of self-destructiveness. More generally, self-deception about immorality can undermine the basis for self-respect by corrupting our integrity. In addition, an interest in preserving self-esteem sometimes motivates self-deception: The desire for a high estimate of ourselves can prompt us to deceive ourselves.

These connections among self-respect, self-esteem, self-deception, and immorality will be explored in this chapter. First, however, we must clarify what self-deception is and illustrate the psychological tactics it involves; thereby resolving some of the paradoxical elements implicit in the idea of deceiving ourselves.

Definitions and Tactics

To deceive other people is to purposefully mislead them, to conceal some truth from them. This can be accomplished by keeping them ignorant about a topic, leading them to believe something false, diverting their attention from an important matter, or distorting their attitudes and emotions. Similarly, *to deceive oneself* is to purposefully mislead oneself, to avoid an unpleasant truth or a painful topic. It can be accomplished by keeping oneself ignorant about a topic, persuading oneself to believe something false, avoiding paying attention to an important matter, or distorting one's attitudes and emotions.

An example should help clarify what self-deception is and how we engage in it. In his memoirs, entitled *Inside the Third Reich,* Albert Speer tries to explain his participation in Nazi Germany. Speer tells us that he was chosen by Hitler to serve as the official state architect. His extraordinary talents in managing large bureaucracies quickly thrust him into higher positions of authority, and within seven years he was appointed to the powerful position of Minister of Armaments. By the end of World War II he was in complete charge of all war productions, and second only to Hitler in power. At the Nuremberg trials following the war Speer was sentenced to twenty years in prison for forcing war prisoners to work under slave conditions in his munitions factories.

Perhaps it would be comforting to regard Speer as a sociopathic monster, lacking any conscience, and bearing no resemblance to people we know. Yet he was a remarkably intelligent man who was sensitive and caring with his family and friends. How could such a person participate in a profoundly immoral government?

Speer's own explanation is that he systematically deceived himself using familiar psychological tactics. For example, he *refused to reflect* on his moral responsibilities while serving Hitler. He *rationalized* (that is, reasoned in a biased way) that questions of morality pertained to his family and personal relationships, not to his leader's decisions. He thoroughly *compartmentalized* his life, thinking of himself solely as an architect and bureaucrat, with no interests in political issues. Motivated by ambition, pride, and a sense of duty, he managed to deny any personal sense of wrongdoing at the time. In this respect he bears a disturbing resemblance to many bureaucrats and business people who loyally obey their superiors' orders to do immoral acts.

Surely, we insist, Speer must have been in a position to know about the Jewish holocaust, which should have shattered the complacency of any minimally decent person. Yet he somehow managed to keep himself ignorant, *willfully ignorant,* of any information that would have disturbed his web of self-deceit. Difficult as it is to believe, he deliberately avoided learning about the existence of the extermination camps. On one occasion, toward the end of the war, a friend alluded in a conversation to a terrifying visit he had just made to a concentration camp, which, after the war, Speer inferred must have been Auschwitz. The friend advised Speer never to accept an invitation to inspect the camp. Speer recalls: "I did not query him, I did not query Himmler, I did not query Hitler, I did not speak with personal friends. I did not investigate—for I did not want to know what was happening there."[1]

Equally important to Speer's self-deception was his ability to control his attention to and emotions concerning those horrors he did know about. He would *selectively attend* to what he wanted, especially by keeping his mind focused on his immediate duties. He would distract himself from the killing, a maneuver made easier by his lack of any direct observation of it. Often he would numb his emotions by engaging in *emotional detachment* from unpleasant realities. Other times, especially in response to the war prisoners he used as slave laborers, he would keep his emotions at the level of pure sentimentality, for example by feeling sorrow without being motivated to action. All these tactics were reinforced by his circle of friends and acquaintances. As he suggested, the Third Reich was like a hall of distorting mirrors that multiplied his self-deceptions.

Speer, of course, represents an extreme example of self-generated moral delusion. Yet the avenues to that delusion are quite familiar. All of us have sometimes evaded acknowledging to ourselves information that we suspected would be unpleasant or onerous to confront head-on. We are all aware of the various evasion tactics: willfully ignoring, selectively attending, detaching emotionally, sentimentally manipulating our emotions so as to avoid acting, working compulsively in order to avoid other responsibilities, compartmentalizing our lives into separate channels that we avoid relating to one another, allowing our biases to shape rationalized belief and attitudes, and acquiescing to peers who mold our opinions and self-images in comforting ways.

Paradoxes

Even though these ways of deceiving ourselves are familiar, the idea of deceiving oneself has proven puzzling to some philosophers. They have argued that it is paradoxical—not just in the literary sense of paradoxes as merely apparent absurdities, but in the sense of paradoxes as contradictions. Literally deceiving oneself, they argue, is an impossibility, especially if it means telling a lie to oneself and coming to believe it.

In a situation in which one person deceives another person, there is a deceiver who is aware of a truth and a deceived person who is not aware of it (and who is prevented from becoming aware of it by the lie). For example, consider an employee who lies to his employer about his alcoholism, and suppose that the employer is in fact deceived by the lie. The employee is fully aware he is an alcoholic: He believes it, he knows it, and he is fully conscious of it (that is, he can and does attend to the fact that he is an alcoholic). The employer, by contrast, is not aware that the employee is an alcoholic: She does not believe it, she does not know it, and she is not conscious of it.

When we try to imagine the alcoholic lying to himself, we must, it seems, imagine him functioning simultaneously as the deceiver and as the victim of the deception. That seems impossible for three reasons. First, he would have to believe and not believe the same thing at the same time—an apparent impossibility. Second, he would have to know and not know the truth at the same time—a further impossibility. Third, he would have to *use* his awareness of the truth as part of the process of hiding the truth from another person. Both the content of the lie ("I am not abusing alcohol") and the way the lie is told (with apparent conviction) are guided by awareness on the part of the alcoholic of the truth that must be kept concealed from the employer. But how could the alcoholic use his awareness of the truth in pursuing his intention to deceive the employer? It seems he would have to maintain awareness of the truth even as he tried to lie to himself. But to say to himself "I am not an alcoholic" at a moment when he is fully aware that he is an alcoholic obviously would represent a futile attempt to deceive himself.

These three paradoxes all stem from trying to interpret self-deception on the model of a lie. By why should that model be accepted? After all, "deceiving" and "lying" are not synonymous terms, as we noted in Chapter 4. A lie is a false statement told with the intention to deceive. If, however, the lie is not believed, no deception occurs. Hence, there can be lies without deception. There can also be deception without lies. To deceive is to intentionally mislead someone (whether by leading them to hold a false belief, by keeping them ignorant of a truth, by distracting them for a while, and so on). Such deception can be achieved without lying, perhaps by saying nothing in a situation in which the truth should be spoken or by engaging in pretense (using "body language").

The expression "lying to oneself" is a metaphor that if taken too literally leads to the paradoxes we mentioned. The concept of "deceiving oneself," however, is meaningful and nonparadoxical even when taken literally to mean purposefully misleading oneself. It need not involve full awareness of the truth at any time. Instead, the self-deceiver often has only a suspicion that something might be true, or perhaps an intimation that an entire topic (such as the details about a pattern of conduct) might prove deeply troubling if examined closely. This was illustrated by Speer when he sensed that something was amiss at Auschwitz and as a result refused to ask questions. Similarly, an alcoholic might deceive himself by refusing to reflect fully and honestly (without bias) about his pattern of drinking and its effects on his life.

These suspicions may involve fleeting moments of consciousness of the truth or just a vague, peripheral awareness that something may be amiss in certain areas of our lives. Moreover, if we engaged in honest reflection, we could in many cases obtain a clearer and fuller awareness. The self-deceiver avoids precisely this kind of honest self-scrutiny, for it threatens to reveal truths or topics that are deliberately being avoided.

If Sigmund Freud was correct, there are also other forms of self-deception in which honest self-scrutiny by itself may not be enough to bring truths to consciousness. He postulated that there are psychological "defense mechanisms" that keep truths out of our conscious awareness and that themselves operate without consciousness. Moreover, we cannot become conscious of the mechanisms and the truths they conceal without (in most cases) the special help of psychoanalysts or other types of psychotherapists.

For example, *repression* is the process through which ideas are blocked from entering consciousness and from being accessible to our attention. Repression operates unconsciously, unlike the act of *suppression,* in which we consciously avoid attending to something ("I must stop worrying about that exam and get my mind back on my work"). Another example is *projection,* in which people unconsciously ascribe their problems, hostility, or other attitudes to other people (often in modified forms). Thus, paranoid people who irrationally think everyone is out to get them are unconsciously ascribing both their own fears and their feelings of aggression to other people they come in contact with.

Responsibility

Self-deception proceeds in the absence of full awareness of what one is deceived about and to the activity of deceiving oneself. It involves, for example, ignoring things without attending to the fact that one is ignoring them. Or it involves the unconscious process Freud described. Does this absence of full awareness mean that one is not responsible for any harm done while self-deceived? Is Speer, for example, not blameworthy for the harm he did while deceiving himself? Is self-deception an excuse, or partial excuse, for immorality?

Herbert Fingarette, in his book *Self-Deception,* suggests that self-deceivers' moral responsibilities are at best ambiguous. Usually, when people are deemed responsible for their conduct, two conditions are met. First, they were aware, or at least able to be aware, of what they were doing. Second, they acted voluntarily, that is, without coercion and without uncontrollable inner compulsions. Self-deceivers, by contrast, render themselves incapable of becoming aware of what they are doing, thereby weakening their capacity to fully control their actions. Fingarette writes:

> There is thus in self-deception a genuine subversion of personal agency and, for this reason in turn, a subversion of moral capacity. The sensitive

and thoughtful observer, when viewing the matter this way, is inclined
not to hold the self-deceiver responsible but to view him as a "victim."[2]

In Fingarette's view self-deception is a morally puzzling state about which
it is impossible to make our usual moral judgments. Self-deceivers are not
clearly acting voluntarily, because they lack the ability to become aware of
what they are doing. Nor are they clearly acting involuntarily, however, because they are, after all, the source of their own deception. Should we accept
this view?

Fingarette was especially interested in neurotic forms of self-deception in
which mental illness is involved. Such persons do sometimes lack the capacity
to gain full awareness of their self-deception and then to control their actions.
They may need the help of a psychotherapist, or just a supportive friend, in
order to confront the truths they are avoiding.

Yet Fingarette's perspective on self-deception is not convincing with
respect to much self-deception in which individuals *are* able to become
conscious of their self-deceiving activities and the truths they are evading.
Certainly mere ignorance and lack of consciousness are not automatically excuses for immorality. Each of us is responsible for knowing what our obligations are and for obtaining information relevant to meeting them. Blinding
oneself to those obligations and facts does not cancel or lessen moral account-
ability. Speer is guilty for the harm he caused—period.

In fact, when the obligations involved are especially important, as with
Speer's responsibility not to support a racist government or employ slave labor, self-deception about the obligations is itself immoral. Thus, Speer was
blameworthy for two reasons: (1) because of the cruelties he participated in
and (2) because he deceived himself about those cruelties in order to proceed
with them without a troubled conscience.

Joseph Butler (1692–1752) made this point. Self-deception about
wrongdoing and character faults, he wrote,

> is essentially in its own nature vicious [that is, a vice] and immoral. It is
> unfairness; it is dishonesty; it is falseness of heart: and is therefore so far
> from extenuating guilt, that it is itself the greatest of all guilt in propor-
> tion to the degree it prevails; for it is a corruption of the whole moral
> character in its principle.[3]

Butler's expression "moral character in its principle" refers to conscience, that
is, a sense of right and wrong. Self-deception about immorality corrupts conscience by preventing it from properly guiding conduct and character
development.

Furthermore, Butler said that self-deception about immorality represents
unfairness and hypocrisy. It is unfairness in that it involves cheating on our
own moral standards. We gain undeserved advantages through wrongdoing
and through an unwarranted view of our own character. Self-deception about

immorality is "inner hypocrisy"—hypocrisy before ourselves—in that we appear better in our own eyes than we really are. Our unjustified self-esteem is bolstered by false beliefs about our conduct and character.

Self-Respect, Self-Esteem, and Immorality

Now that we have clarified the nature of and responsibility for self-deception, let us draw together the connections between self-deception, self-respect, self-esteem, and immorality.

First, self-respect is based on self-understanding and on appreciating our true character and moral worth. Whereas mere self-esteem (a favorable view of ourselves) is often based on illusions or self-deceptions, self-respect requires that we value ourselves as morally concerned persons whose characters are based on moral commitments. Accordingly, self-respect is eroded when self-deception grossly distorts understanding of our character. Thus, whatever positive feelings of self-esteem Speer might have had during his service to the Third Reich, he nevertheless lacked genuine self-respect based on moral self-understanding.

Second, the desire to retain a sense of self-respect and self-esteem is a major motive for self-deception. We deceive ourselves about our wrongdoing and character flaws in order to avoid the pain that results from acknowledging those flaws to ourselves, as well as burden of having to alter them. Speer, for example, would have had little reason to deceive himself about the Third Reich if he had been a callous sociopath who lacked all moral concern. It was because he did have some degree of moral decency, coupled with a desire to think of himself as decent, that he found it necessary to deceive himself.

Third, a desire to maintain a sense of self-respect also motivates us to avoid acknowledging our own self-deceptions: We like to think of ourselves as having the courage to willingly face the truth, not as cowardly and hypocritical evaders of the truth. Of course, many other motives generate or support self-deception, including fear, laziness, envy, a desire for self-esteem, and so on. Perhaps no motive is stronger or more common, however, than the desire to sustain an attitude of self-respect. Thus, in everyday life we employ an array of devices for bolstering an unjustifiably high estimate of our own character and the sense of self-respect based on it. Two centuries ago Samuel Johnson (1709–1784) identified several of these devices:

1. We selectively emphasize our occasional good deeds, eagerly treating one isolated act as if it were a habit constituting a virtuous character trait.

   A miser who once relieved a friend from the danger of a prison, suffers his imagination to dwell for ever upon his own heroic generosity; he yields his heart up to indignation at those who are blind to merit, or insensible to misery . . .

and though his whole life is a course of rapacity and avarice, he concludes himself to be tender and liberal, because he has once performed an act of liberality and tenderness.[4]

2. We dismiss our wrongdoing as uncharacteristic lapses or else as flaws that everyone has. Nights of debauchery, Johnson notes, are easily excused by noting that even great people have similar lapses. Such lapses, we tell ourselves, do not detract from our essential goodness.
3. We confuse lip service to virtue with the real thing: "There are men who always confound the praise of goodness with the practice, and who believe themselves mild and moderate, charitable and faithful, because they have exerted their eloquence in commendation of mildness, fidelity, and other virtues."[5]
4. We tend to focus our attention on the worst deeds of other people as a way to downplay our faults. Dwelling on the worst faults of our acquaintances, or attending to the vicious deeds of criminals reported on in the daily newspaper, brings a comforting sense of our superior virtue.
5. We choose friends who share our vices, and we eagerly listen to the words of flatterers. This reinforces our vices and enables us to avoid that serious self-reflection that Johnson calls "communion with our own hearts."

A fourth connection between self-respect and self-deception concerns overcoming self-deception about our faults. We must honestly acknowledge our lack of moral commitment before we can reclaim our self-respect. Initially, this acknowledgment diminishes feelings of self-respect, assuming we are morally concerned. Within limits, this is as it should be, for at such times we feel guilt for the wrongdoing concealed by the self-deception and guilt for having deceived ourselves about it. There may sometimes be a devastating sense of self-disillusionment—surely we would expect something like that in the case of Speer if his remorse were genuine. Yet remorse and diminished feelings of self-respect can prepare the way for a renewed and stronger basis for self-respect. Genuine remorse should prompt a resolve to try to make some form of amends and to avoid similar self-deceptions in the future.

Fifth, even if we do not succeed in overcoming self-deception about our faults, we may still experience diminished self-respect because of a haunting sense of our "inner dishonesty." Just as we can have a suspicion of the truths we are evading, we can have a sense that we are evading the truth—that we are not being fully honest with ourselves in acknowledging truths important to our lives. In severe cases of habitual self-deception the consequences can be worse than mere anxiety, as Fyodor Dostoevsky (1821–1881) suggested in his novel *The Brothers Karamazov:*

Above all, don't lie to yourself. The man who lies to himself and listens to his own lie comes to such a point that he cannot distinguish the truth within him, or around him, and so loses all respect for himself and for others. And having no respect he ceases to love. And in order to distract himself without love he gives way to passions and coarse pleasures and sinks to bestiality in his vices—all this from continual lying to other men and to himself.[6]

Sixth, some self-deception is damaging to our own talents, happiness, and self-development in ways that undermine self-esteem and sometimes self-respect. For example, self-deception can be used to conceal the motives and significance of tendencies to belittle ourselves—to "put ourselves down" with irrational condemnations. Painful feelings of inferiority can be generated in part by applying self-deceivingly unrealistic standards to ourselves. Many of the examples of masochism and servility discussed in the previous chapter involved self-deception of this sort. In such cases self-deception conceals our capacities for goodness.

Here is a further example of how self-deception can hurt ourselves more than anyone else by weakening appreciation of our own talents and possibilities. In her autobiography entitled *From Housewife to Heretic,* Sonia Johnson describes her struggle to escape submissiveness to a male-dominated culture and servility toward a patriarchal religion. She writes, "I was a person who had unconsciously known for a very long time that something was wrong with patriarchy, but because my entire culture, to say nothing of my church, was based upon it almost as given, I hadn't had the courage to face what I knew."[7]

For the most part, she made innumerable accommodations and sacrifices that undermined her own opportunities and talents. These included the familiar one-sided burden of household chores and responsibility for her four children; the assumption that she was responsible for caring for her husband without comparable reciprocity; the automatic and largely uncritical dependence on the views of her husband and the male bishopric of her church; indulgence not only of her husband's childish habit of emotional withdrawal when problems arose but also of his frequent absences from home for work-related reasons (especially when he had the option not to go on business trips); a blind trust in her husband of twenty years to the point where she was an easy dupe when he connived a plot to divorce her in a way minimizing his legal responsibilities—the act that finally shocked her into sustained self-reflection.

In retrospect Johnson was able to see that her primary tactic of evading the truth about her submissiveness was a systematic suppression of her emotions:

I was living a sort of half life, in half light, a grayish, half-awake limbo of neither clouds nor sunlight, a gray same numbness. . . . I accomplished this great reductionist feat by lowering the threshold of my awareness, allowing very little stimuli into my consciousness for fear of inadvertently letting in the scary things. At the same time, I unconsciously dulled my perception of the stimuli I did choose so that I would not see clearly what I did not want to see, would not feel what I did not want to feel, would not have to face what I feared to face.[8]

Suppression of so many of her own ideas, attitudes, and needs prevented her from emerging as fully authentic through fidelity to her own talents and aspirations.

Seventh, and finally, it should be pointed out that self-deception may in some situations be beneficial and supportive of self-esteem and self-respect. Although Jean-Paul Sartre condemned all self-deception as inauthentic, deceiving ourselves sometimes can actually aid our personal growth and the development of our talents without having harmful side effects.

A familiar example is overcoming the fear of public speaking. Even without self-deception, ignoring one's stage fright by pretending not to be afraid can increase one's self-confidence and thereby strengthen one's speaking ability. Deceiving oneself into believing one is a better speaker than in fact one is may yield similar results. Likewise, an athlete might "psyche up" for a race by engaging in a bit of innocent self-deception about his or her abilities to win. Indeed, we frequently approach difficult tasks by self-deceivingly magnifying our abilities to succeed or minimizing the difficulties ahead. Such self-deception enables us to at least try things we otherwise might turn away from in discouragement. Undoubtedly, some distinctively moral commitments can be strengthened in this way as well. Many parents engage in some useful self-deception to help sustain their efforts in caring for their children—self-deception about the difficulties involved in raising children, for example.

Perhaps such forms of self-deception are not entirely rational in the sense of showing a full devotion to truth. Perhaps it would be more rational to proceed on the basis of hope and faith that did not involve any self-deception. Certainly, habitual self-deception threatens to undermine the standards of rationality essential to living up to moral and other values—standards like respect for evidence, concern for consistency, impartiality, clarity of thought, rigor of argument, and so on. Nevertheless, where isolated instances of self-deception do not contribute to general habits of irrationality, and where they are beneficial rather than harmful, it seems the element of irrationality (avoiding the truth) may be outweighed by other values.

Summary

Self-deception is the evasion of truths or topics, whether specific or general, that should be confronted, however painful it might be. It is typically refusal to acknowledge truths to ourselves, whether through ignoring something we suspect is true, avoiding inquiry into disturbing topics, engaging in rationalization (biased reasoning), emotionally detaching ourselves from difficult situations, or using other tactics. These tactics are employed without attending to them with full consciousness. Understood in this way, self-deception does not involve paradox or self-contradiction.

Sartre thought that all self-deception is "inauthentic" in that it involves a lack of genuineness, honesty, and courage in confronting truth. Yet some self-deception may be beneficial as it contributes to personal development without having bad side effects. Self-deception is immoral, as Joseph Butler suggested, when it conceals wrongdoing, character faults, or facts needed for meeting our obligations. In that context our self-deception prohibits us from honestly confronting the morally harmful aspects of our lives. As such, the self-deception is a kind of derivative wrong—its badness derives from its support of other wrongdoing. In addition, apart from being a form of dishonesty about the truth, it reflects an "inner hypocrisy"—thinking better of ourselves than is warranted by our character.

Insofar as we can refrain from or overcome self-deception about immorality, we are responsible for both the immorality and the self-deception. Precisely how blameworthy we are depends on the answers to several questions: How serious is the immorality about which we deceive ourselves? Are we aware of being in a situation where self-deception threatens to do harm (as with Speer)? How much control do we have over the self-deception, and are we capable of facing the truth? Is there mental illness involved that weakens our capacity to confront the truth, and if so, is there help available that we can be expected to take advantage of? As these questions suggest, responsibility for self-deception mirrors the complexity of morality in general.

Self-deception is related to self-respect (appreciating our moral worth) and self-esteem (thinking well of ourselves) in a number of ways. First, because self-respect means appreciating our moral worth accurately, based on self-understanding, self-deception about our faults undermines self-respect. Second, one major motive for self-deception is the desire to maintain a high opinion of our own character. Third, the desire to sustain self-esteem and a sense of self-respect motivates us not to acknowledge we are self-deceivers, because recognizing our cowardly evasions of truth is not flattering. Fourth, overcoming self-deception can bring a temporary deflation of self-esteem and self-respect, even as subsequent remorse and efforts to make amends can strengthen them. Fifth, habitual self-respect sometimes creates a nagging sense that we are not being honest with ourselves—a sense that weakens self-respect. Sixth, some self-deception damages self-development and the basis for self-esteem. Finally, some self-deception (as with the public speaking example) can contribute to self-development and can strengthen self-esteem.

DISCUSSION TOPICS

1. Suppose someone argued that the idea of "teaching oneself" is confused and self-contradictory because a person would have to know (as teacher) what he or she does not know (as learner). Respond to this argument, and in doing so compare and contrast what is involved in teaching oneself and in deceiving oneself.

2. Consider the argument that we should not punish people who cause accidents while under the influence of alcohol and other drugs because at the time of the crash they were unable to have prevented the accident. Respond to this argument, noting any similarities and differences you see between responsibility for harm done through alcohol use and through self-deception.

3. We suggested that self-deception can be permissible, benign or even beneficial. But could it ever be morally obligatory? Jack Meiland has argued that it can be. In an essay entitled "What Ought We to Believe? or The Ethics of Belief Revisited," he offers the following two examples of when he thinks self-deception is obligatory. Do you agree with his view?

   Case 1. Suppose that Jones and Smith have been business partners and exceptionally close friends for more than thirty-five years. One day Jones discovers a discrepancy in the business's accounts. Upon investigation he comes into the possession of evidence which is sufficient (in anyone's eyes) to justify the belief that Smith has been secretly syphoning off money from the business. Now Jones is in the following predicament. He is, and knows he is, the type of person who is unable to conceal his feelings and beliefs from others. He thus knows that if he decides that Smith has indeed been stealing money from the firm it will definitely affect his behavior toward Smith. Even if Jones tries to conceal his belief, he knows that he will inevitably act in a remote, cold, censorious and captious manner toward Smith and that eventually both the friendship and the business partnership will break up. Jones decides that this price is too high and therefore decides not to believe that Smith stole money from the firm. In fact, he goes farther: he decides that Smith did not steal money from the firm.

   Case 2. Take the classical case in which a wife finds a blonde hair on her husband's coat, a handkerchief with lipstick on it in his pocket, a scrap of paper with a phone number scrawled on it, and so on until everyone would agree that the evidence is sufficient that the husband has been seeing another woman. However, the wife believes that their marriage is basically sound and can weather this storm. Like Jones, she knows that she cannot conceal her suspicions and hence decides to believe that her husband is not being unfaithful to her.[9]

   In defending your agreement or disagreement with Meiland, consider two possibilities: (1) Things turn out as hoped for—that is, Smith stops stealing and the friendship remains intact; and the husband stops having affairs and the marriage grows stronger than ever. (This is the situation Meiland had in mind.) (2) It is not known what consequences are likely to result from the self-deception.

4. Accusing someone of self-deception usually means accusing them of (1) holding a false belief or being ignorant of something they should have known (given the evidence available) and (2) purposefully avoiding the truth. What should be said about the use of the concept of self-deception to criticize people's religious beliefs, which are based on faith and not on proven fact?

In *The Future of an Illusion,* for example, Freud criticized theists (people who believe in God) for engaging in self-deceptive forms of wishful thinking (that is, believing what makes them happy). Jean-Paul Sartre made similar sweeping criticisms of theists, as did Karl Marx when he portrayed religion as "the opiate of the people."

Many theologians and ministers have made the opposite charge: Atheists are guilty of evading the recognition of God's existence. For example, the Protestant theologian Reinhold Niebuhr stated that rejecting belief in God is a sin of pride in basing human concerns above God. He traced this "sin" to willful dishonesty and self-deception: "Man loves himself inordinately. Since his determinate existence does not deserve the devotion lavished upon it, it is obviously necessary to practice some deception in order to justify such excessive devotion." [10]

In making such charges and counter-charges, is the concept of self-deception being properly used or misused?

SUGGESTED READINGS

Butler, Bishop Joseph. "Upon Self-Deceit." In W. E. Gladstone (ed.), *The Works of Joseph Butler.* Oxford: Clarendon Press, 1896.

De Sousa, Ronald. *The Rationality of Emotion.* Cambridge, MA: MIT Press, 1987.

Dilman, Ilham. *Freud and the Mind.* Oxford: Basil Blackwell, 1984.

Elster, John (ed.). *The Multiple Self.* Cambridge: Cambridge University Press, 1986.

Fingarette, Herbert. *Self-Deception.* Atlantic Highlands, NJ: Humanities Press, 1969.

Freud, Sigmund. *The Future of an Illusion.* New York: Norton, 1960.

Goleman, Daniel. *Vital Lies, Simple Truths: The Psychology of Self-Deception.* New York: Simon & Schuster, 1985.

Haight, M. R. *A Study of Self-Deception.* Atlantic Highlands, NJ: Humanities Press, 1980.

Johnson, Samuel. *The Rambler.* In Arthur Murphy (ed.), *The Works of Samuel Johnson,* vol. 2. London: S. and R. Bentley, 1823.

Lockard, Joan S., and Delroy L. Paulhus (eds.). *Self-Deception: An Adaptive Mechanism?* Englewood Cliffs, NJ: Prentice-Hall, 1988.

Martin, Mike W. *Self-Deception and Morality.* Lawrence, KS: University Press of Kansas, 1986.

Martin, Mike W. (ed.). *Self-Deception and Self-Understanding: New Essays In Philosophy and Psychology.* Lawrence, KS: University Press of Kansas, 1985.

Mele, Alfred R. *Irrationality: An Essay on Akrasia, Self-Deception and Self-Control.* New York: Oxford University Press, 1987.

Sartre, Jean-Paul. "Bad Faith." In *Being and Nothingness*. New York: Washington Square Press, 1966.

Sloan, Tod S. *Deciding: Self-Deception in Life Choices*. New York: Methuen, 1987.

Steffen, Lloyd H. *Self-Deception and the Common Life*. New York: Peter Lang, 1986.

Szabados, Béla. "The Morality of Self-Deception." *Dialogue,* vol. 13 (1974).

CHAPTER 7

Weakness of Will

Knowing what is right is one thing. Doing it is something else. No aspect of morality is more poignant than the struggle to live up to our moral convictions. Convinced that we are obligated to do something, we nevertheless fail to do it, even though it is in our power to do it. This is *weakness of will:* judging that an act should be performed, all things considered, and then voluntarily doing something else. When the judgment is a moral evaluation, the weakness of will is called *moral weakness.*

Understanding moral weakness is important for several reasons. For one thing, it enriches our grasp of the virtues of perseverance, self-control, and self-discipline. For another, it adds to our comprehension of inner conflicts and how those conflicts relate to both self-respect and our sense of personal identity. In addition, it enhances our perception of the role of excuses in protecting self-esteem and a sense of self-respect. And yet, as we shall see, weakness of will is itself difficult to understand or even paradoxical.

Loss of Self-Control: Occasional Versus Habitual

Weakness of will can be occasional or habitual. Occasional weakness of will is one act (or omitted act) or a few occurrences of a given type of act. An example is found in Plato's story about a man named Leontius. While on a walk, Leontius's attention was sharply diverted:

> He noticed the bodies of some criminals lying on the ground, with the executioner standing by them. He wanted to go and look at them, but at the same time he was disgusted and tried to turn away. He struggled for some time and covered his eyes, but at last the desire was too much for

him. Opening his eyes wide, he ran up to the bodies and cried, "There you are, curse you; feast yourselves on this lovely sight!"[1]

Habitual weakness of will, by contrast, involves a longer-term pattern of actions of a given type. In his autobiography, written at age ninety-two, Will Durant (1885–1981), the historian and philosophy popularizer, recounts a once deeply distressing habit:

> By the age of twelve—probably earlier—I had become an expert in masturbation; by the age of fourteen I was carrying this manual art to an extreme that alarmed my confessor—that same beloved Father Mooney who had nominated me for the priesthood. I did not dare hide these terrible sins in my weekly confession. This perfect priest seemed not much surprised by my first avowals; he let me off with a gentle reproof and an easy penance; but when, as my fever progressed, I confessed to him that I had broken all my records by relieving my congestion eighteen times in a week, he refused me absolution—without which I could not receive the Eucharist. Even so he spoke with sympathy, and when we met a few days later he greeted me with his usual quiet friendliness. My addiction to baseball, running, and other sports helped me to moderate the habit, but not to overcome it. Nature will out, with or without aid.[2]

Moral weakness, as it is usually understood, involves four elements: (1) a moral judgment or evaluation that an act is wrong and ought to be avoided; (2) a desire to perform the act anyway; (3) intentionally acting on that desire;* (4) doing so voluntarily, without external coercion or irresistible inner compulsions. The first three of these elements are clearly illustrated in the examples of Leontius and Durant. Leontius believed that he should not look at the corpses but nevertheless wanted to and intentionally did so. The young Durant evaluated masturbation as being wrong (indeed, as a sin) but intentionally acted on his desire to engage in it.

It is perhaps less obvious whether the two examples illustrate the fourth element of moral weakness. Did Leontius and Durant act voluntarily in the sense of being able to do otherwise and without coercion or overwhelming inner compulsions? Or were they forced to act as they did by an irresistible compulsion? Some of the language used implies a loss of self-control: "the desire was too much" for Leontius, and Durant concluded that "nature will out." Does a loss of self-control, however, establish the presence of an irresistible compulsion?

The answer depends on clarifying the meaning of the term *self-control*. In one sense "self-control" simply means living on the basis of one's values and

---

*That is, knowingly and purposefully acting to satisfy the desire, although usually not specifically intending (or seeking) to be weak of will.

standards of rationality. Leontius and Durant lost self-control in this sense, because they gave in to impulses contrary to their value standards. That does not imply, however, that these impulses were irresistible and could not have been resisted with greater effort.

In another sense "self-control" means having the psychological ability, drawing on one's best efforts, to live up to one's better judgment in situations in which one is tempted to do otherwise. Perhaps the passages quoted provide insufficient information to determine whether Leontius and Durant lost self-control in this sense. Durant seems to imply that he was able to avoid individual acts of masturbation only by postponing them—"nature will out" in the sense that sooner or later he was bound to give in to the impulses. Whether this was indeed the case will depend on our general understanding of his life and the qualities of self-restraint he showed in other areas of his life at this time. Similarly, fuller knowledge of Leontius's capacities for self-restraint might shed light on his self-control on this occasion.

Most of us are familiar with instances in our own lives when we surely could have exercised self-control (in both senses) but failed to do so because we did not try hard enough. If we afterward offer the excuse "I lost control" or "I was weak-willed," our excuse may be true only in the first sense of "control"—that is, we failed to guide our acts by our standards, even though we were able to do so. Familiar examples include neglecting to write a thank-you letter that we knew was owed, failing to keep a promise, overeating, abusing alcohol, and missing an important appointment.

Paradoxes

Despite the familiarity of these examples of acting against our better judgment, some philosophers find weakness of will paradoxical. They question whether one can really judge or evaluate an act as right and then voluntarily fail to do it. Surely, they insist, the judgment or evaluation is not sincere or genuine. This skepticism about weakness of will takes several forms depending on how judgments or evaluations are understood: (1) as knowledge or beliefs, (2) as commitments, or (3) as entailing wants.

Value Judgments as Knowledge or Beliefs

One group of skeptics about weakness of will view value judgments as consisting essentially of knowledge or beliefs about what ought to be done or what constitutes good conduct. They then argue that the concepts of knowledge and belief make weakness of will, as ordinarily understood, a self-contradictory notion.

Socrates, for example, held that "knowledge *is* virtue": To know what is morally right is to do it (when the opportunity arises, and unless outside forces prevent one).[3] This dictum leaves no loopholes for failures to live up to what is known to be virtuous. As Socrates stated, "Knowledge is a fine thing quite capable of ruling a man, and . . . if he can distinguish good from evil, nothing will force him to act otherwise than as knowledge dictates, since wisdom is all the reinforcement he needs."[4]

Aristotle's view was more complex, but he agreed with Socrates that knowledge about how we ought to act, together with awareness of relevant information about our situation, leads us to act accordingly unless external obstacles interfere. He suggested that "incontinent [i.e., weak-willed] people must be said to be in a similar condition to men asleep, mad, or drunk."[5] Either they are momentarily blinded to the reality of what they are doing or they temporarily lose awareness of its wrongness.

Socrates and Aristotle's perspective on weakness of will do fit some cases. They remind us, for one thing, of how an intense pleasure close at hand can momentarily distort judgment or deflect attention from what we otherwise know is right. Yet their perspective seems to rule out some cases of weakness of will. People can know, for example, that they ought to write more letters to their aging parents and, without losing awareness of this responsibility, simply fail to do so. If Socrates and Aristotle then insist that such people did not really know or believe this was their responsibility, they are stipulating unusually stringent standards for what counts as knowledge and belief. They are redefining knowledge such that only the self-controlled person can be said to know what is morally right.

The important distinction here is between (1) knowing, believing, or judging something to be right and (2) being motivated to do it. More generally, evaluations are one thing, motivations are another. We can know what we ought to do and yet not make a sufficient effort to do it. The explanation for why we failed to try hard enough may be that we did not care deeply enough about our responsibilities, or that we were tired or anxious. (As we saw in the previous chapter, self-deception often clouds our judgment and knowledge as well.)

Value Judgments as Commitments

More recent writers like R. M. Hare view value judgments as more closely resembling commitments than beliefs or knowledge. In Hare's opinion, to evaluate an act as being obligatory is to commit oneself to doing it when the occasion arises. Moreover, this commitment entails doing the act unless prevented by external forces, by an absence of any opportunity to act, or by a psychological inability to so act. The idea of weakness of will, which requires that one could have acted differently but failed to do so because of a lack of effort, is a self-contradictory notion.

Hare certainly is correct in stating that sometimes when we think we could have acted differently at a given moment, we are mistaken. For example, drug addicts or gluttons may feel sure that their actions were avoidable, but in fact they are suffering from addictions. No doubt if they had developed different habits of self-discipline in the past, they could have acted differently in the present. Habits do indeed have a certain psychological force or motivating power that enables us to eat appropriately or to overindulge, or to easily resist impulses to use a drug or to not be able to at a given moment.

Hare's view also has more plausibility than Socrates and Aristotle's when applied to simple cases like failing to write letters to one's parents. Hare forces us to ask, "Are persons sincerely committed to writing the letters if they repeatedly fail to write them when the opportunity arises?" The familiar saying "Actions speak louder than words" in determining what a person is really committed to is relevant here.

Yet is Hare correct in equating moral judgments or evaluations with commitments, especially fully sincere commitments? Judging something to be wrong is not the same as fully committing ourselves to avoiding it. Moreover, even when we are fully committed, we may have momentary lapses of effort and caring. One may be sincerely committed to the principle that one ought to keep promises and fail to do so only rarely. Guilt feelings and efforts to make amends following the failures may confirm the sincerity of the commitment.

Value Judgments as Entailing Wants

A third type of skepticism about weakness of will interprets value judgments as entailing wants or desires rather than commitments. According to this view, judging that one act is better than another entails wanting to do the first act more than the second, which in turn entails acting on that want when the opportunity arises (and assuming one does either act at all). Thus, a person who evaluates keeping a promise as right will want to do it more than not keeping the promise. Presumably, however, one always does what one wants most to do, and therefore, how could one fail to keep the promise (when one is able to do so)? In general, it seems impossible to act contrary to one's evaluations about what ought to be done.

This view is based on confusing two senses of "wants more." In one sense it means "morally prefer" or "value more highly." This has to do with evaluating, and with ranking the value of things. Although one may value promise keeping more than promise breaking, it does not necessarily follow that one always makes the effort to keep one's promises.

In a second sense "wants more" means "is most strongly motivated by." This is a psychological notion pertaining to the strength of a want or desire.

In this sense people do, by definition, always do what they want most to do (when they are able).* That does not mean, however, that weakness of will is impossible. We judge that we ought to keep the promise, but our strongest motivating desire may be to break it. Again, people may "want most" to preserve their marriages by avoiding adultery—they want this most in the sense of judging it most desirable, all things considered. In a moment of weakness of will, however, they may "want most"—in the sense of being most strongly motivated by—to have an affair.

Note that it is within our power to increase the motivational power of our moral judgments or evaluations. In part this is accomplished by forming habits of action that support our judgments, commitments, and desires. Even on the occasion of a specific action, however, we can strengthen our degree of self-control by making efforts of the sort summarized by Alfred Mele:

> An agent can, for example, keep clearly in mind, at the time of action, the reasons for doing the action that he judged best; he can refuse to focus his attention on the attractiveness of what might be achieved by performing a competing action, and concentrate instead on what is to be accomplished by acting as he judges best; he can refuse to entertain second thoughts concerning matters about which he has just very carefully made up his mind; he can seek to add to his motivation for performing the action judged best by promising himself a reward (e.g., an expensive dinner) for successfully resisting temptation. Such exercises of self-control can have a desirable effect upon the balance of his motivation at the time of action.[6]

Mele refers to these tactics as *skilled resistance* to impulses that threaten to prevent us from doing what we judge best. They constitute rational attempts to strengthen our motives, in addition to the sheer *brute resistance* of exerting our effort not to give in to a temptation. Most weakness of will results from failing to exercise a combination of skilled and brute resistance to impulses contrary to our best judgment. Thus, we are often able but unwilling to try hard enough and "skillfully" enough to do what we know we should. A great many of the impulses that we fondly call "irresistible" are in fact resistible by strengthening our motives and desires.

---

* It is important not to confuse this sense of "wants most"—most motivated by—with a third sense. A want can "feel" strongest (carry more psychological agitation with it) and yet not necessarily motivate most strongly.

Inner Conflict and Self-Respect

Leontius and Durant illustrate the most perplexing aspect of weakness of will: inner conflict, or the self divided against itself. By definition, weakness of will involves a split between our judgments (or evaluations) and the desire that most strongly motivates us to act. Typically, it also entails a conflict among our desires. Usually we have at least some desire to do what we judge is right, a desire that conflicts with a second desire to act otherwise. Leontius had a desire not to look at the corpses and also a desire to look at them; Durant had a desire not to masturbate as well as a desire to do so.

These inner conflicts are inherently disturbing. Unless they are successfully resolved, we suffer not only feelings of shame for being unable or unwilling to live up to our own standards but also feelings of guilt when our failures harm other people. Such feelings may compound the damage to our self-respect if we respond to them in unhealthy ways. Some of these ways were mentioned in Chapter 5: drug use, masochism, ongoing self-hate. If continued long enough, habitual weakness of will can cause a sense of self-alienation—a sense of being out of touch with who we are—because our sense of identity depends largely on the commitments around which we shape our lives. Habitual weakness of will can erode our confidence in the genuineness of those commitments. And inner conflicts may wreak even more serious psychological havoc if they undermine our confidence in pursuing a vision of the good and the right.

There are several ways to avoid these negative responses to weakness of will: (1) honestly rethinking one's values, (2) trying harder in the future, (3) accepting one's flaws, or (4) making excuses.

First, we might sometimes do well to reflect on and modify our value judgments and attitudes. As the Durant example suggests, sometimes this is the most appropriate response: weakness of will need not be about conduct that is actually bad. The Victorian taboo against all masturbation, a taboo still present in some religions and cultures, has caused enormous and needless suffering. With a few exceptions,* it is not masturbation but taboos against autoeroticism that deserve condemnation.

Second, we can simply try harder in the future to live up to our moral convictions and other standards of conduct. "Trying harder," as we noted, includes focusing attention on what we ought to do and using effective techniques for summoning our energies in that direction.

Dealing with habitual weakness of will requires long-term adjustments of conduct and attitudes, as anyone who has successfully gone on a diet knows. Certain kinds of food can no longer be brought home, and other foods need

---

*For example, masturbation that is accompanied by, and strengthens, obsessive fantasies about rape and other cruelty.

to be made available in abundance. Hunger can be deflated by drinking water before meals. Eating in front of a television, which invites casual munching, should be avoided. Taking smaller bites and chewing longer helps. Emotionally based attitudes, inherited from childhood, about food as a reward need to be rethought. And so on.

This appeal to hard work and self-discipline has an old-fashioned ring to it that is contradicted by the daily barrage of messages from our consumer-oriented society: "Do what comes naturally." "It's right if it feels good." "Grab for all the gusto you can, because you only go around once." Old-fashioned or not, much everyday moral behavior consists of self-restraint and moral effort.

Third, on some occasions, and with respect to some habits, it may not be worth the effort necessary to avoid weakness of will altogether. Or it may be worth only a moderate effort that only partially succeeds. At these times an informal cost-benefit analysis of effort may be warranted. When the degree of effort required for achieving complete self-control would use up energies needed for more important endeavors, the best compromise might be to accept one's failings, at least at this point in one's life.

Although pursuit of this option can easily degenerate into apathy covered by self-deception about what we are capable of, it need not. Sometimes self-acceptance is creative and enables us to maintain self-respect while channeling energies where they can do the most good. Ironically, there can be strength in accepting some weakness of will, as Friedrich Nietzsche (1844–1900) suggested:

> To "give style" to one's character—a great and rare art! It is practiced by those who survey all the strengths and weaknesses of their nature and then fit them into an artistic plan until every one of them appears as art and reason and even weaknesses delight the eye. Here a large mass of second nature has been added; there a piece of original nature has been removed—both times through long practice and daily work at it. Here the ugly that could not be removed is concealed; there it has been reinterpreted and made sublime. . . . For one thing is needful: that a human being should *attain* satisfaction with himself, whether it be by means of this or that poetry and art; only then is a human being at all tolerable to behold. Whoever is dissatisfied with himself is continually ready for revenge, and we others will be his victims.[7]

Each of these first three responses—rethinking our values, trying harder, and accepting ourselves—is subject to abuse. They can be made dishonestly, in self-deception rather than with genuine moral concern.* Rethinking our

---

*Self-deception, we might add, is at times itself a form of weakness of will. Self-deception most often involves some degree of awareness of or suspicion about the truth or the painful

values may amount to little more than rationalization (biased reasoning). As in Aesop's fable of the fox and the grapes, when we cannot reach the grapes (the good to which we aspire), we may persuade ourselves that the grapes are too sour to be worth seeking. Again, the belief that we are trying hard may be only self-deception masking idle handwringing and token gestures of effort. And self-acceptance may be sheer complacency rather than creative resignation based on a reasonable apportionment of energies.

Excuses

The fourth response to weakness of will in failing to live up to our standards is excuse making. This response deserves a fuller discussion because of the importance of excuse making in protecting self-esteem and self-respect. Our discussion will rely on the work of C. R. Snyder and his colleagues, who co-authored an important psychological study entitled *Excuses*.[8]

An excuse is an explanation of a failure to live up to our standards or to what seems at first to be such a failure. Some excuses are made primarily to protect us from criticisms by other people. Most are designed to maintain our own self-image, our own sense of self-esteem and self-respect. They may represent reasonable explanations, or be made dishonestly using self-deception, as we shall see.

To be human is to be prone to make excuses, as the Biblical account of human origins nicely illustrates. It is written that God had the following interchange with Adam and Eve:

> Hast thou eaten of the tree, whereof I commanded thee that thou shouldst not eat?
>
> And the man said, The woman whom thou gavest to be with me, she gave me of the tree, and I did eat.
>
> And the Lord God said unto the woman, What is this that thou hast done? And the woman said, The serpent beguiled me, and I did eat.[9]

Note how Adam and Eve both try to excuse their conduct by explaining it in a manner designed to lessen their blameworthiness. Knowing full well that they have violated what they believed were God's commandments, they plead extenuating circumstances. Adam alludes to the psychological power of Eve's temptations, and he also reminds God that he gave Eve to be with him as a

---

topic we are avoiding. If we fail to make an effort to confront the truth more directly, to struggle against our biases in reasoning, and to "open up" to other viewpoints that might help us arrive at the truth, then we are being weak of will in the actions that self-deceivingly shape our beliefs.

helpmate (perhaps trying to implicate God in the sin?). Eve alludes to the notorious wiles of the devilish serpent. Let us refer to such attempts as *blame-lessening strategies,* in which one admits wrongdoing (explicitly or tacitly) and tries to lessen the amount of blame and negative response for the wrongdoing.

With even greater boldness Adam and Eve might have tried to deny that they did anything wrong. They might have asked, "What's so bad about eating an apple, anyway?" Or, understanding the apple as a symbol for the knowledge of good and evil, they might have asked, "Isn't it good to have such knowledge?" These would have been attempts to justify the acts as either permissible or desirable. These are *justifying-intended strategies.* This label means the excuse is intended to justify the act, though not, of course, that the act really is justified.

Blame-lessening and justifying-intended excuse strategies were illustrated by the thirty-eight people who witnessed the murder of Kitty Genovese in 1964 in Queens, New York. At 3:20 A.M. Kitty Genovese returned home from her job as a manager at a bar. As she walked the hundred feet to her home, she noticed a man in a parking lot nearby. Concerned, she turned in the direction of a police call box, but before she reached it, the man attacked her with a knife. She screamed, "Oh, my God, he stabbed me! Please help me! Please help me!" [10]

The screams awoke thirty-eight people living in a seven-story apartment house overlooking the scene. One man yelled, "Let that girl alone." No one else did anything. The attacker was scared away by the lights that went on, the windows that opened, and the excited talk that ensued. He walked toward his car but a few minutes later returned to find Kitty Genovese staggering toward her apartment. He then stabbed her again, and she again screamed loudly, "I'm dying!" And again no one did anything. The man went to his car and drove away, only to return yet a third time. Kitty Genovese was still alive. This time he killed her.

Over half an hour passed from the first to the final, fatal stabbing. When the police were finally called, they arrived within two minutes. Any of the thirty-eight witnesses had plenty of time to prevent the murder by making a phone call. Most of the witnesses, when interviewed later, gave justifying-intended excuses to the effect that "It wasn't my responsibility to get involved." One witness went further in saying that he thought it was a lovers' quarrel with which it would be wrong to interfere. A few witnesses, however, admitted that they should have called the police. They used blame-lessening strategies in making excuses such as "Frankly, we were afraid." Some also indicated that it was the middle of the night and they were too tired and upset to think clearly.

Snyder distinguishes between two categories of what are referred to here as blame-lessening strategies. *Consensus-raising strategies* appeal to how most people act in similar situations. The idea is to lessen blame by portraying one's actions as in keeping with what can be expected. This would be illustrated by a witness who comforted her- or himself by saying, "Everyone else did what I did, too." Many everyday excuses fall into this category: "I know the joke was racist, but everyone else laughed at it too." "Sure, adultery is wrong, but the majority of married people do it sometime—so don't come down hard on me." "I'm awfully sorry I knocked over your vase, but it was right where you had to walk to get to the dining room."

In contrast, *consistency-lowering strategies* portray one's failure as a rare lapse that is inconsistent with one's general good character (in light of which one should be judged). This strategy is illustrated by the witnesses who claimed that fear or fatigue preventing them from acting with their normal degree of involvement and concern. This appeal to one's overall integrity and good character is also common in everyday excuse making: "I know I didn't pitch in to help clean up the mess, but I had on my best suit." "I know I didn't try very hard to resist the temptation to have the affair, but I've never done it before and I'll never do it again." "It was a cruel remark, but I'm usually nicer to people." "All right, I'm a drunk, but I don't hurt anyone and I'm usually a good-natured drinker."

Excuses, we have said, are explanations of failures or apparent failures that are intended either to describe acts as not really bad or, alternatively, to lessen blame for admittedly bad acts. These intended portrayals sometimes succeed and are justified: The act was in fact not bad, contrary to appearances, or we are in fact not as blameworthy as it first seemed. These are *valid excuses*. Other excuses, however, are not justified. How do we tell which are valid and which are not?

Unfortunately, the only answer to this question yields no specific guidance. We distinguish valid from invalid excuses by drawing on our understanding of what generally ought to be required of people, given their abilities. That is, the validity of excuses is measured by our standards of responsibility, conscientiousness, self-control, and virtues. Our assessment of excuses is as complicated as our moral sensitivity itself.

To complicate matters further, we assess excuses using criteria other than their validity. Giving and accepting excuses has major implications for sustaining relationships with people and for maintaining self-esteem. These social and psychological aspects of excuses generate what might be called pragmatic considerations in assessing excuses. The struggle to maintain self-esteem is often difficult and sometimes demands any kind of excuse—valid or not. It may warrant a certain generosity in dealing with other people's excuses or our own, especially in light of the increasing complexity of contemporary life. Furthermore, there are occasions when encouraging excuse making may help maintain ties with each other. Consider the teenager who tells his parents he didn't show up for an exam because he didn't feel like it and he hates the class. Not only is he defying his parents, he is threatening to drop out of the educational system. Friends or parents might ease tensions by offering excuses as a kind of social lubricant that will help bring the student back into the school community: "I know it's tough staying with that class given all your other worries right now . . ."

Giving and accepting excuses, Snyder concludes, is a necessary way of coping with our imperfections. Without excuses life would be unbearable. Personal ties would weaken. People would take fewer risks, knowing they might result in inexcusable errors. And preservation of self-esteem would become impossible without drastically lowering our value standards. Within limits, excuse making is justifiable as a part of self-acceptance and tolerance of others' weakness of will.

Summary

Weakness of will is a failure to live up to our value standards and has four elements: (1) a judgment or evaluation that an act is wrong and ought to be avoided; (2) a desire to do it anyway; (3) intentionally acting on that desire; and (4) doing so voluntarily, without external coercion or irresistible inner compulsions. When the judgment or evaluation is a moral one, the weakness of will is called moral weakness.

By definition, weakness of will involves a loss of self-control in the sense that we fail to guide our acts in light of our values, but it does not entail a loss of self-control in the sense that we are unable to act otherwise. Perhaps most weakness of will can be avoided by making a greater effort to resist impulses contrary to our value standards, whether by exerting our energies (brute resistance) or by strengthening our motivation by concentrating attention on what we ought to do and why it is important (skilled resistance).

Weakness of will seems paradoxical when very strict connections are stipulated to hold between judgments or evaluations and actions. Evaluations, however, are one thing; motivations strong enough to induce conduct to conform to those evaluations are another.

Weakness of will and the inner conflict it involves threatens self-esteem and a sense of self-respect. Its harmful effects can be lessened in four ways: (1) rethinking our values, (2) trying harder in the future, (3) accepting our flaws, and (4) making excuses. Each of these ways can have a legitimate role in our lives, but each is also subject to abuse and self-deception.

Excuses represent explanations of our failures to live up to our standards. Blame-lessening strategies appeal to extenuating circumstances that lower blameworthiness. Justifying-intended strategies portray an act as not really wrong, contrary to first appearances. Some justifying-intended strategies are consensus-raising in that they try to lessen blame by portraying a failure as in line with similar failures by most other people. Others are consistency-lowering in that they portray the failure as a rare lapse in our otherwise admirable character.

Whether or not an excuse is valid (that is, justified) can only be determined by reference to our standards of responsibility and the details of the circumstances and capacities of the individual involved. In addition, excuses can be assessed in "pragmatic" terms for their effects on social relationships and the preservation of a desirable degree of self-esteem and self-respect.

DISCUSSION TOPICS

1. In the Kitty Genovese example, are any of the excuses cited valid? Are they acceptable for "pragmatic" reasons connected with their social usefulness or psychological effectiveness in promoting self-esteem? Explain your answers by discussing whether you think there was a minimal standard of decency in helping other people that the thirty-eight witnesses violated.

2. Suppose half of the students in a class are cheating on an exam that will determine one-half of the course grade. Explain how they might attempt to excuse their cheating using each of the following excuse strategies: (1) justifying-intended strategies and (2) blame-lessening strategies, including (a) consensus-raising strategies and (b) consistency-lowering strategies. Are any of the excuses valid or otherwise acceptable to you?

3. Procrastination is a familiar way of being weak of will. It may be defined as unreasonably postponing pressing matters, thereby threatening one's ability to give them the care they deserve. It does not always cause harm, because last-minute efforts may succeed, but it does often lead to a failure to live up to our standards. Describe an example of procrastination from your own experience that fits the following description given by Søren Kierkegaard (1813–1855). Also, do you see anything misleading or paradoxical in the language Kierkegaard uses?

   In case then a man the very second he has known what is right does not do it—well, then, first of all, the knowledge stops boiling. And next comes the question how the will likes this thing that is known. If it does not like it, it does not follow that the will goes ahead and does the opposite of that which the intelligence understood, such strong contrasts occur doubtless rather seldom; but the will lets some time pass, there is an interim, that means, "We'll see about that tomorrow." All this while the intelligence becomes more and more obscured, and the lower nature triumphs more and more. . . . And then when the intelligence has become duly darkened, the intelligence and the will can understand one another better; at last they agree entirely, for now the intelligence has gone over to the side of the will and acknowledges that the thing is quite right as it would have it. And so there live perhaps a great multitude of men who labor off and on to obscure their ethical and religious understanding which would lead them out into decisions and consequences which the lower nature does not love.[11]

4. Four general responses to weakness of will were described in the chapter: Revise one's values, try harder in the future, accept one's flaws, and make excuses. Illustrate how each of these responses might be used in (1) an honest way and (2) a

self-deceiving and dishonest way, by a chain-smoker who is unwilling to make the effort necessary to stop smoking.

5. We noted that it is best to rethink one's moral views when one's conscience is mistaken, and not to exert an effort in obeying conscience. When a person's conscience is seriously distorted, is it perhaps obligatory not to live up to it? Would it be positively immoral to obey one's conscience?

Consider Huck Finn's decision not to return his friend, the slave Jim, to his master. As Huck was helping Jim escape on a raft down the Mississippi River, his conscience began to disturb him:

> Jim said it made him all over trembly and feverish to be so close to freedom. Well I can tell you it make me all over trembly and feverish, too, to hear him, because I begun to get it through my head that he *was* most free—and who was to blame for it? Why, *me*. I couldn't get that out of my conscience, no how nor no way. . . . I tried to make out to myself that *I* warn't to blame, because *I* didn't run Jim off from his rightful owner; but it warn't no use, conscience up an says, every time: "But you knowed he was running for his freedom, and you could 'a' paddled ashore and told somebody." [12]

Huck's conscience tells him that he ought to return Jim—that is what he takes to be morally obligatory. Nevertheless, he refuses to live up to his conscience, instead accepting himself as a sinner. Should we say that his weakness of will is virtuous, and that he would have displayed a vice by exercising greater strength of will in following his conscience?

6. Are self-control, self-discipline, perseverance, and strength of will always virtues? Clearly, deeply immoral people sometimes have great self-control and strength of will: Witness Hitler, Stalin, and the Ayatollah Khomeni. The strength of will of these people gave them the power to accomplish their horrors. If we condemn their conduct, should we not also condemn the traits that enabled them to succeed?

The same question arises with respect to other words commonly used to refer to virtues, because many of them allude to self-control and strength of will. Courage, for example, entails showing self-control in situations involving danger; temperance means showing self-control when the appetites urge otherwise; and prudence involves manifesting self-control over one's thoughts and conduct rather than "losing one's head." Villains can show self-control in pursuing evil ends. When they do so, are they displaying virtues, and are they in that respect admirable?

There are several options in answering this question. (1) We might admit evil people can be virtuous in the limited respects these traits identify, embracing the irony that virtues (admirable traits) can promote vice. (2) We might refuse to call something a virtue when it directly serves evil ends, and interpret the traits as good only when they serve good ends. In a sense they are "dependent virtues": They depend on being found in connection with a restricted range of goals and intentions. [13] (3) We might refuse to call them virtues at all, even dependent ones, and think of them instead as "powers" that, like all power, can serve either virtuous or immoral ends.

Which of these options is preferable? Is there a still better option?

SUGGESTED READINGS

Audi, Robert. "Weakness of Will and Practical Judgment." *Nous,* vol. 13 (1979).

Aristotle. *Nichomachean Ethics.* Trans. W. D. Ross. In Richard McKeon (ed.), *The Basic Works of Aristotle.* New York: Random House, 1941.

Davidson, Donald. "How Is Weakness of the Will Possible?" In Joel Feinberg (ed.), *Moral Concepts.* New York: Oxford University Press, 1970. Reprinted in Donald Davidson, *Essays on Actions and Events.* Oxford: Clarendon Press, 1980.

Dunn, Robert. *The Possibility of Weakness of Will.* Indianapolis, IN: Hackett, 1987.

Hare, R. M. *Freedom and Reason.* New York: Oxford University Press, 1970, pp. 67–85.

King-Farlow, John, and Sean O'Connell. *Self-Conflict and Self-Healing.* New York: University Press of America, 1988.

Mele, Alfred R. *Irrationality: An Essay on Akrasia, Self-Deception, and Self-Control.* New York: Oxford University Press, 1987.

Milgram, Stanley. *Obedience to Authority.* New York: Harper and Row, 1974.

Milo, Ronald D. *Immorality.* Princeton, NJ: Princeton University Press, 1984, pp. 115–139.

Mortimer, G. W. (ed.). *Weakness of Will.* New York: St. Martin's Press, 1971.

Murphy, Arthur E. "The Moral Self in Sickness and in Health." In A. I. Melden (ed.), *The Theory of Practical Reason.* La Salle, IL: Open Court, 1964.

Santas, Gerasimos. "Plato's *Protagoras* and Explanations of Weakness." *Philosophical Review,* vol. 75 (1966).

Snyder, C. R., Raymond L. Higgins, and Rita J. Stucky. *Excuses.* New York: Wiley, 1983.

Thalberg, Irving. "Questions about Motivational Strength." In E. Lepore and B. McLaughlin (eds.), *Actions and Events.* Oxford: Basil Blackwell, 1985.

Watson, Gary. "Skepticism about Weakness of Will." *Philosophical Review,* vol. 86 (1977).

CHAPTER 8

Courage

Self-respect requires one to care about oneself (avoiding masochism), to be honest with oneself (avoiding self-deception about moral values), and to have the strength of will to live up to one's commitments (overcoming moral weakness). It also requires courage on occasions when one's commitments are challenged by dangers and hardship. Courage is as important for preserving self-respect and moral integrity as it is for contributing to the good of other people.

What is courage? We begin this chapter by clarifying courage using two examples. Then we examine why and when courage is a moral good, and we trace its connections with moral integrity.

Acts and Patterns of Action

Nelson Mandela is South Africa's leading opponent of apartheid, the system of racial oppression that treats black people as morally and legally inferior. Prior to his 1962 arrest by South African police he repeatedly risked his life by opposing the racist South African government. Although he was sentenced to life imprisonment, he could easily have escaped and left the country. Indeed, while in jail, he was offered his freedom more than once if he would renounce violence against the government. He refused these offers, and he has continued to sacrifice his personal freedom until the government ceases its violent repression of black people.

Four years before his imprisonment Nelson married Winnie Mandela, the first black female social worker in South Africa. Winnie's opposition to racism has been equally intense and has led to comparable suffering and risk taking. She has been arrested dozens of times, continuously watched by police, and restricted by numerous petty "banning regulations." She was banned from being with more than one person at a time, and she was prevented from attending church without a special permit each time. Since 1977 she has been banished to a remote and highly conservative province where she lives under harsh conditions.

The Mandelas have displayed *physical courage:* courage in the face of risks to body and life. Consider, for example, a description of Winnie given by a member of the Black Parents Association, one of the many organizations she directed:

> As the only woman on the executive, she was more than a man; Winnie is powerful; she is faithful and honest. But above all, she is brave; she has got the kind of guts I don't have, many of us don't have. She would stand before police captains with machine guns and tell them to go and get stuffed. . . . When this Major Visser in Protea police station said to her that she had started the riots, she threw a book at him, her shoe, anything and everything she could lay her hands on—"You bloody murderer, killer of our children, and you tell us *we* started the riots. You go and stop those bastards killing our children in the street!"[1]

The Mandelas' physical courage is based on their *intellectual courage,* or *courage of convictions,* which refers to having the courage to act on one's beliefs and commitments even in the face of enormous pressure not to. For example, repeated attempts to silence Winnie Mandela, including seventeen continuous months of solitary prison confinement under degrading conditions, have failed. She recalls that experience as among the worst of her life: "that uncertainty, that insecurity: there is such a sense of hopelessness, the feeling that this is now the end. The whole thing is calculated to destroy you, not only morally but also physically."[2]

The Mandelas manifest long-term patterns of physical and intellectual courage in their actions. But heroism can also be shown on a single occasion. Here is one example of physical courage.

In a wilderness area near the city where I live, a woman was hiking with her five-year-old daughter in 1986. A mountain lion attacked the girl and dragged her into some bushes. The mother's frantic screams were heard by Gregory Ysais, a thirty-six-year-old electronics technician who happened to be hiking in the same area. Without any hesitation Ysais ran to the scene to find the cougar gripping the bloody and squirming child by the back of her neck. Ysais grabbed a branch and repeatedly swung it over the head of the cougar. The full-grown cougar responded with threatening roars and quick strikes with his huge paws. After a few minutes the cougar dropped the child long enough for her to be pulled away.

Ysais later reported that he had never been in a life-and-death situation before and had never thought of himself as a hero: "I didn't give it much thought. I just heard people crying for help, and I just ran as fast as I could. I was just doing what I had to do. I couldn't think of anything else."[3]

Courage, Cowardice, and Fear

Aristotle defined courage as the tendency to do good in situations where fear is involved. The courageous person tends to "hit the mean," that is, to find the reasonable middle ground between excess (too much) and deficiency (too little). Aristotle writes: "In the field of Fear and Confidence the mean is Courage; and of those who go to extremes the man who exceeds in fear-lessness has no name to describe him . . . the one who exceeds in confidence is called Rash, and the one who shows an excess of fear and a deficiency of confidence is called Cowardly."[4] In other words the courageous person avoids the excess of feeling too much fear (cowardice) and the defect of feeling too little fear (rashness); in addition, the courageous person avoids too much confidence or risk taking (rashness) and too little confidence (cowardice).

Note that courage as defined by Aristotle differs somewhat from the courage outlined in our two examples, for two reasons. First, Ysais performed only one good deed in the face of danger, albeit a highly admirable one in an extremely dangerous situation. Not only is his *act* courageous, but *he* is courageous—we can say this without knowing whether courage is a tendency or habit in his life (apparently he had never displayed similar courage simply because the occasion had never arisen). If in a subsequent situation he was to act cowardly, we would describe him, more cautiously, as a person who sometimes acts courageously and sometimes does not. As long as he is not a coward later, however, we are perfectly justified in calling him a courageous person because of his one extraordinary act. There need not be a habit or pattern of courageous deeds of the sort Aristotle had in mind.

Aristotle's view, then, might be modified to allow for the one-time hero whom we call courageous even in the absence of a demonstrable tendency to do courageous deeds. People are courageous if they either (1) show a tendency to do admirable acts in situations they see as dangerous or (2) do so to an extraordinary degree on one occasion, without acting cowardly on other occasions.

Second, Aristotle defines courage in terms of fear (avoiding too much and too little fear, or avoiding unreasonable fears). We have referred instead to being in a situation regarded as dangerous, whether or not one actually feels fear in response to the danger. Recall that Ysais acted spontaneously, without taking time to deliberate. At the time he may not have felt fear. His courage consisted not in overcoming or controlling his fear but simply in acting effectively in an emergency involving danger. This is not uncommon; indeed, many people report feeling afraid only after an emergency is over. At the time they were too involved in the situation to feel anything except a sense of urgency. In short, courage may or may not involve controlling or subduing fear.

Cowardice, by contrast, is logically connected with fear. By definition cowardice is moral failing due to fear—fear that motivates one to flee, to freeze one's responses, or to otherwise fail to confront the danger. People who fail to meet their obligations in dangerous situations because of sheer laziness are not cowards—they are just lazy. Cowardice arises when fear is the specific motive for the failure.

A Definition of Courageous Actions

We have defined courageous people as those who perform courageous acts (either a pattern of them or an extraordinary act in the absence of subsequent cowardice). But what is a courageous act? In *Virtues and Vices* James Wallace offers the following defining criteria for courageous acts. Each criterion is set forth as a necessary condition (that is, one that must be met for an act to be courageous), and taken together the six criteria are intended to be sufficient (that is, enough to distinguish an act as courageous).

(a) A [a person] believes that it is dangerous for him to do Y [an action].
(b) A believes that his doing Y is worth the risks it involves.
(c) A believes that it is possible for him not to do Y.
(d) The danger A sees in doing Y must be sufficiently formidable that most people would find it difficult in the circumstances to do Y.
(e) A is not coerced into doing Y by threats of punishment, which he fears more than he fears the dangers of doing Y.
(f) A is under self-control, at least in the sense of not being in a frenzy, stupor, or intoxication.[5]

Focus on condition (b), which requires only that the person believe the act to be worth doing despite the risks, not that the act actually be good. Aristotle, however, would require that courageous acts be good. Who is correct?

Wallace's definition seems preferable when we think of soldiers who fight with valor on an immoral side during a war. For example, Field Marshal Rommel was a highly distinguished and intrepid soldier for Hitler's side during World War II. Rommel repeatedly won battles by using daring tactics to infiltrate Allied lines with small numbers of soldiers, and he frequently risked his own life. The Allied officers both feared and respected him for his bravery and his military genius. Because his acts were for an evil cause, Aristotle's definition would not allow us to call him courageous. Yet it does seem natural to ascribe courage to him, and Wallace's definition allows us to do so.

Consider, however, examples of playing deadly games of "chicken." In a movie role made famous by James Dean, a teenager races at breakneck speed toward a high cliff, competing with a teenager in another car to see who "chickens out" first. Or two youngsters act on each other's dares to see who will take the larger dose of a dangerous drug. Also consider cruel actions. A rapist overcomes his fears of being caught and punished, and, after an inner struggle, manages to commit his crimes with chilling efficiency. Again, a professional killer undergoes great personal risks in carrying out daring assassinations of world leaders. Simply stated, such acts are foolhardy, tragically stupid, or grossly cruel. They show excessive, unjustified, and irrational risk taking and are anything but morally good acts. Here Aristotle's definition of courage seems preferable because it sees nothing courageous in such acts, whereas Wallace's definition seems to require us to call such acts courageous because the individuals presumably believe their acts are worth the risks involved.

Our hesitation or refusal to ascribe courage to the "chicken games" and to the acts of cruelty reflects an important linguistic fact: The word *courage* carries strongly positive connotations. To ascribe courage to a person expresses some approval—at least with respect to the risk taking involved. There is, however, nothing worth approving in the cases of the risks undertaken by the rapist and the murderer. The same is probably true of the "chicken game" players.

Wallace seems partly right, then, but so does Aristotle. One way to proceed at this point would be to add a further condition to Wallace's list of criteria:

(g) We admire [person] *A* for [act] *Y*, at least for the risk taking involved in *Y*.

This would allow us to ascribe courage to Field Marshal Rommel (in that we admired his risk taking) but not to the rapist, murderer, or players of chicken games.

A complementary approach, suggested by Douglas Walton in his book *Courage,* is to pinpoint the kinds of risk taking we admire and to modify Wallace's criteria accordingly. Walton agrees in part with Aristotle: There must be something admirable about courageous acts. He suggests that courageous persons must act with at least some good reasons and intentions. Thinking along these lines, we could modify Wallace's condition (b) as follows:

(b') *A* believes that doing *Y* is worth the risks it involves *and A* has at least some good reason for believing *Y* is worthwhile. Acting on these intentions, he intends *Y* to be good.

Having a good reason for believing an act is justified is not the same as actually knowing it is justified. Field Marshal Rommel was mistaken in believing his acts were good and worthwhile. Perhaps, however, he believed that it was his duty as a soldier to act as he did, and perhaps he had an intention (however misguided) to make the world better. Thus, his acts were courageous, meaning that the risk taking had something admirable about it, even though the acts were not admirable in all respects. In contrast, we refuse to call the rapist, murderer, and players in the chicken games courageous because there is nothing admirable about their risk taking.

The Good of Courage

Based on our revised version of Wallace's definition, courage always involves some good, for it entails an *intention* to do something good or right, which is itself good. Risk taking on behalf of such intentions is good, even though the act may be bad in other respects.

Courage is also good insofar as it preserves moral integrity, that is, the consistency of our actions with our moral commitments. The courage of the Mandelas enabled them to pursue their commitments to human rights and dignity when confronted by danger and hardship. It is likely that Ysais's act of heroism reflects a general concern for other people, a concern central to his moral integrity. Furthermore, courage is good insofar as it contributes to the good of other people. This is obvious in the case of Ysais's rescue of the child. It is equally obvious in the moral leadership provided by the Mandelas for an entire nation of persecuted black people.

Courageous benevolence is especially admirable because of its intentions and its consequences, and also because of the risk taking involved. Douglas Walton makes some insightful comments about how risk taking on behalf of altruistic aims is especially admirable. He asks us to consider two men who perform acts with equally good intentions and consequences. In one case all that is required is for the man to pull a child from a shallow pond into which the child has fallen. In the second case the man saves a small child trapped in a burning auto following a crash. When he arrives at the scene of the accident, he sees a group of people shouting and waiting for a rescue team. Fearing that the gas tank is about to explode, he rushes into the flames and, at considerable risk to himself, pries the child free from the burning wreckage. In doing so he is seriously burned and cut. Commenting on why we admire the second man even more than the first one, Walton writes:

> What is of moral import in evaluating actions over and above the goodness of an intention in itself is the commitment of the agent to carrying out that intention. The depth of that commitment is indicated by the time, effort, ingenuity, and sacrifice the agent is willing to put into the carrying out of his good intention. Hence factors like altruism, deter-

mination, and persistence in the face of painful consequences are all characteristics . . . of truly courageous acts. The greater the sacrifice, risk, and danger of carrying out a good objective, the more meritorious is the course of action directed to that end.[6]

The second man's willingness to undergo extreme personal danger suggests that the degree of his moral concern and commitment is exceptional. Admittedly, other facts might be brought to light that make us suspect the presence of ulterior motives, such as an inordinate desire for fame as a hero. Lacking such facts, however, we recognize in the risk taking on behalf of others something especially praiseworthy.

Courage, however, does not always involve altruism, that is, a desire to promote the good of other people. It is also shown in fulfilling our duties to ourselves and in pursuing our self-interest. W. D. Falk pointed out that prudent or cautious pursuit of self-interest is not always the best way to attain what is good for us:

> Prudence is only one way of looking after oneself. To act prudently is to play safe, for near-certain gains at small risks. But some good things one cannot get in this way. To get them at all one has to gamble, taking the risk of not getting them even so, or of coming to harm in the process. If one values them enough, one will do better by oneself to throw prudence to the winds, to play for high stakes, knowing full well the risk and the price of failure. Explorers, artists, scientists, mountaineers are types who may serve themselves better by this course. So will most people at some juncture.[7]

Courage in promoting one's own good can also be shown during a crisis in which suicide is ultimately averted; or during a struggle to overcome drug or alcohol addiction; or in ending a paralyzing depression that threatens personal relationships; or in asserting one's needs in the face of peer or parental pressure.

To summarize, the value of an act of courage, and the degree of praiseworthiness appropriate for courageous people, increases depending on several factors:

1. the good intentions of the agent
2. the contribution of the courage to preserving moral integrity by sustaining moral commitments in the face of danger or hardship
3. the extent to which the act contributes to the good of other people
4. the extent to which the act supports duties to oneself or one's own self-fulfillment.
5. the degree of moral commitment shown in
   a. the type of danger or risk undertaken

b. the specific motives of the agent
c. the degree of skill, judgment, and effort shown in the difficult situation

Integrity, Fanaticism, and Hypocrisy

In concluding this chapter, let us draw together the main themes explored in Part II and, in doing so, relate courage more fully to moral integrity. Moral integrity might be understood as a virtue lying between the excess of fanaticism (including courageous fanaticism) and a cluster of defects that include cowardice, hypocrisy, moral weakness, self-deception about immorality, and lack of moral concern.

Moral integrity entails having moral commitments and seriously striving to live up to them. Fanaticism refers to the excess of losing balance and proper perspective in how one pursues commitments, whereas deficiencies of moral commitment, including the main vices explored in Part II, fall at the opposite end of the moral commitment spectrum. Moral integrity, which includes the balanced pursuit of moral commitments, is a mean lying between these two extremes. This idea is adapted from the following thesis, set forth by Jay Newman in his book *Fanatics and Hypocrites:*

> With regard to the acceptance of a world view, healthy and socially con-
> structive commitment is profitably regarded as a virtue, i.e., a mean or
> an intermediate state of character between a vice of excess (fanaticism)
> and a vice of defect (hypocrisy). . . . To the extent that an individual is a
> fanatic or a hypocrite, he is prevented from living a good and happy life
> and from contributing to the stability and progress of his society.[8]

We have changed "healthy and socially constructive commitments" to the moral commitments at the core of moral integrity, and we focus on hypocrisy and fanaticism concerning moral values. We also recognize defects in addition to hypocrisy as failures to be sufficiently morally committed.

Moral fanatics, we have stated, pursue moral commitments with an excessive zeal, to the detriment of other important obligations. A South African terrorist, for example, who is willing to indiscriminately kill white people, including children, is using immoral means in pursuing a good end—overthrowing a racist government. Similarly, Palestinian terrorists who seek to win their homeland have a justified end but violate obligations not to kill innocent people.

Terrorists often undertake great personal risks in pursuing their ends. When their overall intentions are good, our earlier definition of courage allows us to call their risk taking courageous. Yet their moral understanding suffers from tunnel vision: They see only one moral imperative and are insensitive to equally important ones. As a result their one commitment reveals excess: it is pursued with misguided and intolerant zeal.

There are also defects of commitment. One is hypocrisy. Hypocrites (concerning moral values) present themselves to the world as being morally committed but fail to strive honestly to live up to their commitments. Frequently, the cause of their failure is cowardice. White South Africans who profess that apartheid is evil but who are unwilling to take any risks whatsoever to oppose it are open to the charge of hypocrisy. As we stated earlier, courage in the face of dangers is a litmus test for the depth of our moral commitments.

Hypocrisy, however, represents only one of several defects of moral commitment. There is also the failure to make a full effort to live up to one's commitments. This is moral weakness. There is the failure to recognize honestly what our responsibilities are, which often involves self-deception about our immorality and character flaws. And there is failure to be morally concerned and caring, whether about duties to respect oneself or about duties to respect other people—the topic of Part Three.

Summary

Courageous acts are performed in the face of danger or hardship in pursuit of what one believes, with some good reason, to be a good end. When the reason is insufficient to justify the act, the courage is misguided and not entirely good (as with Field Marshal Rommel).

Courage is especially valuable when it promotes other people's good or one's own moral integrity. In addition, it is valuable insofar as it is prompted by good intentions and motives, and to the degree that it reveals skill and judgment in the face of great danger.

Courageous people either show a tendency to perform courageous acts or perform one extraordinary act of heroism not followed by cowardly acts. In contrast, cowards are motivated by fear to avoid dangers and risks they ought to confront.

Moral integrity and moral commitments are ideally pursued with a balanced moral perspective. The moral fanatic pursues one commitment in excess, at the expense of other important obligations. There are several opposing defects of insufficient commitment: professing but not pursuing commitments (hypocrisy); failing to make sufficient effort to meet commitments (moral weakness); failing to act on commitments in the face of danger or hardship (lack of courage), especially when one is motivated by fear (cowardice); purposefully failing to acknowledge obligations (self-deception about moral values); and failing to care about oneself (masochism and self-destructiveness) or about other people.

DISCUSSION TOPICS

1. Are the following people courageous? Explain, using your definition of courage. (1) A man who invests all his family's earnings in high-risk stocks with the aim of making his family wealthy. (2) A mountain climber who risks her life for the sake of the joys and challenges of the hike. (3) A man who commits suicide by igniting his gasoline-soaked clothes to protest his government's immoral policies.

2. Was Ysais morally obligated to risk his life in order to save the child from the cougar? Would every adult in that situation have a moral duty to act as he did, just as every adult had a duty to call the police to save the life of Kitty Genovese (in the case described in Chapter 7)? Or was Ysais's act supererogatory, that is, more than is required by duty?

3. Is it more admirable to display courage without feeling any fear ("fearlessness") or to feel fear and act courageously despite it? Or is there no moral difference between the two? Consider, for example, two variations on the Ysais example: Ysais felt terror and struggled to overcome it before rushing to the aid of the child; or Ysais felt no fear whatsoever.

4. The first of Wallace's six criteria for courageous acts was that "*A* [a person] believes that it is dangerous for him to do *Y* [an action]." Consider cases in which this belief is irrational, as with acts motivated by phobias. For example, a person with a spider phobia irrationally believes it is dangerous for him to be within yards of a perfectly harmless garden spider. Is the person showing courage by approaching the spider despite the fear? Or should we modify Wallace's criterion to require that the belief about the danger must be reasonable?

5. We sometimes say that cowards compromise their moral principles and their moral integrity. But "compromise" has two meanings. In one sense it has negative connotations: to undermine one's integrity, or appear to do so, by engaging in scandalous conduct or entering into situations that present an appearance of immorality. In another sense "compromise" can have positive connotations: to settle differences by mutual and reasonable concessions. It was this latter sense that John F. Kennedy had in mind when he wrote, in *Profiles in Courage,* that "compromise need not mean cowardice. Indeed it is frequently the compromisers and conciliators who are faced with the severest tests of political courage as they oppose the extremist views of their constituents."[9] Think of two situations, one in which cowardice leads a person to compromise in the first sense, and one in which courage is shown in compromising in the second sense.

SUGGESTED READINGS

Aristotle. *Ethics.* Trans. J. A. K. Thomson and Hugh Tredennick. New York: Penguin Books, 1976.

Falk, W. D. "Morality, Self, and Others." In Hector-Neri Castaneda and George Nakhnikian (eds.), *Morality and the Language of Conduct.* Detroit, MI: Wayne State University Press, 1965.

Foot, Phillipa. *Virtues and Vices and Other Essays in Moral Philosophy.* Berkeley, CA: University of California Press, 1978.

Kennedy, John F. *Profiles in Courage.* New York: Harper & Row, 1956.

Newman, Jay. *Fanatics and Hypocrites.* New York: Prometheus, 1986.

Pears, David. "Courage as a Mean." In Amelie Oksenberg Rorty (ed.), *Essays on Aristotle's Ethics.* Berkeley, CA: University of California Press, 1980.

Rachman, S. J. *Fear and Courage.* San Francisco: Freeman, 1978.

Taylor, Gabriele. "Integrity." *Aristotelian Society Proceedings,* supplementary vol. 60 (1981).

Tillich, Paul. *The Courage to Be.* New Haven, CT: Yale University Press, 1952.

Urmson, J. O. "Saints and Heroes." In A. I. Melden (ed.), *Essays in Moral Philosophy.* Seattle: University of Washington Press, 1958.

Wallace, James D. "Courage, Cowardice, and Self-Indulgence." In *Virtues and Vices.* Ithaca, NY: Cornell University Press, 1978.

Walton, Douglas N. *Courage: A Philosophical Investigation.* Berkeley, CA: University of California Press, 1986.

PART THREE

Respect for Others

Our self-respect normally depends upon the respect of others. Unless we feel that our endeavors are honored by them, it is difficult if not impossible for us to maintain the conviction that our ends are worth advancing.

. . .

[There is a] duty of mutual respect. . . . This is the duty to show a person the respect which is due to him as a moral being, that is, as a being with a sense of justice and a conception of the good.[1]

John Rawls

Respect for other people can mean two things. First, it might mean valuing or admiring them for their character, either their entire character or some specific virtues. Let us call this *character-respect*. Second, it might mean recognizing the worth of people as (in Rawls's words) "moral beings," that is, beings who have a sense of moral values or the potential for acquiring it. Let us call this *minimal-respect* because this recognition (through attitude and conduct) is the least that is owed to other morally responsive people. Minimal-respect is the topic of Part Three.

Character-respect and minimal-respect differ in two important ways. First, character-respect is highly selective. It is directed toward specific persons whose virtues, moral accomplishments, or endeavors evoke our admiration and perhaps inspire us to emulate them. In this sense we might respect Martin Luther King because of his extraordinary courage in leading the Civil Rights Movement, and we might respect Mother Teresa for her compassion and self-sacrifice in helping the desperately poor people in Calcutta, India. In contrast, minimal-respect is highly inclusive: It is owed to everyone who has any sense of morality.

Second, character-respect can come in varying degrees. The respect felt for Martin Luther King and for Mother Teresa is probably much greater than the respect felt for someone who takes care of his family but is indifferent to wider moral issues. In contrast, minimal-respect has a set (minimal) degree—it is the least we owe to all people having any sense of moral values. Minimal-respect is based on the concept of equality of moral worth. In Kantian terms minimal-respect implies a duty to treat all moral beings with dignity and decency; in terms of human rights ethics all moral beings have equal rights; in utilitarian terms all people ought to be taken into account equally in deciding how to produce the most good.

Why does Rawls state that respect is owed to "moral beings," that is, to creatures with a capacity or potential for having some sense of moral values? Are not all humans worthy of respect—period? And is Rawls suggesting that some nonhumans may be worthy of respect?

Such questions may be more important to general ethics than to applied ethics. Nevertheless, a brief "thought experiment" helps explain Rawls's view. Suppose that we encounter a group of creatures from outer space who are highly intelligent and in many respects quite similar to us. The only difference is that they lack any capacity for moral decency, not only in dealing with us but also with one another. They are utterly cruel and completely indifferent to the claims of morality. We also discover that neither they nor their children have any potential for moral relationships. It seems plausible to assert that we would not owe them minimal-respect of the kind we owe to beings who do have a potential for moral relationships.

Tragically, some humans may fit this description of alien creatures. Sociopaths, for example, lack any sense of moral right and wrong and may be capable of murder without suffering any guilt. Moreover, no known therapy can cure sociopathy. Are sociopaths owed the same respect due "normal" people? If we say they are owed minimal-respect, is it because we believe (or hope) they have some potential for becoming morally responsible—if only new therapies could be discovered to help them?

Now imagine that we encounter outer-space creatures who are very unlike humans in appearance and many behavior patterns, perhaps looking and acting somewhat like reptiles. Yet they have significant capacities for rationality and for entering into responsible relationships with us and with one another. Would not they be owed minimal-respect? It seems so. Indeed, some animals we are familiar with in this world may deserve minimal-respect, a topic we shall discuss in Chapter 21.

In any case, here we shall accept Rawls's suggestion that minimal-respect is owed to people and other beings who have some moral potential. We shall explore minimal-respect by examining how the moral requirements defining it are violated. Since those requirements represent minimums, we can gain insight into them by seeing how people fail to meet them.

We begin with some blatant violations: In Chapter 9 we discuss cruelty and coercion as shown in rape and sexual harassment, and in Chapter 10 we look at racial and sexual prejudice. Then in Chapter 11 we explore envy as an attitude and emotion involving hatred. We emphasize how envy differs from jealousy, even though both involve wanting something that other people have. And in Chapter 12 we focus on a contrasting form of disrespect—inconsiderateness—as exhibited in rudeness, snobbery, and put-downs of other people. Taken together, these topics comprise a rich sampling of the forms of disrespect in everyday life.

CHAPTER 9

Rape and Sexual Harassment

Fear of rape is part of the daily life of many women. Unfortunately, the fear is fully warranted: It is believed that one in three women alive today will be raped, and the percentage of rapes is even higher in some American cities already. These statistics represent estimates, because only about one in ten rapes is even reported. Whatever the exact statistics, rape is as shockingly common as it is horrifying. Recent studies have suggested that sexual harassment is also a problem on a much greater scale than is commonly believed.

Rape is both cruel and coercive. Sexual harassment is coercive and frequently cruel. As such, rape and sexual harassment constitute failures to maintain minimal standards of decency; they involve direct assaults on the dignity of people. We will preface our discussion with some general comments on cruelty and coercion.

Coercion and the Right to Personal Autonomy

Coercion entails unjustified interference with another person's freedom. It is an infringement on one's legitimate efforts to determine one's own destiny, a violation of one's right to personal autonomy.

Personal autonomy is a wider notion than moral autonomy, a concept introduced in our discussions of Kohlberg, Gilligan, and Kant. Recall that moral autonomy means exercising the ability to make one's own moral judgments based on some degree of moral caring. Personal autonomy focuses on moral reasoning and judging rather than on action per se, although reasoning, judging, and acting certainly are closely connected. *Personal autonomy,* by contrast, pertains to all reasoning and acting, not just moral reasoning. Its close synonyms are *self-determination* and *self-governance.*

As Lawrence Haworth points out, "personal autonomy" (and its synonyms) has two senses, one purely descriptive and one normative. The descriptive sense refers to certain facts about people who exercise personal autonomy:

> In some contexts, saying a person is autonomous is a way of attributing to him the personal characteristic of being in charge of his own life. He is not overly dependent on others and not swamped by his own passions; he has the ability to see through to completion those plans and projects he sets for himself. He has, one may say, procedural independence, self-control, and competence. In these contexts, "autonomy" is a descriptive term. It is an empirical [i.e., purely factual] question whether, in what respects, and to what degree a person is autonomous.[1]

According to this definition personal autonomy has three main aspects. First, it involves "procedural independence." This means that the person is not coerced into doing things by force, duress, fraud, deception, or other forms of constraints imposed by individuals or society. The idea is that the procedures used by the autonomous person in making decisions are not undermined by external intervention.

Second, autonomous persons are competent to guide their own lives. They have the ability to choose their actions by exercising capacities for making rational decisions and acting on them. Their reasoning is not, for example, distorted by major biases that deflect them from the truth, and they are able to live up to their convictions without frequent weakness of will.

Third, they have "substantive independence" in that they are not overly dependent on other people. "Overly dependent" is a vague term, but it refers, for example, to persons who willingly give up any attempt to think for themselves, relying on someone else to think for them. This is vividly illustrated by the persons who join cults in order to escape the difficulties they have found in governing their own lives.

The normative sense of personal autonomy refers to the moral right to exercise personal autonomy in the descriptive sense. When we claim that someone has violated our autonomy, we mean they have violated our right to guide our own lives. We can also fail to be autonomous by improperly exercising our right to autonomy: Weakness of will and self-deception undermine personal autonomy just as much as do manipulators and deceivers. In discussing rape and sexual harassment, however, our focus will be on violations of another person's right to personal autonomy.

Why is the right to personal autonomy morally important? In Kant's view, violating that right amounts to treating persons as mere means to one's own ends, thereby violating the duty to respect their dignity. In Mill's view (expressed in *On Liberty*) personal autonomy is the primary avenue to pursuing happiness, and hence to undermine autonomy is to lessen the opportunities for finding happiness. In Locke's view, the right to personal autonomy is essentially the same as the right to liberty—the fundamental human right that needs no further justification. While Locke would view it as a negative right (a right to not be interfered with), Melden might say it implies a positive right to have society create an environment where rape and sexual harassment are strongly discouraged.

Haworth believes that personal autonomy is intrinsically good—good in and of itself. The ability and willingness to guide one's own life is desirable for its own sake, apart from any further appeal to duties, happiness, or human rights. We might say it is a virtue: It is a human excellence that should be preserved despite pressures from other people and temptations from within. For it makes possible creativity, individuality, and innovative personal relationships.

Cruelty

We can be briefer in introducing cruelty, even though it takes innumerable forms. One form is omitted actions, such as when we speak of the "cruel indifference" of an insensitive bureaucrat or of the callousness of some people concerning world hunger. There are cruel emotions, such as the enjoyment of the suffering of an innocent victim (a form of sadism); cruel attitudes, such as those of the racist and sexist; cruel hopes, such as the hope to see an innocent child hurt; and cruel motives and desires, such as the desire to augment one's reputation by unfairly criticizing someone.

The most familiar type of cruelty is deliberate infliction of suffering without justification. When the suffering is one's own, masochism is involved. When the suffering is that of another person, as in rape and some sexual harassment, sadism—that is, the enjoyment of the suffering of another person—may be involved.

Most modern moral perspectives, from the Renaissance on, have regarded cruelty as the worst form of immorality. It is noteworthy, however, that this was not true of the predominant attitudes during the Middle Ages. In particular, medieval Christianity viewed pride, not cruelty, as the worst sin. Cruelty was not even listed as one of the Seven Deadly Sins, even though lesser vices like gluttony and lust were. Much of contemporary moral thought consists of identifying subtle forms of cruelty as well as blatant forms that have been unduly tolerated. Some sexual harassment falls into the first category, while rape falls into the second category.

Motivations to Rape

A rapist may have a variety of motives in committing his act, but most of them fall into four general categories: (1) maliciousness, that is, cruelty prompted by the desire to hurt; (2) means-to-end motivation, that is, cruelty as the means to some further desired purpose; (3) unintended cruelty that arises incidentally to the pursuit of other purposes; and (4) cruelty based on indifference to the suffering of the victim. (Note: In our discussion we refer to the rapist using male pronouns because the overwhelming majority of rapes are committed by men against women. Even though homosexual and lesbian rapes do occur, especially in prisons, and rape of men by women is possible, these instances are comparatively rare.)

Malice is the motive when the rapist deliberately seeks to degrade and injure the victim and (sadistically) takes pleasure in dominating her and causing her to suffer. Means-to-end motivation occurs when the rapist seeks some further goal, for example, when he seeks peer approval from fellow gang members who have dared him to commit the rape. Unintended cruelty results when the rapist thinks he is not using coercion, as when he believes that a woman wants him to engage in forcible intercourse with her despite her protestations. And cruelty based on indifference is illustrated by a sociopathic rapist who is completely indifferent to the feelings of the victim.

According to the traditional male-oriented perspective the act of rape depended primarily on means-to-end motivation. Rape was regarded as a sex-oriented crime in which the rapist used the victim as the means to attain his own sexual satisfaction. Both feminists and experimental psychologists have refuted this view, however, asserting that nearly all rapes are malicious or intentionally cruel acts of violence against women. The end sought is not sexual satisfaction per se. Instead, it is either (1) pleasure in the violence or (2) self-esteem derived from power over the victim (often vicariously experienced as power over all women).

Of course, the rapist often deceives himself about his malice. For example, he embraces the myth that women secretly want to be raped and that their protests are not genuine. Or he convinces himself that a particular woman invites the rape by her clothing and behavior. As we saw in Chapter 6, self-deception does not mitigate culpability. In fact, it compounds guilt, because the rapist is blameworthy both for cruelty and for easing his conscience at the expense of the victim and the truth.

What Is Wrong with Rape?

Rape is a clear-cut paradigm of immorality. But precisely why is it immoral? Part of the answer has already been given: The rapist's motives are vicious, such as enjoyment of the suffering of the victim and derivation of self-esteem from seeking to degrade an innocent person. Most of the answer, however, pertains to the act of rape itself and its effects on the victim rather than to the motives for it.

In an insightful essay on rape Susan Griffin offered the following explanation of why it is immoral:

> Rape is an act of aggression in which the victim is denied her self-determination. It is an act of violence which, if not actually followed by beatings or murder, nevertheless always carries with it the threat of death. And finally, rape is a form of mass terrorism, for the victims of rape are chosen indiscriminately, but the propagandists for male supremacy broadcast that it is women who cause rape by being unchaste or in the wrong place at the wrong time, by behaving as though they were free.[2]

Griffin suggests that rape is immoral because it causes at least three kinds of harm to women. First, the act is a violation of a woman's right to self-determination or personal autonomy, a view that follows logically from the definition of rape as sexual intercourse against or without a person's consent. Second, rape inflicts suffering of several kinds: terror, fear for one's life, immediate physical pain, and trauma that endures years after the assault. Third, because rape is widespread, it creates warranted fear that restricts the range of women's activities, thereby again violating their right to autonomy.

There is yet another reason why rape is deeply immoral. In our culture sexuality is regarded as central to a person's identity. Sexuality is also an area where freedom and self-determination are very highly valued. In violating this area of private life, the rapist directly assaults the self-respect of his victim. Usually he is well aware of this fact, and he intends to communicate utter disrespect and contempt for the victim *as* a woman.

Date Rape Versus Consent

Susan Griffin's essay, which appeared in 1971, focused on rapists who choose their victims indiscriminately. Since then it has been learned that many, perhaps most, rapists are acquainted with their victims prior to the rape. This is especially true when the victim is a college student. Such "acquaintance rape" frequently occurs on dates, as in the following examples taken from studies done by the sociologist William B. Sanders:*

Case 4. A blind date had been arranged between the victim and suspect. The couple went out to dinner together and then for drinks. At the apartment, the man began making overtures to the victim, and she declined. Then the suspect began slapping the victim and took her into the bedroom where he raped her.

Case 13. Victim picked up suspect in a bar and drove him in her car to a college parking lot. The suspect propositioned the victim, and the victim said she was "in the mood for some loving." At the parking lot, the victim changed her mind since the man's demeanor became ugly—he offered her money. The suspect then grabbed the victim and demanded she take her pants off, which she did after repeated demands and in fear for her safety, and he raped her.[3]

In the first case there is clearly no consent at any time. What should be said, however, about the second case, in which there is initial consent that is later withdrawn? Does the victim's initial agreement constitute a tacit consent to the man's subsequent conduct, especially if they had already voluntarily engaged in some sexual activity? Surely not. Agreeing to a pleasurable game of tennis does not constitute consent to having one's partner force one to finish the game against one's subsequent wishes. And the same is even more true of sexual activity.

Is the woman nevertheless partially responsible and blameworthy for "precipitating" the rape with provocative behavior? Susan Brownmiller offers the following answer in *Against Our Will: Men, Women, and Rape,* a book that has drawn increased attention to rape:

Some men might consider a housewife who lets a strange man into her house for a glass of water guilty of precipitant behavior, and more men would consider a female hitchhiker who accepts a ride from an unknown male guilty of precipitant behavior. Rape-minded men would consider both actions tantamount to an open invitation. I, on the other hand, consider the housewife and hitchhiker insufficiently wary, but in no way would I consider their actions provocative or even mildly precipitant. Similarly, most men seem to consider a woman who engages in sex play but stops short of intercourse guilty not only of precipitant behavior, but of cruel, provocative behavior with no excuse, yet I and my sister

---

*From *Rape and Woman's Identity* by William B. Sanders. © 1980 by Sage Publications, Inc. Reprinted by permission of the publisher.

feminists would argue that her actions are perfectly allowable and quite within the bounds of human decency and rational decisions.[4]

Brownmiller here argues that women have the same right to control over their lives and sexual conduct that men take for granted over theirs. The right to self-determination is held equally by women and men, despite the unfair double standard concerning sexual activities.

This double standard, we might add, has even entered into the traditional legal definition of rape. That definition explicitly excluded forcible and violent intercourse within marriage after a wife refused her husband's sexual advances. The exclusion was based on the assumption that wives are the sexual property of their husbands, and it also presupposed that consenting to marriage entailed a sweeping consent to sexual intercourse at any time. Laws are changing, but it remains difficult to prove in court that a rape took place when a married or unmarried victim consented on previous occasions to sexual intercourse with the rapist.

Sexual Harassment

Sexual harassment is any sexually oriented act or practice involving intimidation, coercion, or unfair sexual conduct.* In everyday speech the word *harassment* suggests repeated aggravation or persistent annoyance. But as part of the expression "sexual harassment" it carries the special connotation of misuse of power or authority, and this can occur in a single episode that is not repeated. The primary habitat of sexual harassment is authority relationships, in particular at work and school. Before focusing on these authority contexts, however, let us mention cases involving unequal power that do not involve authority (that is, institutionally granted forms of power).

When a man leers, jeers, or whistles at a woman in a public setting, he may be "hassling" her, that is, bothering or irritating her. Hassling becomes sexual harassment when similar acts occur in threatening situations. One such situation is when the two are strangers alone on an isolated street at night; another is when the man is part of a group of men confronting and blocking the path of the woman. Whatever the actual intentions of the man, his conduct is reasonably interpreted in such situations as involving danger or disruption of the woman's life.

---

*This definition applies to sexual assault, although sexual assault is sometimes treated as an offense distinct from sexual harassment.

The Workplace

Sexual harassment by an employer (usually though not always male) of an employee (usually female) involves abuse of institutional authority, that is, the abuse of power given to the employer by the institution. Recent legislation and Supreme Court rulings define sexual harassment in the workplace as essentially any sexually oriented practice that threatens jobs or job performance.

Obvious examples include threats to fire or demote an employee unless sexual favors are granted, deliberate touching in unwanted ways, and inappropriate comments on the clothing and physical appearance of an employee. A different kind of sexual harassment occurs when employers reveal details about their personal sex lives to their employees against their wishes. And the courts have also ruled that harassment occurs when a male supervisor or colleague posts *Playboy* centerfolds in an office to which women have access. All these forms of behavior are restricted by sex discrimination laws prohibiting differential treatment of women and men in unfair ways.

Academia

Academia, like the workplace, is structured according to authority relationships. This fact is occasionally overlooked on campuses where faculty are encouraged to give personal attention to students, where there is general trust between students and professors, and where eccentric behavior is tolerated. Thus, we must emphasize that professors have considerable control over their students through grading practices as well as because of their general authority to guide the educational process. In addition, professors are granted an exceptionally high degree of personal autonomy in carrying out their functions.

As was noted, sexual harassment need not involve assault on or physical restraint of persons against their will. In what way or ways, then, is sexual harassment in academia coercive? Let us consider three types of sexual harassment: (1) threats of penalties, (2) annoyance, and (3) offers of rewards.

Sexual threats are the clearest example of coercion. In extreme cases, professors either hint or directly state that unless students sleep with them, the students will not receive as high grades as their work warrants. This interferes with the agency of the student in that a threat suggests that something unwanted will occur unless one complies. When students do not want to have sex with professors, their situation has been worsened by the threat: Either they must accede to the professor's wishes and do something unwanted or they run the risk of not getting the grade deserved. If the student does want to sleep with the professor, the professor is nevertheless trying to manipulate unfairly, using means outside the bounds of understood professional ethics. The threat is coercive, even when the student does not experience it as such.

Sexual annoyance occurs when a professor's sexual overtures cause a student to feel uncomfortable or anxious, or when the overture in any other way creates a climate that distracts from the learning process. Such an overture normally raises (quite reasonable) fears that the professor might retaliate if the student objects to the advance. Sexual annoyance is wrong precisely because it impedes or threatens to impede the learning relationship between student and professor. In this way it also violates the right to self-determination of the student who has chosen to be in that situation to learn. Sexual annoyance is also wrong because of the disrespect demonstrated by focusing attention on one aspect of the student—the sexual one—in a context where that is understood to be inappropriate.

Sexual offers represent attempts to influence behavior by promising a benefit. For example, the professor who offers to raise a student's deserved grade from a C to an A on the condition that the student agree to a date has acted unethically. Not only is the professor violating the standards of integrity required in grading, but the professor is treating all students in the class unfairly. But is there coercion involved in such cases? After all, a desired good (the higher grade) is being offered, and the student seemingly is free to accept or reject the offer. Indeed, Michael Bayles argues that such offers are not coercive when the student wants what is offered:

> Assume there is a mediocre woman graduate student who would not receive an assistantship. Suppose the department chairman offers her one if she goes to bed with him, and she does so. In what sense has the graduate student acted against her will? She apparently preferred having an assistantship and sleeping with the chairman to not sleeping with him and not having an assistantship. So it would appear that she did what she wanted in the situation. . . . The fact that a choice has an undesirable consequence [i.e., having to sleep with the chairman] does not make it against one's will. One may prefer to have clean teeth without having to brush them; nonetheless, one is not acting against one's will when one brushes them.[5]

Bayles concludes that the student's situation is actually improved by the offer because her options are preferable (in her eyes) to what they were before, and in any case Bayles claims that she is free without coercion to choose either way.

This view fails to take account of the fact that such situations often generate fear. In particular, there is fear that the professor might penalize the student for refusing the offer, a valid fear considering the professor has already (in making the offer) violated the professional standards of fairness in allocating assistantships. Moreover, such bribes exert an undue influence that distorts the choices the student should have to confront. In addition, as John Hughes and Larry May argue, such offers constitute a form of sex discrimination. As such, they directly hurt the victim, who is usually a woman, and also indirectly hurt all women:

Sexual harassment is a form of sex discrimination because (1) the policy is based on a sex-plus criterion of classification, which adversely affects members of only one sex-class, and (2) the policy is based on and perpetuates a sex stereotype [of women as weak and vulnerable] which stigmatizes the class of women and thus, potentially, all of its members.[6]

Here is one final situation. What should be said of the professor who flirts with students and, upon receiving a positive response, asks them to bed? Assume there are no threats, no annoying overtures, and no offers amounting to undue influence. Can we then conclude that this is not sexual harassment, but rather the exercise of free choice in sexual matters? Before accepting that conclusion, the following argument by Billie Dziech and Linda Weiner should be considered:

> Whatever the intent, sexual give-and-take is based on mutual consent of equals. This is obviously not the case in sexual harassment. Normal sexual give-and-take is not possible in student-teacher relationships because the power imbalance and role disparity are too great.[7]

Later, Dziech and Wiener add the following comment:

> Attraction between professor and student may occur, but it is almost impossible for that attraction to be acted on successfully given the average campus environment and the restrictions on student-teacher roles. If legitimate attractions do occur, the couple's regard for the relationship should lead them to restrain themselves until their roles change.[8]

Is this excessive caution? Is it perhaps an infringement of the rights of both students and faculty in matters of sex and love? Or does the risk of coercion in student-faculty relationships warrant the restraint recommended by Dziech and Wiener? We will return to these questions in the "Discussion Topics" section.

Summary

Whereas *character-respect* means admiring specific individuals for their good character or virtues, *minimal-respect* entails recognizing the value of all moral beings, that is, persons having a sense of moral values. Minimal-respect for other people requires honoring their right to personal autonomy or self-determination. This right creates obligations not to interfere in people's legitimate areas of personal prerogative, as well as obligations to contribute to making society supportive of personal autonomy. *Personal autonomy* includes *moral autonomy* (the ability and willingness to form reasonable moral judgments and to act on them), but it encompasses much more. It requires procedural independence (not being coerced or deceived by others), competence (self-control and the exercising of rationality), and substantive independence (not being overly dependent on others).

Rape violates personal autonomy by violating sexual choice, an area of self-determination central to personal identity and self-respect. This is true of individual acts of rape, which by definition involve the violation of consent. But it is equally true of rape as a widespread practice, because the very real threat of rape forces women to restrict their activities.

Rape is also a form of cruelty in which suffering is deliberately and without any justification inflicted on a person. The suffering includes immediate physical pain, terror and fear for one's life, and trauma that lasts for years afterward. The rapist's intentions are violent rather than primarily sexual per se and involve the cruel motives of enjoying the violent subjugation of women and deriving self-esteem though sexual dominance.

Although sexual harassment often involves cruelty, it is of special interest because of the ways it violates self-determination. It can be defined as any sexually oriented act or practice involving intimidation, coercion, or unfair sexual conduct. Most often it involves abuse of authority relationships at work and school. Sexual harassment is most commonly exhibited through sexual threats, sexual annoyance, and sexual offers, each of which creates conditions that disrupt work and learning.

DISCUSSION TOPICS

1. Identify and discuss the moral issues raised by the following case from studies done by William B. Sanders:

> Victim met the suspect at a party. She had met him about two years previously but did not know him very well. They left the party together and went to a drive-in movie where they began necking. The victim willingly performed oral copulation on the suspect and masturbated him while at the drive-in. When they left the drive-in, the suspect tried to pull the victim's pants down and have intercourse with her, but she fought back and was able to escape, going to her boyfriend's house where she spent the night.[9]

2. Date rape sometimes occurs when the rapist is drunk or on drugs, and it also occurs when the victim is intoxicated. Explain what you see as the problems in determining whether there is consent when the victim is partially or completely intoxicated. Should it be assumed that when individuals are intoxicated, they cannot give voluntary consent to intercourse? Also, is an intoxicated rapist less blameworthy than a sober one?

3. Widespread rape is a product of cultures like our own in which male violence is tolerated and even encouraged. Studies show that it is linked to other forms of physical violence on dates—hitting, pushing, squeezing—as well as to verbal abuse. Studies also show that although women sometimes engage in such violence, they do so much less frequently and with far less intensity. What should society (especially schools and law enforcement) do to create a climate discouraging male violence?

4. Should there be absolute (that is, exceptionless) prohibitions on sexual relationships between students and their professors (or other academic supervisors, such as advisors)? Do such prohibitions violate the sexual freedom of consenting adults? Does permitting the relationships create harmful conflicts of interest for professors in grading and also foster exploitation of students? Is your view the same or different with respect to high school students and their teachers?

5. Is there any moral difference between a man forcing his wife to have sexual intercourse and a man raping a stranger?

6. There seem to be humans who lack a potential for moral responsibility. Does this mean they do not deserve even minimal respect? In your answer consider the following three cases.
   a. Some human infants are born without a brain and lack any potential to interact with other people. (Left alone, these "anencephalics" usually die within a day, but with medical technology they can live for years.)
   b. Some sociopathic rapists commit multiple rapes without any remorse whatsoever and are not "curable" by any known psychotherapeutic remedy.
   c. There are sadistic torturers who delight in cruelty and revel in inflicting suffering on others. Consider, in particular, the Nazi officer portrayed in William Styron's novel *Sophie's Choice* who set out to discover an imaginative new form of cruelty. His discovery was to force a mother to choose which of her children will be executed and to execute both children if she refused to make a choice.

SUGGESTED READINGS

Brownmiller, Susan. *Against Our Will: Men, Women and Rape.* New York: Simon & Schuster, 1975.

Cranor, Carl. "On Respecting Human Beings as Persons," *Journal of Value Inquiry,* vol. 17 (1983).

Downie, R. S., and Elizabeth Telfer. *Respect for Persons.* New York: Schocken, 1970.

Dziech, Billie Wright, and Linda Weiner. *The Lecherous Professor: Sexual Harassment on Campus.* Boston: Beacon Press, 1984.

Griffin, Susan. *Rape: The Politics of Consciousness.* 3rd ed. New York: Harper & Row, 1986.

Hallie, Philip P. *Cruelty.* Rev. ed. Middletown, CT: Wesleyan University Press, 1982.

Hughes, John C., and Larry May. "Sexual Harassment." *Social Theory and Practice,* vol. 6 (1980).

MacKinnon, Catharine A. *Sexual Harassment of Working Women.* New Haven, CT: Yale University Press, 1979.

Midgley, Mary. *Wickedness: A Philosophical Essay.* Boston: Routledge & Kegan Paul, 1984.

Mill, John Stuart. *On Liberty.* Indianapolis, IN: Hackett Publishing, 1978.

Pennock, J. Roland, and John W. Chapman (eds.). *Nomos XIV: Coercion.* New York: Aldine, Atherton, 1972.

Sanders, William B. *Rape and Women's Identity.* Beverly Hills, CA: Sage, 1980.

Shafer, Carolyn M., and Marilyn Frye. "Rape and Respect." In Mary Vetterling-Braggin, Frederick A. Elliston, and Jane English (eds.), *Feminism and Philosophy.* Totowa, NJ: Rowman & Allanheld, 1977.

Tong, Rosemarie. *Women, Sex, and the Law.* Totowa, NJ: Rowman & Allanheld, 1984.

Williams, Bernard. "The Idea of Equality." In *Problems of the Self.* Cambridge: Cambridge University Press, 1973.

CHAPTER 10

Prejudice

Prejudice is an unfair and unreasonable attitude toward members of a group of people. The attitude is manifested in emotions and conduct of individuals (individual prejudice) or in practices, laws, and institutions (institutional prejudice). The group of people can be identified by racial, ethnic, national, religious, aesthetic (for example, "ugly" people), or ideological criteria. Racism and sexism are the two types of prejudice emphasized here.

The term *racism* was coined during the 1950s to refer to racial prejudice. *Sexism* was adopted during the 1960s to refer to misogyny (hatred of women), patriarchy (socially sanctioned male dominance), and unfair discrimination against women. The term is also now applied to misandry (hatred of men) and unfair discrimination against men. Interestingly, the expression "male chauvinist" was coined during the late 1960s by women working in the civil rights and students' movements to apply to male colleagues who relegated women to secondary roles in the fight against racism.

Overt Versus Covert Prejudice

One form of individual prejudice is overt—that is, it is easily discernible and involves consciously held prejudiced attitudes. For example, the racist bigot self-confidently asserts that black people are inferior; the anti-Semite passionately denounces Jews as dangerous; and the male chauvinist insists that women are delicate creatures who should be protected and kept safely in the home away from business and politics. Overt institutional prejudice has its origin in widespread negative attitudes toward groups, attitudes that generate or support repressive laws, rules, and practices. Not infrequently it involves violence, both in its personal forms (as when a gang of white youths attacks a stranger simply because he is black) and in its institutional forms (as when laws continue to protect wife-battering husbands).

The form of prejudice we will emphasize, however, is more covert or concealed. It is also called "visceral," not just because it is deep-seated and difficult to remove, but because it is somewhat hidden, especially to the prejudiced person. Covert prejudice may result from self-deception. Just as often, however, it results from uncritically adopting prejudiced attitudes or engaging in prejudiced social practices.

In this chapter, three varieties of covert prejudice are discussed: (1) accepting stereotypes about the personality, character, capacities, or roles of people, (2) using prejudicial forms of language, and (3) restricting social roles available to people. In the next chapter we will discuss a fourth form: prejudiced humor.

Stereotypes

Ralph Ellison's *Invisible Man* explores how stereotypes prevent white people from understanding black people. The central metaphor of the novel is set forth in the opening passage:

> I am an invisible man. No, I am not a spook like those who haunted Edgar Allan Poe. . . . I am invisible, understand, simply because people refuse to see me. Like the bodiless heads you see sometimes in circus sideshows, it is as though I have been surrounded by mirrors of hard, distorting glass. When they approach me they see only my surroundings, themselves, or figments of their imagination—indeed, everything and anything except me. . . . That invisibility to which I refer occurs because of a peculiar disposition of the eyes of those with whom I come in contact. A matter of the construction of their *inner* eyes, those eyes with which they look through their physical eyes upon reality.[1]

These distorting inner mirrors reflect preconceived beliefs and attitudes about black people. In contemporary psychological terms they represent biased "cognitive schemas" through which experiences are filtered. In ordinary language they are negative stereotypes, that is, simplistic outlooks based on false beliefs, incomplete information, or unjustified value judgments.

Later in the novel the Invisible Man relates the incident that forced him to grasp how cognitively distorting mirrors rendered him invisible. Walking alone at night, he accidentally bumped into a white man who called him "an insulting name." He exploded in rage, attacking the man and demanding an apology. During the ensuing fight the white man continued to shout racist obscenities even after the Invisible Man held a knife to his throat. Suddenly he realized that "the man had not *seen* me, actually; that he, as far as he knew, was in the midst of a walking nightmare" involving an insane assailant who had no reason (that the white man would grasp) for attacking him.[2] He also realized that the man's verbal assault resulted from a stereotypic view that operated outside the man's full awareness.

Was the Invisible Man blameworthy for the violence? In the beginning of the novel he denies responsibility, arguing that "responsibility rests upon recognition."[3] In other words moral responsibility presupposes there is at least minimal mutual respect among groups of people, and that is just what the white man refused to give him. By the end of the novel, however, the protagonist modifies this view, accepting partial responsibility for his own invisibility because of his passivity and naiveté.

Is the white man responsible? According to the Invisible Man, that depends on whether he could be expected to recognize the meaning and the danger of his racial slur: "He, let us say, was lost in a dream world. But didn't *he* control that dream world—which, alas, is only too real!—and didn't *he* rule me out of it?"[4] This relates to the question raised in Chapter 6 concerning responsibility for self-deception and preventable ignorance. As was argued there, we are responsible for much of our self-deception and we can be held accountable for too easy conformity to social pressures. Rather than repeating that argument, let us turn to the question of how prejudiced stereotypes are supported by self-deception.

Marilyn Frye makes some helpful suggestions about how this occurs. Although she uses the example of sexism, her remarks are easily extended to other forms of prejudice. In her essay "Male Chauvinism—A Conceptual Analysis" Frye first points out that not all sexism and prejudice involve self-deception. Rather, some sexism is unthinkingly absorbed from parents, friends, and society. She offers the example of a man who, in always opening doors for women but not for men, has simply adopted the practice unreflectively. He may not even be a sexist but merely be engaged in a discriminatory practice. People who develop and sustain prejudiced attitudes even when they have every opportunity to abandon them, however, typically engage in some degree of self-deceptive evasion and distortion of facts.

The tactics of self-deceiving prejudice include straightforward deception about the behavior of individuals with whom one comes in contact, either by ignoring or by downplaying the abilities they display. One can also disregard the special obstacles others confront. More insidious tactics include self-deceivingly rigging the circumstances against a person. Consider, for example, how fathers, in teaching their daughters to throw a baseball, may "go through various superficial maneuvers and declare failure (her failure) without having engaged in anything like the perseverance and ingenuity which would have been engaged in the training of sons."[5] A racist parallel would be an employer who deliberately placed a trainee in difficult situations that made poor performance more likely, or who gave less help and attention to a minority trainee than to a white male.

Frye offers a second example of creating unfair circumstances. Without acknowledging it to oneself, one refrains from the kinds of personal contact in which one's prejudice might be uncovered or challenged:

One cannot, for instance, manifest certain kinds of intelligence in interactions with a person who enters with a prior conviction of one's stupidity, lack of insight, absence of wit; one cannot manifest sensitivity or loyalty in interactions with someone who is distrustful and will not share relevant information. . . . He [the male chauvinist] can in one fell swoop avoid seeing the critical central range of a woman's . . . abilities simply by being uncooperative and uncommunicative, and can do it without knowing he has done it by self-deceptively believing he has been cooperative and communicative.[6]

There are parallels here with the ways of avoiding honest personal interactions with people having particular racial identities. If challenged, one might claim to be acting on one's own tastes concerning people. Don't we all have a right to choose our associates? Yet having rights is not the issue. Quite simply, it is wrong to exercise our rights in ways that show disrespect for an entire group of people.

Language

A second way in which prejudice is expressed covertly is through language. One form of "linguistic prejudice" is telling racist and sexist jokes, as discussed in the next chapter. Another form is using certain familiar terms and expressions, at least as many people now argue.

Language is used to formulate and express thoughts, but it also shapes thoughts. Words and ways of speaking are to a large extent historical products that embody assumptions, attitudes, and emotional responses. As Ludwig Wittgenstein (1889–1951) argued, linguistic practices are intimately joined to "ways of life" defined by communal practices, beliefs, and attitudes. Wittgenstein's later philosophy emerged after he traced his early errors in doing philosophy to naiveté about how language influences thought. In reflecting on those errors, he remarked, "A *picture* held us captive. And we could not get outside it, for it lay in our language and language seemed to repeat it to us inexorably."[7] Earlier thinkers like Francis Bacon (1561–1626) were also sensitive to this danger: "People believe that their reason governs words. But words turn and twist the understanding."[8]

One of the most important applications of how language embeds and sanctions misleading "pictures"—that is, perspectives and ways of thinking—has been made by feminists who uncovered sex biases built into language.

This linguistic sexism still permeates everyday language use and raises moral questions about whether we should feel comfortable in allowing it to continue. Consider some of the ways in which linguistic practices reflect and reinforce sexist as well as racist biases:

1. Men are referred to as *Mr.* while women are identified by marital status: *Mrs.* or *Miss* (a problem now easily solved by using *Ms.*).
2. According to custom and continuing social pressure, after marriage only the woman is encouraged to change her last name, thereby symbolically expressing a new identity oriented toward the man.
3. Everyday locutions place the male first, as in *husband and wife* (not *wife and husband*), *men and women*, and *son and daughter*.
4. Until recently, names for occupations were male-oriented, as in *fireman* (versus *fire fighter*), *mailman* (versus *mail carrier*), *congressman* (versus *member of congress*), and *chairman* (versus *chair* or *chairperson*).
5. Adult women office workers are often referred to as *the girls in the office,* while male workers are called men. (Compare the racist use of *boy* to refer to adult black men.)
6. The same personality traits are labeled positively when found in males and negatively when found in females: males are assertive but females are bitchy; men are blunt but women can't hold their tongues; men discuss but women gossip.
7. Far more than men, women are referred to with terms that tie them to their anatomy or to animals, often vulgarly so: *broads, chicks, piece.*
8. God is referred to as *He,* even in religions that officially find it blasphemous to ascribe human properties to God.
9. *Man* (versus *humans* or *persons*), its variants (*mankind, men*), and male pronouns (*he, his*) are used in contexts referring to both men and women, while the reverse would not convey the same universal meaning.

Despite the systematic and varied ways in which male biases enter into language, there are some people who see no need to change our ways of speaking. They insist that language should be preserved as it is, and they deny that anyone's thoughts or attitudes are influenced by such trivial linguistic customs.

There are two rejoinders to this linguistic conservatism. First, commonsense or naive beliefs about how language affects thought and attitude need to be examined in light of scientific studies. A classic sociological experiment challenges the naive view that using "man" to apply to both men and women has no effect on thought and action:

> Some three hundred college students were asked to select from magazines and newspapers a variety of pictures that would appropriately illustrate the different chapters of a sociology textbook being prepared for publication. Half the students were assigned chapter headings like

"Social Man," "Industrial Man," and "Political Man." The other half were given different but corresponding headings like "Society," "Industrial Life," and "Political Behavior." Analysis of the pictures selected revealed that in the minds of students of both sexes use of the word man evoked, to a statistically significant degree, images of males only—filtering out recognition of women's participation in these major areas of life—whereas the corresponding headings without "man" evoked images of both males and females. In some instances the differences reached magnitudes of 30 to 40 percent. The authors concluded, "This is rather convincing evidence that when you use the word man generically, people do tend to think male, and tend not to think female."[9]

Second, even those who seek to honor custom must recognize that customs are changing dramatically in this area, and presumably, once established, those emergent customs will warrant the same respect claimed for the older ones. Increasingly, publishers, writers, public speakers, and conversationalists are paying heed to ways to root out sexism in language. In such a climate of change it is, at the least, rude to refuse even to try to adjust one's language and such a refusal may indicate sexist attitudes.

Gender Roles

A third way prejudice is manifested is through restrictive social roles. Gender or sex roles represent socially created expectations for males and females, just as racial roles represent socially created expectations for members of particular racial groups. Strong differentiation of roles for black and white people was practiced well into this century. It was only a few decades ago, in 1954, that the Supreme Court ruled in *Brown* vs. *Board of Education* that "separate but equal" schools were inherently unequal and unfair. In principle, and officially, our society has recognized that it is insulting to keep a minority separated—in schools, restaurants, restrooms, buses, and other public settings—from social interaction with a privileged group.

Although the equal rights of minorities have now been at least officially recognized in our society, the same cannot be said for women. Since they were first formulated in 1923, the following two dozen words have continually been blocked from being entered into the Constitution as the Equal Rights Amendment: "Equality of rights under the law shall not be denied or abridged by the United States or by any State on account of sex." In 1982 this proposed amendment failed to pass in three-fourths of the state legislatures, even though it was passed by the U.S. Senate and House of Representatives and had the approval of the majority of Americans.

The defeat of the ERA and the presence of sexism in the grammar of our language have suggested to some thinkers that sexism is more firmly entrenched in our society than is racism, although it would be difficult to prove that. It is, however, worth considering some of the differences between racism and sexism, as identified by Richard Wasserstrom in his essay "On Racism and Sexism." Wasserstrom draws attention to the substantial psychological literature documenting how we respond differently to boys and girls from the time they are born. For example, girls are handled more delicately as babies; from infancy on boys are encouraged to be more independent and strong; and girls and women are taught to be dependent and passive and are generally more restricted in the kinds of activities in which they can engage.

Wasserstrom sees the key difference between racism and sexism as lying in the greater complexity of the attitudes and valuations involved. Racist stereotypes of black people are wholly negative—that is, racists regard black people as having less worth than white people. Sexist attitudes, by contrast, are mixed in a manner that enables sexists to believe they view women as having equal or greater worth than men:

> Women are both put on a pedestal and deemed not fully developed persons. They are idealized; their approval and admiration is sought; and they are at the same time regarded as less competent than men and less able to live fully developed, fully human lives—for that is what men do. At best, they are viewed and treated as having properties and attributes that are valuable and admirable for humans of this type. For example, they may be viewed as especially empathetic, intuitive, loving, and nurturing. At best, these qualities are viewed as good properties for women to have, and, provided they are properly muted, are sometimes valued within the more well-rounded male.[10]

Wasserstrom urges that in order to determine which roles are sexist and racist, we must determine which roles would be present in a morally ideal society. As an aid in thinking about this question, he distinguishes three types of gender roles: (1) those concerning political rights, such as the right to vote and hold political office; (2) those pertaining to economic and nonpolitical practices, such as work and marital roles; and (3) those involving personal traits, tastes, interests, and interactions, including the selection of friends and personal entertainment and the encouragement of sex-stereotyped traits of temperament and character.

With respect to all these areas Wasserstrom suggests that a morally ideal society would regard racial and sexual differences as completely irrelevant. Just as eye color is almost entirely ignored in our society (completely so in areas 1 and 2, and mostly so in area 3), so too racial and sex traits would be equally insignificant if our society were morally ideal. Wasserstrom refers to this as the "assimilationist ideal."

For example, concerning the third area of personal characteristics and interactions, Wasserstrom makes the following assertions:

On the attitudinal and conceptual level, the assimilationist ideal would require the eradication of all sex-role differentiation. It would never teach about the inevitable or essential attributes of masculinity or femininity; it would never encourage or discourage the ideas of sisterhood or brotherhood; and it would be unintelligible to talk about the virtues as well as disabilities of being a woman or a man. Were sex like eye color, these things would make no sense. Just as the normal, typical adult is virtually oblivious to the eye color of other persons for all major interpersonal relationships, so the normal, typical adult in this kind of nonsexist society would be indifferent to the sexual, physiological differences of other persons for all interpersonal relationships.[11]

This is a striking claim. Apparently, in seeking to abolish all differentiation as masculine and feminine, Wasserstrom is recommending a kind of androgynous and bisexual ideal society in which even clothing, hair styles, use of make-up, and sexual preferences would not be developed along sex lines.

Wasserstrom gives two arguments in support of this ideal society. First, he notes that the roles given to women have historically been the lesser, inferior ones in terms of social power. Second, and more important for thinking about ideal societies, gender roles are inherently harmful: "Sex roles, and all that accompany them, necessarily impose limits—restrictions on what one can do, be or become. As such, they are, I think, at least prima facie wrong."[12]

It will be left for the reader to determine whether Wasserstrom is correct. In doing so consider a rejoinder to Wasserstrom by Elizabeth Wolgast in *Equality and the Rights of Women.* Wolgast contends that, at the very least, the biological possibility of pregnancy provides one focal difference that should be openly acknowledged in assessing the comparative rights of women and men: for example, rights to guaranteed pregnancy leaves that secure employment at the same job when women return to work, and funded day care for the children of working mothers. Moreover, special economic benefits to widows are justifiable, especially when women have worked at home as homemakers. With respect to Wasserstrom's third category Wolgast urges that we should not be disturbed by how biological differences encourage some social differentiation in roles:

> *Could* we treat the sexes alike as Wasserstrom proposes? We normally respond differently to members of the opposite sex than to members of our own. Even putting sexual attraction aside, we still have different relations to members of different sexes. With members of our sex, we have and anticipate having, a good deal in common. To a child we say, "When I was a little girl . . ." (if we are women) with the implication that we lack the same identification with boys. While with members of the opposite sex we perceive contrasts and divergent points of view, for some areas of common experience are lacking. Understanding those other perspectives is often a tenuous matter, ignorance and mystery

being the conditions it must work against; but it is also one that fasci-
nates, challenges, delights, and amuses us.[13]

Summary

Prejudice, in the sense of unfair and unreasonable attitudes toward members
of a group, can be overt (consciously held and easily discerned by others) or
covert (less conscious and more concealed). Most prejudice has cultural origins, and much covert prejudice is partially caused and supported by self-
deceptive beliefs and hatreds. Self-deception supports cultural stereotypes
through the tactics of ignoring and downplaying the abilities of others, disregarding the special obstacles they confront, and rigging the circumstances
so as to deny them fair opportunities to overthrow the stereotypes.

In addition to self-deceptive stereotypes, language is a second potent form
of covert institutional prejudice. Familiar grammatical practices, such as using
male pronouns to refer to both women and men, convey language-embedded
images of men as superior to women.

A third form of both institutionalized and personal covert sexism is encouraging women and men into differential roles that deny them equal opportunities, just as racism denies the same opportunities to minorities that members
of the dominant group in a society enjoy. As the disagreement between
Wasserstrom and Wolgast reflects, our society is currently in the midst of determining whether all differential roles impose unfair and hurtful restrictions.

DISCUSSION TOPICS

1. Do you agree with Wasserstrom that all gender roles that create different expectations for females and males impose harmful limits on what they can do and become? Or is Wolgast correct in believing that some differential expectations for
females and males are both inevitable and desirable? Consider a range of examples,
from dress codes and hair styles to differences in personality traits.

2. Is there sexism involved in allowing sports teams to restrict members to one sex?
In answering this question, consider each of the following contexts: junior and
little league sports supported by communities; elementary school teams; high
school teams; college teams; professional sports. Is your answer the same when
you use race as a criterion for team membership?

3. Studies have shown that a large majority of American couples prefer to have boys
for their first babies. Is this preference a form of sexism? What if a couple insists
they like boys and girls equally but assert they need a boy in order to carry on the
family name?

Suppose that a couple learns the sex of their fetus several months into a pregnancy (as is possible using amniocentesis, the process by which cells from a sample of the fluid surrounding the fetus are analyzed to discover its chromosomes). Upon learning that the fetus is female, they plan to have an abortion because they want a boy and plan to have only one child. Is the abortion an act of sexism?

4. Review Carol Gilligan's care-perspective and justice-perspective, which she correlates (loosely) with women and men, respectively, as discussed in Chapter 2. Do you think that these two perspectives are gender-linked (assuming they are) because of covert institutional sexism that pressures women and men to develop their characters in different directions?

5. Wasserstrom believes that a just society would abandon racial roles as well as gender roles. In fact, he thinks that all racial differences would be irrelevant to how people responded to one another in such a society. Do you agree or disagree? In your answer consider the objection that even though racial differences have been used to hurt members of minorities, they need not do so in an ideal society. A perfectly just society might allow a plurality of racial groupings and responses that bring an enriching diversity of subcultures.

6. Elizabeth Wolgast contends that women should have special rights, such as the right to pregnancy leave with a guaranteed job upon return to work. Do you agree? Is her view compatible with the Equal Rights Amendment?

7. Given that much racism is covert, is there a moral obligation for each of us to study racism in order to become better able to uncover it in ourselves? In general, are we responsible, as the Invisible Man suggests, for our failures to identify racism in ourselves?

8. Prejudice entails holding unfair and unreasonable attitudes toward members of a group. Is the black person or the Mexican-American who is raised as a second-class citizen in a ghetto or barrio prejudiced if that person is hostile toward white people and chooses to associate with them as little as possible in his or her personal life?

9. In 1988, on the birthday of Martin Luther King, Jimmy ("the Greek") Snyder commented during an interview that black athletes have special physical prowess because they were "bred" to have strong thighs during the days of slavery in the United States. In widely quoted remarks Snyder said that "the slave owner would breed his big black [man] with his big woman so that he would have a big black kid." Snyder, a prominent sports broadcaster, was fired from his job because of these remarks. Some people defended Snyder on the grounds that he had portrayed black athletes as superior, praising them rather than intending to make a racial slur. Is Snyder's remark racist? Is it unfair that he was fired? (In your answer take account of the fact that there is no evidence supporting his "pop" evolution theory.)

10. From 1986 to 1988 a number of incidents on college campuses created a concern that a "new racism"—that is, renewed racism—confronts black students. For example, a brawl between white and black students occurred at the University of Massachusetts at Amherst following the final game of the 1986 World Series; a fraternity at the New Jersey Institute of Technology held a party advertised with handbills glorifying violence against blacks; a fraternity at the University of Wisconsin at Madison placed a caricature of a black man with a bone through his nose on the fraternity's front lawn; vandals carved "KKK" in a black student's dormitory room at the University of California at Berkeley.[14] Related events occurred elsewhere, such as in the Queens section of New York City, where a black man was killed by a car while fleeing a group of white teenagers who believed they had a right to keep black people away, and in Forsyth County, Georgia, where an all-white area insisted on keeping black people out of their neighborhood. How would you explain this renewal of overt racism in recent years, especially among students at schools that attract well-educated students? What should be done about it?

SUGGESTED READINGS

Baker, Robert. "'Pricks' and 'Chicks': A Plea for Persons." In Robert Baker and Frederick Elliston, *Philosophy and Sex*. Rev. ed. Buffalo, New York: Prometheus, 1984.

Boxill, Bernard. *Blacks and Social Justice*. Totowa, NJ: Rowman & Allanheld, 1984.

English, Jane (ed.). *Sex Equality*. Englewood Cliffs, NJ: Prentice-Hall, 1977.

Fausto-Sterling, Anne. *Myths of Gender: Biological Theories About Women and Men.* New York: Basic Books, 1985.

Frye, Marilyn. "Male Chauvinism—A Conceptual Analysis." In Mary Vetterling-Braggin (ed.), *Sexist Language: A Modern Philosophical Analysis*. Totowa, NJ: Littlefield, Adams, 1981.

Illich, Ivan. *Gender*. New York: Pantheon, 1982.

Lipman-Blumen, Jean. *Gender Roles and Power*. Englewood Cliffs, NJ: Prentice-Hall, 1984.

Miller, Casey, and Kate Swift. *Words and Women*. Garden City, NY: Anchor, 1976.

Sartre, Jean-Paul. *Anti-Semite and Jew*. New York: Schocken, 1965.

Spender, Dale. *Man Made Language*. Boston: Routledge & Kegan Paul, 1980.

Thalberg, Irving. "Visceral Racism." *Monist*, vol. 56 (1972).

Vetterling-Braggin, Mary (ed.). *"Femininity," "Masculinity," and "Androgyny": A Modern Philosophical Discussion*. Totowa, NJ: Littlefield, Adams, 1982.

Vetterling-Braggin, Mary (ed.). *Sexist Language: A Modern Philosophical Analysis*. Totowa, NJ: Littlefield, Adams, 1981.

Vetterling-Braggin, Mary, Frederick A. Elliston, and Jane English (eds.). *Feminism and Philosophy*. Totowa, NJ: Rowman & Allanheld, 1977.

Warren, Mary Anne. *Gendercide: The Implications of Sex Selection*. Totowa, NJ: Rowman & Allanheld, 1985.

Warren, Virginia L. "Guidelines for the Nonsexist Use of Language." *Proceedings and Addresses of The American Philosophical Association*, vol. 59 (February 1986).

Wasserstrom, Richard A. "On Racism and Sexism." In Richard A. Wasserstrom (ed.), *Today's Moral Problems*. 3rd ed. New York: Macmillan, 1985.

Wolgast, Elizabeth H. *Equality and the Rights of Women*. Ithaca, NY: Cornell University Press, 1980.

CHAPTER 11

Ridicule, Rudeness, and Snobbery

"Put-downs" are among the most familiar indignities of everyday life. Although some put-downs may be justified as appropriate responses to arrogance and conceit, most put-downs reflect unjustified and malicious forms of showing disrespect. Such put-downs result from people trying to elevate themselves (either their social standing or their self-esteem) by lowering others.

In this chapter we examine how rudeness and ridicule in the form of malicious amusement represent common forms of put-downs. Then we focus on snobbery, an especially distressing form of elevating oneself at the expense of others.

Ridicule Through Bigoted Humor

To ridicule is to mock or arouse scorn by portraying someone (or something) in a negative way. Usually, one ridicules through malicious humor; humor through ridicule constitutes a seductive and camouflaged way to spitefully mock an individual or a group. It is seductive because it can catch us off guard, evoking spontaneous reactions of amusement. It also camouflages prejudice with apparently innocent pleasure: the physical pleasure of laughter, the social pleasure of sharing laughter with others, and the intellectual pleasure of wittiness. Because bringing people pleasure seems good, ridicule through humor appears to have at least something good about it. But does it?

In fact, telling and enjoying jokes is a virtual haven for expressing covert prejudice. Consider several examples, beginning with the following episode from recent American history. In October of 1976, Earl Butz resigned as President Ford's secretary of agriculture. The resignation was caused by one joke he told on a flight to Los Angeles following the Kansas City Republican convention: As reported in *Newsweek* magazine,

Butz found himself sitting with Watergate veteran John Dean (who was covering the convention for *Rolling Stone* magazine) and singer Pat Boone. At one point Boone mused, "It seems to me that the party of Abraham Lincoln could and should attract more black people. Why can't that be done?" The "coloreds," Butz replied jokingly, were only interested in three things, and his punch line hit in a grossly obscene way at their preferences in sex, shoes, and bathroom arrangements.[1]

John Dean reported the racist slur in his magazine article, ascribing it to an anonymous Ford cabinet officer. Later, another reporter identified Butz by tracing airline passenger records. When questioned, Pat Boone confirmed the incident, adding that he did not find the joke funny and was offended by it. President Ford reprimanded Butz, and despite Butz's popularity with his constituency in the Farm Belt, he was forced by mounting public pressure to resign.

An example of sexist humor is recorded for all posterity by James Boswell in his *Life of Samuel Johnson*. While walking with Johnson one day, Boswell remarked, "I had been that morning at a meeting of the people called Quakers, where I had heard a woman preach." Johnson replied, "Sir, a woman's preaching is like a dog's walking on his hind legs. It is not done well; but you are surprised to find it done at all."[2]

Light bulb jokes, which became popular in the United States during the late 1960s and 1970s, were used to portray Polish-Americans as stupid: "How many Polacks [to use the offensive slur] does it take to change a light bulb? Three: one to hold the bulb and two to turn the ladder." And anti-Semitic jokes frequently portray Jews as cheap while mocking their physiognomy: "Why do Jews have big noses? Air is free." As Holocaust jokes, the slur becomes ghastly: "Why did so many Jews go to Auschwitz? The fare was free."[3]

Also consider humor involving prejudice toward the disabled. Often it takes sick forms, as with quadriplegic jokes of the early 1980s: "What is the hardest part of the vegetable to eat? The wheelchair."[4] And as a final example, here is a joke that mocks physical deformity, ethnic language abilities, and women: "What do you call a woman with one leg shorter than the other? Eileen. What is a Japanese woman with one leg shorter than the other? Irene."[5]

The Ethics of Humor

Telling these jokes in the presence of members of the groups being ridiculed will generally directly insult those persons and cause both hurt and resentment. But what if no members of the group are present? Is any harm done?

Whether we tell a bigoted joke or laugh at one, we are usually sharing the prejudiced attitudes expressed in the joke. In finding the joke enjoyable, we embrace, at least for that moment, the derogatory attitudes underlying the negative stereotype of a group of people. Earl Butz insisted that he was not a racist and did not intend to express a racist attitude—he was just having fun. But the fun came through "making fun of" all black people by affirming a negative stereotype of black people and inviting his hearers to do likewise. Simply stated, bigoted humor endorses or condones bigoted attitudes. It supports a social climate contributing to disrespect and degradation of groups of people. Telling and laughing at bigoted jokes usually joins speaker and hearer in a conspiracy of social oppression.

We should, however, qualify this point with several observations. For one thing, in special circumstances it is possible to tell or enjoy some otherwise bigoted jokes without being prejudiced. Much depends on the context. For example, there is such a thing as having a *right to laugh* at a particular joke in a particular situation. Members of a minority group often have the right to tell and enjoy a joke about their group that outsiders do not have (unless they have been accepted by the group). The Jewish nose joke, for example, may be permissible for some Jews to tell, but not for non-Jews. Yet there are limits even here: It is highly unlikely a Jew would tell the Holocaust joke, and if he or she did, we would suspect anti-Semitism. (It is possible for members of a minority group to hold prejudiced attitudes toward their own group.)

Furthermore, white people may be justified in laughing at racial jokes told by Richard Pryor, even though laughing at the same jokes told by Earl Butz would be wrong. This is due to the differences in motives and attitudes being expressed through the telling of the joke. Whereas Butz is putting down and alienating black people, Pryor is trying to overcome alienation among races through self-understanding about racism, mutual understanding, and sympathetic identification. Butz would have us laugh at black people; Pryor would have us laugh with him. As Ronald de Sousa suggests:

> First, we claim a right to laugh, by virtue of shared experience or community, at some things but not others. Second, we distinguish between laughing *at* and laughing *with* someone. These are different distinctions, but they are related in the following way: I cannot really laugh with you, unless I have the right to laugh; and I only have a right to laugh *at* you if there is a clear possibility of identification *with* you. Although Cyrano de Bergerac makes fun of his own nose, he threatens with death anyone else who makes fun of it."[6]

Butz had no right to tell or laugh at the racist joke because he did not identify in good will with the black people his joke was about; rather, he intended to alienate them. Lacking the right to laugh, he was laughing with contempt at black people, not with them.

In short, the ethics of humor is complex because so much depends on context. Context largely determines what attitudes and emotions are being conveyed, as well as the likely consequences of a joke. A joke told by one per-

son in one way in a certain setting is a source of human unity and friendliness; when told by another person in a different way on a different occasion,
however, the same joke will be divisive and degrading.

Definitions of Humor

Let us consider some possible objections to the points just made. For example, are we perhaps guilty of overmoralizing? Are we undervaluing the joys
that humor brings? After all, doesn't all humor involve put-downs? As long as
we do not directly insult people, shouldn't we be allowed to enjoy all jokes?
Not only would that relieve boredom and tension, but it would also provide a
healthy outlet for racial and other anxieties.

In addressing these objections, we need to clarify what humor is. Some
theorists define all humor as a form of put-down, which means every joke has
a "butt" that brings pleasure to others. Thus, Thomas Hobbes (1588–1679)
wrote that "The passion of laughter is nothing else but sudden glory arising
from a sudden conception of some eminency in ourselves."[7] Hobbes thought
laughter expressed the delight of seeing ourselves as superior to the person
being mocked. We laugh at the person slipping on the banana peel because
we enjoy feeling ourselves to be more competent than such awkward fools.

Although Hobbes's theory applies to some examples of humor (including
bigoted humor), it does not fit many others. When we laugh at puns, funny
sounds, and the awkward walk of a toddler, we need not be enjoying any
thought about being superior. Humor is better defined, following the lead of
Arthur Schopenhauer (1788–1860), as a form of enjoyment of incongruities. An incongruity is any real or imagined silliness, inappropriateness, absurdity, irrationality, or failure to meet some standard. Through humor,
incongruities are enjoyed (at least partly) for their own sake through laughter, pleasant inclinations to laugh, and moments of cheerfulness.[8]

There are infinite possibilities for enjoying laughable incongruities for
their own sake, without insulting or degrading anyone. Moreover, when
jokes do involve seeing someone as inferior or flawed, we can often focus on
the incongruity itself as humorous, without expressing degrading attitudes.
That makes it possible sometimes to have a right to laugh at otherwise bigoted jokes in special circumstances where the incongruity itself, rather than a
put-down, is being enjoyed.

Our main response to such objections, then, is to deny any legitimacy to
bigoted humor. There are enough enjoyable incongruities—an infinity of
them—to enrich our lives without the need for degrading forms.

Another response, however, deserves mention before leaving it as a discussion topic. We focused on bigoted humor, which is based on general stereotypes. Perhaps a softer line should be adopted concerning derogatory humor

aimed at individuals. Certainly, much daily humor consists of poking fun, behind their backs, at individuals who annoy us or who are difficult to live with. The humor can often become quite mean-spirited, and we would hardly make such "humorous" comments in the presence of the individual being ridiculed. Some of it cannot be condoned. But does much of this jesting provide an acceptable release of negative feelings that might otherwise find less innocent outlets? Some of these feelings might fester inside us and harm relationships with the mocked individuals. Isn't it all right, for example, for workers to poke outrageous fun at their employer, at least as long as it does not involve bigoted humor? If there is bad involved in such derogatory humor, isn't it often outweighed by good? We will leave these questions for the "Discussion Topics."

Rudeness

Rudeness is a major violation of decorum, that is, of the generally accepted standards for proper behavior, dress, and speech in a given culture. That makes rudeness seem a matter of "mere etiquette" rather than morality, and it also explains why rudeness goes unmentioned in most ethics books. But rudeness is sometimes a moral offense, even when it is also a violation of etiquette, because it entails showing disrespect through violations of etiquette.

The ethics of rudeness is complicated in at least five ways. First, some rudeness is justifiable, or at least excusable. Although it can be noble to turn the other cheek to an insult, it can also be a legitimate expression of one's dignity to give a witty and sarcastic rejoinder that is as rude as the insult itself.

Second, rudeness can be either intentional or unintentional. Examples of intentional rudeness include contemptuously tramping across a newly cleaned carpet and chattering during a lecture or speech. An example of unintentional rudeness is making obscene gestures or degrading insults to the host of a party after having too much wine to drink. As this example suggests, we are accountable for unintentional rudeness insofar as we are expected to avoid getting into the situation causing it (in this case by not drinking so much). Yet deliberateness is one factor that tends to make rudeness more blameworthy.

Third, as with malicious humor, the offense involved in rudeness depends greatly on context. The same behavior can be rude or not rude depending on the circumstances. Normally, it is permissible to leave one's shoes on when entering friends' homes. If, however, the friends happen to be a traditional Japanese couple or unusually finicky about clean carpets, not removing shoes is rude. Likewise, a frank sexual overture that is flattering to one person can be a devastating insult to another. Even crass physical behavior that would be gross in polite company can be acceptable in some circles of friends. As these examples suggest, avoiding rudeness requires sensitivity concerning both publicly understood conventions of etiquette and the personal tastes of individuals.

Fourth, the ethics of rudeness is complicated by the potential conflict between authenticity and conformity to conventions of etiquette. Social conventions can cramp and suppress individuality and the expression of personal tastes. For example, in most circles etiquette demands more somberness at funerals than an individual may be comfortable with. Is one insensitive if one chooses to wear brighter-colored clothes as opposed to the traditional dark colors?

Fifth, the conventions of etiquette are often uncertain or undergoing change. Not long ago it was considered rude if a man failed to open doors for women, offer to help carry a woman's packages, give up a seat on a bus to a woman, or pay the lunch bill for women friends. For some, these rules still apply. For others, the rules represent a strong symbolic message that is itself insulting to women: that they need special help because they are weaker than men.

Taken together, these five considerations suggest that avoiding rudeness is more a matter of sensitivity than of rule following. Even when rules of etiquette are involved, showing respect and avoiding rudeness is a matter of being considerate of the feelings of individuals. As John Rawls suggested, respect requires a

> willingness to see the situation of others from their point of view, from the perspective of their conception of their good. . . . Also respect is shown in a willingness to do small favors and courtesies, not because they are of any material value, but because they are an appropriate expression of our awareness of another person's feelings and aspirations.[9]

Snobbery

Snobbery is an attitude and character trait that constitutes a put-down of other people. It is the attitude that one is superior in worth to all other people except an in-group to which one belongs. One can, of course, truthfully and humbly recognize that one is superior in talents or achievements without being a snob. Snobbery results when one wants others to suffer—to feel inferior—because of one's alleged superiority. The snob regards others as inferiors to be treated with contempt and disdain, or at best with pity and condescension.

The basis for snobbery can be almost anything: wealth, intellectual capacity, skill in sports or chess, or taste in clothing or fine china. Sometimes it has nothing to do with abilities or achievements but instead is based on inherited name, social standing, or club membership.

Whatever its basis, snobbery is usually accompanied by arrogance. Arrogance can take one of two forms: (1) making unwarranted claims to superiority or (2) flaunting one's genuine superiority in offensive ways. The first form is objectionable because it claims an unfair basis for social esteem, the second because it threatens others' self-esteem.

Snobbery is also frequently accompanied by hypocrisy, as when one pretends to be better than one is. Snobs thus make ready-made targets for satire aimed at ridiculing and deflating their pomposity. Even when their accomplishments are genuine, snobs exaggerate them beyond any reasonable perspective, making themselves vulnerable to the satirist's way of providing perspective. In his nineteenth-century classic, *Book of Snobs,* William Thackeray satirizes most major varieties of snobbism, including academic varieties. Here, for example, in his portrayal of college president Crump:

> Crump thinks Saint Boniface [College] the centre of the world, and his position as President, the highest in England. He expects the fellows and tutors to pay him the same sort of service that Cardinals pay to the Pope. I am sure Crawley would have no objection to carry his trencher [i.e., academic cap], or Page to hold up the skirts of his gown as he stalks into chapel.[10]

Closer to our own day, Vice President Spiro Agnew became something of a professional debunker of snobs. With bitter wit he defended President Nixon's Vietnam policies against liberal journalists whom he derided as pretentious and hypocritical snobs. But of all his targets, student radicals were dealt with most viciously. The leaders of the student protest movement were, according to his famous phrase, "an effete corps of impudent snobs who characterize themselves as intellectuals."[11] As he explained, "I call them snobs for most of them disdain to mingle with the masses who work for a living. They mock the common man's pride in his work, his family and his country."[12]

In retrospect, however, Agnew can be seen as a snob who set himself above honest critics of the war. Beneath his eagerness to debunk anyone who disagreed with him was hypocrisy about his own pettiness. On October 10, 1973, he was forced to resign as vice president because of charges of bribery and tax evasion during his earlier career as county executive of Baltimore County in Maryland. In that role he had awarded county engineering contracts on the basis of lucrative kickbacks. As the example of Agnew suggests, both snobs and people who are eager to call others snobs can be hypocrites.

Snobbery can involve other vices in addition to cruelty, arrogance, and hypocrisy. It may be accompanied by cowardice and disloyalty when, for example, one fears being seen in the company of certain relatives and friends lest they lower one's social status among the "in-group" to which one belongs. It can express a lack of collegiality when one snubs colleagues and co-workers in order to be accepted by a small group of "superior" people. It can lead one to ignore the needs of entire groups of people from whom one turns away as part of a preoccupation with a selected social group.

Summary

Put-downs are attempts to hurt by making people feel inferior or by encouraging other people to view them as inferior. Three common forms of put-downs are acts of rudeness, emotions of malicious amusement, and attitudes of snobbery.

Humor is the enjoyment of incongruities for their own sake through laughter or episodic cheerfulness. It is bad when the enjoyment comes at the expense of others, and malicious when others are intentionally degraded. Bigoted humor expresses prejudice and reinforces negative stereotypes. We have no right to laugh at groups in ways that alienate them, although in special circumstances we can laugh with someone who does have the right to tell an otherwise inappropriate joke. Everything depends on the context and motives.

Rudeness is a concept overlapping etiquette and ethics. Although rudeness typically involves violating the conventions of etiquette, it is really a matter of being insensitive to the feelings of other people rather than a matter of rules. As with the ethics of humor, the ethics of rudeness requires attention to context, awareness of changing norms, and balancing of authentic expressions of one's tastes with the requirements of social decorum. Occasionally, rudeness is justified, as with some rude responses to insults.

Snobs feel superior to people outside their in-group, whether that group is defined by intellect, tastes, wealth, social status, or any number of other things. Often, snobs are cruel in making others feel inferior. Usually, they are arrogant hypocrites who fail to have a reasonable perspective on the modest nature of their own achievements. Frequently, they betray relatives and former friends as they aspire to be seen only with their in-group.

DISCUSSION TOPICS

1. It was charged that Earl Butz expressed prejudice toward black people, but this claim was made without supplying any autobiographical details showing he was a racist. It was also argued that sometimes telling what would normally be a bigoted joke is morally permissible. How could we know that Butz's joke expressed prejudice?

2. Describe a situation in which telling the following jokes would be morally objectionable and a situation (if there is one) in which they would not:

   What's black and catches flies?
   —Willie Mays (former centerfielder of the San Francisco Giants).[13]

   Who are the three most dangerous men in the world?
   —An Italian with a gun, a Mexican with a driver's license, and a Frenchman with a chipped tooth.[14]

What is the difference between a Jewish Mother and a vulture?
—A vulture waits until you are dead to eat your heart out.[15]

Men have only two faults: Everything they say and everything they do.[16]

3. When, if ever, is it all right to use humor to ridicule behind their backs people who are difficult to live with?

4. How would you respond to someone who justified laughing at a sexist joke because it was so funny he or she could not help laughing? In general, is laughter a spontaneous reaction not under our control? If it is, should we refrain from criticizing people for feeling amused by bigoted jokes that other people tell them?

5. Is it rude not to open doors for women, or does opening doors for them express or support the assumption that women are weak and in need of help?

6. Is much snobbery inevitable, as the following passage from Judith N. Shklar suggests?

> Our most genuine experiences of equality, of intimacy, and of fraternity occur only within a "clique"—that is, in an excluding group of like-minded people, modeled on that most irreducible and necessary of all societies, the family. Many groups do not have exclusion as their main object, and some are hardly aware of it; but whatever their real ends may be, they exclude by including selectively. Snobbery is the by-product of this multiplicity, and it is a personal price that must occasionally be paid for the sake of freedom. Not all doors are or can be open.[17]

SUGGESTED READINGS

De Sousa, Ronald. "When Is It Wrong to Laugh?" In *The Rationality of Emotion*. Cambridge, MA: MIT Press, 1987.

Dundes, Alan. *Cracking Jokes: Studies of Sick Humor Cycles and Stereotypes*. Berkeley, CA: Ten Speed Press, 1987.

Martin, Mike W. "Humor and Aesthetic Enjoyment of Incongruities." In John Morreal (ed.), *The Philosophy of Laughter and Humor*. Albany, NY: State University of New York Press, 1987.

Morreall, John (ed.). *The Philosophy of Laughter and Humor*. Albany, NY: State University of New York Press, 1987.

Morreall, John. *Taking Laughter Seriously*. Albany, NY: State University of New York Press, 1983.

Philips, Michael. "Racist Acts and Racist Humor." *Canadian Journal of Philosophy*, vol. 15 (1984).

Schopenhauer, Arthur. *The World as Will and Representation*. Trans. E. F. J. Payne. New York: Dover, 1969. Vol. I, pp. 58–61; Vol. II, pp. 91–101.

Shklar, Judith N. "What Is Wrong with Snobbery?" In *Ordinary Vices*. Cambridge, MA: Harvard University Press, 1984. Pp. 87–137.

Thackeray, William M. *The Book of Snobs*. In W. P. Trent and J. B. Henneman (eds.),

The Complete Works of William M. Thackeray. Vol. XIV. New York: Thomas Y. Crowell [undated]. Pp. 1–240.

Warren, Virginia L. "Elitism in Higher Education." Unpublished manuscript, Chapman College, 1988.

Woodruff, Paul. "Rousseau, Molière, and the Ethics of Laughter." *Philosophy and Literature,* vol. 1 (1976–77).

CHAPTER 12

Envy and Jealousy

Envy is a potent motive for engaging in put-downs, whether through insults, ridicule, or rudeness. It is a form of unjustified hatred and a desire for others not to have their good fortune. As such, envy is immoral, even when it is not expressed in outward attacks on others. Moreover, envy is based on a perception that one is inferior or a feeling that one's self-esteem is threatened by someone else's well-being: Whereas the snob feels superior, the envious person feels inferior. Envy is the experience of feeling diminished by someone else's possessions, achievements, or virtues. It means hating them for their good fortune and wanting to see it taken away or destroyed. Because envy involves both disrespect for others and lessened self-esteem, our discussion in this chapter joins together the topics in Part Two and Part Three of this book.

Envy as a Vice

The word *envy* has several meanings, two of which do not concern us and will be set aside: (1) envy as admiration and (2) envy as merely desiring what someone else has. When a person we respect wins a contest or receives an award, we might compliment them by saying, "I envy you." This conveys our admiration and expresses a wish that we had been worthy to be recognized in a similar fashion. Using the word *envy* adds to the compliment by making it more personal, as if we were saying, "What you have done is so superb I wish I had been able to do it." In contrast, *envy* in the more traditional sense used here is something we would be unlikely to acknowledge openly. As mentioned previously, this type of envy entails unjustified hatred of others because of their good fortune, as well as desire to see that fortune taken away. The good fortune of the other person strikes us as a personal affront that intimidates and rankles us and makes us feel inferior or even worthless.

Envy differs substantially from justified resentment and indignation. When someone steals from us, we are justified in responding with indignation, that is, anger over the injustice. And when someone wins an award that we deserved, it is appropriate to feel resentment, that is, indignant displeasure. Envy, by contrast, is unjustified spite. For example, we despise a colleague who won an award we wanted, we become less friendly toward a classmate who was accepted into the fraternity or sorority we wanted to join, we hate a brother for his professional achievements, or we detest all people who graduate from universities having a higher reputation than does our college.

Envy should also be distinguished from jealousy. When we feel envy, we perceive ourselves as being inferior to others and desire that they be brought down to or below our level. When we feel jealousy, however, we feel injured and hurt rather than inferior. And as we shall see, jealousy, unlike envy, is not always unjustified and bad. It is no surprise that medieval Christians included envy as one of the Seven Deadly Sins. Envy is malicious; it is unwarranted hatred manifested in disrespect and contempt for other human beings who have done nothing to wrong us—except to prosper in ways we don't want them to. When envy is not overcome, it has the potential to endure indefinitely and even to dominate an entire life.

Particular Envy

Envy takes two forms, particular and general.[1] General envy entails hating entire classes of people because they have a type of good thing that we want for ourselves and that we want them not to have. For example, we hate all rich people or we detest all people with greater intellectual or athletic abilities. Particular envy, by contrast, is directed toward specific individuals with whom we compare ourselves or against whom we compete.

A vivid example of particular envy is found in Salieri, a character in Peter Shaffer's play and movie *Amadeus*. The character is based on a composer who was a contemporary of Wolfgang Amadeus Mozart during the late eighteenth century. Salieri rose to prominence and became the official court composer for Austria's emperor. From his youth on he burned with the ambition to become the greatest composer of his day, but that ambition was shattered when he encountered Mozart, whose talents were vastly superior to his own.

It was a tribute to Salieri's genuine abilities that he, unlike most of his peers, could fully appreciate the majesty of Mozart's inspired music. His appreciation was tainted, however, with intense bitterness. Not only did confronting Mozart make him feel inferior, empty, worthless, it also generated rage against Mozart and a desire to see Mozart's superiority overthrown. The rage was accompanied by a sense of powerlessness to do anything about his inferiority. These, then, are the primary ingredients of particular envy: feelings of inferiority, hatred, and impotence.

Tortured by the envy, Salieri sets out to destroy Mozart. When asked about Mozart's talents, he downplays his musical compositions. Using his influence as court composer, he prevents Mozart from obtaining the work and public recognition he deserved. When he learns later that Mozart is suffering from guilt and hallucinations following the death of his father, he proceeds to push him over the edge of sanity. Discovering that Mozart's hallucinations contain a father figure wearing a black mask and cape, he mimics the figure and appears at Mozart's apartment to requisition a "death mass." Then he forces Mozart to complete the work at a frantic pace, periodically appearing outside the window of the apartment. The combination of alcoholism, overwork, poverty, and tortured guilt causes Mozart to die at the young age of thirty-five, but even Mozart's death does not end Salieri's self-imposed suffering. Rather, his envy continues as Mozart's reputation grows following his death.

Amadeus, we might add, explores envy within a religious context. When Salieri devoted his life to music at age sixteen, he promised God he would be morally conscientious if only God would grant him sufficient fame to enjoy his work as a composer. When he realized that Mozart's accomplishments would undermine his fame, he swore vengeance against God. God, he reasoned, had chosen to make Mozart rather than himself his musical mouthpiece. Hence, God could be attacked by destroying Mozart. Recast in secular terms, the play suggests that in envy it is *as if* we are outraged over a fate that made us inferior. In retaliation we assault the person who received the superiority we want for ourselves.

General Envy

Whereas particular envy is directed toward rivals and competitors, general envy is aimed at entire groups of people who possess a good. For example, a person may hate all rich people or despise all owners of BMW cars. Much class hatred is of this sort, such as blue collar workers' hostility toward white collar workers and white collar workers' contempt for anyone who inherits great wealth.

Some philosophers claim that general envy underlies strict egalitarianism; that is, the insistence on all people being the same, especially in wealth or prestige. Strict egalitarians despise anyone better off than them, as well as anyone with greater virtue. In their eyes everyone with unusually good fortune has an unfair advantage, and anyone claiming higher virtues is a snob. Friedrich Nietzsche, for example, viewed strict egalitarianism as a moral distortion that expresses the self-interest of mediocre people who feel impotent to strive for greatness. The person who constantly downgrades and criticizes as unjust anyone better off than them is probably expressing envy:

> You preachers of equality, the tyrannomania of impotence clamors thus out of you for equality: your most secret ambitions to be tyrants thus shroud themselves in words of virtue. Aggrieved conceit, repressed envy . . . erupt from you as a flame and as the frenzy of revenge.[2]

Nietzsche was alarmed by how societies were becoming increasingly uniform and morally bland. Democratic ideals, in his view, were being misused to justify the attitude that everyone is equally virtuous and no one is more noble or heroic than everyone else.*

This aspect of Nietzsche's thought was developed by the Spanish philosopher José Ortega y Gasset (1883–1955). In *The Revolt of the Masses* Ortega argued that modern societies pull down everything valuable to the level of average persons who make up the masses. A contemporary illustration is the almost uniformly mediocre programming offered by commercial television and radio in response to advertisers' demands for mass audiences. This "herd mentality," as Nietzsche contemptuously referred to it, undermines the higher standards that societies ought to promote. In such an atmosphere, Ortega suggests, noble individuals strive to achieve excellence, even when it is beyond their grasp:

> For me, then, nobility is synonymous with a life of effort, ever set on excelling oneself, in passing beyond what one is [at a given moment] to what one sets up as a duty and an obligation. In this way the noble life stands opposed to the common or inert life, which reclines statically upon itself, condemned to perpetual immobility, unless an external force compels it to come out of itself.[3]

Because general envy leads to hatred on a large scale, involving entire classes of people, it has the potential to disrupt societies. For this reason it is an important issue in social ethics (which explores how to achieve good societies) as well as everyday ethics. In this regard two very different approaches to envy are reflected in a fundamental disagreement between John Rawls and Robert Nozick over social justice.

Rawls and Nozick agree that all people ought to have the same basic liberties, such as the right to speak freely, to vote, and to have educational opportunities. But they differ sharply over how far government should intervene in economic systems to redistribute wealth from the rich to the poor. Rawls thinks there should be limits on how much people are allowed to keep from their earnings: Differences in wealth are justified only as they ultimately work to everyone's benefit. For example, people should be allowed to become mil-

---

*Some of my students have insisted that there are no real heroes, and that everyone is basically alike—an attitude that Nietzsche would abhor.

lionaires if this practice leads to investments that help disadvantaged people, perhaps by creating jobs through investments in companies. It is unjust, however, to allow vast disparities in wealth between millionaires and people below the poverty line who are not benefited in any way by millionaires.

In this connection Rawls contends that the envious hostility felt by impoverished people is understandable:

> Sometimes the circumstances evoking envy are so compelling that given human beings as they are no one can reasonably be asked to overcome his rancorous feelings. . . . Indeed, we can resent being made envious, for society may permit such large disparities . . . that under existing conditions these differences cannot help but cause a loss of self-esteem. For those suffering this hurt, envious feelings are not irrational.[4]

Perhaps this "reasonable envy" is better viewed as a form of justified indignation. In any case Rawls is clearly worried about the possibility of general envy being disruptive within societies like ours where differences in wealth are enormous. He believes that governments have an obligation to find ways to prevent such painful disparities in wealth so as to minimize the harm done by general envy.

In sharp contrast, Robert Nozick insists that envy should never be used to restrict the economic rights of others. As a libertarian Nozick believes that people should be left alone to earn and spend as they choose within a free economy without interference. Government should have only the minimal role of providing the prerequisites for people to earn as much as they choose within a free enterprise system (for example, by providing for national defense and enforcing laws about contract agreements). Government has no right, however, to restrict the wealth of some groups merely because it might cause envy among other groups.

> It would be objectionable to intervene to reduce someone's situation in order to lessen the envy and unhappiness others feel in knowing of his situation. Such a policy is comparable to one that forbids some act (for example, racially mixed couples walking holding hands) because the mere knowledge that it is being done makes others unhappy.[5]

"Ressentiment" and Self-Deceiving Envy

Just as we are unlikely to admit our envy openly, we tend not to acknowledge it to ourselves. Doing so would force us to confront several unflattering truths: that we hate without justification, that we feel painfully inferior, and that our sense of self-esteem is so flimsy as to depend on the misfortune of others. In avoiding these painful truths, we tend to deceive ourselves about envy, and when we do, the envy often finds devious ways of expressing itself.

Nietzsche used the French word *ressentiment* to refer to unconscious envy and other forms of repressed hatred. His insights were clarified and developed by the philosopher-sociologist Max Scheler (1874–1928) in a book entitled *Ressentiment*. According to Scheler, *ressentiment* arises not only when we feel inferior, hostile, and impotent to better our situation, but also when we feel unable to suffer and confront these feelings. We lack a way to remove the feelings through improved self-understanding, or to express them openly in a way that will help weaken their intensity:

> Revenge, envy, the impulse to detract, spite, *Schadenfreude* [i.e., enjoying someone's misfortune], and malice lead to *ressentiment* only if there occurs neither a moral self-conquest . . . nor an act or some other adequate expression of emotion (such as verbal abuse or shaking one's fist), and if this restraint is caused by a pronounced awareness of impotence. . . . *Ressentiment* can only arise if these emotions are particularly powerful and yet must be suppressed because they are coupled with the feeling that one is unable to act them out.[6]

Self-deception about envy and other forms of hatred leads to a loss of conscious supervision over such emotions, but the hate does not go away. It is merely released through more subtle avenues than Salieri's open campaign of vengeance. For example, under the guise of moral criticism a snide remark is made about a rival's despicable dishonesty in attaining recognition we wanted for ourselves. Or hate finds an outlet through explosive fits of anger over minor inconveniences, only the hate and anger are rechanneled toward other objects—we kick the dog or yell at a friend.

Sometimes an entire personality is taken over by *ressentiment,* with envy erupting in the form of hostility toward anyone better or more successful than oneself. But its most devastating effect, according to Scheler, is in distorting values: Value standards are lowered or corrupted so as to make us look good in our own eyes. Thus, for example, strict egalitarianism represents a sweeping attempt to level all values to the lowest common denominator. Another approach is to say that all values are subjective, which implies that one person's values are as good as anyone else's. On a more restricted scale someone might attack the practice of grading because it unfairly tries to distinguish and rate work that is essentially all the same—and because professors are all biased anyway.

Creative Responses to Envy

Because envy involves feelings of hatred, inferiority, and impotence, it can be overcome or weakened by removing any of these feelings. Occasionally, rational reflection by itself enables us to purge the feelings by seeing their unreasonableness. Usually, however, deeper emotional adjustments are required. Hating other people for their good fortune is best tackled with a combination of the following: (1) increasing confidence in one's ability to achieve one's own good fortune; (2) strengthening the basis of one's self-esteem so it becomes more durable and less prone to collapse when confronted by others' well-being; and (3) increasing one's capacity to appreciate, rather than hate, others' achievements.

First, one can strengthen one's self-confidence simply by taking risks and by learning about one's abilities through reflecting on one's successes and failures. Of course, the capacity to take risks presupposes having some self-confidence to begin with. But one's resources, together with the support of friends and family, usually suffice to get things underway.

Second, one can develop a more stable sense of self-worth in several ways. One way is to discover one's talents and to develop them through work and relationships. Kant recommended a second way: Focus on values themselves rather than on how well other people excel.[7] Directing attention to ideals and standards of excellence will no doubt make one feel humble for failing to live up to them. But feeling humble—recognizing our imperfection—differs from feeling inferior. Humility is a creative attitude and emotion that motivates us to continue our efforts, whereas envy is a destructive emotion that motivates us to harm others.

Sometimes, further effort is impossible or unlikely to help. Resigning oneself to one's true nature thus may be both necessary and liberating. For example, elderly persons may find this the only way to release their envy of the young. And at every stage of life there is a need for self-acceptance of personal limits instead of an undertaking of unrealistic competitions. Nietzsche put the point nicely in a passage quoted in Chapter 7 and requoted in part here:

> For one thing is needful: that a human being should *attain* satisfaction with himself, whether it be by means of this or that poetry and art; only then is a human being at all tolerable to behold. Whoever is dissatisfied with himself is continually ready for revenge, and we others will be his victims.[8]

Third, the noblest way to overcome envy is to transform it into admiration and emulation. Salieri would have displayed nobility had he found a way to transform his hostility toward Mozart into enjoyment of Mozart's music. Doing so would also have enriched his life by replacing hostility with new sources of delight. Envy, after all, already contains the seeds of admiration because it typically involves appreciating the values realized in other lives. Certainly this was true of Salieri, who was at least able to see Mozart's genius. In fact, with this in mind, envy may be surprisingly close to another life-enriching attitude: gratitude for the presence of gifted people who inspire and challenge us to do our own personal best.

Jealousy

Jealousy and envy often occur together, and it is easy to confuse them even though they are distinct emotions and attitudes. For one thing, whereas envy centers on hatred, jealousy centers on a sense of injury and loss. We are jealous when we believe we have lost or are threatened with losing something important to us. Most often we fear the loss of affection, love, or respect that we see going to someone else. Although jealousy may involve hatred, it need not. Frequently, we express a sense of injury or loss through the emotions of anger, sadness, depression, or an aroused desire to assert ourselves in order to regain lost affection.

Furthermore, whereas it only takes two people for envy to occur, jealousy normally requires three—a triangle. For example, a brother is jealous of a brother because only one receives what both need: attention and recognition from their father. A worker is jealous of a co-worker because the latter received an award or bonus from the employer. A lover is jealous because the beloved favors a rival suitor.

Finally, whereas envy is tied to feelings of inferiority, jealousy derives from feelings of insecurity. It entails a fear that one will lose something dear, or it brings a painful collapse after losing a hoped-for relationship. The vulnerability caused by love renders even the most secure person vulnerable to the insecurities of jealousy. For example, in Shakespeare's tragedy *Othello,* the title character, Othello, the secure and successful military leader, becomes intensely jealous when he (mistakenly) suspects his wife Desdemona of having an affair with his lieutenant, Cassio. (Note that Iago, who plots to make Othello feel this way, is motivated by envy, not jealousy.) Othello's jealousy and doubts about Desdemona's faithfulness become an obsession. He cannot work, love, or think rationally, and in a final rage he kills Desdemona.

Evaluating Jealousy

Is jealousy, like envy, always bad? It certainly has a bad reputation. Othello reminds us of its potential to foster destructive anger and hate. More recently, the 1960s free-love movement attempted to portray jealousy as based on an ugly attitude of possessiveness. The jealous person was viewed as treating his or her lover as a commodity that can be owned. Love, the free-love movement insisted, must be freely given and received as a gift, never claimed as a property right. As recently as 1982, Richard Taylor defended this assessment of jealousy:

> Jealousy is the most wrenching and destructive of human passions. Not only is it painful, but the pain is self-inflicted; and unlike most other emotions, no good ever comes from it. . . . Jealousy always has its source in something almost as ugly as itself; namely, in the attitude of possessiveness towards another person.[9]

Taylor viewed jealousy as destructive of love, or at least of erotic love (which was his main concern):

> Possessive love, as it might be called, is no real expression of love at all, but its perversion. Loving an *object* is not really loving *it* at all; instead, it is an expression of self-love. A person who takes pride in his possessions, who glories in them, quite clearly does not love them for their own sake, but for his. They are just ornaments.[10]

Is this entirely negative evaluation of jealousy fair? Granted, jealousy can become pathological and involve immoral attitudes of owning other people and their affection. But it need not. In fact, jealousy is very often a sign of love! Consider the traditional "love game" designed to test whether someone really cares about us. We contrive a situation in which the person being tested sees us with some attractive rival. Our goal is that the person will show displeasure, thereby confirming our hope that the person desires our affection, and that the person will become more ardent in pursuing us.

To be sure, this is a *game,* most often a childish game of the sort encountered in soap operas. It can even cause harm when it backfires by causing the beloved to feel betrayed or abandoned. Nevertheless, it provides a clue to a deeper truth: Feeling jealousy shows we care about the attention and affection of another, and this is frequently a sign of love. Imagine a married couple who are utterly incapable of feeling jealousy toward each other. No matter how much time, affection, and sexual attention both spouses devote to others, the partners never feel a twinge of jealousy. Either they are extraordinarily confident about never losing whatever it is they need from each other, or they do not care very deeply about each other.

Jerome Neu put the point this way: "Behind jealousy lies love. . . . [For] 'jealousy' includes a positive evaluation of, or attachment to, the person (or thing or property) one is jealous over or about. One can be jealous only of something that it highly valued."[11] As Neu also emphasizes, jealousy may be an inevitable aspect of some personal relationships. Intimate love relationships usually demand large amounts of time and energy, and time and energy are limited quantities. It is understandable that jealousy will play a role when these quantities become too diffused away from the relationship.

Even if we grant that jealousy is frequently a sign of love, and perhaps an inescapable aspect of intimate relationships, does any real good ever come from it? Would anything be lost if all jealousy suddenly disappeared from human experience?

Something might indeed be lost. Two good things can be said about at least some jealousy, assuming it does not become obsessive and cruel. First, jealousy provides a helpful vehicle for self-discovery: Honest reflection on jealousy can yield insights about who we love and how deeply we love them (as the previous comments imply). Second, jealousy sometimes helps to protect and preserve love and friendship. It functions as an emotional alarm warning us that caring relationships may be at risk from outsiders. As with the emotion of fear, jealousy can provide a painful but prompt warning before we can even articulate our concern for a relationship. Moreover, jealousy can strengthen, albeit temporarily, the ardor with which love is expressed, because we put more attention into valuable things when we believe they are at risk. In this role it serves on occasion to help sustain intimate and caring relationships.

Summary

Envy entails hating a person (particular envy) or a group of people (general envy) because they have something we do not want them to have (and usually want for ourselves). When self-deception causes envy to be expressed through unconscious spite, it is called *ressentiment*. Jealousy, by contrast, means feeling that we have lost or may lose something dear to us.

Envy and jealousy differ in several ways. First, envy need involve only two parties; jealousy usually involves three (we are jealous of rivals because they have received a benefit from a third party). Second, envy is always accompanied by hatred; jealousy may lead to hatred, but more often it causes anger (as well as fear, sadness, and depression). Third, envy derives from a feeling of inferiority or lowered self-esteem (because someone is perceived as fortunate); jealousy derives more from fear or from loss of hope in obtaining something valuable. Fourth, envy entails feelings of impotence to change the good fortune of others; jealousy more often sparks an angry impulse to prevent a competitor from winning or keeping the good one seeks.

The moral statuses of envy and jealousy also differ. Envy is always bad because at its core is unwarranted hate (unlike resentment, in which one's anger may be fully justified). Jealousy is sometimes very bad, as when it becomes obsessive and destroys loving relationships. But sometimes it has good effects: aiding self-understanding, warning of dangers to relationships, and evoking increased attention to a relationship.

Envy is overcome or weakened when one of its three aspects is removed or lessened. Feelings of hate, inferiority, and impotence can be overcome through strengthening self-confidence, self-esteem, and the capacity to appreciate the talents and achievements of other people.

DISCUSSION TOPICS

1. This chapter emphasized the bad of envy and the good of jealousy. Based on your own experience, is this emphasis unjustified? Have you found that jealousy tends to do far more bad than good, and can you see some possible good effects of envy (such as stimulating us to compete more fiercely)?

2. Read the following passage:

> Consider a relationship stricken by envy. A friend joyfully shares the news of her fine achievement. The less successful friend wishes to, wants to, intends to, and indeed tries to create a sincere congratulation fitting with the excellence of her accomplishment and the warmth of their friendship. But he botches it. The congratulations come out forced, choked, diminished, and cool.[12]

Describe two possible aftermaths, one in which the envy destroys the friendship and one in which the envy is overcome and the relationship stays intact. That is, what might lead things to develop in the one way rather than the other?

3. It was suggested that strict egalitarianism is often motivated by envy. But what if the central motive for affirming egalitarianism is a desire to help impoverished people rather than to hurt advantaged people. Where the motive is to "pull up" the poor rather than to "pull down" the rich, need there by any envy involved?

4. Apply the following passage, written by Henry Fairlie, to Salieri:

> The envious man does not love himself, although he begins with self-love. He is not grateful for, or happy in, what he is or what he has. The sin is deadly, less because it destroys him, than because it will not let him live. It will not let him live as himself, grateful for his qualities and talents, such as they are, and making the best and most rewarding use of them. His disparagement of others is a reflection of his disparagement of himself; he regards himself with as much malice as he regards them.[13]

5. Kant wrote that "the three vices which are the essence of vileness and wickedness are ingratitude, envy, and malice. When these reach their full degree they are devilish."[14] What connections do you see among these three vices? Do they perhaps share a common core?

6. To covet is to desire another's possessions excessively or in an otherwise improper manner. How is coveting related to envy and to jealousy?

SUGGESTED READINGS

Fairlie, Henry. *The Seven Deadly Sins Today.* Notre Dame, IN: University of Notre Dame Press, 1979.

Farber, Leslie H. *Lying, Despair, Jealousy, Envy, Sex, Suicide, Drugs, and the Good Life.* New York: Basic Books, 1976.

Friday, Nancy. *Jealousy.* New York: Morrow, 1985.

Gaylin, Willard. *Feelings: Our Vital Signs.* New York: Ballantine Books, 1979.

Kant, Immanuel. "Jealousy and Its Offspring—Envy and Grudge." In Lewis White Beck (ed. and trans.), *Lectures on Ethics.* New York: Harper & Row, 1963.

Klein, Melanie. *Envy and Gratitude and Other Works.* London: Hogarth Press, 1975.

Lyons, William. *Emotion.* Cambridge: Cambridge University Press, 1980.

Neu, Jerome. "Jealous Thoughts." In Amèlie Oksenberg Rorty (ed.), *Explaining Emotions.* Berkeley, CA: University of California Press, 1980.

Nietzsche, Friedrich. "On the Tarantulas." In *Thus Spoke Zarathustra,* trans. Walter Kaufmann. New York: Penguin, 1978. Pp. 99–102.

Nisbet, Robert. "Covetousness" and "Envy." In *Prejudices.* Cambridge, MA: Harvard University Press, 1982. Pp. 63–66, 107–109.

Nozick, Robert. "Self-Esteem and Envy." In *Anarchy, State, and Utopia.* New York: Basic Books, 1974. Pp. 239–246.

Ortega y Gasset, José. *The Revolt of the Masses.* New York: Norton, 1957.

Rawls, John. "The Problem of Envy" and "Envy and Equality." In *A Theory of Justice.* Cambridge, MA: Harvard University Press, 1971. Pp. 530–541.

Sabini, John, and Maury Silver. "Envy." In *Moralities of Everyday Life.* Oxford: Oxford University Press, 1982. Pp. 15–33.

Scheler, Max. *Ressentiment.* Trans. William W. Holdheim. Lewis A. Coser (ed.). New York: Schocken, 1972.

Schoeck, Helmut. *Envy: A Theory of Social Behavior.* Trans. Michael Glenny and Betty Ross. London: Secker & Warburg, 1969.

Shaffer, Peter. *Amadeus.* New York: New American Library, 1984.

Shakespeare, William. *Othello.* New York: New American Library, 1963.

Solomon, Robert C. *The Passions.* Notre Dame, IN: University of Notre Dame Press, 1983.

Tov-Ruach, Leila. "Jealousy, Attention, and Loss." In Amelie Oksenberg Rorty (ed.), *Explaining Emotions.* Berkeley, CA: University of California Press, 1980.

PART FOUR

Sexual Morality

It is through sex . . . that each individual has to pass in order to have access to his own intelligibility . . . to his own identity. . . . Hence the importance we ascribe to it, the reverential fear with which we surround it, the care we take to know it. Hence the fact that over the centuries it has become more important than our soul, more important almost than our life.[1]

Michel Foucault

Sexual desire, according to traditional attitudes, is a valuable but danger-ous force needing control through a swarm of prohibitions. Its moral status centers on the biological purpose of producing children and is specified by five mandates: (1) to refrain from sexual activity until marriage, (2) to en-gage in marital sex without preventing the conception of children, (3) to refrain from sex with anyone but one's spouse, (4) to choose a spouse of the opposite sex, and (5) to love one's sexual partner, that is, one's spouse. One variation on this traditional view emphasizes that sex is morally significant in supporting love between married partners, in addition to its role in creat-ing children.

The sexual revolution of the 1960s challenged these mandates by ques-tioning the requirement to join sex with love, marriage, and children. It accepted or advocated sex outside marriage, contraception, sex with more than one person, homosexuality, and sex without love. In the name of free-dom (autonomy, self-determination) and respect for others' freedom, proponents of the sexual revolution accepted virtually all forms of sexual expression by consenting participants.

Philosophical thinking about sex emerged largely in response to the sexual revolution. Prior to the 1960s few philosophers regarded sex as a worthy topic.* Since 1970, however, philosophers have devoted increasing attention to the topics dealt with in the following four chapters: the moral relationships between sex and love, marriage and adultery, homosexuality and homophobia, and pornography and fantasy, respectively.

Some have argued that the sexual revolution is over and that the horrifying epidemic of AIDS (Acquired Immune Deficiency Syndrome), as well as the increase in other, albeit less deadly, sexually transmitted diseases, is forcing a renewed interest in more traditional values. Others hope that sexual attitudes are undergoing a gradual evolution that will bring about a synthesis of the best ideas and attitudes of the sexual revolution and traditional perspectives. In any case sexuality is a central topic for everyday ethics and for understanding our personal identity and relationships.

---

*A notable exception was Bertrand Russell (1872–1970), whose defense of sex outside marriage—"free love"—prompted universities to ban him from teaching for over two decades.

CHAPTER 13

Sex and Love

What is the moral relationship between sex and love? Is there an obligation to restrict sex to relationships involving love? Is the insistence that sex be accompanied by love based on a degrading view of sexuality—that sex is bad and in need of redemption by love? Is so-called true love a kind of illusion and trap, or at least so fraught with peril that it is best avoided?

In Marilyn French's novel *The Women's Room* a character named Val contends that sex ought to be separated from love. Val, a thirty-nine-year-old Harvard student, has come to believe that erotic love is a biological illusion and a trap for women:

> Love is insanity. . . . It is the taking over of a rational and lucid mind by delusion and self-destruction. You lose yourself, you have no power over yourself, you can't even think straight. That's the reason I hate it.[1]

By the time people recover from this insanity—and sooner or later they always do—they are often married and have children. According to Val this works out well for men who wish to have wives at home with their children, but less well for women, who usually end up getting hurt.

Even though she rejects erotic love, Val is not cynical about sex once it is freed from love. Indeed,

> for her, sex was almost a philosophy. She saw the whole world in terms of it. . . . Val slept with people the way other people go out for dinner with a friend. She liked them, she liked sex. She rarely expected anything from it beyond the pleasure of the moment. At the same time, she said it was overrated: it had been so tabooed, she claimed, that we had come to expect paradise from it. It was only fun, great fun, but not paradise.[2]

189

Definitions of Love

By "love" Val seems to mean romantic idealization: the process whereby two lovers exaggerate each other's beauty and goodness and become oblivious to each other's faults. We sometimes refer to such love as an infatuation that distorts one's normal degree of reasonableness. But is that true love?

Most of us distinguish "true" or "genuine" love—the "real thing"—from a variety of more superficial infatuations. We draw the distinction in different ways, however, reflecting differences in the values we hold. "True love" is a value-laden expression: It refers to what is most valuable in intimate human relationships, and we can disagree about what that is. Consider just three different views of true love.

From the romantic perspective passion above all else is to be valued. Passion reflects an intense longing for someone accompanied by an obsessive preoccupation with that person. It contains large degrees of frenzied attention to everything about the beloved as being glorious. It is the state most often referred to as "falling in love," but we might just call it the "in love" state. This is the conception of love that Val rejects.

A contrasting conception stresses "loving" rather than being "in love." Loving means caring and commitment as opposed to passionate attention, although the caring on occasion is expressed through passion. In *The Art of Loving* the humanistic psychologist Erich Fromm developed a strongly moralized view of love along these lines. Love, he suggests, is the attitude characterized by giving, caring, responsibility, and respectfulness while maintaining one's own integrity and individuality. "Falling in love," by contrast, is an immature and selfish preoccupation. In fact, Fromm continues, any form of intense preoccupation with one individual can be a distortion of true love, which is always a general attitude of caring about people:

> Love is not primarily a relationship to a specific person; it is an *attitude,* an *orientation of character* which determines the relatedness of a person to the world as a whole, not toward one "object" of love. . . . If I truly love one person I love all persons, I love the world, I love life.[3]

It is difficult, however, to see how Fromm's attempt to view all love as general humanitarian caring (or as he calls it, "brotherly love") can apply to erotic love. Humanitarian caring is inclusive: It is addressed to many people at the same time. Erotic love is exclusive: It focuses great concern and attention on one person (or at most a few persons), excluding most others.

A third conception of love combines some elements from the romantic and humanitarian views while discarding others. Erotic love involves preoccupation with one individual, but in a caring and committed way. Thus, according to feminist Shulamith Firestone, erotic love entails an intermingling and reshaping of the personal identity of two equal partners. Each becomes "psychically wide-open" to the other, in terms of both complete emotional vulnerability and intellectual openness to the experience of the other. Commitment is crucial in order to create the trust and security needed to sustain this vulnerability. Yet the commitment is not entirely selfless. Instead, it is based on a mixture of caring and self-interest:

> The self attempts to enrich itself through the absorption of another being. . . . Love between two equals would be an enrichment, each enlarging himself through the other: instead of being one, locked in a cell of himself with only his own experience and view, he could participate in the existence of another—an extra window on the world.[4]

In addition, Firestone insists that true love involves mutual understanding, not illusion of the sort typical of romantic infatuation. In fact, love is a form of creative vision in which value is discerned (in the beloved) as well as affirmed and bestowed:

> Because of this fusion of egos, in which each sees and cares about the other as a new self, the beauty/character of the beloved, perhaps hidden to outsiders under layers of defenses, is revealed. . . . Increased sensitivity to the real, if hidden, values in the other . . . is not "blindness" or "idealization" but is, in fact, deeper vision.[5]

Yet Firestone would agree with Val that love is easily distorted in ways hurtful to women. She argues that until women have economic status and power equal to that of men, true love will remain difficult to achieve. Unequal power tends to make women vulnerable to exploitation by men, who tend to have difficulty in giving the commitment and the emotional openness required by love.

These three conceptions of love—a romantic, a humanitarian, and a feminist conception, respectively—are intended only as illustrations of how the expression "true love" is used to convey contrasting values. Love is not some simple "feeling," contrary to what contemporary popular music and romance novels assume. For the purposes of discussing the relationship between sex and love, however, it will be helpful to develop some minimal, simplifying definitions.

Erotic love or *sexual love* is love expressed through sex, which includes sexual arousal, desire, and activity (ranging from kissing to intercourse). The adjective *sexual* thus refers to bodily states involving genital excitement and to thoughts, pleasures, and desires (especially for other people) associated with that excitement. In contrast, *love* refers to an attitude that involves deeper affection for and commitment to the good of one's partner than is suggested by the term *liking*. *Liking* means having a positive attitude toward someone based on some attraction—finding that person "to one's taste." *Affection* is an emotion of concern for another person's well-being, an emotion that may last for a shorter time than does the attitude of liking.

Arguments for Sex Without Love

Russell Vannoy provides a philosophical defense of Val's attitudes in his book *Sex Without Love*. Vannoy focuses on people whom he calls "authentic" and "humanists." In keeping with Sartre's definition (Chapter 2), Vannoy defines authentic individuals as people who make decisions based on self-knowledge, with a minimum of external influences and in full awareness of relevant information. Humanists are individuals who value other people as having intrinsic worth and who display sensitivity, simple decency, and some generosity.

Vannoy believes that traditional views of sex are based on a simplistic dualism: Either sex is loving or it is a degrading indulgence for selfish purposes. He argues that there is a large middle ground between these two extremes. For example, sex can express simple affection, liking, friendship, sheer delight in the beauty of another person, and physical recreation based on mutual consent and desire. In this sense sex need not be degrading or exploitative, nor need it involve anything as serious as love, which implies deep emotional ties and commitment. Traditionalists, Vannoy argues, have simply failed to acknowledge the full possibilities of nonloving sex:

> It can be an evening of sensuous eroticism that may continue for hours and include all the foreplay, afterplay, kisses and caresses that actual lovers enjoy, perhaps done simply out of deep mutual admiration for each other's sensuous qualities and out of gratitude for having been chosen by the other for such an evening. Yet the pair may go their separate ways in the morning and never see each other again, perhaps because they prefer their own independence and singlehood to permanent emotional involvement and marriage.[6]

Furthermore, Vannoy defends sex without love outside of love relationships. Masturbation and fetishes, for example, provide pleasurable experiences for people who prefer more private modes of sexual expression. To deny that sex has many legitimate forms of expression outside love relationships is to embrace a degrading view of sex as redeemed only through love, marriage, and procreation.

In addition to arguing that sex without love is morally permissible for authentic humanists, Vannoy defends two further theses. On the one hand, he contends that much sex without love is better than sex with love—better in terms of pleasure and contribution to well-being. The practice of sex without love can yield higher degrees of excitement by allowing greater newness, variety, and romantic adventure, whereas sex between married partners tends to become boringly routine. Inevitably, the initial romantic intensity fades, leaving at best lukewarm companionship and at worst mutual hostility because other romantic options are lost. Also, love burdens sex with demands that partners perform satisfactorily. It threatens the delights of sex by burying them within delicately balanced and emotionally complex love relationships.

In this context affectionate sex without the burdens of commitment is far preferable.

On the other hand, Vannoy attacks erotic love as an incoherent ideal riddled with inconsistent demands and illusions that inevitably cause frustration and unhappiness. For example, love seeks to endure forever ("until death do us part" or "for all eternity") and simultaneously to be ecstatically exciting. But it cannot be both: The initial intensity always fades. Again, lovers want their partners to be overwhelmed with emotions so intense as to blind them to their flaws, and yet simultaneously to choose rationally to love them based on understanding them as they really are. They also want partners who feel a deep need to be dependent on them and a desire to serve their interests out of pure altruism, and yet who are secure and independent individuals with interests of their own.

In short, Vannoy argues for three theses: (1) All sex without love is morally permissible when engaged in by consenting and decent people; (2) much sex without love is better than sex with love; and (3) sexual love is an incoherent ideal. Can defenders of traditional views refute these theses?

Arguments for Sex with Love

Many defenses of traditional views of sex rely on appeals to God's commandments as interpreted by particular religions. Although it is understandable that religious faith will influence one's views of sexual morality, is it possible to defend traditional views without making controversial appeals to God?

Roger Scruton attempts such a defense in his book *Sexual Desire*. His defense is based on the Aristotelian view that virtue and self-fulfillment go together, as well as on the claim that sex has a natural role in contributing to self-fulfillment.

Scruton first reminds us that sexual desire is not merely a desire to engage in intercourse with a *body*. Instead, it is a desire for another *person* who is, like oneself, an embodied consciousness, that is, a conscious being in a body. More specifically, sexual desire entails a longing to unite with a person, whether the longing is focused in a desire to kiss, caress, or have intercourse or whether it is a less focused desire. It also implies a desire to have our partner desire us in similar ways and to enjoy being desired by us.

Sexual desires are satisfied through experiences of shared sexual excitement in which the consciousnesses of both partners are focused on the pleasures of their bodies. Scruton eloquently describes this "mutual embodiment, the other's 'being in' his body and I in mine": "In our excitement we sense each other's animation, and become acquainted with the pulsing of the spirit in the flesh, which fills the body with a pervasive 'I', and transforms it into something strange, precious and possessible."[7]

But what moral relevance does this experience have? When joined with love, it provides a unique way for two people to affirm each other's value. In doing so it teaches them to appreciate the basis of morality: the value of people as conscious beings with bodies. Without erotic love we would "appreciate less vividly the fundamental premise of morality: that the repository of infinite value which is the other self, exists not in some Platonic supersphere, but here in the flesh."[8] Thus, Scruton asserts, giving and receiving this form of appreciation and affirmation is a crucial aspect of fulfilling oneself:

> Erotic love involves an element of mutual self-enhancement; it generates a sense of the irreplaceable value, both of the other and of the self, and of the activities which bind them. To receive and to give this love is to achieve something of incomparable value in the process of self-fulfillment. It is to gain the most powerful of all interpersonal *guarantees;* in erotic love the subject becomes conscious of the full reality of his personal existence, not only in his own eyes, but in the eyes of another.[9]

Sex without love cannot yield this mutual affirmation of personal worth, which Scruton thinks is essential for self-fulfillment. Love affirms the interests of the beloved through a long-term commitment to promote them. Within love relationships sex becomes an expression and symbol of this enduring affirmation. In contrast, sex as a one-night stand, as a temporary recreation, or even with affection, is incapable of conveying the profound affirmation of the other person. Nor can masturbation and perversions (such as sex with animals and sex with dead people), which do not even involve two mutually excited conscious beings, convey any such affirmation.

Scruton elaborates on his ideal of "sexual integrity" based on mutual self-fulfillment by arguing against premarital sex. Postponing sexual activity until long-term marital commitments are possible is a way to preserve the connection between sex and love. He also argues against adultery on the grounds that it inevitably generates jealousy, which disrupts love. These topics will be addressed in subsequent chapters, as will be the qualms he expresses concerning homosexuality. For now, let us simply emphasize Scruton's belief that there is an obligation to join sex and love because doing so makes it possible for individuals to affirm each other's moral worth in a singularly important way that contributes to their self-fulfillment. How, then, would he respond to Vannoy's claims that sex without love is more exciting and that erotic love is an incoherent ideal?

Recall that Vannoy viewed much sex without love as more exciting because it offers greater variety, newness, and romance than does sex within long-term loving relationships. A traditionalist might admit there is a loss of newness and romance as partners become well acquainted with each other's bodies, but nevertheless insist that the loss is outweighed by the security and mutual affirmation offered by loving sex. Scruton, however, has a more positive rejoinder. He reminds us that erotic love offers unlimited variety, because sexual desire is focused on a conscious person, and consciousness is not something fixed:

> Sexual curiosity . . . renews itself endlessly; for the object of curiosity is not the bodily region as such, but the region "as inhabited by a pleased consciousness," and pleasure is a dynamic thing, which has a constantly shifting significance in the experience of the person who feels it.[10]

Sex within long-term relationships is as varied in what it expresses and affirms as are the two consciousnesses it joins together.

Is love an impossible ideal? Scruton might agree that it is when it involves the conflicting desires Vannoy lists: that love both last forever and provide constant ecstasy; that one's partner be overwhelmed by emotion and thereby blinded to one's flaws and yet rationally understand and appreciate one; that one's partner be perfectly altruistic and dependent on one and yet be an interesting and independent individual. But he would probably view these desires, in contrast with the rational desires involved in the kinds of self-fulfilling love he describes, as unreasonable and immature.

Scruton might also point out that mature love relationships provide recurring moments of ecstasy interspersed with caring support for partners' endeavors, allow for honest recognition of faults, and admit to elements of both strong dependency and independence. Scruton does agree with Vannoy on one point: Love requires a thoroughgoing union of interests. Whereas Vannoy finds that stifling, however, Scruton finds it liberating. This disagreement strikes at the heart of contemporary concerns to reconcile individuality and unity, or distinct and shared identities, in love relationships.

True Love: Obligations or Ideals?

We noted that *love* is a term whose meaning is tied to one's value perspective on human relationships, and we have mentioned several such perspectives. In conclusion let us ask whether the values that enter into conceptions of "true love" are universal obligations, as Scruton suggests, or moral ideals that individuals are free to embrace but that are not incumbent on everyone.

Scruton's defense of the traditional view of sex rests on the assumption that human sexuality has one "natural" aim in promoting self-fulfillment: to foster erotic love and its unique form of moral affirmation. Drawing on that assumption, he tries to demonstrate a general obligation to link sex and love. But is there any one "natural" role of sex in contributing to human fulfillment? Isn't sex capable of serving many legitimate roles in different lives, or in the same life at different stages?

There are many roads to self-fulfillment, and many avenues to finding affirmation of one's moral worth. Perhaps for some people the suppression or sublimation of sex is the best avenue, as with priests and nuns who take vows of chastity as part of a religious commitment. For other people (like Vannoy), who value variety and intensity of sexual passion, avoiding long-term commitments may contribute to self-fulfillment. For some, a variety of types of relationships, some long and some short, may be best. And for those who value the constancy, support, and depth of long-term relationships, the lifetime commitments advocated by Scruton will be best.

According to this line of thought there is no universal obligation to link sex and love in any one way. Instead, there are many permissible moral ideals concerning sex that individuals may choose among in seeking their self-fulfillment (and hopefully do so wisely, based on self-understanding). These are *moral* ideals in that they express visions of valuable forms of human relationships, ones that involve various combinations of affection, caring, mutual understanding, mutual respect, and long-term mutual commitments. Moreover, once embraced, some of the ideals generate obligations. In particular, when two people accept Scruton's ideal of long-term commitments, they acquire special obligations to conform to the ideal. The same is true for other moral ideals. When individuals devote themselves to special causes like alleviating world hunger and promoting world peace, they also acquire special obligations (as we shall discuss more fully in Chapter 20). There is, however, no one degree of commitment to these ideals that is obligatory for all individuals.

Recognizing a plurality of permissible sexual ideals should not be confused with embracing the attitude put forth in the 1960s that anything goes (as long as there is consent). For again, the sexual ideals can be evaluated by reference to the self-fulfillment and personal well-being of individuals and couples. There are often very good reasons for recommending to certain individuals and couples (given their psychological make-ups, and preferred lifestyles) that they pursue one ideal rather than another.

This pluralistic model of sexual morality would certainly complicate sexual relationships, because individuals would bring to relationships different ideals about what is desirable for them. But that is already largely true in our society. In any case, ideals are open to discussion and criticism by couples. They are also open to compromise, in the best sense of the term: reconciliation of differences by mutual concessions.

Summary

True love is a term used to express value perspectives concerning what relationships are most desirable. The romantic perspective focuses on passionate preoccupation with the beloved; Erich Fromm's humanitarian perspective stresses general caring for all people, even when expressed through a relationship with one person; and Shulamith Firestone's feminist perspective emphasizes emotional sharing between equals in a way that reshapes personal identity.

When is sex without love morally permissible? Russell Vannoy argues that it is permissible whenever the participants freely consent. He rejects the simple dichotomy between sex as expressing love and sex as a selfish indulgence, drawing attention to how sex can express affection, liking, and friendship. Roger Scruton argues that erotic love makes a unique contribution to self-fulfillment through mutual affirmation of the moral worth of embodied conscious beings. Perhaps, however, sex can contribute in a variety of ways to the fulfillment of individuals and couples, allowing for several morally permissible ideals concerning sex.

Is sex without love more exciting because it allows greater variety and romance with different partners? Perhaps it is for some individuals. But as Scruton points out, sexual desire is directed toward persons whose consciousness is as alive as one's own, and this enables long-term relationships to offer unlimited variety in what is enjoyed and expressed through sex.

Is sexual love an incoherent ideal, as Vannoy charges? Must it involve conflicting desires, such as for constant ecstasy and lastingness, overwhelming emotions and calm rationality, dependence and independence for both partners, unity and individuality? Although immature forms of love are characterized by incompatible demands, mature love need not be. As Shulamith Firestone suggests, love involves a profound reshaping of personal identity within a caring relationship with another person.

DISCUSSION TOPICS

1. Is there a universal moral obligation to refrain from sex except when it expresses deep affection and lasting commitment? Or are all forms of sexual expression morally permissible, so long as they are based on consent and respect for one's partner's consent?

2. In what ways is sex with love better than sex without love, and vice versa?

3. Firestone believes that (genuine) erotic love is possible only between individuals who are equal in the kinds of power that mutual economic independence provides. Presumably, two people need not earn the same income, but both must be able to live from their own incomes; otherwise, harmful forms of dependency arise. In contrast, Robert Solomon contends that love only requires equality of consent— that is, both partners agree to the roles they play in the relationship. Do you agree with what he says in the following passage?

   But what does "equality" mean in relations? It does not mean "being the same." It does not exclude all sorts of asymmetrical and uneven roles and relationships, including the absolute domination of one person by the other. It does not require, as such, the equal division of housework or "bread earn-ing" tasks. . . . Equality in love essentially means a mutually-agreed upon indeterminacy . . . in which one's self-images and personal roles and identity are up for grabs, in negotiation with one other person, in which there are no preordained roles or predestined status relationships.[11]

4. Is it possible to erotically love more than one person at the same time? Before answering this question, first discuss what you take it to mean. Are we asking whether one person could experience certain emotions at the same time toward more than one person? Are we asking a practical question about whether there is enough time and energy to pursue more than one relationship at a time? Or are we asking a value question concerning which kind of relationships have the highest value?

5. The French romantic novelist Stendhal (1783–1842) argued that passionate romantic love is the highest form of love and that it always involves an element of illusion: "From the moment he falls in love even the wisest man no longer sees anything *as it really is*. He underrates his own qualities, and overrates the least favour bestowed by his beloved."[12] Love is a combination of illusion and valuing of the beloved and involves a process he called "crystallization." When a tree branch is thrown into the salt mines near Salzburg and remains there for a few months, it is transformed into a shimmeringly beautiful crystalline laticework. Analogously, the lover's imagination ascribes one perfection after another to the beloved. Does the process of falling in love always or usually involve illusions? Or can the intense preoccupation with the beloved be based primarily on insight into the special value the person has, as both Scruton and Firestone suggest?

6. *True love* is an expression used to express a value perspective on the most desirable forms of erotic relationships. Put into words your conception of true (erotic) love. Include in your discussion a response to the following questions (which combine some of the preceding questions):
   a. Is true love something that has to last a lifetime, or can it exist for a few years and then end?
   b. Can a person love two people at the same time?
   c. To what extent does genuine love require sharing the interests of one's lover?
   d. Is true love purely altruistic, that is, completely selfless? Or does it involve a strong element of self-concern or self-love?
   e. In what sense, if any, does true love require equality?
   f. Must true love be based on mutual understanding, or does it admit to large degrees of illusion and error about one's partner?
   g. Do we "choose" to love, or does love "happen" to us?

7. It is sometimes claimed that AIDS is "changing sexual morality." It is certainly altering many people's behavior patterns, but is this due to prudence about one's self-interest or to fundamental changes in moral beliefs and attitudes concerning sex?

SUGGESTED READINGS

Baker, Robert, and Frederick Elliston (eds.). *Philosophy and Sex*. Rev. ed. Buffalo, NY: Prometheus, 1984.

Bertocci, Peter A. *Sex, Love, and the Person*. New York: Sheed & Ward, 1967.

Brown, Robert. *Analyzing Love*. New York: Cambridge University Press, 1987.

Cancian, Francesca M. *Love in America: Gender and Self-Development*. New York: Cambridge University Press, 1987.

Firestone, Shulamith. *The Dialectic of Sex: The Case for Feminist Revolution*. New York: Morrow, 1970.

Foucault, Michel. *The History of Sexuality*. Vol. I, trans. Robert Hurley. New York: Vintage, 1980.

Fromm, Erich. *The Art of Loving*. New York: Harper & Row, 1956.

Hunter, J. F. M. *Thinking about Sex and Love: A Philosophical Inquiry*. New York: St. Martin's Press, 1980.

Norton, David L., and Mary F. Kille (eds.). *Philosophies of Love*. Totowa, NJ: Rowman & Allanheld, 1983.

Pierce, Christine, and Donald VanDeVeer (eds.). *Aids: Ethics and Public Policy*. Belmont, CA: Wadsworth, 1988.

Pope, Kenneth S. (ed.). *On Love and Loving: Psychological Perspectives on the Nature and Experience of Romantic Love*. San Francisco: Jossey-Bass, 1980.

Russell, Bertrand. *Marriage and Morals*. New York: Liveright, 1929.

Scruton, Roger. *Sexual Desire: A Moral Philosophy of the Erotic*. New York: Free Press, 1986.

Singer, Irving. *The Nature of Love*. 3 vols. Chicago: University of Chicago Press, 1984, 1987.

Snitow, Ann, Christine Stansell, and Sharon Thompson (eds.). *Powers of Desire: The Politics of Sexuality*. New York: Monthly Review Press, 1983.

Soble, Alan (ed.). *Philosophy of Sex: Contemporary Readings*. Totowa, NJ: Littlefield, Adams, 1980.

Solomon, Robert C. *About Love: Reinventing Romance for Our Times*. New York: Simon and Schuster, 1988.

Sternberg, Robert J., and Michael L. Barnes (eds.). *The Psychology of Love*. New Haven, CT: Yale University Press, 1988.

Vannoy, Russell. *Sex Without Love: A Philosophical Exploration*. Buffalo, NY: Prometheus, 1980.

Verene, D. P. (ed.). *Sexual Love and Western Morality: A Philosophical Anthology*. New York: Harper & Row, 1972.

Whiteley, C. H., and W. N. Whiteley. *Sex and Morals*. New York: Basic Books, 1967.

Wilson, John. *Love, Sex, and Feminism*. New York: Praeger, 1980.

CHAPTER 14

Marriage and Adultery

Despite the sharp criticisms of it since the 1960s, marriage continues to be a dominant form of sexual relationship. Ninety percent of Americans marry. Half of those marriages end in divorce, but 80 percent of divorced people remarry, usually within five years. Perhaps no form of social relationship has greater demands placed on it and as a result is more burdened with difficulties. One difficulty is adultery, which is present in half of all marriages—most males and many females have extramarital affairs at some time during their marriage. Yet sexual exclusivity in marriage—that is, restricting sex only to one's spouse, excluding others—is only one aspect of traditional marriages. Even more central is the lifetime commitment to join one's life intensively and intimately to one other person.

Five elements enter into the traditional conception of marriage in Western culture: (1) commitments to life-long companionship (2) and to sexual exclusivity, (3) initiated by a formal ceremony and given legal or religious status, (4) made mutually by two people, (5) one male and one female. We will focus on the first four conditions, postponing the question of homosexual marriages to the next chapter. Our interest is in the moral significance of two people formally committing themselves to life-long companionship and sexual exclusivity.

Is Marriage a Moral Issue?

Some religions regard marriage as a *religious* obligation (assuming the opportunity for it arises). It seems clear, however, that there is no general *moral* obligation to marry. Marriage is an option, not an obligation. Does that mean marriage is primarily a matter of personal preference rather than morality?

In our society, of course, decisions about marrying are based in large part on personal preferences (in contrast to societies favoring arranged marriages). Some people choose to marry because they believe it is the best avenue for finding love, emotional support, sexual satisfaction, an enriched sense of self-worth, and economic well-being. For example, in *Women and Love* Shere Hite quotes one woman as reporting, "I didn't like being single. No emotional security, no stability, no financial security, no companionship, no closeness, no love or sharing."[1] For other people, however, marriage is the end of happiness and the beginning of frustration (and possibly abuse). Many of the women Hite interviewed reported a preference for being single:

> Life is much better for me as a single woman. I can choose my friends, plan my social life, plan my private life, do and say what I please at home, make my home MINE (reflective of me), and I don't have to answer to anyone or explain my actions to anyone. Isn't it funny how long it takes to find out that freedom feels so good? Why do we rush into marriage like we do?[2]

Yet marriage decisions are not solely expressions of personal preference and self-interest. They are also moral decisions. Even though there is no obligation to marry, marriage is a moral ideal and involves moral commitments. There is also an obligation for some people in some circumstances *not* to marry: Unless one is willing in good faith to undertake the commitments involved, one may be guilty of deceit and betrayal. There is also an obligation to make marital decisions wisely, because the good of one's partner, oneself, and often others (children, family members, and so on) is at stake.

Potential Drawbacks to Marriage

Conventional thought asserts that marriage is worth the sacrifices it requires, because it offers the best hope for most people to find love and emotional richness, satisfying sex, and support and self-esteem. Many critics of this view, however, urge that most marriages are bad overall and that they would not exist if people thought more clearly and honestly. In particular, John McMurtry in "Monogamy: A Critique" argues that marriage is bound to adversely affect most people's chances of finding love and happiness, for four reasons.

Outside Control

McMurtry's first criticism concerns state and religious control of marriages: "Centralized official control of marriage . . . necessarily alienates the partners from full responsibility for and freedom in their relationship."[3] For the Romans, marriage was a matter of personal agreement between the partners, and it automatically dissolved by similar mutual agreement. In contrast, our tradition, which allows government and churches to control marriage ceremonies and relationships, restricts freedom and encourages individuals to think of their relationship as partly the responsibility of larger social institutions, as well as being influenced by peer pressure deriving from those institutions.

Certainly, such external forces do come into play. In allowing society to have any control over marriages, there can arise coercive pressures and a sense that marital commitments are not entirely one's own responsibility. There continue to be social pressures, especially on women, to marry and to stay married, even in extremely destructive relationships that ought to be dissolved. Yet much has changed since 1972 when McMurtry wrote his essay. There is greater social tolerance for people who live together before marriage (nearly half of recently married couples). It is also easier to end a marriage because of changing divorce laws. And when couples do marry, it is usually by choice and with the aim of expressing their commitments through a public ceremony. Some couples may regard public ceremonies and legal ties as superfluous or hurtful in the way McMurtry suggests. For others, however, the symbolism provides a significant way to solemnize their commitments in the eyes of society and also in their own eyes—it is, or can be, a highly personal mutual expression between partners.

Let us set aside this question about ceremonies in order to focus on a purely moral concept of marriage defined by life-long commitments, whether or not legal and religious rites are involved. McMurtry's other criticisms are directed toward these commitments and their consequences.

Sexual Confinement

Far from supporting erotic love, McMurtry maintains, marriage frustrates it: "Formal exclusion of all others from erotic contact with the marriage partner systematically promotes conjugal insecurity, jealousy, and alienation."[4] It does this by creating "a literally totalitarian expectation of sexual confinement" of one's spouse that is bound to create anxiety about potential violations of the commitment of sexual exclusivity by either spouse. Spouses become fearful of losing the spouse, jealous about attention paid to others, and emotionally distanced from each other. In any case the confinement is impractical: Affairs occur with accompanying deception and antagonism between partners.

These effects do sometimes occur. But are they the result primarily of the commitment to sexual exclusivity? Certainly, for many couples, that commitment provides a stable context that promotes sexual satisfaction, not just through engaging in regular sex but by creating an atmosphere in which trusting sexual expression can take place. It also lessens jealousy by allowing partners to feel confident that outside affairs will not occur. The ill effects that McMurtry emphasizes are due primarily to the personality and character of individuals rather than to the nature of marital commitments per se. Yet he is right about one thing: Traditional marriage does limit the possibility of erotic love relationships through extramarital affairs by spouses; we will discuss this idea further in a subsequent section.

Sexual Ownership

Quite apart from consequences, McMurtry states, marriage is based on degrading attitudes that spouses "own" each other's sexual activities: "The ground of our marriage institution . . . is this: the maintenance by one man or woman of the effective right to exclude indefinitely all others from erotic access to the conjugal partner."[5] Marriage is a state of "indefinite, and exclusive ownership by two individuals of one another's sexual powers" and as such is "a form of private property" that treats people as if they were things to be possessed.[6]

Once again, McMurtry raises a valid criticism of some marriages. Certainly, some husbands treat their wives as chattel. Yet it is entirely possible for spouses to view themselves as the beneficiaries of each other's gift of free commitments rather than as having ownership rights. If there is a right, it is the right created by freely given promises and commitments, not ownership. And there is an awareness and appreciation that each is dependent on the other for on-going renewal of those commitments.

Psychological Constriction

The marriage vows of the Church of England's *Book of Common Prayer* require the man to answer affirmatively to this question: "Wilt thou love her, comfort her, honor and keep her, in sickness and in health; and, forsaking all others, keep thee only unto her, so long as ye both shall live?" In addition to making these same vows, the woman is also asked to obey and serve—an inequality best avoided in contemporary vows! No doubt some couples speaking these words understand them as a kind of pleasant poetical expression rather than a literal commitment. Most couples, however, fully intend to make the commitment to life-long companionship. But is such a commitment wise? Not according to McMurtry:

> The restriction of marriage union to two partners necessarily prevents the strengths of larger groupings. Such advantages as the following are thereby usually ruled out: (a) the security, range, and power of larger socioeconomic units; (b) the epistemological [i.e., mental] and emotional substance, variety, and scope of more pluralist interactions.[7]

Feminist critics of marriage emphasize that these losses hurt women more than men. All too often, women's identities are based only on their roles as wives (and mothers), whereas men find greater enrichment through their work—even when both partners have jobs. For most wives, one-sided dependency leads to more sacrifice than self-fulfillment.

These criticisms reach deeper than the superficial idea that marriage takes away freedom in the sense of reducing options. Marriage does not automatically reduce overall options; instead, it changes them—dramatically. Marriage does close some options. Single (and childless), one can come and go as one chooses without having to notify or negotiate with anyone. But marriage opens other options, such as for steady companionship and the sharing of daily activities (including sex). Of course, only good marriages offer this, but then, only some forms of being single offer happy options.

McMurtry, and some feminists, are concerned more with the quality of options within marriages than with the quantity. In their view marital options are psychologically constrictive: Dependency on just one partner restricts the intellectual and emotional stimulation offered by a wider network of relationships. We have all seen marriages in which this constriction occurs. But must it occur? Is there some quality inherent in marriage that causes it to occur?

Although contemporary marriages are too diverse to permit generalized characterization, they include three general types, as distinguished by sociologist Francesca M. Cancian. Cancian suggests that two models have been overemphasized: "(1) the traditional family, based on restricting individual freedom, especially for women, and (2) the contemporary pattern of limited commitments between independent individuals, each focused on his or her own self-development."[8] Yet a third model, which is increasingly popular, views long-term love and self-development as equally important and mutually reinforcing: "(3) Love and self-development both grow from the mutual interdependence of two people, not from extreme independence nor from the one-way dependency of a woman on a man encouraged by traditional marriage."[9] This model of interdependence stresses growth through intimate and caring relationships with as much equal sharing as possible. According to Cancian such relationships break down role differentiation based on gender stereotypes of women as submissive, gentle and tender, sensitive and supportive, and of men as assertive and dominant, emotionally reserved (except perhaps in showing anger), and economically and intellectually independent. In this sense both marital roles and love itself are *androgynous*.

Interdependent relationships require *mutuality* of effort, sensitivity, and adjustment, as well as commitment to mutuality as an on-going process. The philosopher S. I. Benn earlier described this process, which is found among friends as well as spouses:

> It is of the essence of this relation that it is fully participatory. Each respects and values every other as a full partner, and exerts his own effort in the expectation and trust that the other will do likewise. . . . [The

relation is one of] mutuality, the extent to which each is sensitive to the others' response to his own effort, is prepared to monitor his own attitudes to his partners and to the partnership, and to adjust to changes in the interests, tastes, values and personalities of the others. . . . [The goal of] the enterprise is to keep the partnership moving, to make it a vehicle through which the personalities of the partners can develop autonomously, without destroying it.[10]

This kind of relationship need not foster isolation from other enriching relationships. Rather, it allows marriages to function as emotional anchors that strengthen capacities for friendships and community involvement. A sense of permanence makes partners feel confident that the relationship will not be destroyed by change and disagreements, but rather that they will eventually enter into a sense of shared history together.

Having emphasized that marriage for many people is enriching, not constricting, we can agree with this much of McMurtry's criticism: Marriage is not for everyone. It requires an ability and a willingness to continuously and intensively join one's activities with those of another person. Usually, it requires a personal decision to value that relationship over attractive career options and other forms of relationships, and for some individuals that can be constrictive.

Extramarital Affairs: Two Cases

McMurtry's second and fourth criticisms express a dissatisfaction with how traditional marriages destroy the possibility of extramarital love affairs. And he implies that these affairs can be vastly enriching—not just sexually, but in terms of affection, love, and elevated self-esteem. Is he right in thinking that such affairs do not deserve their negative reputation, as conveyed by the pejorative connotations of the word *adultery*?

In 1987 we saw a revival of these questions due to widespread press coverage of the cases of Jim Bakker and Gary Hart. The differences between the cases remind us that extramarital affairs take many forms, making it difficult to generalize about their moral status.

Jim Bakker was a successful television evangelist ("televangelist") who created and directed the PTL (for "Praise the Lord" and "People That Love") Club. His affair was a one-night stand six years earlier with Jessica Hahn, a twenty-one-year-old former church secretary. Bakker followers portray Hahn as a temptress who seduced Bakker during a troubled time in his marriage to Tammy Faye Bakker. Hahn's version, as recounted in *Newsweek* magazine, differed sharply:

She was flown to Florida to meet Bakker by another evangelist, John Wesley Fletcher; she had baby-sat with Fletcher's children, and he knew she idolized Bakker. But at a hotel, so the story went, she was given drugged wine. Bakker appeared, dressed only in a white terry-cloth swimsuit, and she was told to give him a back rub. Dazed and sick, she resisted, but was unable to fight off Bakker's advances.[11]

Whichever version is true, the story is sordid (even setting aside the $265,000 in hush money Bakker paid to Hahn a few years later and the subsequent charges against Bakker of fraud and abuse of ministry funds). The Bakkers' marriage was based on traditional vows of sexual exclusivity, vows that were violated in a sexual episode that involved no love and possible abuse of authority.

In 1987 Gary Hart was the leading Democratic candidate for president. Early in May he challenged reporters to scrutinize his private life by following him around. In mid-May he was seen entering and leaving his townhouse on Capitol Hill with model Donna Rice. The next day it was reported that in March he had gone on an overnight trip to Bimini (aboard a boat named *Monkey Business*) with a male friend and two women, one of whom was Rice. Hart and Rice insisted their relationship was platonic. Yet Hart's friends had worried for years that he was destroying his political career by womanizing: "'It's no secret among Hart staffers that Hart has had these romances,' said one campaign official. 'But we felt it wasn't anybody's business except his and [his wife] Lee's.'"[12]

Hart's political sense is open to challenge, but how about his sexual ethics? If we assume that Gary and Lee Hart, unlike Jim and Tammy Bakker, did not have a traditional commitment to sexual exclusivity, is there anything immoral about Hart's having extramarital sexual romances? In general, aren't extramarital affairs immoral when and only when they involve a violation of commitments or promises?

A Defense of Extramarital Affairs

According to Richard Taylor in *Having Love Affairs* extramarital affairs should not automatically be condemned. Taylor's basic argument is simple: Love is the highest good, and extramarital affairs based on love therefore are intrinsically good, although admittedly their good might occasionally be outweighed by bad effects. Unlike McMurtry, Taylor sees great value in marriages (based on love), but he vigorously defends McMurtry's favorable view of affairs as offering enriching human relationships, even for couples who began their marriages with traditional vows:

The joys of illicit and passionate love, which include but go far beyond the mere joys of sex, are incomparably good. And it is undeniable that those who never experience love affairs, and who perhaps even boast of their faultless monogamy year in and year out, have really missed something.[13]

Just as marital love offers the special goods deriving from close companionship, extramarital affairs offer a unique combination of excitement, affection, recognition, and strengthened self-esteem. Few things are more flattering and exhilarating than being loved by someone willing to take risks in surmounting conventional pressures against extramarital affairs.

Of course, affairs do sometimes hurt spouses. Jealousy is natural, even though according to Taylor it is always bad and destructive (contrary to the view expressed in Chapter 12). But affairs need not hurt marriages: "No good marriage relationship can be threatened by a love affair so long as others keep out of it."[14] Good marriages are based on mutual love, which presumably is strong enough to survive affairs.

Taylor admits that love affairs are not for everyone, and certainly not for those who prefer orderliness and security over the excitement and risk offered by affairs. He insists, however, that the risk of harm from affairs can be minimized if spouses and lovers follow some basic rules.

For example, spouses of people having affairs should heed the following guidelines: (1) "Do not spy or pry." Not only is that self-degrading, but it shows a lack of trust in the spouse's exercise of autonomy. (2) "Do not confront or entrap," because doing so is based on a cruel impulse to humiliate the spouse. (3) "Stay out of it," cultivating instead an attitude of confidence that the love involved in the marriage will sustain it after the affair has run its course. (4) "Stop being jealous," for jealousy is an inherently ugly and self-torturing emotion (contrary to what was argued in Chapter 12).

Spouses engaged in love affairs should heed the following rules, among others: (1) "Stop feeling guilty"—such feelings are irrational products of centuries of prejudice against affairs. (2) "Be aware of the needs of the other" (that is, of one's lover), because that is central to love. (3) "Be honest" (with one's lover), because absolute honesty is required by the special intimacy involved in affairs. (It is especially wrong to lie about one's marital status.) (4) "Do not exhibit and boast," but rather restrain the natural tendency to broadcast the joy the affair has brought.

Taylor's view of extramarital affairs turns traditional morality on its head! But what about the deception involved in most affairs? And what about infidelity? Doesn't his view neglect the virtues of truthfulness and fidelity?

Taylor in fact defends concealing the truth from one's spouse: "Candor is *not* the first obligation of husbands and wives. The first obligation is to love, and a direct consequence of that love is the desire not to injure."[15] When revealing the truth is likely to injure one's spouse and one's marital relationship, love justifies concealment—including lying if necessary.

As to fidelity to one's spouse, Taylor is adamant that it has nothing to do with sexual exclusivity: "The real and literal meaning of fidelity is *faithfulness;* and what thinking person could imagine that there is only one way in which someone can fail to keep faith with another? Faithfulness is a state of one's heart and mind," rather than a matter of rule following.[16] Infidelity represents a betrayal of love and the commitment to love. It takes many forms, such as neglecting the sexual needs of one's spouse, being uncaring, being unappreciative of the spouse's talents, and diverting shared money into a secret savings account for one's selfish use. According to Taylor, however, love for one's spouse is not betrayed by extramarital love affairs.

Many extramarital affairs are entered into without serious thought. Taylor is the first major philosopher to view them as so important as to warrant a book-length examination. Even if one disagrees with his arguments, as many people do, he raises important questions, some of which will be included as discussion topics.

Summary

The traditional form of marriage in Western culture is based on mutual commitments between a man and a woman to life-long companionship and sexual exclusivity (sex only with one's spouse). While there is no moral obligation to marry (although some people believe there is a religious obligation), marriage nevertheless raises moral questions involving permissible moral ideals.

John McMurtry argues that traditional marital commitments are inherently harmful in four respects. First, allowing government or churches to exercise regulatory control over marriages lessens spouses' sense of full responsibility for their relationship. Second, the commitment to sexual exclusivity leads to sexual confinement that causes insecurity and jealousy. Third, the exclusivity commitment leads to degrading attitudes of ownership of the spouse's sexual activities. Fourth, the commitments prevent enriching emotional and intellectual relationships with other people.

McMurtry's criticisms are important because each of these bad effects can occur, although they need not. Many marriages are based on mutual trust and support that, together with intensive and continuous interdependence of two lives, reduce insecurity and jealousy while promoting affection and companionship. In addition, premarital living together and less stringent divorce laws have encouraged marital partners to make fully autonomous decisions about their marriages, despite continuing pressures from society.

Richard Taylor defends extramarital affairs insofar as they are based on passionate love. He argues that such affairs are singularly exciting, supportive of self-esteem, and valuable for the affection and love they provide. They need not involve either infidelity or immoral deception. Infidelity is a betrayal of love, but one can love a partner in an affair while continuing to love one's spouse. Moreover, loving one's spouse entails not wanting to hurt her or his feelings, and that may justify concealing the affair with secrecy and deception. These provocative claims, however, are open to challenge, as the following "Discussion Topics" suggest.

DISCUSSION TOPICS

1. An "open marriage" is one in which spouses mutually agree to permit each other to have extramarital affairs. In some open marriages there is an agreement to tell each other about the affairs; in others telling is left to the discretion of the spouse having the affair; and in still others there is an agreement not to tell each other about the affairs. Without appealing to religious beliefs (about divine commandments) is there anything immoral about any of these forms of open marriage?

2. One objection to traditional marriages is that they are based on unrealistic commitments. No matter how intense one's feelings may be at the time of the marriage, no one can know for sure whether one will still love one's spouse twenty or fifty years, or even one year, later, because feelings are not entirely under one's control. Therefore, such commitments are either foolish or dishonest (based on pretense). Do you agree? In presenting your answer, clarify what you mean by "love." Also, compare and contrast marriage vows to other lifetime promises, such as a promise made to a parent that one will become (and stay) a doctor, or a promise made to God to undertake a lifetime of humanitarian service.

3. Comment on sayings like "True love will last," "Love is all we need" (to make our relationship work), and "Love will keep us together." Distinguish different things that might be meant by "love" (some of which perhaps make the cliché false, and some true). In this connection discuss whether marriage and other long-term love commitments require cultivation of virtues such as patience, persistence, flexibility, willingness to compromise, sensitivity, honesty, courtesy, and even a sense of humor. What about the willingness to "fight fair" during disagreements by not attacking one's partner in emotionally vulnerable areas, as well as the skill not to allow daily problems to escalate out of all proportion? And what about the virtue of wisdom in identifying when a marriage has become hopeless and is best dissolved?

4. Taylor argues compellingly that marital infidelity can take forms having nothing to do with sexual exclusivity. That does not prove, however, that breaking marriage vows of sexual exclusivity is not also infidelity. Isn't having a sexual affair after one has promised (to one's spouse) not to have such affairs a form of infidelity? If it is, can the obligation of fidelity sometimes be overridden by other reasons that justify sexual affairs?

5. Taylor contends that affairs do not threaten good marriages, that is, those based on love. If "love" implies the willingness to indulge a spouse's affairs, the claim is

true by definition. But Taylor seems to be making an empirical claim (one based on experience) about the impact of affairs on marriages characterized by a deep sense of caring. He bases the claim on his own experience together with some sixty to seventy questionnaires filled out by people who answered an ad he placed in three newspapers. (The ad stated that a professor of philosophy was researching extramarital love affairs and called for people willing to answer a questionnaire.) Do you agree with Taylor's claim that extramarital affairs do not threaten good marriages? What kind of scientific studies of marriages are needed to determine whether Taylor is correct?

6. Many people are currently experimenting with various forms of "marriage con-tracts." For example, prior to marrying a couple might sign a legal document spec-ifying the distribution of money and property in the event of divorce. (See Lenore Weitzman's book *The Marriage Contract* for details.) Critics of these contracts contend that they convey doubts about whether the relationship will survive and thereby weaken the hope for a permanent relationship based on trust. (They might even constitute a kind of self-fulfilling prophecy.) Defenders believe that the contracts are based on an attitude of realism (in facing the fact that one in two marriages ends in divorce) and that such an attitude may actually benefit the rela-tionship. What is your view and why?

7. Does the fact that traditional marriages involve commitments to life-long compan-ionship mean that divorce always represents a kind of moral failure? Isn't it pos-sible to be morally justified in withdrawing a lifetime commitment in light of major changes in one's life and the relationship with one's spouse? Is divorce sometimes a very good thing, even where children are involved?

SUGGESTED READINGS

Bardwick, Judith M. *In Transition: How Feminism, Sexual Liberation, and the Search for Self-Fulfillment Have Altered America*. New York: Holt, Rinehart & Winston, 1979.

Bayles, Michael D. "Marriage, Love, and Procreation." In Robert Baker and Freder-ick Elliston (eds.), *Philosophy and Sex*, rev. ed. Buffalo, NY: Prometheus, 1984.

Bernard, Jessie. *The Future of Marriage*. New York: Bantam, 1973.

Cancian, Francesca M. *Love in America: Gender and Self-Development*. New York: Cambridge University Press, 1987.

Gregory, Paul. "Against Couples." *Journal of Applied Philosophy*, vol. 1 (1984).

Guggenbuhl-Craig, Adolf. *Marriage: Dead or Alive*. Trans. Murray Stein. Dallas: Spring Publications, 1986.

Hite, Shere. *Women and Love*. New York: Knopf, 1987.

Hunter, J. F. M. *Thinking about Sex and Love*. Toronto: Macmillan of Canada, 1980.

McMurtry, John. "Monogamy: A Critique." *The Monist*, vol. 56 (1972). Reprinted in Robert Baker and Frederick Elliston (eds.), *Philosophy and Sex*, rev. ed. Buffalo, NY: Prometheus, 1984.

O'Driscoll, Lyla H. "On the Nature and Value of Marriage." In Mary Vetterling-

Braggin, Frederick A. Elliston, and Jane English (eds.), *Feminism and Philosophy.* Totowa, NJ: Rowman & Allanheld, 1977.

Palmer, David. "The Consolation of the Wedded." In Robert Baker and Frederick Elliston (eds.), *Philosophy and Sex,* rev. ed. Buffalo, NY: Prometheus, 1984.

Russell, Bertrand. *Marriage and Morals.* New York: Liveright, 1929.

Taylor, Richard. *Having Love Affairs.* Buffalo, NY: Prometheus, 1982.

Wasserstrom, Richard A. "Is Adultery Immoral?" In Richard A. Wasserstrom (ed.), *Today's Moral Problems,* 3rd ed. New York: Macmillan, 1985.

Weitzman, Lenore J. *The Divorce Revolution: The Unexpected Social and Economic Consequences for Women and Children in America.* New York: Free Press, 1985.

Weitzman, Lenore J. *The Marriage Contract: A Guide to Living with Lovers and Spouses.* New York: Free Press, 1981.

CHAPTER 15

Homosexuality and Homophobia

Homosexuality is the sexual orientation centered on a primary attraction to members of one's own sex. Gays are men primarily attracted to men, and lesbians are women primarily attracted to women. In heterosexuality the primary sexual attraction is to members of the opposite sex, and in bisexuality the attraction is to both men and women. Sexual orientation and attraction is defined by predominant patterns of sexual behavior, desires, emotions, fantasies, and the cues or stimuli that lead to sexual arousal.

Sexual orientation differs from biological sex type (male versus female) and gender identity (one's conviction of being male or female).[1] It also differs from sex roles, that is, the social roles conventionally expected for men and women (as defined by physique, voice, clothing, personality, occupation, parenting styles, and so on). Although homosexuality is a minority orientation, a great many individuals are homosexual: roughly 10 percent of males and 4 percent of females.

Classical Greek culture accepted homosexuality, indeed preferred it as the most desirable sexual orientation. Most Western societies, however, have sought, often violently, to suppress homosexuality and have treated homosexuals with contempt. Homosexuality has been viewed as a sickness, and homosexual acts have been condemned as deeply immoral. In this chapter we discuss whether those attitudes are justified or whether they comprise negative attitudes toward homosexuality based on ignorance, prejudice, and fear, that is, homophobia. Homophobia is the *irrational* fear and hatred of homosexuality, homosexual acts, and homosexuals. Often, it leads to acts of prejudice and persecution: ridicule, discrimination, support of social policies oppressing homosexuals, and violence against gays and lesbians. Is hatred of homosexuality irrational (homophobic)? Is it a form of immoral prejudice? Is homosexuality or homophobia the moral problem?

Closets and Coming Out

Let us begin with two case studies illustrating the difficulties confronting gays and lesbians. Negative social attitudes lead many homosexuals to live "closeted" lives of sexual isolation, loneliness, fear, and frustration. Not only does this compound the normal difficulties associated with finding sexual partners, it also encourages short-lived affairs rather than long-term relationships (which are publicly visible). Publicly affirming a homosexual identity—"coming out"—would risk reprisals: shunning, derisive laughter, physical assault, and violation of rights in buying or renting homes.

Social pressure also can make it difficult to "come out to oneself," that is, to acknowledge and affirm to oneself one's sexual orientation. Whatever one's sexual identity, adolescence is a turbulent time in terms of awakening to, accepting, and expressing one's sexuality. For gays and lesbians, however, the obstacles are multiplied. The difficulties continue well into adulthood, as is illustrated in the autobiography of Malcolm Boyd, *Take Off the Masks.*

During the 1960s and 1970s Boyd was well known as a nonviolent civil rights activist, Vietnam War protester, and religious thinker. As a prominent Episcopalian priest he crusaded for the rights of women to enter the priesthood, and he also sought to strengthen ties between Christians and Jews. Yet accepting his own sexuality was a painful and gradual process.

At age ten he knew he was attracted to boys and men, but he suppressed the thoughts and impulses. During high school he took a rare (and spontaneous) gamble in hinting to his closest friend that he was attracted to him. The friend never spoke to him again. In college and early adulthood he grew contemptuous of homosexuals and was willing to laugh derisively at them. Yet later he occasionally experimented with gay relationships, which led only to feelings of intense guilt and self-contempt.

Boyd was thirty-three when he began to accept his sexual orientation. He was able to do so through a love relationship with a man who reciprocated his feelings. The affair lasted eight months until circumstances forced the two men apart. About the experience Boyd wrote:

> Could I not stand, alone before my God, and say, "This is who I am.
> I can be no other." Wasn't this the essence of Christianity—a direct and
> personal relationship between a human being and God? "Listen, for
> whatever reason you made me, I am part of your creation. I have found
> a capacity to love. I do not believe that that is sin."[2]

During the next decade Boyd fell in love twice more, but again it was impossible to pursue the affairs publicly in a way that would enable them to last. Gradually, he was able fully to accept his homosexuality and the form of love it made possible:

I cannot recall a sexual relationship that was ever simply casual for me. Always I felt an intensity, a yearning to belong and love, and an awesome sense of universal meaning in *this* act. Surely this has brought me sadness as well as joy.[3]

For lesbians, acceptance of homosexuality can be an even more difficult process because of additional general social pressures against female assertiveness in overcoming expected social roles for women. Those individuals who achieve self-acceptance without major trauma tend to be unusually strong. One such woman is Martina Navratilova, the champion tennis player. Navratilova says she is bisexual (although she hates that "creepy sounding" label), but her primary adult sexual attachments have been with women.

During her early teenage years Navratilova had crushes on both female and male teachers. Later she felt strong attachments to a few women tennis players. Only when she turned eighteen, however, did she recognize and accept these crushes as involving a sexual interest. At that time she also had her first love relationship, one initiated by an older and more assertive woman:

When it finally happened, I said, this is easy and right. And the next morning—*voilà*—I had an outright, head-over-heels case of infatuation with her. When will I see you again? What will we do with our time together? I was in love, just like in the story books, and everything felt great.[4]

Things were not so great when her parents learned about the affair. Her father immediately referred her to a book about her "sickness." There were violent arguments. During one argument her father said he would rather see her become a hooker than a lesbian (and he meant it). Navratilova also worried that her sexual orientation would disrupt her attempts to become an American citizen after defecting from her native country, Czechoslovakia (where, incidentally, gays were sent to insane asylums and lesbians never came out of the closet). Yet overall, Navratilova's process of self-acceptance seems to have been much easier than Boyd's.

The Reproductive Purpose of Sex

Is there anything immoral about homosexual acts? One view, held by the Catholic church and some other major religions, is that homosexuality is *unnatural* in that it departs from (or "perverts") the proper role of sex in human life. That role is procreation—having children. Because homosexual acts do not have the potential to generate children, they constitute a misuse of sex and are therefore immoral. According to *Leviticus* in the *Old Testament*, homosexual acts are an abomination warranting death by stoning.[5] And according to *Romans* in the New Testament, homosexuals are guilty of a "vile affection" that alters "the natural use [of sex] into that which is against nature."[6]

If homosexual acts are immoral simply because they cannot lead to children, then it follows that all kinds of sexual acts that cannot lead to children are also immoral. Masturbation and heterosexual intercourse using contraceptives, for example, would also have to be viewed as immoral. Leaving aside certain religious views, it is hard to see how they could be. Masturbation and sexual intercourse using effective contraception cannot generate children. If we accept, however, that such acts are not immoral (at least not always), the statement that all nonreproductive sex is immoral becomes false. And therefore, the mere fact that homosexual acts cannot generate children does not make them immoral.

This type of argument is known as *reductio ad absurdum* ("reduction to absurdity"). It attempts to refute a view by showing that it entails a falsehood, drawing on the logical point that true views do not entail falsehoods. The argument should be convincing for anyone who believes that masturbation and the use of birth control devices are not immoral per se. But what if someone does not hold these beliefs?

For example, Saint Thomas Aquinas would not be convinced by the reductio ad absurdum argument. According to him all use of sex except for procreation is immoral:

> The emission of semen ought to be so ordered that it will result in both the production of the proper offspring and in the upbringing of this offspring.
>
> It is evident from this that every emission of semen, in such a way that generation cannot follow, is contrary to the good for man. And if this be done deliberately, it must be a sin. . . . For which reason, sins of this type are called contrary to nature.[7]

In fact, Aquinas believed that masturbation and homosexuality constituted even worse sins than did heterosexual rape, because heterosexual rape could at least generate children. Today the Catholic church does not share that view. Nor does it agree with Aquinas that the *sole* legitimate use of sex is procreation: Sex also should express love. Nevertheless, the official Catholic view concurs with Aquinas that masturbation, heterosexual sex using contraceptives, and homosexual acts are all immoral for the same reason: They are not the type of acts that can lead to reproduction.

One way to proceed at this point is to argue that masturbation is surely morally permissible when it leads to pleasure and has no bad side effects. And intercourse with contraceptives is morally permissible and often desirable when it supports loving relationships and yields no harmful side effects (as are other nonreproductive sex acts based on mutual consent, such as oral sex).

Utilitarianism, duty ethics and mutual respect, and rights ethics all seem to offer support for this view.

Let us shift the burden of proof, however, by asking whether there are any good reasons for believing that nonreproductive sex is bad. What could be morally objectionable about using sex solely to express affection and love, at least within long-term relationships of the sort that Boyd and Navratilova sought to establish in their lives? Doesn't sex have (at least) two entirely "natural" functions in human life? In fact, aren't there several natural and legitimate uses of sex in addition to procreating, such as obtaining pleasure, relieving stress, strengthening self-esteem, showing affection, and expressing love?

Notice that the question about moral reasons does not disappear by appealing to God or by stipulating that "natural" means "what God commands" and "unnatural" means what God forbids. Even setting aside religious disagreements about what God commands and whether God exists, recall the point raised in Chapter 1: It makes sense to ask *why* God commands certain things rather than others. Presumably, a morally perfect being would make commandments on the basis of good moral reasons rather than on whim or from prejudice. Are there any good reasons to believe that a morally perfect being would forbid all nonreproductive types of sex acts? This is essentially the same question as above: Are there any good reasons for believing that all nonreproductive sex acts are bad? This question will be left as a discussion topic.

Other Senses of "Unnatural"

If we set aside the senses of "unnatural sex" that mean "nonprocreative" and "contrary to God's commands," are there any other senses in which homosexuality is unnatural—senses that have some moral relevance? The words *natural* and *unnatural* do have other meanings, but it is doubtful that they have any moral significance or relevance for thinking about homosexuality.

First, one could define *natural* in terms of "the *primary* biological function." Thus, the natural function of the digestive system and of eating is to provide nutrition for the body; similarly, the natural function of genitals and sexual intercourse is procreation. If we adopt this definition, nonreproductive sex is unnatural (assuming the most important evolutionary role of sex is reproduction). Although this may be true, however, it is morally irrelevant to the topic of homosexuality. Just because the primary function of the digestive system and of eating is nutrition, it does not follow that it is immoral sometimes to eat just for pleasure or during an enjoyable luncheon with a friend or spouse, even though one is not hungry or in need of food. Similarly, even if the primary biological purpose of sex is procreation, it does not follow that anything is bad about using sex solely for pleasure or for expressing love.

Second, *natural* might mean "healthy," both mentally and physically.

Prior to 1974 the American Psychiatric Association viewed homosexuality as a mental disorder and listed it as such in its *Diagnostic and Statistical Manual of Mental Disorders*. In 1974, however, the APA acknowledged that they had made a mistake and emended the *Manual*. Today the vast majority of health professionals do not view homosexuality as unhealthy. Insofar as homosexuals suffer from any greater anxiety or depression, the cause is now understood to be society's rejection of homosexuals.

The physical health of many gays, of course, has been devastated by AIDS. But homosexuality is not the cause of AIDS, and homosexual acts by themselves do not cause AIDS. AIDS is spread by the failure to use precautions (especially condoms) during homosexual *or* heterosexual intercourse (as well as by drug addicts sharing needles, blood transfusions using contaminated blood, and so on).

Third, some people see a kind of naturalness in how genitals "fit together" during heterosexual intercourse. Here "natural" seems to mean "geometrically congruent." This notion of genital geometry, however, has no relevance to the debate over homosexuality as unnatural and provides no grounds for moral objections to homosexuality. Rather, it seems to express heterosexual bias and ignorance about homosexual experiences.

Fourth, *natural* might mean "common" or "usual." This sense is also irrelevant morally. Just because 90 percent of people are heterosexual does not make it immoral to be in a sexual minority. If it did, all left-handed people would be immoral too, because they represent a minority orientation to space and activities; likewise, windsurfing would constitute an immoral use of the sea.

Fifth, *natural* might mean "feels natural" in the sense of being based on an inclination that one feels and with which one identifies. True, many heterosexuals do lack or are uncomfortable about homosexual impulses, which seem alien and repulsive. Yet that is a statement about heterosexual tastes and orientation. To illustrate, eating snails undoubtedly is not something that most of us have a spontaneous desire to do, but it does not follow that eating escargot is immoral. Tastes in sex, food, wine, books, and friends involve deep feelings that can be as strong as moral emotions. Because of this it is sometimes easy to confuse issues of taste and morality—but they are distinct.

Sixth, *natural* might be defined as what conforms to the appropriate roles for men and women. Homosexuality, it is claimed, is morally objectionable because gays tend to be effeminate in gesture and voice, violating masculine role models; conversely, lesbians tend to be unfeminine. This argument is weak for several reasons. It falsely stereotypes the mannerisms of gays and lesbians, most of whom do not fit this profile. (Just to mention one example: Rock Hudson was gay but hardly effeminate.) It falsely assumes that all males and all females have a moral obligation to fit a particular sex role. And it misappropriates the word *natural* by applying it to what are primarily society-created (not nature-created) sex roles.

Promiscuity

Another stereotypic view of gays—that all gays are promiscuous due to something inherent in male homosexuality—merits a separate discussion. Whereas lesbians tend not to be promiscuous, there are in fact gay men who have hundreds of sexual partners during a lifetime. Yet most gays have fewer partners than this stereotype suggests, and of course many heterosexual males are promiscuous, having sex as often as they can find a willing partner.

Nevertheless, Roger Scruton argues that male homosexuality *tends* to encourage promiscuity and thereby discourages long-term love relationships of the kind he values (as we saw in Chapter 13). According to Scruton all males have a high degree of natural sexual predatoriness, which means they will desire many sexual partners during a lifetime. This instinct is tamed through attraction to the mysteries of the opposite sex. Because members of the opposite sex are radically unlike oneself (physically, mentally, and so on), in pursuing sexual relationships with them one knowingly undertakes great risks—the risks of the unknown. This risk taking encourages commitment and fidelity of the sort Scruton values (as we saw in Chapter 13).

> The opening of the self to the mystery of another gender, thereby taking responsibility for an experience which one does not wholly understand, is a feature of sexual maturity, and one of the fundamental motives tending towards commitment. This exposure to something unknown can resolve itself, finally, only in a mutual vow. Only in a vow is the trust created which protects the participants from the threat of betrayal. Without the fundamental experience of the otherness of the sexual partner, an important component in erotic love is therefore put in jeopardy. For the homosexual, who knows intimately in himself the generality that he finds in the other, there may be a diminished sense of risk. The move out of the self may be less adventurous, the help of the other less required.[8]

In short, Scruton thinks that mystery heightens risk, and risk encourages mutual commitment to sustain the partners in taking the risk. Homosexual relationships offer less mystery because the participants are already familiar with the gender of their partners; therefore, the need for commitment is lessened, and promiscuity is encouraged.

The argument is ingenious, but is it sound? One difficulty is that if the argument works for gays, why shouldn't it also work for lesbians? Scruton is aware that lesbian promiscuity is rare, and he implies that the real problem lies in the sexual predatoriness of all males. But his mystery-of-the-opposite-sex argument seems to imply that lesbians are less inclined to form commitments than are other women, and no evidence supports that conclusion. A second difficulty is that the promiscuity of some gays has more plausible explanations. As previously mentioned, the harsh social condemnations of homosexuality have made it very risky (often dangerous) for gays to be identified publicly, thus discouraging open, long-term relationships and encouraging brief and secretive sexual encounters.

In assessing the mystery-and-risk argument, two further points need to be considered. There may be deep mysteries (and unknowns worth exploring) between any two lovers, whatever their sexual orientation. Were society to remove its taboo on homosexuality, couldn't the emotional and intellectual differences between two individuals suffice to encourage trust and commitment?

Furthermore, shouldn't heterosexuals allow the possibility that homosexuality may contain its own domains of new and "mysterious" experience for those who choose to explore it? In this connection consider the words of the poet and feminist Adrienne Rich concerning lesbian experience:

> Lesbian existence comprises both the breaking of a taboo and the rejection of a compulsory way of life. It is also a direct or indirect attack on male right of access to women. But it is more than these. . . . I perceive the lesbian experience as being, like motherhood, a profoundly *female* experience, with particular oppressions, meanings, and potentialities.[9]

Homophobia and Sexual Tastes

We have not uncovered any convincing moral reasons for being against homosexuality. Let us conclude with some comments about homophobia. It is one thing to believe that homosexual acts are bad. It is quite another to hate, detest, degrade, and condone repression of homosexuals.

Not everyone who objects to homosexuality (perhaps because of religious beliefs) is homophobic. They might object to hatred of homosexuals as much as they object to homosexuality itself. Many people, however, feel justified in "putting down" gays and lesbians in a variety of ways, ranging from tasteless jokes and derisive laughter to indifference to their legal rights. Isn't this a form of prejudice equally as bad as prejudice based on race, religion, or physique?

Imagine someone arguing that the hatred involved in homophobia is no more immoral than that involved in other phobias. According to this argument it is not immoral to have and to act upon phobias about spiders or snakes, about open spaces or closed spaces, or about heights and airplane rides. Similarly, nothing is immoral about hating gays and lesbians (whatever the moral status of homosexual acts). In fact, this argument is based on a weak analogy. Homophobia is directed toward people, not animals, spaces, spacial locations, or modes of transportation. The argument is akin to asserting that one is not a racist but just has a phobia about black people. Such an assertion would be based on self-deception or hypocrisy.

Consider another argument that appeals to the right to pursue one's own tastes. Just as we have tastes in food, sex, and clothing, we all have tastes in the kinds of people with whom we interact. Some people, so the argument goes, are uncomfortable with gay people and have a right to dislike them, avoid them, and joke about them. We do of course have a right to pursue our tastes, including those concerning people. There are limits to those rights, however, and they do not justify violating the rights of homosexuals. An equally important point is this: Having a right to pursue a taste does not mean that the taste is "all right" (i.e., morally permissible). The right to pursue our tastes means that others should not interfere in an attempt to coerce us to act otherwise. Our tastes and actions may nevertheless be objectionable because they are prejudiced. Hatred of all homosexuals is a form of dismissing and shutting out people on the basis of one of their attributes—their sexual orientation. In that respect, at least, it is similar to racism and sexism.

Summary

Homosexuality is the sexual orientation of being primarily attracted to members of one's same biological sex category. Homophobia is the irrational fear and hatred of homosexuality, homosexual acts, and homosexuals.

The primary traditional ethical argument against homosexual acts is that they are unnatural or perverted in that they cannot cause reproduction. Sexual intercourse and orgasm, it is contended, are morally permissible only when they involve the kinds of acts that could lead to children. If this view were true, masturbation and sexual intercourse using contraceptives must likewise be condemned as unnatural or perverted. Although some religions hold this view, we found no sound moral theory or principle that supports it.

Various other arguments supporting the idea that homosexual acts are unnatural include the following: (1) The primary biological function of sex is reproduction; (2) homosexual acts are unhealthy; (3) only in heterosexual acts is there genital congruence; (4) heterosexual acts are usual or most common; (5) only heterosexual acts are based on an inclination with which most people identify; (6) and only heterosexual acts conform to gender roles. None of these senses, however, yield moral objections to homosexual acts. Moreover, arguments using these other senses often involve heterosexual biases (for example, concerning proper genital geometry) and dubious claims (for example, that homosexuality is an illness).

Roger Scruton argues that male homosexuality encourages promiscuity, making it objectionable in light of the traditional view that sex should be joined to long-term erotic love relationships. His argument is that homosexuals miss out on the mysteries involved in a relationship with a member of the opposite sex (with whom one is less familiar than one's own sex type).

His argument fails, however, on several counts: The main mysteries of sex derive from an exploration into the unknown of another person, whatever their sexual orientation; most homosexuals are more promiscuous than are heterosexuals; the stronger tendency to promiscuity in some gays may be due to social pressures against publicly visible, long-term gay relationships.

Homophobia is unlike most phobias in that it is directed toward people. There are limits to how far one can go in acting on one's tastes. Even when one has a right not to be interfered with by others in pursuing one's tastes, those tastes may involve prejudice based on religion, race, or sexual orientation.

DISCUSSION TOPICS

1. Are there good reasons for believing that the only morally permissible sex acts are procreative kinds (that is, acts of the general kind that could lead to children)?

2. Sexual orientation is something that is usually not "chosen." (If you are heterosexual, did you ever choose to be so?) Most likely it is caused by a combination of genes and environment. Moreover, sexual orientation is usually impossible to change completely, because it involves fundamental types of desires, fantasies, and interests that are not easily removed. Do these facts have any moral relevance to the question of whether homosexual and heterosexual acts are morally permissible?

3. One objection raised against homosexuality is, "What if everyone (or most people) became homosexual? There would not be enough children to sustain society." Is this a good argument?

4. Heterosexuals take for granted the legal right to marry in any state in the United States, but homosexuals are denied this right. Is this unjust discrimination? In your answer take note of the fact that even if homosexuality is believed to be immoral, that does not settle the question about the right of homosexuals to marry. (And consider as well the following analogous situation: Many people believe that the use of contraceptives is immoral but not that laws should prohibit their use and prohibit people who use them from marrying.)

5. Some people say that they have nothing against homosexuals, but they morally object to homosexuals "flaunting" their sexuality by holding hands in public. The same people do not object to heterosexuals holding hands in public. Are their views morally consistent?

6. Assess the following claim: "Homosexuality is immoral because homosexuals caused the AIDS epidemic in the United States." In your assessment take account of the following facts: It is not known how AIDS originated in the world, and the existence of the AIDS virus was not even suspected (by homosexuals or by anyone) during the early years in which the epidemic spread.

SUGGESTED READINGS

Aquinas, St. Thomas. *On the Truth of the Catholic Faith*. Book 3: *Providence,* Part I, trans. Vernon J. Bourke. New York: Doubleday, 1956.

Batchelor, Edward (ed.). *Homosexuality and Ethics*. New York: Pilgrim Press, 1980.

Bentham, Jeremy. "An Essay on 'Paederasty.'" In Robert Baker and Frederick Elliston (eds.), *Philosophy and Sex,* rev. ed. Buffalo, NY: Prometheus, 1984.

Boyd, Malcolm. *Take Off the Masks*. Philadelphia: New Society, 1984.

Elliston, Frederick. "Gay Marriage." In Robert Baker and Frederick Elliston (eds.), *Philosophy and Sex,* rev. ed. Buffalo, NY: Prometheus, 1984.

Engelhardt, H. Tristram. "The Disease of Masturbation: Values and the Concept of Disease." In Tom. L. Beauchamp and LeRoy Walters (eds.), *Contemporary Issues in Bioethics,* 2nd ed. Belmont, CA: Wadsworth, 1982.

Koertge, Noretta (ed.). *Philosophy and Homosexuality*. New York: Harrington Park Press, 1985.

Kosnik, Anthony, et al. *Human Sexuality: New Directions in American Catholic Thought*. New York: Paulist Press, 1977.

Levy, Donald. "Perversion and the Unnatural as Moral Categories." In Alan Soble (ed.), *The Philosophy of Sex*. Totowa, NJ: Littlefield, Adams, 1980.

Rich, Adrienne. "Compulsory Heterosexuality and Lesbian Existence." *SIGNS: Journal of Women in Culture and Society,* vol. 5 (1980). Reprinted in Catharine R. Stimpson and Ethel Spector (eds.), *Women: Sex and Sexuality*. Chicago: University of Chicago Press, 1980.

Ruse, Michael. "The Morality of Homosexuality." In Robert Baker and Frederick Elliston (eds.), *Philosophy and Sex,* rev. ed. Buffalo, NY: Prometheus, 1984.

Scruton, Roger. *Sexual Desire: A Moral Philosophy of the Erotic*. New York: Free Press, 1986.

Weinberg, George. *Society and the Healthy Homosexual*. Garden City, NY: Anchor, 1973.

CHAPTER 16

Pornography and Fantasy

Sexually explicit magazines, books, and movies pervade our society. During the sexual revolution of the 1960s supporters argued that such materials liberated sexual repressions and affirmed sex as good. President Johnson's 1970 Commission on Obscenity and Pornography concluded that pornography is not harmful but instead is a positive influence in releasing inhibitions, helping married couples with sexual difficulties, and encouraging frank discussions between parents and children about sex. Critics of this attitude were regarded as puritanical reactionaries who would have us retreat into the sexual hypocrisy and repression of the 1950s.

A decade later, however, these comfortable generalizations were being seriously challenged by two groups that had little else in common. Both conservatives and liberal feminists were alarmed by the sheer magnitude of the multibillion-dollar pornography industry that was churning out obscenity on an alarming scale. Of greatest concern were two dramatic trends: mixing sexual and violent images and using children in pornography. Liberation, it seemed to many, had turned into degradation of women and exploitation of children.

During the past decade attempts have been made to control pornography by passing laws against its makers, by allowing civil suits against its distributors, and by supporting economic boycotts and demonstrations against its merchandisers. Debates over such attempts address important and complex issues. Yet they should not deflect attention from everyday questions we all face concerning the use of pornography. Whether or not censorship of pornography violates rights to expression and privacy, we still need to examine the moral effects of pornography on our lives. Even if legal and moral rights forbid others from interfering with the use of pornography, we still need to ask whether that use is sometimes morally harmful. A right to use something does not automatically mean it is all right to use it.

We begin with a question of definition: Just what is pornography? We then ask several specific questions concerning everyday pornography use. Because many anxieties about pornography pertain to wider issues about fantasy pleasures, we next raise those issues. The chapter concludes by sorting out categories of pornography to enable readers to pinpoint which kinds they find morally objectionable.

A Definition of Pornography

Disputes over pornography, whether between friends or among legislators, are often hamstrung by unclarity about the meaning of the term. It would be unreasonable to expect a definition to resolve uncertainties about what material is pornographic: There will always be difficult cases, whatever definition we adopt. Yet if verbal disputes are to be avoided, it is crucial to begin with some shared definition.

Conservative thinkers and many lawyers and judges use *pornography* as a close synonym for *obscene* in the sense of disgustingly offensive to decency. In this usage to label something as pornography is to condemn it or to express a negative attitude toward it. For example, in 1986 Attorney General Meese's Commission on Pornography wrote a letter to the owners of 7-Eleven stores suggesting that by selling *Playboy* and *Penthouse* magazines they were distributing pornography. It was understood that this was intended as a criticism of the magazines as obscene, and for a while it caused the stores to stop selling them.

Feminists have also built negative attitudes into their definition of pornography, usually defining it as any sexual material that is degrading, especially to women (about 90 percent of pornography uses female models). They invoke the term *erotica* to refer to morally acceptable sexually arousing material. One definition of pornography along these lines is given by Helen Longino:

> I define pornography as verbal or pictorial explicit representations of sexual behavior that . . . have as a distinguishing characteristic the degrading and demeaning portrayal of the role and status of the human female . . . as a mere sexual object to be exploited and manipulated sexually. In pornographic books, magazines, and films, women are represented as passive and as slavishly dependent upon men. The role of female characters is limited to the provision of sexual services to men.[1]

Other feminist definitions are narrower and specifically single out images of sexual violence against women. Robin Morgan implied such a definition when she entitled an essay with what quickly became a feminist slogan: "Theory and Practice: Pornography and Rape."[2]

Conservative and feminist definitions are "persuasive definitions" in that they define *pornography* in a way that implies negative attitudes intended to persuade us to view pornography in a certain way. In the discussion that follows, however, we do not presuppose negative attitudes toward pornography. In fact, a more neutral definition is employed by most philosophers, literary critics, social scientists, and some people in everyday discourse. According to this neutral sense *pornography* refers to sexually explicit material that is intended primarily to be sexually arousing. Nudity shown in medical textbooks would not count as pornography because its intended use is educational. Similarly, explicit depictions of highly erotic scenes in serious works of fiction, such as James Joyce's *Ulysses* or Philip Roth's *Portnoy's Complaint,* would not be considered pornographic because the intended role of these depictions has a serious aesthetic purpose (beyond sexual arousal). As used here, *pornography* means any writing or image (in pictures, film, sculpture, music, and so on) that is sexually explicit and created with the primary intention of sexually arousing the reader, viewer, or audience. We will also speak of a "pornographic use" of nonpornography. This means using as an object of sexual arousal any sexually explicit nonpornography (such as a photograph in a medical textbook, a scene in a serious novel, or an ad for lingerie).

These definitions are somewhat vague. They do not, for example, spell out what "sexually explicit" means. But there will always be some uncertain or borderline instances of pornography, and this definition will at least enable us to proceed with some shared understanding.

Examples of Pornography

When is the use of pornography, or the pornographic use of sexual material, morally permissible, and when is it morally objectionable? Let us replace this general question with a few more specific questions, using several examples.

First consider a married couple watching an X-rated video about another couple who in real life happen to be married. The movie depicts the time from when they first meet through their honeymoon. The last half of the movie is devoted to graphic depictions of honeymoon lovemaking scenes. The lovemaking is lively, involves a remarkable variety of physical positions and locations, is visually explicit and somewhat exaggerated in terms of the moaning and exclamations of pleasure, and depicts mutual assertiveness and equal ecstasy for the two participants. The viewers struggle to contain themselves until the movie is over, at which time they jump into bed to engage in a considerably shorter version of what they have just seen.

This example is highly atypical. Only a small percentage of X-rated movies depict men and women as sexual equals, or focus on sex between married people, or use actors who are married in real life. But the example provides a useful starting point for reflection. Is there anything morally objectionable about the couple viewing the movie? Assuming that both partners wanted to watch the film and did so in order to enhance their relationship, is there anything problematic about watching another couple make love on film? Should the answers to these questions be based solely on considerations of the good and bad effects on the couple's relationship and character?

Let us look at another situation. A high school student buys photographic art magazines containing nude pictures that art critics would consider to be in good taste. The student appreciates the beauty of the models and has a strong interest in imagining what the women are like in real life. In his own mind, at least, he regards the pictures as depicting people with whom he feels some sense of personal connection. He is especially attracted to those models who convey in their facial expressions and bodily postures a sense of warmth, love, and ease with their bodies. Nevertheless, his use of the magazines is pornographic in that he buys them primarily because they are sexually exciting and uses the pictures as the basis for his fantasies about making love.

Examples of this sort are part of the personal history of most people. If the student is criticized for treating the models as "mere sex objects," then some account must be given of the role of the personal dimension of the fantasies. No doubt some individuals come to rely on fantasies to such an extent that they lose touch with reality, or else they allow the fantasies to foster distorted expectations of or attitudes toward women or men. But when that does not occur, is there anything morally objectionable about this use of pornography?

Suppose about once a week a young woman reads a romance novel, preferably a sexually explicit one. She takes some interest in the plot and character development, but she regards such elements primarily as a warm-up for the more sexually arousing scenes involving explicit sexual depictions. Her main use of the novels is pornographic. Occasionally, the scenes form the basis for sexual fantasies, but for the most part they heighten her sexual life with her husband. Is there anything morally problematic about married partners enjoying fantasies about having love affairs with people other than their spouses, especially where the overall effects on the relationship are beneficial?

Next consider a single, middle-aged man who subscribes regularly to several hard-core pornography magazines because they feature pictures showing close-ups of female genitals. His sex life consists of occasional affairs and regular masturbation sparked by fantasy images of the sort depicted in the magazines. Is it immoral to have a fantasy about one part of the body? Or is it immoral to become preoccupied with such fantasies to the point where they become the center of one's sexual life?

Finally, let us consider a man who takes intense pleasure in watching snuff films, that is, films showing actresses playing characters who are murdered ("snuffed out"). His all-time favorite is the 1976 film entitled *Snuff*, which was advertised as showing the actual murder of a woman, although its distributors denied a real murder was filmed (and let us assume they were right). The film is about a man named Satan who heads a South American cult of young women who are allowed to enter the group only after an initiation involving torture. The cult plans a slaughter of a mother and her near-birth fetus. Following the graphic and violent scene in which the mother and baby are stabbed, the camera pulls back to show the production crew. A young production assistant tells the film director that she was greatly aroused by the scene, and the director responds by asking her to bed to play out her fantasies about the stabbing scene. Here is what follows, in the words of Beverly LaBelle, who saw the film:

> They start fumbling around in bed until she realizes that the crew is still filming. She protests and tries to get up. The director picks up a dagger that is lying on the bed and says, "Bitch, now you're going to get what you want." What happens next goes beyond the realm of language. He butchers her slowly, deeply, and thoroughly. The observer's gut revulsion is overwhelming at the amount of blood, chopped-up fingers, flying arms, sawed-off legs, and yet more blood oozing like a river out of her mouth before she dies. But the climax is still at hand. In a moment of undiluted evil, he cuts open her abdomen and brandishes her very insides high above his head in a scream of orgasmic conquest.[3]

Beverly LaBelle felt only revulsion, but the male viewer in our example (like many other men who watched the film) felt intense sexual arousal.

Is our horror and revulsion toward this man due to a belief that he is likely to harm women? Or isn't there something inherently immoral about delighting in such movies and fantasies, and about the attitudes toward women that underlie such fantasy pleasures?

Fantasy

In these and other cases, is pornography immoral insofar as it stimulates pleasurable fantasies about immorality? To answer this question we must first ask a more basic question: Is a fantasy immoral when (and because) it consists of pleasurable thoughts about immorality (whether or not pornography is involved)? Does the immorality of what is thought about transfer in some way to the fantasy itself?

Fantasy as Morally Neutral

We do sometimes *feel* guilty or ashamed for enjoying thoughts about doing something we believe is wrong. But it does not follow that we actually are guilty of wrongdoing. Feelings, after all, can be inappropriate, excessive, and irrational (as we saw in Chapter 5). According to many popular psychology books, fantasies are harmless passing thoughts about which people should not feel guilt and for which they should not be criticized. Insofar as fantasies produce pleasure, they are good, and by themselves they cannot cause harm.

Furthermore, according to this view, fantasies are involuntary—they happen to us—and in this respect they are unlike voluntary actions with which morality is concerned. To be anxious about fantasies reflects a superstitious attitude. It is akin to the unreasonable anxieties of children who believe their nightmares or daydreams can magically cause events without further agency on their part. Indeed, criticizing fantasies on moral grounds is actually harmful, for it encourages repression of thoughts that should be freely brought to consciousness as aids to understanding ourselves.

This view is expressed by Nancy Friday in her collection of women's sexual fantasies, *My Secret Garden*. According to Friday, fear of enjoying sexual fantasies is a sign of inhibitions that have been forced on women. Some sexual fantasies provide a healthy outlet ("catharsis") for unrealized sexual desires, for desires for greater variety of partners and experiences, for desires for greater intensity of pleasure, for desires to control sexual encounters, and for the need for sexual approval and esteem.

Other sexual fantasies, according to Friday, do not express serious desires to do what is imagined:

> "Fantasy need have nothing to do with reality, in terms of suppressed wish-fulfillment. Women . . . whose fantasy life is focused on the rape theme, invariably insist that they have no real desire to be raped, and would, in fact, run a mile from anyone who raised a finger against them, and I believe them."[4]

Women who have such fantasies are expressing only a desire for a ravishing sexual experience, while maintaining in their imaginations full control over what happens (unlike what happens in rapes).

Fantasy as Sometimes Immoral

A sharply opposed religious view, however, does not accept all sexual fantasies as morally neutral. In a familiar passage in the *New Testament* we read:

> Ye have heard that it was said by them of old time, Thou shalt not commit adultery:
> But I say unto you, that whosoever looketh on a woman to lust after her hath committed adultery with her already in his heart.[5]

Whatever the intent of the author of these lines, many Christians have interpreted them as condemning pleasurable fantasies about certain sexual activities as immoral.

Is this religious view excessively moralistic? Not according to Herbert Fingarette in his essay "Real Guilt and Neurotic Guilt." Fingarette points out that it is both common sense and central to Freudian psychoanalysis that fantasies express and are caused by wishes. Such wishes, rather than fantasies per se, are subject to moral appraisal:

> Moral guilt accrues by virtue of our wishes, not merely our acts. . . . The question of moral guilt does not wait for acts; it is in profound degree a question of what one harbors in one's heart. . . . One only need wish evil in order to be genuinely guilty.[6]

Fingarette adds some important qualifications, however, that bring him somewhat closer to Friday's view. First, he is sensitive to the complexities involved in interpreting fantasies in order to uncover the wish or desire they express. As Freud emphasized, wishes are often distorted and disguised before they reach consciousness as fantasies and daydreams. Hence, the wish being expressed in the fantasy may not be a wish actually to do what is fantasized, a notion compatible with Friday's interpretations of women's rape fantasies as not expressing a desire to be raped.

Second, Fingarette develops his thesis primarily with respect to neurotics who deceive themselves about their wishes. He emphasizes that in order to confront these wishes, individuals must be willing to bring them to consciousness and reflect on them honestly. Here again he would agree with Friday about the importance of exploring rather than repressing dreams, daydreams, and fantasies of all sorts. He would also agree that an overly harsh judgmental attitude toward fantasies can prevent honest self-exploration.

Third, the degree of guilt for having the wish is obviously far less than for actually doing an immoral act. Common sense alone tells us that murdering someone is infinitely worse than wishing to murder them: The murder harms another person, whereas the wish need not affect others at all. Moreover, the murderer, by acting, has accepted and endorsed the wish to kill, thereby making his or her character far worse than that of the fantasizer.

This last comment suggests that guilt should be measured in part by how extensively a person endorses and identifies with wishes to do immoral things. Although Fingarette might agree with this point concerning healthy people, he draws attention to a complication: Neurotics refuse to acknowledge and identify with troublesome wishes and instead deceive themselves about them. In this connection Fingarette notes that the disavowed wishes can wreak havoc in the neurotic's life, as well as harm others through actions that express those wishes. Hence, Fingarette suggests that the degree of guilt for wishes depends not just on how far they are identified with but also on the degree of harmful effects of the wishes.

To sum up, Fingarette asserts that we should feel guilt for wishes to do what is immoral. Although he does not offer a complete answer on how to measure this guilt, he suggests we should consider more than merely how bad the imagined immorality is and how strongly felt the wish is. We should also consider how firmly rooted the wish is in the personality of the individual. And we should take into account the actual impact the wish has on individuals and their relationships.

A Synthesis of Opposing Views

Which is correct, Friday's complete demoralization of fantasies or Fingarette's guarded moralization of them? However we answer this question, three points seem clear.

First, the crux of the matter, as both Friday and Fingarette agree, lies in how dramatically fantasies influence lives—in particular how they influence actions, attitudes, emotions, and relationships. Fantasies vary considerably in how they function within individuals' personalities, characters, and relationships. No doubt Friday is overly optimistic here (in her effort to make us more accepting of sexual fantasies), and Fingarette unduly somber (perhaps as a result of focusing on neurotics).

Second, Friday and Fingarette also agree that we must take care in interpreting exactly what wish is being expressed in fantasies. Consider, for example, adultery fantasies. Some of them involve desires to hurt one's spouse and thereby raise moral concerns. Others, perhaps most, involve no desire to hurt. They merely express a wish for an exciting experience, and they need have no adverse effects on relationships. Many adultery fantasies do not express a serious desire for an affair but merely represent a wish to enjoy a pleasurable thought. Yet some adultery fantasies involve obsessive and anxiety-generating feelings and may contribute to temptations to have affairs that betray the trust of one's spouse.

Third, we have varying degrees of control over our fantasies. Some fantasies arise involuntarily and then drift out of consciousness, never to reappear. Adopting a censorious attitude toward them is surely inappropriate, not only because they come uninvited and have no further implications in our lives, but also because preoccupation with judging them deflects attention from matters of greater importance.

Other fantasies are intentionally brought to mind or reveled in once they enter consciousness. Occasionally, doing this provides an effective release for an impulse that would otherwise boil within. Deliberately feeding the imagination with images of violence, however, is more likely to have the opposite effect of strengthening impulses. It is not prudishness, but common sense, that men who eagerly and repeatedly seek out violent sexual pornography are fostering desires and attitudes that they should instead work to control.

In sum, the moral status of sexual fantasies about immoral acts is complex. These fantasies are not automatically immoral; neither are they always immune from moral criticism. Similarly, the moral status of pornography to stimulate fantasy is equally complex. Each of us must assess our fantasies and the fantasies of others in light of overall patterns of behavior and attitude, avoiding the extremes of viewing fantasies either as always harmless or always subject to moral criticism.

Obscenity

Fantasy represents only one dimension of pornography use. There is another: the public reality of massive amounts of pornographic material. Pornography entails explicit *depiction* of sex through words or images intended to arouse sexually. Depiction requires the use of a medium or representational form, whether books, magazines, pictures, movies, taped telephone recordings, computer programs, or whatever. The extensive buying, renting, and using of pornography contributes to this social practice. It would seem that repeated use of violent and degrading forms of pornography for pleasure constitutes a tacit endorsement of the objectionable attitudes underlying immoral forms of pornography.

Most of us do not object to all pornography, but we do regard some pornography as obscene. Obscenity is not defined solely in terms of the emotions it provokes, such as disgust, nausea, and abhorrence. After all, we can recognize obscenity even after becoming desensitized and jaded toward it. Obscenity refers to that which goes beyond decency and hence refers to standards of decency and beliefs about those standards.

Obscenity is a wider concept than pornography. An action or a remark as well as a depiction may be regarded obscene. Also, obscenity comes in nonsexual forms. There are obscene ways of eating (gluttonously), and obscene depictions of excretion and defecation. Although "obscene" can be used as an aesthetic term alluding to nonmoral standards of beauty and taste, in discussing pornography it has moral connotations. Obscene kinds of pornography violate standards of *moral* decency.

When is pornography obscene in morally objectionable ways? And when does using it constitute participation in a morally objectionable practice?

These questions will be left as discussion topics, but before we conclude this chapter, a few additional comments should be made. First, it is important to distinguish between depicting something indecent and depicting something in an indecent way. Obscene things can be depicted in nonobscene ways. For example, depictions of rape and other forms of extreme sexual violence can be decent if they reveal the horror of the act, and good literature and art does just that. Conversely, nonobscene things can be depicted in obscene ways. Human nudity is not obscene, but in much pornography it is depicted obscenely.

Furthermore, our discussion suggests that pornography comes in many forms. Four general categories—loveless sex, child pornography, nonviolent sexist pornography, and violent sexual imagery—deserve separate consideration.

First, much pornography is intended to convey the message that sex without love, affection, or commitment is permissible and desirable. It sympathetically portrays and tacitly endorses sex solely for pleasure, sex outside marriage, casual and anonymous sex, group sex, or public sex. Conservatives' objections to pornography have tended to center on this category, alleging that all such pornography is obscene. Is it?

Second, pornography that uses children as sex objects and that involves child nudity is immoral. It exploits the children used as models, and it condones and encourages child abuse. This is the one area in which conservatives and liberals can agree on the need for strict censorship laws. Yet many forms of advertising and modeling use sexually provocative pictures of children. Is the use of twelve- and thirteen-year-old models in sexually suggestive poses morally objectionable? How about fifteen- or sixteen-year-olds? Is it objectionable to use adult models who look as if they were children?

Third, much pornography falls into the category of nonviolent but potentially sexist. The difficult question here is, What is sexist? Is it always sexist to portray a nude woman with a snake wrapped sensuously around her or with bunny ears on (or with other animal suggestions)? Is every picture emphasizing or exclusively showing women's sex organs sexist and degrading? What about the nude photos in *Playboy* that show a complete figure in poses suggesting that women are primarily sexual playmates for men?

Finally, much pornography features the use of violent sexual images. In recent years this form of pornography has proliferated, mostly involving obscene and violent images of women. With good reason, feminists have directed most criticism against it and have struggled to define it with sufficient precision to pass laws against it. One influential definition of obscene pornography (or what the authors call simply "pornography") was developed by Andrea Dworkin and Catharine MacKinnon. It was presented as part of a model civil rights statute for permitting civil suits against makers and distributors of obscenity. One version of the model statute was adopted in Indianapolis, but in 1984 the Supreme Court declared it an unconstitutional violation of free speech. Nevertheless, the definition remains morally valuable and reminds us of the kinds of violent pornography being mass produced today:

1. *Pornography* is the graphic sexually explicit subordination of women through pictures and/or words that also includes one or more of

the following: (i) women are presented dehumanized as sexual objects, things, or commodities; or (ii) women are presented as sexual objects who enjoy pain or humiliation; or (iii) women are presented as sexual objects who experience sexual pleasure in being raped; or (iv) women are presented as sexual objects tied up or cut up or mutilated or bruised or physically hurt; or (v) women are presented in postures or positions of sexual submission, servility, or display; or (vi) women's body parts—including but not limited to vaginas, breasts, or buttocks—are exhibited such that women are reduced to those parts; or (vii) women are presented as whores by nature; or (viii) women are presented being penetrated by objects or animals; or (ix) women are presented in scenarios of degradation, injury, torture, shown as filthy or inferior, bleeding, bruised, or hurt in a context that makes these conditions sexual.

2. The use of men, children, or transsexuals in the place of women in (1) above is pornography for purposes of this law.[7]

Defenders of the violent forms of pornography contend that it provides a healthy release or catharsis, rather than encouraging violence. Although the full scientific evidence necessary to fully address such viewpoints has not yet been gathered, this claim is being much more seriously challenged by recent experiments. For example, there is now solid evidence that long-term exposure to images of gross violence does strengthen negative attitudes toward women. Men are affected by repeated exposure to the myth that women want to be raped, a familiar theme in violent pornography. Anyone who reviews recent studies, such as those in *Pornography and Sexual Aggression,* edited by Neil Malamuth and Edward Donnerstein, cannot be altogether complacent about the influence of violent pornography.

Finally, whatever the general experiments show about overall tendencies, it remains true that the use of pornography is a personal matter in the following sense: Its effect on individuals varies. Each of us must achieve a self-understanding of its sometimes beneficial and sometimes harmful effects on our lives.

Summary

The word *pornography* has two very different meanings: (1) obscene (or immoral) smut and (2) sexually explicit material intended primarily to be sexually arousing. We have used the second sense. Nonpornographic materials (such as nude pictures in medical books) also can be used pornographically in the sense of being used primarily for sexual arousal.

Is using pornography morally objectionable? No simple answer is possible, because the uses of pornography are too varied. This general question is best replaced by a series of more focused questions about specific uses of pornography. These uses include: (1) married couples using pornography for enrichment of their sexual relationship; (2) an adolescent using nude photos for sexual arousal but responding to them (through imagination) as representing people for whom he feels affection; (3) a spouse using romance novels to stimulate adultery fantasies; (4) preoccupation with "hard-core" pornography centered on genital pictures of members of the opposite sex; and (5) repeated use of violent pornography that portrays women as objects to be abused.

One way to evaluate these and other uses of pornography is by exploring the role of the fantasies they produce in individuals. Nancy Friday argues that sexual fantasies are in general a healthy sexual expression, while Herbert Fingarette defends the *New Testament* view that fantasies to do immoral acts frequently express immoral wishes. Both agree, however, on several points: Sexual fantasies should be evaluated in light of how they affect an individual's life and relationships; care must be taken in interpreting the wish being expressed in a fantasy (because unconscious wishes are often disguised before they are manifested in a conscious fantasy); and varying degrees of voluntariness may be involved in fantasies (ranging from a spontaneous nonvoluntary fantasy to deliberate, repeated summoning of a fantasy).

The second way to evaluate pornography is as mass-produced and mass-consumed public objects that, by permeating our society, influence attitudes—especially about women. Obscene pornography is sexually explicit material that violates standards of moral decency. Four categories of pornography are often regarded as obscene: (1) material that conveys a message that sex without love is desirable, (2) material that portrays children as sex objects, (3) nonviolent sexist pornography, and (4) violent sexual imagery.

DISCUSSION TOPICS

1. We assumed that it is "prudish" (that is, excessively proper or modest about sexuality) to object to all uses of sexually explicit material for sexual arousal. Is this assumption perhaps unjustified? In defending your view, explain how this question (about moral justification) might be approached within the framework of each of the main types of ethical theory: utilitarianism, duty ethics, rights ethics, and virtue ethics.

2. Pornography is often criticized as treating women (and sometimes men) as "mere sex objects." What do you think is meant by this expression, and is it a valid complaint? Relate your answer to what Kant says about not treating other people merely as a means to our own ends.

3. Are some fantasies, sexual or otherwise, inherently immoral—even though they do not lead to immoral actions? In giving your answer, comment on the views set forth in the *New Testament* and the views of Nancy Friday and Herbert Fingarette.

4. Discuss whether there is anything immoral about each of the following:
   a. A rape fantasy spontaneously enters a man's mind and is quickly dismissed from attention.
   b. A man deliberately and frequently brings to mind rape fantasies, even though he never has any strong urge to rape (and never does so).
   c. Occasionally (about once every few months), a woman has the fantasy of being raped.
   d. A woman has and enjoys recurring fantasies of being raped, even though she sincerely denies any desire to be raped.

5. Five different uses of pornography were presented early in this chapter. Present and defend your answer to the questions raised at the end of each example.

6. Four general categories of pornography are most often criticized as being obscene and immoral: (1) that which recommends sex without love or affection, (2) that which portrays children as sex objects, (3) nonviolent sexist pornography, and (4) violent sexual images, usually of women. Present and defend your view concerning whether each of these types of pornography is obscene.

SUGGESTED READINGS

Attorney General's Commission on Pornography: Final Report. 2 Vols. Washington, DC: U.S. Department of Justice, 1986.

Burstyn, Varda (ed.). *Women Against Censorship*. Vancouver, British Columbia: Douglas & McIntyre, 1985.

Copp, David, and Susan Wendell (eds.). *Pornography and Censorship*. Buffalo, NY: Prometheus, 1983.

Davis, Murray S. *Smut: Erotic Reality/Obscene Ideology*. Chicago: University of Chicago Press, 1983.

Fingarette, Herbert. "Real Guilt and Neurotic Guilt." In *On Responsibility*. New York: Basic Books, 1967.

Friday, Nancy. *Men in Love: Men's Sexual Fantasies, The Triumph of Love over Rage*. New York: Dell, 1980.

Friday, Nancy. *My Secret Garden: Women's Sexual Fantasies*. New York: Pocket Books, 1973.

Garry, Ann. "Pornography and Respect for Women." *Social Theory and Practice*, vol. 4 (1978).

Lederer, Laura (ed.). *Take Back the Night: Women on Pornography*. New York: Morrow, 1980.

Morgan, Robin. "Theory and Practice: Pornography and Rape." In Laura Lederer (ed.), *Take Back the Night: Women on Pornography*. New York: Morrow, 1980.

Report of the President's Commission on Obscenity and Pornography. Washington, DC: U.S. Government Printing Office, 1970.

Singer, Jerome L., and Ellen Switzer. *Mind-Play: The Creative Uses of Fantasy.* Englewood Cliffs, NJ: Prentice-Hall, 1980.

Soble, Alan. *Pornography: Marxism, Feminism, and the Future of Sexuality.* New Haven, CT: Yale University Press, 1986.

Talese, Gay. *Thy Neighbor's Wife.* New York: Dell, 1980.

Tong, Rosemarie. *Women, Sex, and the Law.* Totowa, NJ: Rowman & Allanheld, 1984.

PART FIVE

Caring Relationships

It may be esteemed, perhaps, a superfluous task to prove, that the benevolent or softer affections are estimable; and wherever they appear, engage the approbation and good-will of mankind. The epithets **sociable, good-natured, humane, merciful, grateful, friendly, generous, beneficent,** *or their equivalents, are known in all languages, and universally express the highest merit, which* **human nature** *is capable of attaining.*[1]

David Hume

Caring for someone means desiring their well-being and, when appropriate, seeking to promote their good for their sake. It is more than respecting them and their rights. We want those we care for to prosper, and we enjoy helping them prosper.

To care for someone need not be "purely" or "solely" altruistic in the sense that we are concerned only with their good, and not ours. Nor need it be entirely "selfless" in the sense of involving self-sacrifice. On the contrary, people who are most caring tend to see their own good as intimately tied to the good of those they care about. In caring for others, they see their own good promoted as well.

In this way caring and self-interest can be compatible and mutually reinforcing. When we sustain relationships based on care, we promote both the good of others and of ourselves. That does not, of course, make caring "selfish." Selfishness is excessive concern for oneself at the expense of others. Caring is the opposite of selfishness, but it can also differ from self-sacrificing forms of "selflessness."

Caring relationships involve two or more conscious beings, at least one of whom cares about the other. They take many forms beyond the relationships of sexual love discussed in Part Four. In Part Five we discuss caring relationships between parents and children, friends, colleagues at work, community members, and people and animals.

CHAPTER 17

Parents and Children

Relationships between parents and children are as morally perilous as they are momentous. They are the source of much suffering and cruelty, yet they can also be full of caring and love. At least we think they *ought* to be paradigms of relationships based on care and love.

This "ought" raises interesting questions. Does it mean there is a "duty to love" one's children and, reciprocally, a duty for children to love their parents? Can there in fact be a duty to love? Isn't love something that must emerge spontaneously or not at all, as opposed to being cultivated as a matter of duty? Does the "ought" perhaps express a moral ideal that is better understood in terms other than duties?

Surely parents have some duties to children, but what is their basis, and which duties are most important? Do all grown children have obligations to their parents? In thinking about children, should we emphasize their rights rather than their duties, as the recent childrens' rights movement insists?

Although it is impossible to generalize about family structures, especially with respect to contemporary society, it will help focus our discussion of these issues if we begin with an example of one type of family.

An Example of a Parent-Child Relationship

When he was thirty-six, the Czechoslovakian writer Franz Kafka composed a forty-five-page letter to his father in which he sought to understand and to heal the emotional chasm between them. The letter is a vivid reminder of how relationships with parents have an influence well into adulthood. It begins: "You asked me recently why I maintain that I am afraid of you. As usual, I was unable to think of any answer to your question, partly for the very reason I am afraid of you."[1]

241

The fear arose from the father's thoroughgoing domination in raising his son: "From your armchair you ruled the world. Your opinion was correct, every other was mad."[2] The father defined the rules of the household, the children's behavior away from home, the family business, and the acceptable attitudes toward the world outside the family. His views were the final authority in determining everything important. They were also frequently self-contradictory or even preposterous, and this generated in Kafka the painful awareness of irrational authority that permeates his writings in such short stories as "The Metamorphosis" and such novels as *The Trial*.

His father's edicts were backed by threats, shouts, rage, and spiteful laughter at any sign of disobedience. Young Franz viewed such behavior as more than sheer bluster, as indeed a recurring condemnation of him. When the raging was not followed by the threatened punishment, his feelings of guilt and failure were only compounded.

Even worse was his father's difficulty in showing simple affection and providing emotional support. Returning home from school, Franz's excitement over his ideas or achievements would be disparaged by the father as childish and petty. He received encouragement only when he conformed to his father's image of manliness—as a business-oriented, soldiery, beer-drinking tough guy. Franz's gradual development as a sensitive artist and writer was met with contempt or disregard.

Not surprisingly, Kafka developed a personality grounded in self-doubt and a sense of worthlessness: "Ever since I could think I have had such profound anxieties about asserting my spiritual existence that I was indifferent to everything else."[3] Even as an adult he continued to judge himself in the harsh terms set by his father. Marriage, for example, which he accepted as the sign of full maturity in his society, became impossible for him. Shortly before writing the letter, he could still be deflated by his father's criticisms of his fiancée as being a mediocre girl who seduced his son by wearing a fancy blouse.

After writing the letter to his father, Franz asked his mother to deliver it. This messenger role was in keeping with her subservient status within the family as go-between for the father and the children. She was a paragon of kindness, but always within the limits of her husband's dominance. This kindness served the cruel function, Kafka realized in retrospect, of the beater during a hunt. By constantly seeking to reconcile Franz to his father, his mother drove him back under the father's domination.

The Kafkas were typical of the nineteenth-century family in which the father's authority was both unlimited and unquestioned by wives and children, something much rarer today. The authority of contemporary parents has largely been replaced by the powerful influences of peers, teachers, and mass media, as well as being undermined by greatly increased freedom for children. In fact, according to the Carnegie Council on Children, modern parents are like corporate executives responsible for loosely coordinating the activities of others who shape their children's lives. Confronted with an array of professionals who claim to understand their children better than they do, each parent is also like "a maestro trying to conduct an orchestra of players who have never met and who play from a multitude of different scores, each in a notation the conductor cannot read."[4]

Nevertheless, the fundamental parental role in providing early guidance and emotional support for children remains the same as in previous centuries. In fact, as the Carnegie Council also noted, this role has become even more important. In a world where work is increasingly impersonal, where ties with neighbors are weak, and where religions have lost their grip, the family becomes a haven for emotional and moral nurturing of all family members. With this in mind, we can turn to the question, What are the primary responsibilities of parents toward their children?

Parental Responsibility: Respect Versus Abuse

By *parents* we mean individuals who have primary responsibility and authority in raising a child. They may be biological parents, foster parents, or "significant others" who replace legal guardians as primary providers and protectors. Parents are those people who, by assuming responsibility for a child's development, serve as primary caretakers.

Parents' fundamental duty to their children is to respect them as persons—persons undergoing various stages of development. This may sound odd at first, because we expect so much more from parents than the respect that all people owe to children. Yet just as parents are in a unique position to nurture and support their children, so too are they uniquely well placed to harm them by failing to show them even minimal respect, as we saw in Kafka's case. Furthermore, precisely because parents do contribute so much to their children's development, it is easy for them to rationalize away the harm they do under the guise of exercising parental responsibility. Three areas in which this frequently occurs are in disciplining, showing affection, and giving encouragement.

First, child abuse is sometimes rationalized as discipline or excused as an attempt to teach a lesson. Thus, a spanking turns into a beating without the parent grasping the transition. Kafka reported a related example in recalling his only direct memory from infancy. He had been whimpering for water, and ignoring several warnings to be quiet, when suddenly his father carried him outside and locked him out for a while on a cool evening when he was wearing only a nightshirt. This was devastating to Franz, who remembered the episode as ultimate proof that he was worthless in his father's eyes.

Second, even gross abuse can occur in the guise of showing affection. Father-daughter incest and other forms of sexual abuse, which are estimated to involve one of every six girls, rarely result from the use of overt force. Typically, at first there is enticement: kind words ("Daddy loves you") and gentle touching. Threats aimed at keeping the child quiet usually come after the sexual abuse. Sexual abuse, which so clearly exploits the vulnerability and trust of children, is sometimes rationalized by alleged paternal rights to the sexual satisfaction that the wife "fails" to give, combined with the self-serving belief that no real harm is done. Such beliefs have even been publicly defended: There is a pro-incest lobby, the René Guyon Society, which publicly espouses parent-child sex in the name of the sexual liberation of children.

Third, a great deal of psychological manipulation takes place under the guise of guidance and encouragement. Parents do have the right and responsibility to convey their own sense of moral decency to their children—within limits. That sense of decency may be prejudiced and narrow, and in some respects it almost always is. Nevertheless, it provides the essential foundation of values that children can subsequently modify. What is objectionable, obviously so in the case of Kafka's father, is the use of tactics that crush a child's attempts to assess those values and to modify them as the child develops capacities for autonomous reasoning. Furthermore, overzealous parental concern can mask an attempt to live vicariously through children, deriving esteem and venting frustrations by pressuring children in harmful ways.

Definitions of Child Abuse

As child abuse takes on increasingly subtle forms, it is necessary to become clearer about the meaning of *child abuse,* and thereby clearer about the minimal parental duties to respect children. Traditional definitions of child abuse were developed in the legal context, because courts needed a criterion for justifiable forced removal of children from homes. Studies showed that forced removal of children does more harm than good except when abuse is very severe. This fact, coupled with a concern for preserving family unity, led courts to develop a very narrow definition of child abuse as a pattern of either severe battering or deprivation of necessities such as food, shelter, clothing, affection, and education. Hence, the legal definition does not apply to an array of moral harms that are less severe or not solvable through legal remedies.

At the opposite extreme is a definition of child abuse as any failure to promote the best interests of the child. This definition, however, is much too wide. For one thing, there is always some alternative home where the interests of a given child might be better promoted. This would make most parents abusers because they lacked ideal resources for maximizing their child's interests! For another, according to this definition, parents would be abusers each time they failed to place a given child's interests above all others. Yet what a child should be provided with must always be balanced against the needs and interests of other family members, including parents.

If the definition of child abuse as extreme deprivation is too narrow, and the definition of child abuse as a failure to maximize the interests of the child is too wide, then perhaps child abuse should be defined as handicapping of the basic development of the child by failing to meet the child's needs. This definition would have to be linked to a theory about needs, development, and growth toward maturity. Because these are all value concepts, such a theory would draw on both psychological and value assumptions about mature and responsible conduct, which is the goal of healthy psychological development.

Although this definition is an improvement over the others, Natalie Abrams suggests it is still too limited. In her essay "Problems in Defining Child Abuse and Neglect" Abrams points out that abuse of people in general includes more than simply harming their development. In a legal context, for example, the term *battery* refers to an infringement on the liberty of others against their will or choice. This is wrong because battery also constitutes an assault on their dignity, even if it does not actually handicap their growth. Similarly, she suggests, abuse of children is best conceived as an assault on their dignity as persons:

> It is this concept of an affront to dignity that is totally omitted in the definitions of child abuse or neglect, which focus solely on actual or risked harmful consequences. It is not enough simply to say that the harmful consequences constitute assaults on one's dignity and, therefore, that the child's dignity is indirectly being protected. Although harmful consequences must be prohibited in order to ensure the possibility of the child's development, the prevention of these harms does not amount to respect for the child's dignity, any more than it would amount to respect for adult dignity.[5]

This definition, which is plainly inspired by Kantian rather than utilitarian thought, coheres with our earlier emphasis on respect for children as persons. Yet there is a problem with the definition, Abrams acknowledges. The dignity of adults is defined by reference to their consent. Assaulting their dignity is a violation of their rights without their consent, that is, without their voluntary and informed agreement. But how can this standard be applied to young children who lack the capacity to give consent?

Abrams offers the following suggestions. The concept of consent is indeed inapplicable to very young children, and a minimum standard for the decent treatment of children should be established. Even young children can express their wishes, verbally or nonverbally. These wishes should be respected as far as possible, except when doing so would be detrimental to the development of the child or prohibited by the needs of other family members. Thus, this standard does not require that maximum amounts of money be spent on the child, as the best-interests standard might imply. It only requires that a fair share of family resources be spent on the child in the direction indicated by the child's wishes, except when doing so would harm the child's development.

It follows from this standard that there are limits on how far parents can go in manipulating their children to adopt particular interests, values, careers, religious beliefs, and tastes. The sheer appeal to their best interests, for example, does not automatically justify coercing older children into particular religious practices. Nor are parents warranted in coercing children to pursue careers that, in the parents' judgment, are in the children's best interests. Instead, parents should help provide the conditions that will enable children to make their own career choices.

Next to providing for basic physical needs, the essential ingredients for children's well-being are the skills and enthusiasm for independent thought and action. Note that this is also at the heart of personal and moral autonomy: the active capacity to create and pursue a rational and moral plan of life. Hence, the primary duties of parents include providing conditions that foster the growth of autonomy.

Before turning to the reciprocal duties that children owe to parents, let us briefly consider two further objections to Abrams's emphasis on consent as a moral limit on how children can be treated. The first objection is that the emphasis is unimportant because it allows exceptions whenever harm to the child is involved and because parents will inevitably apply their own views of what this harm is. Thus, for example, parents will continue to force their religious beliefs on their children in the name of their own good, even when the children clearly refuse consent.

This objection highlights a practical difficulty in applying Abrams's standard, though the objection should be qualified. The standard is not parents' views of the proper development of the child but instead the actual healthy development of the child. Parents are required to become informed and intelligent about what that development is! Moreover, the consent requirement clearly does imply increased respect for the child's own views about proper development as the child matures. Eventually, at the morally vague stage of "maturity," the parent should recognize the consent of the son or daughter as final. Between early infancy and maturity, however, children have a gradually developing capacity for consent that should be respected in such matters as religion.

The second objection concerns incest. Suppose there are rare instances when incest does not harm the development of a child and when an older child of fifteen years or more gives consent. Does it follow that the incest is permissible and not an assault on the child's dignity? If so, this might imply that we should no longer regard incest as taboo, that is, as absolutely prohibited in a manner that does not permit exceptions or challenges.

In response to this objection we should emphasize that the chances of psychological and developmental harm from incest are so high, and the degree of possible harm so enormous, that it makes sense to retain an absolute ban on it. (This is a rule-utilitarian argument that recognizes the need for all to adhere to a general rule because of the important good consequences that follow from doing so.) Furthermore, there is the question of whether even a fifteen-year-old child (or young adult) is capable of giving consent freely in a situation combining sexual inexperience on the part of the child and psychological authority on the part of a father or older brother or uncle. Finally, there remains the ideal of parents loving their children as parents, not as sexual partners. Incest threatens the kind of love that for children is both inherently valuable and the basis of self-respect in adult life.

Filial Duties and Gratitude

Let us now shift the moral focus from parental responsibilities to children's duties. What is the appropriate moral attitude of children, especially grown sons and daughters, toward their parents? Recent social thought has stressed that the relationship is largely one of rights. Reacting to the horrors of child abuse and neglect, members of the children's rights movement, such as Abrams, have emphasized children's rights to be given what is necessary for proper development ("positive rights") and their rights to have as much freedom as possible without interference from others ("negative rights"). These human rights are viewed as one justification for saying parents have duties toward children, that is, duties to respect their children's rights.

Duties

Young children, of course, also have duties to obey and cooperate with parents once they grow beyond infancy. The duties are limited, because there is no duty to do everything a parent says, no matter how immoral or inappropriate it might be. Nevertheless, the duties are important because other members of the family have needs that must be recognized and balanced. Young children are not able to balance these other needs and hence should generally defer to their parents' judgment. As they grow older, however, they should be allowed an increasing voice in family decisions in order to aid development of their own autonomy. Furthermore, children's own sense of autonomy can arise only on a foundation of early development guided by their parents.

The traditional Judeo-Christian view of what is owed to parents goes far beyond this, however. Children and adults alike are enjoined, according to one of the Ten Commandments, to "Honor thy father and thy mother." Honoring is usually interpreted as respecting them and being grateful to them. This is a prescription for a lifetime, not just during childhood. Failure to be grateful reflects the vice of extreme ingratitude. Thus, Franz Kafka was accused by his father of ingratitude for becoming estranged from him.

This traditional view has been challenged on several counts. For one thing, being grateful is an emotion, and emotions are not under our direct control. Therefore, we cannot have a duty to feel gratitude, because we do not have duties to things not under our control. One possible reply to this challenge is that the duty of gratitude refers more to *showing* gratitude than to *feeling* grateful. To show gratitude is to perform acts manifesting or expressing gratitude, and these are under our control.

Perhaps, however, this preliminary reply is superficial. The duty of gratitude is a duty to show genuine or sincere gratitude, and that entails actually feeling grateful rather than merely pretending to be. Can there, then, be a duty to be grateful if such a duty entails a duty to have certain emotions?

Gratitude

In order to answer this question, we need to know what the emotion of gratitude is. If it is an inner sensation or feeling (for instance, feeling a warm glow inside) over which we have no control, then it would seem absurd to speak of a duty of gratitude. Fortunately, it is not! Like other important and complex emotions, gratitude is not a set of inner twitches and tingles, but instead a structure involving beliefs, attitudes, and desires.

Gratitude has the following ingredients: (1) believing that one or more people voluntarily did something good for us, or at least intended it to be good for us, (2) having a positive attitude of goodwill toward them (such as a hope for their well-being), and (3) having a desire to show them appreciation (in an appropriate way, whether with a reciprocal gift, a simple thank you, or any other number of signs of appreciation). When what we received is actually good for us, gratitude also requires (4) appreciating and properly using the gift. With the "white elephant" gift, however, which we cannot be expected to appreciate, this last condition does not apply. We are free to dispose of the gift with discretion, that is, without hurting the feelings of the giver.

Understood in this way, gratitude is somewhat under our control—to some extent we can influence our beliefs, attitudes, and desires. We can often allow (or refuse to allow) gratitude to develop within us by attending to the benevolent motives of the giver, dwelling on the value or intended value of the gift, and reminding ourselves of the importance of sustaining our relationship with the person by acknowledging his or her kindness.

Admittedly, there are some occasions when gratitude either cannot or should not be fostered in this way. Perhaps, for example, doing so would add to an already harmful sense of dependence on a parent whose motives in giving were as much an attempt to manipulate as to help. The following statement illustrates this point: "If you do not complete medical school and stay active in our church, then you are an ingrate for all we have given you!"

A second challenge to the traditional view that children owe gratitude to their parents is that the parents were merely doing their duty. They were "just doing their job" in giving their children the necessities for development. Gratitude, it is implied, is owed only when people do something good that is not required by duty.

This argument is unsound. Sometimes, we owe gratitude for acts on our behalf that were required by duty. It would, for example, be callous for someone who was saved by a lifeguard or police officer to dismiss them as not deserving gratitude because they were just doing their duty as professionals. When we benefit from a great good, we should be grateful. For most of us, the greatest goods we receive include those from our parents. Moreover, parents are usually motivated far more by love than by a sense of duty. Raising children requires sacrifices, and parents usually make those sacrifices voluntarily and lovingly. Not to respond with gratitude for being the beneficiary of this love and these sacrifices is a moral failure as well as a betrayal.

A third and more forceful challenge to the view that parents are owed honor and gratitude was given by Jane English, who found it objectionable to talk about *owing* parents for their sacrifices. The notion of owing is appropriate in thinking about repaying debts, meeting contracts, and returning favors. But adult children ought not to think of their relationship with their parents in such ways:

> Parents' voluntary sacrifices, rather than creating "debts" to be "repaid," tend to create love or "friendship." The duties of grown children are those of friends and result from love between them and their parents, rather than being things owed in repayment for the parents' earlier sacrifices.[6]

English makes an important point: The adult son or daughter does not owe parents in the same way they might owe an unpaid debt or owe a favor in return for having received one. This legalistic way of thinking actually threatens the kind of mutual caring about one another's needs that underlies loving relationships.

Moreover, when parents sever an ongoing loving friendship with their children, they should not expect gratitude for the earlier sacrifices they made. As English notes, if biological parents who are fully able to raise their child decide instead to give it up for adoption, they should not expect gratitude for any sacrifices they made in having the child. Again, if parents disavow their children because they refuse to marry within their preferred religion or to pursue their favored careers, and thereafter have nothing to do with them, the children have no obligation years later to pay their medical bills in old age. For similar reasons Franz Kafka's father had no right to expect gratitude from him.

Perhaps, however, we may hesitate in embracing English's emphasis on friendship in thinking about the relationship between parents and grown children. Notice that a consequence of her view is that once friendship ceases on the part of either party, duties of friendship also cease. Yet isn't there a stronger obligation to try to sustain a loving relationship with one's parents than there is to sustain friendships? More basically, isn't construing the relationship with parents as primarily friendship *or* as primarily a matter of rights and duties inappropriate? What about love?

Love

As we saw in Chapter 13, love is as conceptually and morally complex as it is complicated in real life. Here we will mention an aspect of love that warrants further discussion. The issue is whether most of what has been said thus far in this chapter is inappropriate because the relationship between parents and children ought to be one of love, not duties and rights. Parents have children out of love and out of a desire to create an intimate loving relationship. Moreover, successful parenting depends upon raising children with love, and in such a way that children know they are deeply loved and singularly important to the parents.

The failure of Kafka's father was a failure to love, not a failure of duty, and perhaps the same is somewhat true of Franz Kafka with respect to his father. Similarly, talk of a duty of gratitude is insulting to many parents precisely because they seek love, not dutiful respect and gratitude, from their children. For a similar reason mere friendship is not sufficient to capture the hoped-for relationship between parents and children.

Perhaps much of this emphasis on love can be granted without removing the relevance of the preceding discussion of duties, rights, and responsibilities. The *kind* of parent-child love that is most important and worth promoting encompasses and transcends, without replacing, the duties of mutual respect and caring. Love is the aim and ideal of parent-child relationships. It is itself an ideal, not a duty.

The important question at this point is, What kind of love? Is mutual caring for one another's interests sufficient? Is self-sacrifice implicit in the ideal? Is the desire for love a desire for an unconditional love that does not depend upon any particular achievements or traits of character in the family members? These questions will be left as discussion topics.

Summary

Parents are any persons who assume responsibility for the primary caretaking of a child. Their most fundamental duty to the child is respect, which includes providing the basic necessities of life during the time when the child is completely dependent on the parents. In disciplining, showing affection, and giving encouragement, this duty requires avoiding abuse and forms of manipulation that restrict the potential for subsequent autonomous growth.

Child abuse is an assault on the dignity of children, whether by disregarding their needs or by undermining their autonomy as they move toward adulthood. Respect for children involves providing conditions that enable children to develop a capacity for creating and pursuing their own rational plan of life rather than imposing one's own convictions on them.

Children have obligations of gratitude for the benefits and the benevolence from parents. Gratitude has the following ingredients: believing that someone voluntarily did something intended to be good for us, usually motivated by a concern for our good; having goodwill toward them for this; desiring to show appreciation; and appreciating and properly using the gift. Gratitude is under our control and is appropriate even though parents have an obligation to promote their children's good.

Although there are mutual obligations involved in parent-child relationships, the ideal form of the relationship is centered on mutual love and mutual caring about one another's good.

DISCUSSION TOPICS

1. What kind of love between parents and adult children do you see as most desirable? Is it a form of friendship (as Jane English suggests) or is it more like identity-shaping romantic love?

2. Do adult children have an obligation to feel and show gratitude to parents who have greatly contributed to their good? Or is showing sincere gratitude to one's parents a moral virtue that is highly desirable but not obligatory?

3. Is there an obligation to give financial support to your parents in their old age, should they need it? Does the obligation depend upon whether one's parents were caring and loving? Is there an obligation of parents not to become a financial burden on their children?

4. Evaluate the following argument: Parents should not raise their children in any particular religion, because that brainwashes them into the outlook in a matter of great importance. Instead, they should take them to several churches in order to lay a foundation for children to make up their own minds about religion later on. Is your view on this issue the same with respect to early moral training?

5. Two parents who believe that homosexuality is immoral learn that their son or daughter is homosexual. In a rage they sever all ties with their child—emotional, financial, communication, and so on. The last time they talk with their child they disavow their identity as parents, exclaiming, "You are no longer our child." Have the parents done anything immoral? If so, which ethical theory best captures what is wrong: utilitarianism, duty ethics, rights ethics, or virtue ethics?

6. During 1986 and 1987 there were several widely publicized cases of children (teenage and preteenage) who reported their parents to the police for using illegal drugs. Some of the children were given recognition awards by police departments. Identify and discuss the moral issues you see raised by these cases. Are the issues the same or different concerning parents turning in their adult children for drug use?

7. Decisions about whether to have children include decisions to beget, to bear, to keep, and to adopt a child. We speak of such decisions as "deciding to have a baby," reflecting our preoccupation with cuddly, dependent infants (rather than merely reflecting the biological fact that babies are in the early stages of development of childhood). Yet the decision to have a child is or should be a decision to enter into a long-term, complex, dynamically changing, and largely unpredictable intimate relationship with another person. Discuss the main moral considerations that should be weighed by prospective parents in deciding whether to have a child. At the time of making the decision to beget a child, are there obligations to the future child (who does not yet exist)?

8. Ideally, parent-child relationships are based on mutual trust. Does that make it worse to lie to one's parents than to lie to a stranger? Consider several examples, and also review the discussion of lying in Chapter 4.

SUGGESTED READINGS

Abrams, Natalie. "Problems in Defining Child Abuse and Neglect." In Onora O'Neill and William Ruddick (eds.), *Having Children*. New York: Oxford University Press, 1979.

Aiken, William, and Hugh LaFollette (eds.). *Whose Child? Children's Rights, Parental Authority, and State Power*. Totowa, NJ: Littlefield, Adams, 1980.

Berger, Fred R. "Gratitude," *Ethics*, vol. 85 (1975): 298–309.

Blustein, Jeffrey. *Parents and Children: The Ethics of the Family*. New York: Oxford University Press, 1982.

Daniels, Norman. *Am I My Parents' Keeper?: An Essay on Justice Between the Young and the Old*. New York: Oxford University Press, 1988.

English, Jane. "What Do Grown Children Owe Their Parents?" In Onora O'Neill and William Ruddick (eds.), *Having Children*. New York: Oxford University Press, 1979.

Janeway, Elizabeth. "Incest: A Rational Look at the Oldest Taboo." In *Cross Sections from a Decade of Change*. New York: Harcourt Brace Jovanovich, 1977.

Keniston, Kenneth, and The Carnegie Council on Children. *All Our Children: The American Family Under Pressure*. New York: Harcourt Brace Jovanovich, 1977.

Neu, Jerome. "What is Wrong With Incest?" *Inquiry,* vol. 19 (1976).

O'Neill, Onora, and William Ruddick (eds.). *Having Children: Philosophical and Legal Reflections on Parenthood.* New York: Oxford University Press, 1979.

Pagelow, Mildred Daley. *Family Violence.* New York: Praeger, 1984.

Poster, Mark. *Critical Theory of the Family.* New York: Seabury Press, 1978.

Schoeman, Ferdinand. "Rights of Children, Rights of Parents, and the Moral Basis of the Family." *Ethics,* vol. 91 (1980).

Trebilcot, Joyce (ed.). *Mothering: Essays in Feminist Theory.* Totowa, NJ: Rowman & Allanheld, 1983.

Wringe, C. A. *Children's Rights: A Philosophical Study.* Boston: Routledge & Kegan Paul, 1982.

CHAPTER 18

Friendship

Ethics books emphasizing theories about right conduct rarely give friendship more than passing mention. At best, they treat it as one of many sources of obligation or as a context in which moral dilemmas might arise. At worst, they dismiss it as a source of private pleasure that poses a threat to justice in that it involves a kind of favoritism seemingly incompatible with the demands of impartiality and fairness.

Shifting to an emphasis on character and personal relationships, however, invites a different perspective that is closer to common sense. We do, after all, ordinarily think of the caring involved in friendship as having special significance morally; moreover, we are uneasy about people who strike us as incapable of friendship. These considerations led Aristotle to devote two of the ten books of his *Nicomachean Ethics* to friendship. In this chapter we examine both the moral value of and the moral limits on friendship.

An Example of Friendship

Each of us will have in mind personal examples of friendship, but it may be helpful to cite one example here. In her memoirs, entitled *Pentimento*, the American playwright Lillian Hellman describes her friendship with a person she calls Julia. Hellman and Julia were close friends from the time they were twelve until Julia's death almost twenty years later. Their friendship began with mutual interests and enjoyment of each other's company and deepened through shared activities and experiences. Hellman recalls, for example, the first time she was allowed to sleep overnight at her friend's house on a New Year's Eve in New York when they were both twelve:

Each New Year's Eve of my life has brought back the memory of that night. Julia and I lay in twin beds and she recited odds and ends of poetry . . . Dante in Italian, Heine in German, and even though I could not understand either language, the sounds were so lovely that I felt a sweet sadness as if much was ahead in the world, much that was going to be fine and fulfilling if I could ever find my way.[1]

Hellman and Julia spent many hours together, often seeing each other daily. Although their conversations were permeated by their shared love of literature, they "also talked like all young people, of possible beaux and husbands and babies, and heredity versus environment, and can romantic love last, mixing stuff like that in speeches made only for the pleasure of girls on the edge of growing up."[2] They went on several camping trips near Lake Champlain, including a particularly memorable one when they were sixteen. On that trip Julia captured a rabbit that the two young women skinned, cooked, and ate for dinner. The experience left a permanent mark on Hellman: "Even now, seeing any island, I am busy with that rabbit and fantasies of how I would make do alone, without shelter or tools."[3]

As with most friendships, there were disagreements and frictions that periodically strained their closeness. But these were relatively mild. By the time they turned eighteen, however, circumstances separated them: Julia moved to Oxford for undergraduate studies and later to Vienna for medical school, while Hellman attended college in New York where she began writing plays. Yet their feelings for one another never diminished, and they continued to write and occasionally to see each other. During the 1930s Julia had become a socialist and had moved to Berlin to join the anti-Hitler underground and fight fascism. Her socialist principles led her to distribute her considerable wealth to the poor she met in Berlin. Contrary to those principles, she sent frequent and extravagant gifts to Hellman whenever she saw anything she might like.

In 1937, while visiting Paris, Hellman accepted an invitation to attend a theatre festival in Moscow and called Julia to arrange a brief meeting on the way. To her surprise Julia asked her to stay in Paris a few days longer until she could send a messenger with a special request. Despite the mystery Hellman immediately agreed to wait: "It would not have occurred to me to ignore what Julia told me to do because that's the way it had always been between us."[4] When the messenger arrived, he requested that Hellman carry to Berlin $50,000 of Julia's money, to be used to buy the freedom of Jews and other victims of Nazi persecution. The messenger also said that even though every precaution was to be taken, there would be some danger, and Julia would completely understand if she was unable to grant her request.

Hellman agreed to the request and, not without intrigue, smuggled the money into Berlin. For safety's sake she was allowed to meet with Julia only briefly in a restaurant. There she burst into tears when she saw that one of Julia's legs had been amputated following an injury sustained in a Nazi attack. Less than a year later she was informed by telegram that the Nazis had murdered Julia. It was twenty-five years before Hellman was able to write about the incident, and then out of respect for Julia she withheld her true name in order to protect her family and friends who were still alive.

Definition of Friendship

The example of Hellman and Julia illustrates many features typical of friendship. Yet friendship comes in many forms, and it would be futile to try defining it with a simple set of conditions that sharply distinguish it from other relationships based on caring. Our interest is in relationships deeper than mere acquaintance, even though in real life we typically count as friends people we have spoken with only a few times. The best we can do here is to indicate several criteria characterizing central (or "paradigm") examples of friendship.

First, friendship involves sharing: mutual activities, shared experiences, reciprocal interests in each other, and intimate communication. This was notable in the early years of the Hellman-Julia friendship, and it continued during the years when exchange of letters was the main shared activity.

Second, friendship involves reciprocal giving. Hellman and Julia gave freely of their time, attention, and energy, as well as exchanging material gifts. The reciprocal nature of the giving was not diminished by Julia's ability to give far more materially because of her inherited wealth.

Third, the motive for sharing and giving is based on mutual caring. This involves desires on the part of two friends for the well-being of each other, as well as an especially deep affirmation of the importance of the other person. It is true that Julia made a request placing Hellman at risk, but the request derived from a matter of extraordinary moral importance, and Julia took every possible precaution to protect her.

Fourth, friendship entails that special affection we refer to as "liking." Friends enjoy each other's company, enjoy hearing news about each other, accept each other's imperfections, and delight in each other's particular characteristics.

Fifth, friendship is built on a sense of mutual understanding, understanding based on direct acquaintance with each other and shared personal knowledge. In part this understanding arises from the time spent together, and in part from personal conversation and correspondence. The relationship is "intimate" not only in the sense of involving close emotional ties, but also in the willingness of friends to disclose more about themselves than they do to most other people.

Sixth, there is trust on the part of both friends. The trust is based on mutual commitments to care about each other's well-being, together with mutual understanding.

Seventh, friends share mutual respect, especially respect for each other's needs for freedom and self-respect. The friendship is entered into and sustained voluntarily. It is not based primarily on a desire to dominate and manipulate, nor on a desire to be submissive.

Eighth, in friendship there is mutual acknowledgement and affirmation of the relationship (as characterized by the preceding features). Each friend is aware of the ties joining them, hopes that the ties will be maintained, and is committed to making an effort to preserve the friendship. In fact, to some extent the high degree of caring involved depends on an anticipation that the friendship will continue.

The Value of Friendship

Why, and when, is friendship valuable, in particular morally valuable? Aristotle stated that friendship is valuable when based on admiration for the good traits of character in each other rather than on mutual usefulness or mutual pleasure. This is because friendship reinforces and develops good character through mutual inspiration and character building. The same might be said when the shared activities joining the friends are altruistic causes, such as helping the poor, promoting world peace, or working to preserve human rights. However, let us set aside these special cases for a moment and require only that the shared activities be morally permissible (not necessarily admirable) and that the mutual liking not be centered on immoral traits.

In moral terms the most significant aspect of friendship is the mutual caring based on mutual respect and understanding. Each friend is especially concerned about the other's well-being, and each willingly expresses that concern without losing either self-respect or respect for the freedom of the other person. This is morally desirable and admirable in and of itself. Moreover, the degree of moral goodness involved depends upon the degree of caring.

This view contrasts with Kant's narrow claim that the only thing morally good in and of itself is the desire to act for the sake of duty. It also differs sharply from all theories based on Kant's definition of the "moral point of view" as impartial regard for all people equally. The caring involved in friendship is morally valuable precisely because it is grounded in especially deep concern based on appreciating what is unique in the friend. It constitutes a singularly important way of recognizing the worth of individuals, a way that fulfills the human need to feel liked based on intimate knowledge about oneself.

Friendship is also morally valuable because of its general consequences.

Often, it increases our capacities for understanding people who are not our friends. It can provide a quickened sense of why people have moral worth, and it can augment our sensitivity to the needs of strangers. Friendship also offers primary support for self-respect: Our sense of self-worth is more vulnerable than we like to think, and nothing can help it more than a supportive friendship.

In addition to these distinctively moral goods friendship contributes to personal well-being. It increases delight in each other's company, in working and playing together on the basis of mutual concern. There are of course the agonies of friendship: grief in response to the harm befalling a friend, sadness at being unable to help when circumstances prevent us, and anguish when we fail to help because we are apathetic or selfishly preoccupied. Even when friendship is painful, however, it usually adds to the sense of worthwhileness of our lives. It also evokes our interests and enlivens our activities to know that they matter to our friends.

Acknowledging these good aspects of friendship does not mean we should be preoccupied with them. Although they may serve as reminders of the value of friendship, they cannot provide the primary reasons for having friends. To repeat, friendship is based on care and concern, and its origins lie in spontaneous liking. Motivation primarily deriving from an attitude of "What's in it for me?" only inhibits or erodes friendship.

Moral Limits on Friendship

We must qualify some of the points previously made concerning the value of friendship. For one thing, praise for friendship has sometimes been excessive. Writing in the sixteenth century, for example, Montaigne asserted that "a single dominant friendship dissolves all other obligations" and that in an ideal friendship "each one gives himself so wholly to his friend that he has nothing left to distribute elsewhere."[5] Closer to our own time, E. M. Forster expressed a related sentiment:

> I hate the idea of causes, and if I had to choose between betraying my country and betraying my friend, I hope I should have the guts to betray my country. Such a choice may scandalize the modern reader, and he may stretch out his patriotic hand to the telephone at once and ring up the police. It would not have shocked Dante, though. Dante places Brutus and Cassius in the lowest circle of Hell because they had chosen to betray their friend Julius Caesar rather than their country Rome.[6]

It is impossible to assess Forster's remark without first knowing about the particular context—the kind of country, the kind of friendship, the kinds of betrayal at issue and their probable consequences. If the country, for example, were a totalitarian state of the sort George Orwell described in *1984* (in which the government suppressed personal relationships as threatening its absolute power), then Forster's remark is an admirable call for heroism. If, however, the friendship were one among terrorists bent on destroying a democratic society, then his remark is morally grotesque.

Surely, too, Montaigne's assertion represents harmful hyperbole in view of the numerous moral obligations limiting the claims of friendship. Earlier we assumed that the shared activities in friendships were morally permissible. But now consider situations in which they are immoral. For example, there is friendship among criminals and in the "brotherhood" of organized crime. Insofar as these relationships involve genuine mutual caring, they have moral worth. That worth may be overshadowed, however, by the harm to which the friendship contributes.

It would be moral idolatry to elevate friendship to moral supremacy. No simple general ranking system dictates when the loyalties of a friendship should outweigh or temper loyalties to other friends, to family, or to community. Julia provides an interesting illustration of this. When it came to gifts for Hellman, she allowed personal affection to override her socialist principles of egalitarianism, which prohibit exorbitant gifts to financially secure friends. And her generosity seems admirable. In response to the possibility of saving innocent human lives, however, she was willing to request that Hellman make the personal sacrifice of putting herself at risk.

Strict egalitarians sometimes object to friendship as violating what they believe is owed equally to all other human beings, or at least to those having the greatest need. For them, the singling out of a few individuals for special attention conflicts with the ideal of universal love for all. As our earlier discussion of the value of friendship might imply, we strongly disagree with that position. Nevertheless, there are special contexts in which the claims of justice for all people, as expressed in impartiality and fairness, ought to restrict the exercise of generosity to friends. When a public official is responsible for appointing the best person for a job in which competence must be maximized (for example, a police chief or a chief surgeon), allowing friendship to bias the selection represents a violation of public trust.

Yet even in public life—in politics, business, and the professions—we place a high value on friendship and its special loyalties. It is often desirable to work with colleagues who are also friends, and we may give some preference to friends when not strictly prohibited by professional responsibilities. Even the competitive world of profit-making business recognizes the importance of "mentor relationships" involving friendship, whereby an established member of a company aids a younger one to advance in the company. Is this unjustified? Not insofar as friendships serve to humanize work situations that would otherwise be impersonal and even degrading.

Summary

Friendship has several characteristic features: sharing and reciprocal giving motivated by caring (i.e., the desire to promote the well-being of each other); mutual liking (i.e., mutual affection and enjoyment of each other's company); mutual understanding, trust, and respect; and mutual recognition and affirmation of the friendship.

Because of the mutual caring involved, friendship has moral worth. Not only does it represent an important way to appreciate and affirm the worth of other individuals, it also frequently results in good consequences such as contributing to happiness and increasing our capacity to understand people in general. Friendship can be harmful, however, when it leads to the violation of important obligations.

DISCUSSION TOPICS

1. Philosophers influenced by Kant argue that morality, by definition, requires impartiality in how we deal with other people. Consider, for example, the following comment:

   > Morality is, at the very least, the effort to guide one's conduct by reason—that is, to do what there are the best reasons for doing—while giving equal weight to the interests of each individual who will be affected by one's conduct.[7]

   Present and defend your view of whether friendship has a moral importance that justifies (indeed, requires) not being completely impartial in all contexts. Also, identify several contexts in which morality does require strict impartiality and forbids allowing friendships to bias decisions.

2. Just as we speak of "true love," we sometimes speak of "true friendship." Presumably, true or genuine friendships meet some criteria that distinguish them from less valuable relationships. In your view, what are these criteria? That is, what features of some friendships make them especially valuable?

3. Lillian Hellman was willing out of friendship to undertake a course of action that involved some danger. What does this willingness indicate about the nature of the friendship she had with Julia? Also, in requesting that Hellman undertake the action, was Julia being disloyal to Hellman or violating their friendship in any way?

4. Friendship requires mutual caring. Does that mean it requires "pure altruism" in the sense of desiring the well-being of the friend for its own sake and without any ulterior motives of self-interest? Or is friendship ultimately a matter of promoting someone's good in order to get something good for oneself in return? In your answer take account of Lawrence Blum's view in the following passage, and give examples of what you think he means:

   > Caring and the acts of beneficence in friendship are not separate from my own interests, from what is personally a good to me; it is not, in that sense,

'disinterested.' In fact, friendship is a context in which the division between self-interest and other-interest is often not applicable. The friendship itself defines what is of importance to me, and in that sense what is in my interest. In that sense I do not generally sacrifice my own interest in acting for the good of my friend. I act with a sense of the friendship's importance to me, even though it is the friend whose benefit I directly aim at (i.e., which is my motive for acting), and not my own.[8]

5. We can be friendly toward a great many people, but we can be close friends with far fewer people at any given time. Explain why this is, and in doing so clarify the distinction between friendliness and friendship.

6. Express in your own words Aristotle's argument in the following passage:

> Whatever existence means for each class of men, whatever it is for whose sake they value life, in *that* they wish to occupy themselves with their friends; and so some drink together, others dice together, others join in athletic exercises and hunting, or in the study of philosophy, each class spending their days together in whatever they love most in life; for since they wish to live with their friends, they do and share in those things which give them the sense of living together. Thus the friendship of bad men turns out an evil thing (for because of their instability they unite in bad pursuits, and besides they become evil by becoming like each other), while the friendship of good men is good, being augmented by their companionship.[9]

Is Aristotle's argument a good one?

SUGGESTED READINGS

Aristotle. *Nichomachean Ethics*. Trans. W. D. Ross. In Richard McKeon (ed.), *The Basic Works of Aristotle,* Books 8 and 9. New York: Random House, 1941.

Bernikow, Louise. "Friends." Chapter 4 of *Among Women*. New York: Harper & Row, 1981.

Blum, Lawrence A. *Friendship, Altruism and Morality*. Boston: Routledge & Kegan Paul, 1980.

Cooper, John M. "Aristotle on Friendship." In Amelie Oksenberg Rorty (ed.), *Essays on Aristotle's Ethics*. Berkeley, CA: University of California Press, 1980.

Falk, W. D. "Morality, Self, and Others." In Hector-Neri Castaneda and George Nakhnikian (eds.), *Morality and the Language of Conduct*. Detroit, MI: Wayne State University Press, 1965.

Feinberg, Joel. "Psychological Egoism." In Joel Feinberg (ed.), *Reason and Responsibility,* 6th ed. Belmont, CA: Wadsworth, 1986.

Forster, E. M. "What I Believe." In *Two Cheers for Democracy*. New York: Harcourt, Brace & World, 1951.

Hellman, Lillian. *Pentimento*. New York: New American Library, 1974.

Kant, Immanuel. "Friendship." In *Lectures on Ethics,* trans. Louis Infield. New York: Harper & Row, 1963.

Meilander, Gilbert C. *Friendship: A Study in Theological Ethics*. Notre Dame: University of Notre Dame Press, 1981.

Montaigne. "Of Friendship." In *The Complete Essays of Montaigne,* trans. Donald M. Frame. Stanford, CA: Stanford University Press, 1971.

Pogrebin, Letty Cottin. *Among Friends.* New York: McGraw-Hill, 1987.

Raymond, Janice G. *A Passion for Friends: Toward a Philosophy of Female Affection.* Boston: Beacon Press, 1986.

Solomon, Robert C., and Kristine R. Hanson. "The Personal Side of Business." Chapter 14 of *Above the Bottom Line: An Introduction to Business Ethics.* New York: Harcourt Brace Jovanovich, 1983.

Telfer, Elizabeth. "Friendship." *Proceedings of the Aristotelian Society,* vol. 71 (1970–71).

Weil, Simone. "Friendship." In *Waiting for God,* trans. Emma Crauford. New York: Harper & Row, 1973.

CHAPTER 19

Work

In a wide sense work is any form of producing something of value, whether or not one is paid for it. In this sense the unpaid homemaker who spends over eighty hours a week tending children, cleaning, cooking, ironing, and so on certainly works. In the narrower sense used here, however, work is an activity for which one receives financial compensation and that most often occurs (at least in part) outside the family and home.

Because most people work out of the necessity to earn a living, we tend to think of the morality of work as simply doing a job responsibly in return for money. Yet work is equally important in providing a context for caring relationships with colleagues, clients, and members of the public. Although a few types of work are conducted largely in isolation, most work requires shared activities, cooperation, and mutual respect. Collegiality is a virtue essential for both successful and enjoyable work. Moreover, most work situations involve caring relationships with people for whom one performs a service (clients and the public), and these require a range of virtues, from conscientiousness (in performing one's job) to loyalty. Caring relationships provide much of the meaning of work, as the following examples illustrate.

Examples of Two Workers

In his book *Working* Studs Terkel records more than a hundred interviews with workers from many occupations. The first interview is with a thirty-seven-year-old steelworker named Mike Lefevre, who describes his job as "strictly muscle work . . . pick it up, put it down, pick it up, put it down."[1] His steel mill handles from forty to fifty thousand pounds of steel each day, steel whose final destination is unknown to him. Lefevre takes no pride in his work, he explains, because "it's hard to take pride in a bridge you're never gonna cross, in a door you're never gonna open. You're mass-producing things and you never see the end result of it."[2] And he is nagged by a fear of being replaceable at any time by a machine that can do his work more efficiently.

From his supervisor he receives neither respect nor recognition for his endeavors. Instead, the boss "spies" on him, thereby compounding the monotony of the work with anxiety. Nor is there recognition from co-workers and the public: "It's the not-recognition by other people. To say a woman is *just* a housewife is degrading, right? Okay. *Just* a housewife. It's also degrading to say *just* a laborer."[3]

For Lefevre, work lacks intrinsic value—there is nothing in it worth doing for its own sake, nor are there any personal relationships to give it some meaning. Indeed, from his point of view the work is inherently bad. He sees nothing in it that evokes his talents and interests: "My attitude is that I don't get excited about my job. I do my work but I don't say whoopee-doo. The day I get excited about my job is the day I go to a head shrinker. How are you gonna get excited about pullin' steel?"[4] Work for him represents a long series of daily humiliations, frustrations, and resentments that periodically erupt into after-work barroom brawls. He works solely for a livelihood and for the sake of his family, especially in order to send his children to college.

Matters are very different, however, with other workers Terkel interviewed. They do not find their jobs demoralizing, even though their work is seemingly as repetitive and difficult as that of the steelworker. Consider Dolores Dante, a waitress in the same restaurant for twenty-three years, working from 5 P.M. to 2 A.M., six days a week. She suffers from arthritis and on many days goes home physically and emotionally exhausted. Nevertheless, she enjoys her work and takes great pride in serving people.

To outside observers many aspects of her work seem boringly routine, in particular waiting on an endless stream of customers. But Dante takes great interest in her work: "I have to be a waitress. How else can I learn about people? How else does the world come to me?"[5] She creates variety in her work through conversations with customers, and she takes pride in the considerable talents she has developed as a conversationalist.

She also introduces pleasing variations on routine work, such as by developing a repertoire of ways to ask for a customer's order. She also values her skills in dealing diplomatically with temperamental cooks. And at times she even creates an imaginative personal drama in her work: "To be a waitress, it's an art. I feel like a ballerina, too. I have to go between those tables, between those chairs. . . . I do it with an air."[6]

Like Lefevre, Dante is annoyed by people who treat her with the attitude that she is *just* a waitress. But she is able to regard those individuals as failing to see the genuine value in the service she has to offer. She also has to contend with "spying" supervisors and the fear that she is replaceable by others who want her job. Yet she deals with these problems as she does with other difficult aspects of the work, without being overcome by a sense of being superfluous or unimportant.

Unlike Lefevre, Dante finds her work inherently valuable, in addition to being instrumentally valuable, that is, valuable as a means to other good things, such as an income for herself and her children. A large part of the inherent value derives from the personal relationships she has with co-workers and members of the public she serves. These relationships bring recognition and a sense of cooperative endeavor and are for the most part based on mutual respect. She works with a clear sense of connection between her work and the good of the people she serves and works with.

Alienation and Work Ethics

We can state that Lefevre *feels* alienated from his work and *is* alienated from his work, the things he produces, and the people with whom he works. He does not *identify with* his work, nor can he affirm its worth. This subverts the possibility of caring relationships in the workplace; however, the absence of those relationships also contributes to worker alienation, as do some attitudes toward one's work.

Karl Marx (1818–1883), who introduced the concept of worker alienation, describes alienation from work activities in terms that fit Lefevre perfectly:

> What constitutes the alienation of labor? First, that the work is *external* to the worker, that it is not part of his nature; and that, consequently, he does not fulfill himself in his work but denies himself, has a feeling of misery rather than well being, does not develop freely his mental and physical energies but is physically exhausted and mentally debased. The worker therefore feels himself at home only during his leisure time, whereas at work he feels homeless. . . . [Work] is not the satisfaction of a need, but only a *means* for satisfying other needs.[7]

In addition to this characterization of alienation from the activity of working, Marx also analyzes alienation from the product of one's labor (e.g., when Lefevre is unable to experience the steel products as a personal self-expression), alienation from co-workers (i.e., feeling disconnected from colleagues), and alienation from other human beings in general. All these forms of alienation involve a lack of connection with and personal affirmation of the thing from which one is alienated. In Marx's view work should be central to our self-esteem and our sense of identity (i.e., our sense of who we are). Hence, alienation from work is ultimately alienation from ourselves—from who we ideally are.

Marx argued that worker alienation was an inevitable product of capitalism whereby workers sell their labor to someone else for money (which is then used to purchase things satisfying their desires). As the case of Dolores Dante suggests, however, the causes of worker alienation are probably more complicated. In subsequent sections we will focus on one such cause: the nature of the personal relationships at work.

Before continuing, however, we should note a few other attitudes toward work—other "work ethics"—than those of Lefevre (work as a necessary evil) and Marx (work as the primary avenue to self-fulfillment). One is the "Protestant Work Ethic," which the sociologist Max Weber saw as underlying the historical development of capitalism. According to this ethic people are obligated to refrain from pleasures by engaging in work, however onerous and distasteful it may be. This enables us to serve the community, to avoid becoming a social burden, and to accumulate wealth in the service of God. Weber quotes an influential Protestant minister:

> If God shows you a way in which you may lawfully get more than in another way (without wrong to your soul or to any other), if you refuse this, and choose the less gainful way, you cross one of the ends of your calling, and you refuse to be God's steward, and to accept His gifts and use them for Him when He requireth it: you may labour to be rich for God, though not for the flesh and sin.[8]

As this ethic later became secularized, it tended to encourage the seeking of wealth for its own sake. Perhaps it also formed a rationale for workaholics who devote themselves to work beyond reasonable bounds. Both the Protestant work ethic and workaholism elevate work over personal relationships (whether at work or in personal life).

An opposing work ethic is suggested by Gilbert Meilaender, who rejects the idea that we should "live in order to work" and favors instead "working in order to live." Whether or not work is inherently unpleasant, its primary role in human life is to be an instrumental good. Work provides the leisure time necessary for sustaining personal relationships with family and friends:

> When work as we know it emerges as the dominant idea in our lives—
> when we identify ourselves to others in terms of what we do for a living,
> work for which we are paid—and when we glorify such work in terms
> of self-fulfillment, it is time for Christian ethics to speak a good word
> for working simply in order to live. Perhaps we need to suggest today
> that it is quite permissible, even appropriate, simply to work in order
> to live and to seek one's fulfillment elsewhere—in personal bonds like
> friendship.[9]

Probably there is no one work ethic that is obligatory for all people; rather, a variety of attitudes toward work seem morally permissible. Nevertheless, three features of work improve its moral worth wherever they are present: collegiality, loyalty, and caring for members of the public who benefit from one's work.

Collegiality

Collegiality entails more than refraining from unjustly defaming, insulting, harassing, or degrading colleagues. It is a more positive ideal and virtue. Craig Ihara defines it this way:

> The conclusion I have reached is that collegiality is a kind of connectedness grounded in respect for professional expertise and in a commitment to the goals and values of the profession, and that, as such, collegiality includes a disposition to support and cooperate with one's colleagues.[10]

According to this definition the key ingredients of collegiality are mutual respect, connectedness, and cooperation. These ingredients, and hence collegiality, can be present in all forms of work, not just professions like law, medicine, and teaching, which require advanced education.

Respect for one's colleagues is an attitude, not simply a pattern of conduct. One who respects one's co-workers values them for their expertise and for their devotion to serving some public good. As with friendship, Ihara claims respect must be reciprocal; however it seems possible for one person to display collegiality toward a colleague who does not reciprocate with the same attitude.

Connectedness consists of an awareness of being part of a social structure and a community of people who together pursue some shared good. It is a sense that what one does is possible because others are involved along with oneself. There must be at least a minimal sense of shared values concerning the goal being pursued together.

Cooperation is the willingness to work together and to support one another in pursuit of the common goal. Although cooperation is compatible with moderate degrees of competitiveness in which co-workers help stimulate one another's endeavors, it is undermined when competition with co-workers becomes cutthroat.

Collegiality, which thus encompasses the three elements of mutual respect, connectedness, and cooperation, is a moral virtue for two reasons, according to Ihara. One concerns the benefits to the public and the other concerns a benefit to workers. First, collegiality enables professionals (and, we would add, workers in general) to serve the public good by strengthening their motivation at work. It does this by creating an environment that supports mutual endeavors, enlivens shared commitments, and encourages responsible work. Second, it contributes to making work inherently worthwhile for those who engage in it. Dolores Dante found significance in her work in part because of the attitudes of goodwill and shared endeavor of co-workers. Mike Lefevre found work hateful in part because of the absence of a sense of collegiality with co-workers.

Loyalty

Collegiality is one expression of the wider virtue of loyalty. Loyalty in the workplace has several dimensions: loyalty to colleagues, to one's employer, to one's corporation, and to the clients and public one serves. Many of the difficulties of professional life arise because of conflicts among two or more of these loyalties and the obligations they engender.

Loyalties involve obligations or duties, but they have other elements as well. To be loyal is to want to meet one's obligations because of a concern for a person or group. One is motivated by something more personal than Kant's "acting for the sake of duty." There must be caring and concern for the person, group, or cause one is loyal to.

Josiah Royce (1855–1916) proposed the following definition of loyalty: "Loyalty is the willing and practical and thoroughgoing devotion of a person to a cause."[11] As such, according to Royce, loyalty is inherently good. He recognizes that loyalty as practiced by fanatical devotees to evil causes can have very bad consequences, making it "instrumentally bad" (i.e., bad as a means to bad effects). Nevertheless, it is always inherently good in relation to a person's character:

> Whoever is loyal whatever be his cause, is devoted, is active, surrenders his private self-will, controls himself, is in love with his cause, and believes in it. The loyal man is thus in a certain state of mind which has its own value for himself. To live a loyal life, whatever be one's cause, is to live in a way which is certainly free from many well-known sources of inner dissatisfaction. Thus hesitancy is often correct by loyalty; for the cause plainly tells the loyal man what to do. Loyalty, again, tends to unify life, to give it centre, fixity, stability.[12]

It is true, of course, that devotion to both moral and immoral causes can have some good effects on the personalities of particular individuals. But that does not make it inherently good, as Royce goes on to suggest. In fact, insofar as the unifying and stabilizing of a personality strengthens an individual's commitment to immoral causes, they are not desirable.

After raising similar criticisms against Royce, John Ladd suggests redefining loyalty. His definition makes loyalty a virtue, and hence inherently good, without implying there is anything good about immoral fanatics. His definition builds moral duties into the concept of loyalty:

> Loyalty, strictly speaking, demands what is morally due the object of loyalty. . . . Loyalty includes fidelity in carrying out one's duties to the person or group of persons who are the object of loyalty; but it embraces more than that, for it implies an attitude, perhaps an affection or sentiment, toward such persons. Furthermore, at the very least, loyalty requires the complete subordination of one's own private interest in favor of giving what is due.[13]

Because there are no moral duties to pursue immoral ends, the immoral fanatic cannot be called loyal. For example, there cannot be "loyal Nazis." The cause of Nazism is thoroughly immoral, and there are no (moral) duties to serve Hitler; hence, the crucial idea of fidelity to one's duties is missing. Loyalty presupposes that the group, individual, or cause to which one is loyal is morally good or permissible.

Adopting Ladd's definition, we can locate the primary good of loyalty in its role in shaping character in the direction of conscientious, responsible, and caring work and relationships at work. At this point, however, we must consider an objection: Is loyalty obsolete and even harmful in today's work environment?

Modern corporations, especially profit-making ones, are abstract and impersonal entities. Employers have little or no loyalty toward employees: They fire them whenever they deem it necessary for the corporation. This makes it seem unfair to expect loyalty from employees. All that should be required is that employees do a responsible job in return for fair wages.

Furthermore, loyalty can have bad consequences. When combined with employees' self-interest in keeping their jobs, it can lead workers to do whatever the boss orders, often at the expense of the public good. For example, many employees engage in or know about unethical practices at work about which they remain silent, motivated by a combination of self-interest and loyalty to the corporation. There is a need for courageous individuals willing to "blow the whistle" by informing someone outside the corporation of dangers to the public.[14]

To develop this criticism, there are innumerable instances when whistleblowing would serve the public good. One example concerns the first crash of a fully loaded jumbo jet, which occurred in 1974 when a cargo door blew open in midair. The open cargo door depressurized the cargo area, collapsing the floor of the passenger area, along which ran the pilot's steering mechanism. All 346 people on board were killed.

Two years prior to the crash it was known that the door was unsafely designed. The senior engineer in charge of the design wrote a memo to his boss stating, "It seems to me inevitable that, in the twenty years ahead of us, DC-10 cargo doors will come open and I would expect this to usually result in the loss of the airplane." [15] Without disagreeing with the engineer's judgment, top management decided on financial grounds that nothing would be done. The engineer did not whistle-blow (to the government or to a journalist), and many people died.

Do such tragedies mean that loyalty to companies, colleagues, and employers are harmful? Perhaps not. Recall that Ladd's definition of loyalty places moral limits on what is required by loyalty. Loyalty means faithfully and caringly fulfilling one's (prima facie) duties to one's corporation and to the people with whom one works. But there are also (prima facie) duties not to harm innocent members of the public. In the airplane case the duties to the public override those to the employer.

There is, however, some truth in the objection that it is unfair to expect loyalty from employees when employers show little or no loyalty. Insofar as corporations encourage an entirely impersonal contract relationship with employees, then the conditions for reciprocal loyalty and care are subverted, resulting in the depersonalized and alienated work relationships illustrated in the case of Mike Lefevre. Corporations do in fact vary greatly in the extent to which this occurs.

Altruism and Career Choice

Most careers, and all professions, have some impact on the public good. Once one embarks on a profession, one acquires duties to the public. These duties place limits on duties to the corporation for which one works, as we saw in the case of the airplane disaster. But is there a duty to embark on any particular kind of career? More generally, should any moral considerations enter into decisions about careers?

Two points are obvious. First, there is an obligation not to pick careers that are likely to cause more harm than good. This rules out "careers" in crime, and it also rules out careers that violate one's conscience. If one believes that the tobacco industry or the nuclear armaments industry is harmful, then one should not work in those industries. The argument that "if I don't take this job someone else will" does not excuse one from doing what one views as harmful.

Second, individuals have a moral right to select their own careers, at least within a democratic society that values individual liberty. We have a human right to pursue our career interests given the available options, and we are also in the best position to judge what those interests are.

Nevertheless, having a right to select a (morally permissible) career does not mean that one will select the morally best career available. Should we think in terms of the moral good we can achieve through a career, or is career choice entirely a matter of self-interest (as is commonly thought)?

Norman Care contends that the good of the community should enter into career decisions—that is, careers should be selected in light of our membership in a community. Each of us, he urges, is responsible for other people who share this world with us. Obviously, we live in a world where millions of people are destitute, where gross inequities exist, and where not nearly enough is being done to help people in need. Caring for the public good should enter heavily into career decisions.

In developing this view, Care contrasts three approaches to career choice. A purely *self-realization ethics* implies that personal fulfillment should be the sole principle guiding career choice. A purely *service ethics,* by contrast, suggests that careers should be selected on the basis of the maximum good we can do for people. Service to others should have a higher priority than does self-realization. A *mixed ethics* states that self-realization has priority in selected careers but that, once careers are chosen, they should be pursued in ways that serve the public good as much as possible.

Care argues that service ethics is the correct view. A purely self-realization ethics reflects and encourages callousness. It is based on the false moral assumption that we are in the world for ourselves rather than as participants among a community of people having equal worth and importance. Moreover, the mixed-ethics view makes caring relationships with other people secondary to self-interest, when in fact the opposite should be true. At least caring for others ought to have priority as long as we live in a world where "relatively few are able to realize themselves, relatively many suffer destitution in some or many of its desperate forms, and no effective general ameliorating scheme is in place at all."[16]

There is a problem with this view, however, that was voiced much earlier by Hastings Rashdall (1858–1924). Rashdall was a utilitarian who thought we are obligated to select careers that promote the most good for the most people. This would seem to commit him to a service ethics, but in fact Rashdall defended what Care calls a mixed ethics. He reminded us that careers extend over many years and make great demands. These demands can generate frustration and harm unless they fit our talents and interests. Thus, people who wish to succeed in a service career must have a "calling" for it, because selecting a service career out of a sense of duty is probably harmful:

> Certain social functions require for their adequate fulfillment that they should be done in a certain spirit. Such functions demand the possession of certain qualities of mind or heart or character which cannot be summoned up at the command of the will, and cannot be satisfactorily performed merely as a matter of duty. . . . It is for the general good that every man should do the work for which he is most fitted; and as a

general rule, a natural liking for the work or kind of life adopted is one of the most important qualifications for it.[17]

Using this line of reasoning, Rashdall concluded that it is morally permissible, in selecting careers, to place greater emphasis on self-realization than on service. Nevertheless, once a career is selected, caring relationships should be sought and sustained as much as possible in order to promote as much good as possible. Determining whether Care or Rashdall is correct will be left as a discussion question.

Summary

Most work involves caring relationships, at least potentially, and the presence of these relationships adds to the meaning derived from work. This is true whether one's "work ethics" leads one to value work as intrinsically worthwhile or as an instrumental good that serves primarily as a means to other intrinsic goods.

The meaning of work is subverted when workers become alienated from their work activities, the products of their work, or the people with whom they work. Alienation, as Karl Marx analyzed it, involves the inability to identify with something: to see it as a personal involvement or self-expression, and to value it. The absence of caring relationships in the workplace is a major cause of alienation.

Collegiality as a virtue has three aspects: respecting one's co-workers and having that respect reciprocated, having an attitude or sense of being connected with colleagues in a shared enterprise serving some public good, and being cooperative in the sense of being willing to work together with colleagues. It is inherently good as one form of a caring relationship, and also good as a means to whatever public good is served by work.

Loyalty is a wider virtue. It is best understood as faithful devotion to fulfilling one's moral duties, which rules out blind and fanatical service to immoral causes. Loyalty to colleagues, employers, and companies is appropriate if there is reciprocal loyalty and if genuine duties and goods are being served by that loyalty. Loyalties frequently come into conflict in the workplace, however, requiring balanced reflection to identify the primary duty in a given situation.

How far should moral reasons enter into the selection of a career? Self-realization ethics states that one's self-interest is all that needs to be considered (assuming the work is not inherently immoral). Service ethics states careers should be selected on the basis of the maximum good we can do for people. Mixed ethics states that self-realization is most important but that, once a career is chosen, it should be pursued so as to maximize the public good.

DISCUSSION TOPICS

1. What moral considerations should be taken into account in choosing a career? On this issue, do you agree with Norman Care, with Hastings Rashdall, or with neither of them?

2. You are working with a colleague who confesses to you that he has been charging personal long-distance phone calls to the company for several years, against company regulations, but that he recently stopped doing so. Does collegiality obligate you to say nothing about the infraction to your employer? Does loyalty to the company obligate you to report the infraction? What should you do?

3. With respect to the case of the airplane crash in 1974, we stated that the obligation to warn the public of dangers should override the duty to the company to obey one's employer. However, it is likely that if the engineer had engaged in whistle-blowing (by going outside the company to inform the public of the dangerous cargo door), he would have been fired. Most whistle-blowers are fired or demoted, and frequently they are "blacklisted"—that is, they are prevented from obtaining a comparable job by negative evaluations when other companies, to which the fired individual applies for a job, call to check on the references of the individual. Do these facts excuse the engineer from warning the public in view of the extreme self-sacrifice that would be required?

4. In a similar connection consider the tragic explosion of space shuttle *Challenger* on January 29, 1986. The disaster was due largely to unsafe seals joining segments of a booster rocket. A number of engineers for Morton Thiokol, the designer and builder of the rocket, argued against making the launch. One engineer, Allan McDonald, had been a critic of the seals long before the disaster. He urged both Thiokol and NASA officials to postpone the launch because the seals had not been tested under comparable temperatures at the launch site. Unfortunately, his protests were rejected by the Thiokol management, who had authority for making the final launch recommendation to NASA. Identify the obligations and loyalties relevant to McDonald's situation. Which should have priority? In vigorously protesting the launch, did McDonald do everything morally required?

5. Professions are occupations requiring advanced education, sophisticated skills, and service to some important public good. Usually, they involve special caring relationships with clients. Moral dilemmas arise for professionals when two or more professional duties or loyalties come into conflict, or when a professional obligation conflicts with personal conscience. Defend your view about what ought to be done in each of the following cases, basing your answers on an ethical theory about right action. Also, what virtues are at stake in each case?

   a. Judges are responsible for upholding the laws. Suppose, however, that a judge views a particular law as grossly immoral, such as a law requiring excessive punishment for people convicted of using marijuana. Is the judge obligated to enforce laws that violate his or her personal conscience? Can a judge's caring about a particular individual justify departing from the law?

   b. Physicians have obligations to alleviate suffering and promote life. American physicians also work within a legal tradition that forbids euthanasia (that is, the intentional inflicting, motivated by benevolence, of death on a hopelessly ill or injured patient). Consider a physician who disagrees with this tradition and who has a patient suffering from terminal cancer. Safe dosages of morphine are no longer sufficient to stop the pain, and the patient begs for increased dosages, knowing they will hasten death. Assuming the physician is motivated by concern for the patient's good, is the physician justified in granting the patient's request?

c. Politicians sometimes are asked to lie in order to protect national security. One example occurred in 1980 during the U.S. attempt to save fifty-three Americans held hostage in Iran.[18] President Carter believed that if the rescue attempt was to have a chance of success, the Iranians had to believe that no military action was being planned. As a decoy he sent Secretary of State Cyrus Vance to assure U.S. allies publicly that the United States would not engage in military action if the allies would participate in enforcing economic sanctions against Iran. Vance made these deceitful assurances to people with whom he had previous relationships of trust. Before doing so, he submitted a confidential letter of resignation to President Carter, effective after the rescue attempt. Was his resignation inappropriate? Do you think he should have refused President Carter's order?

SUGGESTED READINGS

Anthony, P. D. *The Ideology of Work.* New York: Methuen, 1978.

Best, Fred (ed.). *The Future of Work.* Englewood Cliffs, NJ: Prentice-Hall, 1973.

Bolles, Richard Nelson. *What Color Is Your Parachute? A Practical Manual for Job Hunters and Career Changers.* Berkeley, CA: Ten Speed Press. New edition each year.

Callahan, Joan C. (ed.). *Ethical Issues in Professional Life.* New York: Oxford University Press, 1988.

Care, Norman S. "Career Choice." In *On Sharing Fate.* Philadelphia: Temple University Press, 1987.

Donaldson, Thomas, and Patricia H. Werhane (eds.). *Ethical Issues in Business.* 3rd ed. Englewood Cliffs, NJ: Prentice-Hall, 1988.

Flores, Albert (ed.). *Professional Ideals.* Belmont, CA: Wadsworth, 1988.

Frankena, William K. "The Philosophy of Vocation." *Thought,* vol. 51 (1976): 393–408.

Glover, Jonathan. "Work." In *What Sort of People Should There Be?* New York: Penguin, 1984.

Goldman, Alan H. *The Moral Foundations of Professional Ethics.* Totowa, NJ: Rowman & Littlefield, 1980.

Ihara, Craig K. "Collegiality as a Professional Virtue." In Albert Flores (ed.), *Professional Ideals.* Belmont, CA: Wadsworth, 1988.

Martin, Mike W., and Roland Schinzinger. *Ethics in Engineering,* 2nd ed. New York: McGraw-Hill, 1988.

Marx, Karl. *Economic and Philosophical Manuscripts.* In Erich Fromm, *Marx's Concept of Man.* New York: Ungar, 1966.

O'Toole, James, Jane L. Scheiber, and Linda C. Wood (eds.). *Working: Changes and Choices*. New York: Human Sciences Press, 1981.

Rashdall, Hastings. "Vocation." In *The Theory of Good and Evil,* Vol. II. Oxford: Clarendon Press, 1907.

Terkel, Studs. *Working*. New York: Avon Books, 1975.

Weber, Max. *The Protestant Ethic and the Spirit of Capitalism*. Trans. Talcott Parsons. New York: Scribner, 1958.

Work. Special issues of *The Philosophical Forum,* X, Nos. 2–4.

Work in America. Report of a Special Task Force to the Secretary of Health, Education, and Welfare. Cambridge, MA: MIT Press, 1973.

CHAPTER 20

Community

Voluntary service and giving to communities occurs on a massive scale in the United States. It is not, however, the exclusive domain of a few rich people and wealthy foundations—they account for only 10 percent of private donations. The remaining 90 percent comes from individuals, half of them in families whose income is under $39,000. Moreover, about half of Americans over thirteen years old volunteer an average of 3.5 hours of their time each week.[1]

This aspect of everyday morality—involvement in community—deserves more attention in ethics. When philosophers discuss moral community, they often have in mind an abstraction. The most famous such abstraction is Kant's "kingdom of ends": an imaginary situation in which all rational beings respect one another's autonomy and dignity. Here, by contrast, moral community refers to the moral ties that do or should be sustained by groups of people identified by their place of residence, shared traditions and culture, or common way of life within a neighborhood, state, country, religion, profession, or institution.

Consider, for example, a college. As a moral community it is defined by the moral relationships that do or should exist among students, professors, staff, trustees, local citizens, and alumni (living and dead). These relationships involve *special* ties of loyalty, shared value, and meaning—"special" in that they center on the aims of the college rather than on the general connections among all rational beings to which Kant referred. These ties, in turn, provide a context for moral activity and virtue for members of that community. In fact, with respect to morally concerned individuals—those having a reasonable degree of moral caring—it is plausible to argue that self-fulfillment requires some voluntary service and giving to the community. A dramatic illustration is the life of Jane Addams.

An Example of Community Service

Jane Addams was a pioneer in modern social work, a profession that did not exist in 1889 when she founded Hull-House. Hull-House was a "settlement house," that is, a community center created to serve the immigrant population in Chicago. In 1889 Addams and her friends renovated an old tenement building in an impoverished part of Chicago, moved in, and began offering a variety of services in response to the needs of the local community. Initial services included first aid, a public kitchen for people lacking income, and a day care service for children of working parents (most of whom worked twelve to fourteen hours a day). Later, they built many new buildings, including an art museum, a theatre, and a gymnasium. They recruited hundreds of college students and professors (including John Dewey, the leading American philosopher at the time) to help serve and teach over two thousand people each day.

It became clear to Addams that the needs of the immigrants required more than even this monumental enterprise could provide. She initiated and supported a variety of legal reforms: reducing working hours, prohibiting child labor, funding school playgrounds, improving sanitation, supporting women's voting rights, and creating the first juvenile court in the country. Later, as World War I approached, she devoted her energies to peace activism—the role for which she was the first woman to receive the Nobel Peace Prize.

What motivated Addams and her colleagues at Hull-House? According to her own account three motives were primary. First, they shared a conviction that democracy is more than a matter of political rights; it is the ideal of having everyone participate in the community. This ideal is based on the awareness that in a democracy the good of individuals is interwoven with the good of the masses: "The good we secure for ourselves is precarious and uncertain, is floating in the mid-air, until it is secured for all of us and incorporated into our common life."[2]

Second, Addams (like David Hume) believed that an innate sense of humanity generates altruistic desires. She thus found it entirely natural to help others.

Third, Addams asserted, community service connects us with people in ways that evoke our talents and lead to self-fulfillment:

> Nothing so deadens the sympathies and shrivels the power of enjoyment as the persistent keeping away from the great opportunities for help-fulness and a continual ignoring of the starvation struggle which makes up the life of at least half the race. To shut one's self away from that half of the [human] race life is to shut one's self away from the most vital part of it; it is to live out but half the humanity to which we have been

born heir and to use but half our faculties. We have all had longings for a fuller life which should include the use of these faculties.[3]

Individualism and Community

For Addams, community service was selfless, in the sense of unselfish; but it was not a pure "selflessness" in the sense of forgetting one's own interests and needs. Community involvement helped unfold her interests and capacities so as to create a richer self through relationships within a community. In this sense there are, and should be, mixed motives for volunteerism, and also for giving. Self-interest (one's own good) and altruism (concern for the good of others) combine in ways that are mutually strengthening. And the combination in no way lessens the virtue involved in the acts of altruism.

Pursuit of individual self-interest and commitment to the good of the community have more often been seen as opposed than complementary in American traditions, according to the sociologist Robert Bellah and his co-authors in *Habits of the Heart*. The lone individualist, whether a cowboy or a corporate entrepreneur, is glorified. Social involvement is mistakenly equated with conformity, that is, as passive acceptance of given social practices. The social rebel excites our imagination, whereas the community participant strikes us as a drudge.

Jane Addams reminds us that stunning individual expression is fully compatible with community service, indeed, that community service can be an ideal forum for individual expression. Addams was an extraordinary individualist in precisely the sense honored in American traditions: self-reliant, independent in thought, innovative, and tenacious in pursuit of her ideals.

In their studies of a wide cross-section of Americans, Bellah and his colleagues uncovered many individuals who were engaged in community service of the sort Addams pursued. To mention just one, they discovered Cecilia Dougherty, an activist in the Campaign for Economic Democracy, which educates, advises, and organizes interracial tenement dwellers in Southern California. Her involvement in the group resulted from her sustained concern for the plight of the underprivileged, a concern that stemmed from her family's tradition of participating in worker reforms.

In reflecting on Dougherty and others like her, Bellah points out that individualism and commitment are creatively intertwined in their lives:

> It is characteristic of Cecilia Dougherty and the others . . . that they
> define themselves through their commitments to a variety of communities
> rather than through the pursuit of radical autonomy [that is, separateness
> from community]. Yet Cecilia, like the others, exhibits a high degree of
> self-determination and efficacy. She exemplifies a form of individualism

that is fulfilled *in* community rather than against it. Conformism, the nemesis of American individualism, does not seem to be a problem for Cecilia and the others. Their involvement in practices of commitment makes them able to resist pressures to conform.[4]

By "community" Bellah means a group of interdependent—mutually dependent—people with a shared history, jointly participating in social practices, having a common forum for discussion and mutual decision making, and looking to the future with a sense of shared hope. Understood in this way, a community is changing and responsive to individual initiative. In turn, it enables individuals to acquire extended and enriched identities through relationships with other people.

How Much Should We Give?

Yet, it might be objected, individuality can be enriched and extended in many other ways than through community involvement. Rather than giving our time and resources to the community, why not focus them entirely in pursuing our careers, our families, and our hobbies? After all, isn't the role of government to sustain community, and aren't our community duties fulfilled in voting and paying taxes so that government can fulfill that role?

Moreover, the idea of a duty to give to the community (beyond the minimal requirements of citizenship) seems perplexing in that there seems to be no way that duty can be structured and focused. To whom or to what are we obligated to give? Should our money go to the poor or be donated to the fine arts? And how much of our resources should we give? Does the amount people should give (if anything) depend on their personal preferences, and, if so, how can something so personal or subjective have anything to do with morality?

One way to approach these questions is by applying Kant's distinction between "perfect" and "imperfect" duties. Perfect duties are those that hold for all situations: One ought to keep one's promises, be truthful, pay one's debts, not kill innocent people, and so on. Kant thought there were no exceptions to such duties. A more plausible view, however, as we saw in Chapter 4, is that these are prima facie duties that sometimes have legitimate exceptions when more pressing duties override them. Imperfect duties, by contrast, allow us discretion about when to act on them. In particular, the duty of beneficence or benevolence requires that we help other people who are in distress, but it also allows us to decide when and how much of our time and money we donate to charitable causes.

A difficulty with this view is that it provides no guidance for how our "moral discretion" should be exercised in helping other people. Apparently, we can give much or give little depending on personal choice. In addition, because both those who give much and those who give little are simply fulfilling their "imperfect duty," they can be placed on an equal moral level.

If Kant seems to require too little from us in the way of community involvement, utilitarians seem to require too much. They state that we ought to give as much as we can in order to promote the most good for the most people, considering each person equal with ourselves. Complete impartiality should be our guide in dealing with others in need, and we should not give preference to ourselves or our family.

Peter Singer defends an extreme version of this doctrine. He argues that we should sacrifice luxuries in our lives in order to help save the ten thousand people who die from starvation each day and the many others who live impoverished lives in countries like Bangladesh and Ethiopia. All humans are part of a worldwide community, or "global village," and make a legitimate claim on our wealth. We should respond to that claim by acting on the following utilitarian-inspired principle: "If it is in our power to prevent something bad from happening, without thereby sacrificing anything of comparable moral importance, we ought, morally, to do it."[5] The amount of giving required by this principle, as Singer insists, is considerable:

> I and everyone else in similar circumstances [of having great wealth compared to starving people] ought to give as much as possible, that is, at least up to the point at which by giving more one would begin to cause serious suffering for oneself and one's dependents—perhaps even beyond this point to the point of marginal utility, at which by giving more one would cause oneself and one's dependents as much suffering as one would prevent in Bengal [and other impoverished regions].[6]

Singer's conclusion is radical, even from a utilitarian perspective. Most utilitarians allow that we can give some emphasis to our own needs and those of our family, and that doing so is compatible with the doctrine of impartiality. They believe that doing so will actually lead to more overall good, because each of us is in the best position to promote our own good. Also, if we give the extraordinary quantities recommended by Singer, we will erode our long-term ability to help others. In adopting this position, however, utilitarians fail to resolve the same question that Kant faced: Just how much ought we to give to others?

Rights ethics offers two answers, depending on the kinds of rights recognized. If only negative rights are recognized—rights *not* to be interfered with—then very little giving seems to be required of us. We have a right to what we earn, and no one outside our family has a right to share our resources unless we decide to share them.

A very different conclusion is reached if we recognize positive rights—rights to have the goods needed for a minimally decent standard of living. If each human has these rights, then impoverished people in this country and throughout the world have basic rights to shelter, clothing, and food. Those rights place obligations on people who are advantaged to provide assistance. This positive rights view leaves open the question of whether giving should be done through governments or by individuals. Nevertheless, it also seems to require that we give more than most of us do now, although precisely how much is unclear.

Virtue ethics is often criticized as the least helpful theory when it comes to providing guidance for action in that it does not offer precise rules about how we ought to act and how much we ought to give. But this criticism mistakenly assumes that guidance must come in the form of rules. In fact, it can come in the form of ideals that inspire and focus our efforts. In particular, there is the virtue and the ideal of generosity in giving to the community beyond what is required by the minimal duties of morality, as we will see in the next section.

Generosity and Supererogation

Kant placed all actions into three categories: required by duty (right), forbidden by duty (wrong), and morally neutral (permissible or "all right"—for example, brushing one's teeth):

> A *duty* is an action to which we are obligated. . . . An action that is neither commanded nor forbidden is merely *permissible,* since there is . . . no duty with regard to the action. An action of this kind is called morally indifferent.[7]

This threefold classification, however, overlooks actions that are morally admirable—and hence not "morally indifferent"—but that are not required by duty. These acts are supererogatory, that is, morally good in ways that go beyond the requirements of duty.

David Heyd points out that *supererogation* means giving beyond what is required by duties *to others* rather than to ourselves. It is defined in terms of an altruistic aim or intention. To be sure, there may be mixed motives involved, such as a desire for fame coupled with a desire to help. If a person is to be generous, however, there must be an intention (aim, purpose) to promote the good of others. Accordingly, Heyd defines a supererogatory act as meeting the following conditions:

1. It is neither obligatory nor forbidden.
2. Its omission is not wrong, and does not deserve sanction or criticism—either formal or informal.
3. It is morally good, both by virtue of its (intended) consequences and by virtue of its intrinsic value (being beyond duty).

4. It is done voluntarily for the sake of someone else's good and is thus meritorious.[8]

Generous actions meet these conditions, and generous persons have a disposition to perform generous acts. Generous actions are beyond what is morally required or obligatory. And they are done voluntarily with the intention to promote someone else's good. Admittedly, they may not be good in all respects: Generous acts sometimes fail to help others despite the best intentions. But they are intended to help and as such are admirable.

Generous giving of oneself—of one's time, talents, and money—to the community is one ideal worth pursuing. It represents an important virtue worthy of admiration precisely because it goes beyond the minimal moral requirements in sharing our resources in benevolent and caring ways. It also provides an answer to the question of how much to give. We should give generously—if we want to be generous persons! Although this answer shares the vagueness of the answers offered by duty ethics, utilitarianism, and rights ethics, in a way the vagueness is morally fruitful. It sets forth a positive ideal, it recognizes and praises higher degrees of benevolent giving, and by allowing flexibility it takes account of the personal aspect in giving.

"Degrees" of benevolent giving are frequently understood in terms of greater and lesser quantities. The more generous person seems to be the one who gives greater quantities. This view is reflected in James Wallace's definition of acts of what he calls "economic generosity" (which contrasts with generosity in judging other people):

1. The agent, because of his direct concern for the good of the recipient, gives something with the intention of benefiting the recipient.
2. The agent gives up something of his that has a market value and that he has some reason to value and, therefore, to keep.
3. The agent gives more than one is generally expected, because of moral requirements or custom, to give in such circumstances.[9]

The third condition places an emphasis on giving in quantities beyond what is obligatory or usual. This emphasis on quantities, however, overlooks an insight expressed in a well-known passage in the *New Testament:*

And Jesus sat over against the treasury, and beheld how the people cast money into the treasury: and many that were rich cast in much. And there came a certain poor widow, and she threw in two mites, which make a farthing. And he called unto him his disciples, and saith unto them, Verily I say unto you, That this poor widow hath cast more in, than all they which have cast into the treasure: For all they did cast in of their abundance; but she of her want did cast in all that she had, even all her living.[10]

In other words the widow is more generous than are the rich donors, even though she gives a vastly smaller quantity. This suggests that degrees of generosity must be measured in relation to the resources of the giver rather than primarily in terms of custom or moral rules about what is required. It also suggests that Wallace's third condition needs to be modified:

3′. The agent gives more than is expected of someone having her or his resources and financial situation.

To Whom Should We Give?

Endorsing generosity as an admirable ideal does not answer the question of to whom and to what we should give. Community has many dimensions. Should we give our resources to humanitarian efforts to feed and clothe the poor and to provide shelter for the homeless? Or should we give to the arts, to education, and to environmental causes? Should we give lots of small gifts or combine our resources into a few large ones (the same question could be asked about how we allocate the time we give in volunteering)?

Here we need to remind ourselves that generosity is fully voluntary and beyond the requirements of duty. That means that it is up to each of us where and to what extent we give. It does not mean, however, that giving becomes a matter of whim. For we can give generously only when we are moved by benevolent concern for the good of others, and that means giving thoughtfully in situations in which caring is evoked genuinely and in very personal ways.

The occasions and objects of giving reflect, and should express, our *personal* interests. Some people are most deeply committed to humanitarian goals, some to educational goals, some to the arts, some to scouting and little league baseball. Pursuing these personal loyalties expresses their caring about community better than impartial giving could. In fact, each of us participates in many communities, of different sizes, ranging from membership in a school, company, or church to a city, nation, or the world community. Most of us are able to give generously only to some of these overlapping communities. There seems to be no abstract duty to focus our energies on any one such community (say, the largest one), and hence, here again, much is left up to our judgment and interests.

There is, in short, a large area of highly *personal* morality in deciding where and how we display virtues like loyalty and generosity. But "personal" does not mean "arbitrary." For our judgment and interests are evoked and exercised thoughtfully, not whimsically, as we engage in intelligent and benevolent giving to help others.

Summary

A community is a group of people related by shared history and hopes, location and interactions, interests and values. Loyalty to community is shown in more than minimal participation (such as meeting one's responsibilities as a citizen). It is shown in voluntary giving of one's time, talents, and resources to help others.

America's tradition of individualism is misconstrued when it equates community involvement with mere social conformism. As the life of Jane Addams exemplifies, service to community can express creative individual initiative and development of personality. Moreover, benevolent giving need not be "selfless" in the sense of doing it solely for the good of others. Mixed motives of self-interest and altruism do not remove or lower the moral worth of giving to help others. The volunteer who serves to help others while developing her or his skills and expressing her or his interests is often more vigorously motivated because of the mixed motives.

How much should we give, and to whom? Duty ethics, rights ethics, and utilitarianism do not provide clear-cut answers. Neither does virtue ethics, but it does at least set forth generosity as an ideal that guides and focuses giving. Generosity is supererogatory in the sense of going beyond what is required by moral duty and respect for others' rights. Generosity entails giving with the intention to benefit others, out of concern to promote their good. Degrees of generosity are measured by reference to our resources and ability to help, as well as in terms of the quantities we give beyond the customary or required amount.

DISCUSSION TOPICS

1. Consider the following observation by Brian O'Connell:

   There are some disturbing signs that giving and volunteering may not be held in high esteem by young adults. A recent study . . . has found that people between the ages of 18 and 34 do not place community service high on their lists of values. The Gallup survey confirms that. It found that volunteering declined 11 per cent from 1980 to 1985 among people 18 to 24 years of age and 19 per cent among single people.[11]

   Is this observation supported by your own view of people in this age range, and do you agree with O'Connell that there is something disturbing about it? Does it suggest, for example, that people in this age group are more selfish than before?

2. What, if anything, is wrong about never making any philanthropic contribution or engaging in any voluntary service to help others?

3. Ralph Waldo Emerson was a classic spokesperson for American individualism. Do

you agree or disagree with what he says about philanthropy in the following passage?

> Do not tell me, as a good man did to-day, of my obligation to put all poor men in good situations. Are they *my* poor? I tell thee, thou foolish philanthropist, that I grudge the dollar, the dime, the cent I give to such men as do not belong to me and to whom I do not belong. There is a class of persons to whom by all spiritual affinity I am bought and sold; for them I will go to prison if need be; but your miscellaneous popular charities; the education at college of fools; the building of meeting-houses to the vain end to which many now stand; alms to sots, and the thousand-fold Relief Societies;— though I confess with shame I sometimes succumb and give the dollar, it is a wicked dollar, which by and by I shall have the manhood to withhold.[12]

4. Is it better to give several small charitable gifts or one large one? In answering this question respond to the following claims:

> There are so many good causes that if we try to respond to them all, we dilute our ability to make a difference to any. But more important is the fact that we dilute ourselves. We run the risk of losing touch with what is really important to us.[13]

5. Assess the following argument: All the concern about motives and intentions in giving is entirely irrelevant. All that matters is the good done by acts of giving. Donations to relieve world hunger, for example, keep people alive no matter what motives or intentions lead people to make the donations.

6. One person regularly donates blood to the Red Cross without receiving any payment, while a second person gives blood only to commercial blood banks that pay for the blood. What moral good is present in the giving done by the first person that is absent in the second? In general, what distinctive moral goods are made possible by volunteering and giving?

7. Women have traditionally been encouraged (far more than men) to engage in voluntarism and philanthropy. Do you see any objections to this? In particular, does it or could it lead to exploitation of women who could be doing paid work that has greater economic benefits for them?

SUGGESTED READINGS

Addams, Jane. *Twenty Years at Hull-House*. New York: New American Library, 1981.

Aiken, William, and Hugh La Follette (eds.). *World Hunger and Moral Obligation*. Englewood Cliffs, NJ: Prentice-Hall, 1977.

Bellah, Robert N., et al. *Habits of the Heart: Individualism and Commitment in American Life*. Berkeley, CA: University of California Press, 1985.

Bellah, Robert N., et al. (eds.). *Individualism and Commitment in American Life*. New York: Harper & Row, 1987.

Boyte, Harry C. *Community Is Possible*. New York: Harper & Row, 1984.

Bremner, Robert C. *American Philanthropy*. 2nd ed. Chicago: University of Chicago Press, 1988.

Douglas, James. *Why Charity?: The Case for the Third Sector*. Beverly Hills, CA: Sage Publications, 1983.

Heyd, David. *Supererogation*. Cambridge: Cambridge University Press, 1982.

Kaminer, Wendy. *Women Volunteering: The Pleasure, Pain, and Politics of Unpaid Work from 1830 to the Present*. Garden City, NY: Anchor Press, 1984.

Ladd, John. "Loyalty." In Paul Edwards (ed.), *The Encyclopedia of Philosophy*. New York: Macmillan, 1967.

O'Connell, Brian (ed.). *America's Voluntary Spirit*. New York: Foundation Center, 1983.

Oldenquist, Andrew. *The Non-Suicidal Society*. Bloomington, IN: Indiana University Press, 1986.

Nisbet, Robert. *The Quest for Community*. New York: Oxford University Press, 1970.

Paul, Ellen Frankel, Fred D. Miller, Jr., Jeffrey Paul, and John Ahrens (eds.). *Beneficence, Philanthropy and the Public Good*. New York: Basil Blackwell, 1987.

Royce, Josiah. "The Nature of Community." In *The Problems of Christianity*. New York: Macmillan, 1913.

Shelp, Earl E. (ed.). *Beneficence and Health Care*. Boston: Reidel, 1982.

Wallace, James D. "Benevolence." In *Virtues and Vices*. Ithaca, NY: Cornell University Press, 1978.

Wolff, Robert Paul. "Loyalty" and "Community." In *The Poverty of Liberalism*. Boston: Beacon Press, 1968.

CHAPTER 21

Animals

About half of all Americans and Europeans have pets whom they regard as companions rather than household curios. Generally, they devote large amounts of attention and significant financial resources to them, often far more than they give to their neighbors. They are sensitive to their pets' needs and emotions and interact with them in caring ways that have moral significance, or so it will be argued here.

Our attitudes toward pets contrast sharply with our typical attitudes toward animals in general. Most people eat animals daily without a qualm. Yet the thought of eating their pets may be as horrifying as the thought of eating a human stranger. Clearly, we recognize our pets as having an importance that sets them apart from other animals. Do we perhaps exaggerate the importance of pets, or conversely, underestimate the value of animals we eat?

Animals as Companions

When John Steinbeck approached sixty, the age at which he would receive the Nobel Prize for literature, he felt the need to travel extensively in order to regain contact with the people he wrote about. He planned a trip around and through America in a camper truck, leaving his family during the months he traveled alone. His excitement about the planned trip, however, was dampened by "a very lonely, helpless feeling at first—a kind of desolate feeling."[1] The cure was to take along as a traveling companion his large French poodle, named Charles le Chien, or Charley for short. *Travels with Charley,* the literary offspring of the trip, is in part a record of his interactions with Charley.

Steinbeck already knew Charley well, but on the trip he came to know him better. He was previously aware, for example, that Charley was diplomatic rather than confrontational in dealing with other animals. In Yellowstone Park, however, Charley betrayed his usual good sense by trying to charge a bear: "Bears simply brought out the Hyde in my Jekyll-headed dog."[2]

The trip also led Steinbeck to a greater appreciation of Charley's superior intelligence in some matters. Charley lived in an entire world of smells to which Steinbeck and other humans were oblivious. More interestingly, Charley had an exceptional intuitive understanding of people. He would show contempt for incompetent veterinarians who mishandled him and spontaneous trust in skillful ones. He also avoided people who addressed him using baby talk, revealing, according to Steinbeck, a certain pride in not being a human infant. Yet he displayed a humanlike pride in being well groomed, a vanity Steinbeck shared concerning his own beard.

Charley had an equally subtle knowledge of Steinbeck. His understanding extended well beyond responses to verbal commands, for he could easily anticipate with excitement when he would be included in Steinbeck's plans or discern with chagrin that he would be left alone to guard the camper. His talents included several techniques for awakening Steinbeck in the morning: "He can shake himself and his collar loud enough to wake the dead. If that doesn't work he gets a sneezing fit. But perhaps his most irritating method is to sit quietly beside the bed and stare into my face with a sweet and forgiving look on his face."[3]

Like most people with pets, Steinbeck talked to Charley frequently and on a variety of occasions. He routinely spoke to Charley in greeting him, saying goodbye, comforting him when he was nervous, and in relaxing both of them by chatting about a problem. Charley was also the object of conversations with strangers and served as an ambassador for Steinbeck in meeting people: "A dog, particularly an exotic like Charley, is a bond between strangers. Many conversations en route began with 'What degree [that is, pedigree] of a dog is that?'"[4]

Steinbeck and Charley were emotionally attuned to each other. On one occasion, for example, Steinbeck became depressed following a conversation with someone who had a special knack for sarcastically demolishing the simple pleasures of a sunny afternoon. Charley cheered him up by initiating puppylike games. On another occasion Charley was sick, and Steinbeck postponed the trip for an entire week while he recuperated. During this time Steinbeck reports feeling compassion for the suffering of his traveling companion as well as helplessness for not being able to alleviate the suffering.

The relationship with Charley that Steinbeck reports involves several elements that common sense recognizes as possible for human-animal interactions. It allows that animals are capable of beliefs and emotions, and also that animals of a given type are not alike—they have distinctive personalities. All these features enter into human-animal interactions in selective and personal ways akin to friendships among humans. It is true that in a few places Steinbeck lapses into excessive anthropomorphizing of animals—that is, ascribing human traits where they are not appropriate—as when he speaks of Charley's pride in not being a human. Nevertheless, Steinbeck's descriptions of his interactions with Charley, rather than striking us as poetic fancies, for the most part ring true.

They ring true to common sense. But is this common sense reasonable? If it is, it will make sense to inquire into the moral status of relationships with pets based on mutual caring. But if common sense is mistaken here, relationships with animals may be more akin to children's relationships with dolls rather than to relationships with creatures having some moral significance.

Attitudes Toward Animals

What is the moral status of pets and other animals, at least higher mammals? The attitude of most classical philosophers was that animals have no intrinsic moral worth of any kind. They acquire value and moral relevance only insofar as humans choose to value them for human purposes. It follows that nothing is inherently wrong in hurting animals. Hunting them becomes wrong only when they are the property of other humans whose property rights would be infringed by hurting the animal. According to this attitude attachment to animals may alleviate loneliness, be calming, and provide delight—but so does television. Deep emotional attachment or caring for animals is sentimental—that is, it reflects excessive and inappropriate emotional involvement. Pets are like pens or cars to which one might also become sentimentally attached, but they have value only insofar as humans give them value.

The philosophical basis for this attitude was uncompromisingly set forth by both René Descartes (1596–1650) and Benedict de Spinoza (1632–1677). Descartes viewed animals as "thoughtless brutes," sophisticated machines lacking consciousness.[5] Spinoza, by contrast, recognized that they could feel pain and pleasure, but he joined Descartes in banishing them from the realm of moral concern:

> The rational quest of what is useful to us further teaches us the necessity of associating ourselves with our fellow-man, but not with beasts, or things, whose nature is different from our own. . . . Still, I do not deny that beasts feel; what I deny is, that we may not consult our own advantage and use them as we please, treating them in the way which best suits us; for their nature is not like ours, and their emotions are naturally different from human emotions.[6]

Surely the attitude of Descartes and Spinoza is wrong, tragically wrong. Many animals do feel emotions and have desires and beliefs very similar to our own. Certainly, this is true of the higher mammals on which we will focus. Of course, we admitted the conceptual danger in anthropomorphizing animals by ascribing overly complex mental states to them. But the same forms of behavior that warrant ascribing at least simple psychological states to people are manifested by mammals. Moreover, numerous studies in comparative anatomy and neurophysiology also indicate similarities in the mental activities and functions of humans and higher mammals.

There is no need here to engage in subtle debates about the precise degree to which higher mammals are self-conscious or capable of rational endeavors and communication. What matters is their capacity for social life and also their capacity for feeling. Jeremy Bentham (1748–1832) drew attention to the importance of the capacity to feel when he charged that the refusal of Descartes and Spinoza to grant any moral status to animals was akin to the sweeping blindness of racists. He drafted the following passage shortly after France prohibited slavery in French colonies:

> The French have already discovered that blackness of the skin is no reason why a human being should be abandoned without redress to the caprice of a tormentor. It may one day come to be recognized that the number of the legs, the villosity of the skin, or the termination of the *os sacrum* [that is, the tail bone] are reasons equally insufficient for abandoning a sensitive being to the same fate. What else is it that should trace the insuperable line [between humans and animals]? Is it the faculty of reason, or perhaps the faculty of discourse? But a full-grown horse or dog is beyond comparison a more rational, as well as a more conversable animal, than an infant of a day or a week, or even a month, old. But suppose they were otherwise, what would it avail? The question is not, Can they *reason?* nor Can they *talk?* but Can they *suffer?*[7]

Mammals do indeed suffer, feel pleasure and delight, and have interests based on their desires and needs. They care for their young, interact with sensitivity to one another and sometimes to humans. Surely, at the very least, it is wrong to torture them for fun.

Let us now turn to Immanuel Kant, who agreed that torturing animals was clearly immoral, but who shared Descartes and Spinoza's view that animals have no moral worth. According to Kant only rational beings (humans, and possibly other beings like angels and God) have inherent value. They are ends in themselves in the sense that they are autonomous beings who place moral limits on other rational beings' pursuit of their ends or purposes. Everything else in the universe is a mere means to gratifying the reasoned purposes of rational beings. Animals in particular lack the capacity to reason about general principles of conduct that ought to guide rational living. Hence, we owe them no moral respect and have no moral duties to them.

Nevertheless, Kant believed there are duties *to humanity* and to ourselves that generate indirect duties to treat animals humanely. That is, we have duties concerning animals, but not to animals:

So far as animals are concerned, we have no direct duties. Animals are not self-conscious and are there merely as a means to an end. That end is man. . . . Our duties towards animals are merely indirect duties towards humanity. . . . Thus, if a dog has served his master long and faithfully, his service, on the analogy of human service, deserves reward, and when the dog has grown too old to serve, his master ought to keep him until he dies. Such action helps to support us in our duties towards human beings. . . . Tender feelings towards dumb animals develop humane feelings towards mankind.[8]

Kant's idea is that tenderness with animals helps foster kindness toward humans, whereas cruelty to animals encourages cruelty to humans. Humane responses are a kind of practice exercise for being kind to people.

This is an interesting suggestion, but is it always true? Perhaps some individuals are actually kinder to people because they vent their hostilities on animals, which, in Kant's view, would justify their cruelty to animals. In any case Kant mislocates the basis for condemning cruelty to animals. It is wrong to torture a dog or cat not because doing so may indirectly influence one's subsequent behavior toward people, but because it harms the dog or cat! Furthermore, the act itself reveals cruelty in one's character, even if that cruelty is not also expressed toward people.

Do Animals Have Rights?

Let us turn to two contemporary philosophers who have drawn attention to the plight of animals in a human-centered world. Both are prominent members of the "animal rights movement" that has gained momentum in the last decade, and both sharply disagree with Kant's refusal to grant animals any direct moral status. Yet they offer very different defenses of the humane treatment of animals.

Peter Singer has been called the father of the modern animal rights movement, principally because of his influential book *Animal Liberation*. There is irony in this, however, because Singer denies that animals have rights! Even though in a few passages in *Animal Liberation* he speaks loosely about animal rights, he has since made it clear that for him talk of moral rights is muddled, whether one ascribes them to animals or persons. Like Bentham, Singer is a utilitarian who believes that the only reason acts are right or wrong is because they maximize or fail to maximize good consequences, taking into account the effects of the acts on every conscious being affected. Mammals are conscious beings and as such should be taken into account. Usually, it is wrong to cause suffering to animals because such suffering is rarely justified by some greater good produced for humans.

Animals who are conscious, and hence who are capable of feeling pain or pleasure, have preferences and interests just like humans do. In this respect, according to Singer, their interests should be considered equally with those of humans. To think otherwise is to be guilty of "speciesism," which he defines as "a prejudice or attitude of bias toward the interests of members of one's own species and against those of members of other species."[9] Speciesism has caused harm as terrible as that of sexism and racism: "This tyranny has caused and today is still causing an amount of pain and suffering that can only be compared with that which resulted from the centuries of tyranny by white humans over black humans."[10]

As might be expected, ethicists who regard moral rights as the foundation of morality would develop a very different argument, even if their conclusions are similar to Singer's. Perhaps the most careful argument that animals have moral rights is presented by Tom Regan in *The Case for Animal Rights*. Regan begins with the premise that mammals (at least those who are one year old or older) have inherent value. They have this value not just because they are capable of feeling pain and pleasure but also because they have beliefs, desires, memories, a sense of the future, preferences, the ability to act purposefully in pursuing their preferences, and a welfare (or set of interests) that goes beyond their potential uses for humans.

Regan contends that having inherent value is not a matter of degree—one either has it or one does not. Hence, the value of mammals is equal to the value of humans. Moreover, this inherent value ought to be respected because it creates a valid claim on us. Because these valid claims are what is meant by moral rights, it follows that mammals have moral rights. Their inability to speak for their rights does not alter this fact. It merely makes animals dependent on surrogate agents to defend their rights for them. Their moral situation is in this respect exactly analogous to human babies, infants, and severely mentally handicapped people, who are also dependent on guardians to defend their rights.

Extreme and Moderate Views of the Moral Status of Animals

Even though Singer and Regan represent opposite poles in theoretical ethics, they share an extreme position concerning the moral status of animals—as extreme as the view they attack. Kant, Descartes, and Spinoza approached animals with a similar dichotomy: Either animals share full moral status with humans or, like rocks and other material objects, they lack any moral status. Kant reasoned that because animals lack the rational capacities of humans, they are mere things undeserving of any respect. Likewise, according to

Singer, either animals' interests do not matter at all or else they matter equally with those of humans. According to Regan either animals have no rights or else they have the same rights as humans.

Yet there is a middle ground that enables us to avoid these extreme positions. It affirms that insofar as animals are conscious beings, they have some inherent worth, but nevertheless human beings have greater inherent worth. It recognizes in human consciousness greater degrees of value and potential value, analogously to how John Stuart Mill distinguished between degrees of quality among pleasures. This moderate view might also grant that animals have important rights but deny that they have all the rights of human beings. Thus, although they have the right to be treated humanely and not to be tortured, they lack rights to social support through our welfare system.

Finally, this moderate view also distinguishes degrees of inherent worth among animals depending on the extent of their capacities to feel pain and pleasure, to act purposefully, and to interact socially with one another and with humans. This would support the special status we have granted to higher mammals, who possess these capacities in greater degrees than do many other animals.

Singer and Regan would reject this moderate approach as being "speciesist" in that it explicitly shows favoritism for humans. Nevertheless, the moderate approach to the moral status of animals reflects the considered convictions of most people who are certain that humans have a higher and richer moral status than do other animals. It also provides a firm basis for including animals in the realm of moral concern and for decisively rejecting cruelty to animals.

Mary Midgley, who explored this middle ground in *Animals and Why They Matter*, cautions us about the term *speciesism*. As typically used, the word is ambiguous. It condemns either of two views: (1) Animals have no inherent moral significance or (2) animals have inherent worth, although not as much as humans. Midgley rejects the former view while affirming the latter. It is not, she urges, a sheer prejudice akin to racism and sexism to give some preference to the interests of members of one's own species in situations where interests conflict. Precisely when and how much preference is justified should be explored without presuming that animals lack all moral significance or that they have moral worth equal to that of humans.

Midgley also recognizes some special significance in animals having the capacity to interact with humans. Underlying this attitude is a clear acknowledgment of the special worth of humans, but also underlying it is sensitivity to genuine differences among animals that gives them capacities we equally value among humans. Such a position helps make sense of our attitudes toward pets, as does the fact that a history of personal interactions with specific animals adds to the value of relationships with them.

Furthermore, this moderate view provides a rationale for developing laws to protect dolphins, whales, chimpanzees and gorillas. Such laws are designed to protect individual animals, unlike other laws merely aimed at preserving whole species (of fish, crabs, and so on).

Caring for Pets

Disagreements over the precise moral status of animals should not blur the areas of widespread agreement about the moral worth of animals. Let us now summarize the points of agreement among moderates and extremists in the contemporary animals rights movement.

First, companionship between humans and animals has moral importance. It benefits humans by bringing comfort, security, and daily cheerfulness. It obviously benefits specific animals. But is also creates a bond or relationship based on caring. The importance of this relationship is especially rich within families in which there is an interaction between several humans and pets that exerts a unifying force. The pet becomes a focus of shared concern, including shared activities (petting, feeding, exercising, conversing, playing, and so on). Psychologists also emphasize that pets provide a sense of peace and security. (This goes for cats as well as for guard dogs!) Pets serve as surrogate children for adults, fantasied babies for children, and real friends for all. Pets also generate problems, of course, but even in that regard they are like people, reminding us that all valuable caring relationships require effort.

Second, relationships with animals enliven a sense of kinship with other animals and nature. Living with animals adds to our delight in the simple aspects of biological existence, including pleasure in a good meal or playing a game. The relatively short life spans of pets reminds us of the contingency and fragility of our own lives.

Third, caring for animals can add to a capacity to care for people (as even Kant allowed). This is not always true, to be sure. Occasionally, pets are used to provide a means of escaping from caring about people. But we recognize such cases as unhealthy distortions rather than as typical products of relationships with animals. As Midgley emphasizes, it is a misconception to think that caring for animals somehow takes away from the care available for other people. That would be like arguing that we should not aid a suffering dog hit by a car because our energies could in principle be used to help a human at that moment. As Midgley writes, "The reason why this would be odd is that compassion does not need to be treated hydraulically in this way, as a rare and irreplaceable fluid, usable only for exceptionally impressive cases. It is a habit or power of the mind, which grows and develops with use."[11]

Fourth, recognizing the moral status of animals forces us to rethink the human capacities most fundamental to morality. Ethicists like Spinoza and Kant overemphasized the importance of rationality, to the neglect of relationships based on caring. As a result they disregarded animals altogether or else granted to them a peripheral moral status as the indirect objects of moral duties. Gaining an appreciation of animals' moral worth reverses this entire way of thinking. Mammals have worth because they are capable of feeling, as well as of maintaining relationships with us. Like us they care for their young and have complex forms of social organization. These aspects of their lives evoke our compassion and a sense of kinship. Reflecting on them helps us emphasize our capacities for compassion, kindness, and goodness of heart.

Summary

Most traditional ethical theories have been exclusively human-centered, regarding animals as mechanical playthings that were incapable of feelings (Descartes). Or they regarded animals' feelings as radically dissimilar to human emotions and insufficient to give them moral worth, which only "rational" humans have (Spinoza, Kant). Responses to animals, according to these theories, have moral relevance only as they affect responses to other humans. Thus, torturing animals is bad only because it encourages cruelty to humans, and gentleness to animals is good insofar as it reinforces gentleness to humans.

Jeremy Bentham, however, stressed that the ability to reason and to experience complex emotions links humans and animals. In his view it is morally significant that animals can suffer as well as feel pleasure. To torture an animal for fun is to do moral harm to it and to manifest a character that is cruel, no matter what further implications there are for how one treats humans. Contemporary philosophical advocates of humane treatment of animals differ over whether animals have rights, but they share Bentham's view that torturing an animal is a direct moral wrong—to the animal.

Bentham's view also lays a philosophical basis for appreciating caring relationships between humans and animal companions. Insofar as animals have emotions and needs, it makes sense to care for them and to promote their interests, in the way people do with their pets or "animal companions." Moreover, caring relationships with animal companions take on increased worth insofar as animals are capable of reciprocal responses and interactions with humans.

Does valuing animals require recognizing them as having equal worth with humans? According to some philosophers it does, and treating them as moral inferiors is a form of prejudice that they call "speciesism" (Singer, Regan). Recognizing that animals have inherent worth, however, is compatible with a more moderate position that allows that humans' moral worth is greater and that human interests may legitimately be given greater weight when they conflict with those of animals (Midgley).

DISCUSSION TOPICS

1. Respond to the following argument: People treat their pets *as if* they were people. As long as they do so, it is appropriate to care for them in some ways otherwise appropriate only for humans. Much the same is true, however, of fictional characters in plays and movies: It is appropriate to respond with fear, affection, anger, and other emotions to characters whom we pretend are real people. But in both cases there is a game of pretense involved. Neither pets nor fictional characters are real people, and we know this even at times when we pretend they are. Neither has any kind of inherent moral worth that makes them *deserve* to be treated as people.

2. Many pet owners spend more on their pets than they do on world hunger, even though their money for pet food and supplies could help save human lives. Discuss your view of whether this is morally permissible. If you think it is permissible to spend substantial amounts of money on pets, are there any limits to how much should be spent?

3. It is not uncommon for farmers to become emotionally attached to one animal of a species whose other members they are willing to eat. An example of this millennia-old practice is found in the *Old Testament:*

   > The poor man had nothing, save one little ewe lamb, which he had bought and nourished up: and it grew up together with him, and with his children; it did eat of his own meat, and drank of his own cup, and lay in his bosom, and was unto him as a daughter.[12]

   Is there anything morally inconsistent about having a caring relationship with this one sheep while being willing to eat other sheep?

4. Is there anything morally objectionable about hunting just for sport (and not for food)? In your answer discuss the attitudes of the hunter who (in 1850) wrote the following description of shooting an elephant:

   > The elephant stood broadside to me, at upwards of one hundred yards, and his attention at the moment was occupied with the dogs. . . . I fired at his shoulder, and secured him with a single shot. The ball caught him high on the shoulder-blade, rendering him instantly lame; and before the echo on the bullet could reach my ear, I plainly saw the elephant was mine. . . . I resolved to devote a short time to the contemplation of this noble elephant before laying him low; . . . I quickly kindled a fire and put on the kettle, and in a few minutes my coffee was prepared. There I sat in my forest home, coolly sipping my coffee, with one of the finest elephants in Africa awaiting my pleasure beside a neighbouring tree. . . .
   > Having admired the elephant for a considerable time, I resolved to make experiments for vulnerable points . . . [He bungles this again and again; eventually, after even he has become a little worried, he succeeds in wounding the elephant fatally.] Large tears now trickled from his eyes, which he slowly shut and opened, his colossal frame quivered convulsively, and, falling on his side, he expired.[13]

5. Is it morally permissible to eat animals? Jeremy Bentham thought it was, even though (as we saw) he affirmed the moral worth of animals who can feel pain and pleasure:

There is very good reason why we should be suffered to eat such of them [i.e., animals] as we like to eat; we are the better for it, and they are never the worse. They have none of those long-protracted anticipations of future misery which we have. The death they suffer in our hands commonly is, and always may be, a speedier, and by that means a less painful one, than that which would await them in the inevitable course of nature.[14]

Contemporary mass production of meat, however, does involve considerable suffering for animals. One example that Peter Singer describes in *Animal Liberation* concerns the raising of calves for veal.[15] The calves are taken from their mothers at a very young age and placed in wooden stalls one foot and two inches wide. This prevents them from turning around during the thirteen to fifteen weeks prior to slaughter. During that time their diet is entirely liquid, denying them their need for roughage. The lack of exercise and grass keep their flesh tender. In addition, they are kept anemic to produce the pale pink flesh preferred to gourmets (even though the color does not affect taste). To reduce restlessness, some producers keep them in the dark at all times except for about two hours during feeding. Thus, the calves live in an environment without visual stimulation, physical activity, interaction with their mothers, or social interaction of any other kind. Is their suffering outweighed by the human pleasures in eating them? Would you agree with Bentham about other cases in which suffering to animals is far less extreme?

6. The Food and Drug Administration requires that many kinds of new substances be tested on animals before they are marketed for human use. For example, new cosmetics must be tested for possible eye or skin damage on humans. One test involves using unanesthetized rabbits whose heads are held firmly in place by a neck brace and whose eyes are kept open with metal clips. Concentrated solutions of the substance are dripped into the rabbits' eyes, often repeatedly for several days, and eye damage is measured. Peter Singer writes of such experiments that

while it may be thought justifiable to require animal tests of potentially lifesaving drugs, the same tests are done for products like cosmetics, food colorings, and floor polishes. Should hundreds of animals suffer so that a new kind of lipstick or mouthwash can be put on the market? Don't we already have enough of these products? Who benefits from their introduction, except the companies that hope to make a profit from their new gimmick?[16]

Do you agree or disagree with Singer? What general criteria would you endorse to morally justify experiments on animals?

SUGGESTED READINGS

Bentham, Jeremy. *Introduction to the Principles of Morals and Legislation,* Chapter 17. New York: Hafner, 1948. First published 1789.

Clark, Stephen R. L. *The Nature of the Beast: Are Animals Moral?* New York: Oxford University Press, 1984.

Frey, R. G. *Rights, Killing and Suffering: Moral Vegetarianism and Applied Ethics.* New York: Basil Blackwell, 1983.

Hearne, Vicki. *Adam's Task: Calling Animals by Name.* New York: Vintage, 1987.

Kant, Immanuel. "Duties Towards Animals and Spirits." In *Lectures on Ethics,* trans. Louis Infield. New York: Harper & Row, 1963.

Levinson, Boris M. *Pets and Human Development.* Springfield, IL: Thomas, 1972.

Midgley, Mary. *Animals and Why They Matter.* Athens, GA: University of Georgia Press, 1984.

Regan, Tom. *The Case for Animal Rights.* Berkeley, CA: University of California Press, 1983.

Regan, Tom (ed.). *Earthbound: New Introductory Essays in Environmental Ethics.* New York: Random House, 1984.

Regan, Tom, and Peter Singer (eds.). *Animal Rights and Human Obligations.* Englewood Cliffs, NJ: Prentice-Hall, 1976.

Rollin, Bernard E. *Animal Rights and Human Morality.* Buffalo, NY: Prometheus, 1981.

Singer, Peter. *Animal Liberation.* New York: Avon Books, 1977.

Singer, Peter (ed.). *In Defense of Animals.* New York: Basil Blackwell, 1986.

Spinoza, Benedict de. *The Ethics.* Trans. R. H. M. Elwes. New York: Dover, 1955.

Notes

PART ONE   *Character, Conduct, and Relationships*

1. Iris Murdoch, *The Sovereignty of Good* (Boston: Ark Paperbacks, 1985), p. 52.

CHAPTER 1   *Moral Reasoning and Applied Ethics*

1. Jean-Paul Sartre, "Existentialism Is a Humanism," trans. Philip Mairet, in Walter Kaufmann (ed.), *Existentialism from Dostoevsky to Sartre*, rev. ed. (New York: New American Library, 1975), p. 354.
2. Ibid., p. 356.
3. Ibid., p. 353.
4. Jean-Paul Sartre, *Being and Nothingness,* trans. Hazel E. Barnes (New York: Washington Square Press, 1966), p. 76.
5. Plato, *Euthyphro,* trans. Lane Cooper, in Edith Hamilton and Huntington Cairns (eds.), *The Collected Dialogues of Plato* (Princeton: Princeton University Press, 1961), p. 178.
6. The metaphor of words as tools was used by J. L. Austin in "A Plea for Excuses," in *Philosophical Papers by J. L. Austin* (Oxford: Clarendon Press, 1961), p. 129. The comparison of words and tools was used earlier by Ludwig Wittgenstein in *Philosophical Investigations,* 3rd ed., trans. G. E. M. Anscombe (New York: Macmillan, 1958), p. 6.
7. Gen. 22:1–2, 9–10, King James version.
8. Jean-Paul Sartre, "Existentialism Is a Humanism," p. 351.
9. Søren Kierkegaard, *Fear and Trembling,* trans. Alastair Hannay (New York: Penguin Books, 1985).
10. Gen. 1:31, King James version.

C H A P T E R   2   *Creativity, Autonomy, and Moral Growth*

1. Plato, *Apology,* trans. G. M. A. Grube, in *The Trial and Death of Socrates* (Indianapolis, IN: Hackett, 1975), p. 26.
2. Ibid., p. 39.
3. Ibid., pp. 32–33.
4. Matt. 5:44, King James version.
5. A phrase used by Martin Luther King, Jr. (among other places) in his dedication to *Why We Can't Wait* (New York: New American Library, 1964), p. vi.
6. Elizabeth Cady Stanton et al., "Declaration of Sentiments," in Alice S. Rossi (ed.), *The Feminist Papers* (New York: Bantam Books, 1973), p. 416.
7. Elizabeth Cady Stanton and The Revising Committee, *The Woman's Bible* (Seattle, WA: Coalition Task Force on Women and Religion, 1974), p. 131. First published in two parts in 1895 and 1898.
8. Carol Gilligan, "Moral Orientation and Moral Development," in Eva Feder Kittay and Diana T. Meyers (eds.), *Women and Moral Theory* (Totowa, NJ: Rowman & Littlefield, 1987), p. 25.
9. Lawrence Kohlberg, "Indoctrination Versus Relativity in Value Education," in George Sher (ed.), *Moral Philosophy: Selected Readings* (New York: Harcourt Brace Jovanovich, 1987), p. 88.
10. Plato, *Euthyphro,* trans. G. M. A. Grube, in *The Trial and Death of Socrates* (Indianapolis, IN: Hackett, 1975), p. 6.
11. Mary Midgley, "Creation and Originality," in *Heart and Mind: The Varieties of Moral Experience* (New York: St. Martin's Press, 1981), p. 57.

C H A P T E R   3   *Theories of Virtue*

1. Cf. Richard Norman, *The Moral Philosophers* (New York: Clarendon Press, 1983), pp. 22–28; and Anthony Kenny, "Mental Health in Plato's Republic," in *The Anatomy of the Soul* (Oxford: Oxford University Press, 1973).
2. Aristotle, *Ethics,* trans. J. A. K. Thomson and Hugh Tredennick (New York: Penguin Books, 1976), p. 108.
3. Ibid., p. 104.
4. Ibid., p. 106.
5. Ibid., pp. 108–109.
6. Ibid., pp. 101–102.
7. Cf. Annette C. Baier, "Hume, the Women's Moral Theorist?" in Eva Feder Kittay and Diana T. Meyers (eds.), *Women and Moral Theory* (Totowa, NJ: Rowman & Littlefield, 1987).
8. David Hume, *Hume's Ethical Writings,* Alasdair MacIntyre (ed.) (New York: Macmillan, 1965), p. 29.
9. Alasdair MacIntyre, *After Virtue* (Notre Dame, IN: University of Notre Dame Press, 1981), p. 204.
10. Ibid.
11. Ibid., p. 178.
12. Ibid., p. 204.

13. Ibid.
14. Edmund L. Pincoffs, *Quandaries and Virtues* (Lawrence, KS: University Press of Kansas, 1986), p. 78.
15. Ibid., p. 85.
16. Ibid., p. 89.
17. Plato, *The Republic,* trans. Francis MacDonald Cornford (New York: Oxford University Press, 1945), pp. 141–142.

CHAPTER 4 *Theories of Right Action*

1. Immanuel Kant, *Foundations of the Metaphysics of Morals,* trans. L. W. Beck (New York: Liberal Arts Press, 1959). Printed in A. I. Melden, *Ethical Theories: A Book of Readings,* 2nd ed. (Englewood Cliffs, NJ: Prentice-Hall, 1967), p. 345.
2. Ibid., p. 339.
3. Ibid., p. 348.
4. David Ross, *The Right and the Good* (Oxford: Clarendon Press, 1930), p. 19.
5. Ibid., pp. 21–22.
6. John Stuart Mill, *Utilitarianism* (Indianapolis, IN: Hackett, 1979), pp. 22–23, 25.
7. Ibid., pp. 8–9.
8. Ibid., p. 10.
9. Immanuel Kant, "On a Supposed Right to Lie from Altruistic Motives," in Lewis White Beck (ed. and trans.), *Critique of Practical Reason and Other Writings in Moral Philosophy* (Chicago: University of Chicago Press, 1949), pp. 346–350.
10. Fyodor Dostoevsky, *Crime and Punishment,* trans. Constance Garnett (New York: Bantam Books, 1981), pp. 58–59.

PART TWO *Self-Respect and Integrity*

1. Immanuel Kant, *Lectures on Ethics,* trans. Louis Infield (New York: Harper & Row, 1963), p. 126.
2. John Rawls, *A Theory of Justice* (Cambridge, MA: Harvard University Press, 1971), p. 440.

CHAPTER 5 *Harming Oneself*

1. Immanuel Kant, *Foundations of the Metaphysics of Morals,* trans. Lewis White Beck (Indianapolis, IN: Bobbs-Merrill, 1959), p. 47.
2. Immanuel Kant, *Lectures on Ethics,* trans. Louis Infield (New York: Harper & Row, 1963), pp. 117–118.
3. Fyodor Dostoevsky, *The Brothers Karamazov,* trans. Andrew H. MacAndrew (New York: Bantam Books, 1970), p. 697. The example of Lise is used by Irwin

Goldstein in "Pain and Masochism," *Journal of Value Inquiry,* vol. 17 (1983): 219–223.

4. Fyodor Dostoevsky, *The Brothers Karamazov,* p. 703.
5. Theodore Isaac Rubin, *Through My Own Eyes* (New York: Macmillan, 1982), p. 171.
6. Virginia Woolf, "The New Dress," in *A Haunted House and Other Stories* (New York: Harcourt Brace Jovanovich, 1972), p. 47.
7. Nathaniel Hawthorne, *The Scarlet Letter* (New York: Norton, 1978), p. 107.
8. Robert C. Solomon, *The Passions* (Notre Dame, IN: University of Notre Dame Press, 1983), p. 295.

CHAPTER 6   *Self-Deception*

1. Albert Speer, *Inside the Third Reich,* trans. Richard and Clara Winston (New York: Avon Books, 1971), p. 481. Also see pp. 48, 63–65, 161–163, 379, 480–481. Matthias Schmidt raises questions about Speer's honesty in writing his memoirs in *Albert Speer: The End of a Myth,* trans. Joachim Neugroschel (New York: St. Martin's Press, 1984).
2. Herbert Fingarette, *Self-Deception* (Atlantic Highlands, NJ: Humanities Press, 1969), p. 141.
3. Bishop Joseph Butler, "Upon Self-Deceit," in W. E. Gladstone (ed.), *The Works of Joseph Butler* (Oxford: Clarendon Press, 1896), pp. 177–178.
4. Samuel Johnson, *The Rambler,* in Arthur Murphy (ed.), *The Works of Samuel Johnson,* Vol. 2 (London: S. and R. Bentley, 1823), pp. 181–187.
5. Ibid.
6. Fyodor Dostoevsky, *The Brothers Karamazov,* trans. Constance Garnett (New York: New American Library, 1957), p. 49.
7. Sonia Johnson, *From Housewife to Heretic* (Garden City, NY: Anchor, 1983), p. 94.
8. Ibid., pp. 160–161.
9. Jack W. Meiland, "What Ought We to Believe? or the Ethics of Belief Revisited," *American Philosophical Quarterly* (1980):15–16.
10. Reinhold Niebuhr, *The Nature and Destiny of Man,* Vol. 1 (New York: Scribner, 1964), p. 203.

CHAPTER 7   *Weakness of Will*

1. Plato, *The Republic,* trans. F. M. Cornford (New York: Oxford University Press, 1945), p. 137.
2. Will and Ariel Durant, *A Dual Autobiography* (New York: Simon & Schuster, 1977), p. 30.
3. Plato, *Apology,* trans. G. M. A. Grube, in *The Trial and Death of Socrates* (Indianapolis, IN: Hackett, 1975).
4. Plato, *Protagoras,* trans. W. K. C. Guthrie, in Edith Hamilton and Huntington Cairns (eds.), *The Collected Dialogues of Plato* (Princeton, NJ: Princeton University Press, 1963), p. 344.

5. Aristotle, *Nichomachean Ethics,* trans. W. D. Ross, in Richard McKeon (ed.), *The Basic Works of Aristotle* (New York: Random House, 1941), p. 1041.

6. Alfred R. Mele, *Irrationality: An Essay on Akrasia, Self-Deception, and Self-Control* (New York: Oxford University Press, 1987), pp. 51–52.

7. Friedrich Nietzsche, *The Gay Science,* trans. Walter Kaufmann (New York: Vintage, 1974), pp. 232–233.

8. C. R. Snyder, Raymond L. Higgins, and Rita J. Stucky, *Excuses* (New York: Wiley, 1983).

9. Gen. 3:11–13, King James version.

10. Martin Gansberg, "38 Who Saw Murder Didn't Call Police," *New York Times,* 1964. Printed in Christina Hoff Sommers, *Vice and Virtue in Everyday Life* (San Diego, CA: Harcourt Brace Jovanovich, 1985), pp. 35–39.

11. Søren Kierkegaard, *Fear and Trembling* and *The Sickness unto Death* (Garden City, NY: Doubleday, 1954), p. 225.

12. Mark Twain, *The Adventures of Huckleberry Finn* (New York: Dell, 1960), p. 122.

13. The term *dependent virtues* is used by Michael Slote in *Goods and Virtues* (Oxford: Clarendon Press, 1983), pp. 61–75.

CHAPTER 8   *Courage*

1. Winnie Mandela, *Part of My Soul Went with Him,* Anne Benjamin (ed.) (New York: Norton, 1984), p. 116.

2. Ibid., p. 99.

3. As reported in the local news in Orange County, California.

4. Aristotle, *Ethics,* trans. J. A. K. Thomson and Hugh Tredennick (New York: Penguin Books, 1976), p. 103.

5. James D. Wallace, "Courage, Cowardice, and Self-Indulgence," in *Virtues and Vices* (Ithaca, NY: Cornell University Press, 1978), pp. 78–81.

6. Douglas N. Walton, *Courage: A Philosophical Investigation* (Berkeley, CA: University of California Press, 1986), p. 191.

7. W. D. Falk, "Morality, Self, and Others," in Hector-Neri Castaneda and George Nakhnikian (eds.), *Morality and the Language of Conduct* (Detroit, MI: Wayne State University Press, 1965), p. 103.

8. Jay Newman, *Fanatics and Hypocrites* (Buffalo, NY: Prometheus, 1986), p. 18.

9. John F. Kennedy, *Profiles in Courage* (New York: Harper & Row, 1956), p. 17.

PART THREE   *Respect for Others*

1. John Rawls, *A Theory of Justice* (Cambridge, MA: Harvard University Press, 1971), pp. 178, 337.

CHAPTER 9 *Rape and Sexual Harassment*

1. Lawrence Haworth, *Autonomy: An Essay in Philosophical Psychology and Ethics* (New Haven, CT: Yale University Press, 1986), p. 1.
2. Susan Griffin, *Rape: The Politics of Consciousness,* 3rd ed. (New York: Harper & Row, 1986), pp. 23–24.
3. William B. Sanders, *Rape and Woman's Identity* (Beverly Hills, CA: Sage, 1980), pp. 50–51.
4. Susan Brownmiller, *Against Our Will: Men, Women, and Rape* (New York: Simon & Schuster, 1975), p. 354.
5. Michael D. Bayles, "Coercive Offers and Public Benefits," *Personalist,* vol. 55 (1974): 142–143.
6. John C. Hughes, and Larry May, "Sexual Harassment," *Social Theory and Practice,* vol. 6 (1980): 273–274.
7. Billie Wright Dziech and Linda Weiner, *The Lecherous Professor: Sexual Harassment on Campus* (Boston: Beacon Press, 1984), p. 25.
8. Ibid., p. 77.
9. William B. Sanders, *Rape and Women's Identity,* pp. 50–51.

CHAPTER 10 *Prejudice*

1. Ralph Ellison, *Invisible Man* (New York: Vintage, 1972), p. 3.
2. Ibid., p. 4.
3. Ibid., p. 14.
4. Ibid.
5. Marilyn Frye, "Male Chauvinism—A Conceptual Analysis," in Mary Vetterling-Braggin (ed.), *Sexist Language: A Modern Philosophical Analysis* (Totowa, NJ: Littlefield, Adams, 1981), p. 17.
6. Ibid., p. 18.
7. Ludwig Wittgenstein, *Philosophical Investigations,* 3rd ed., trans. G. E. M. Anscombe (New York: Macmillan, 1953), p. 115.
8. Francis Bacon, *Novum Organum,* Thomas Fowler (ed.) (Oxford: Oxford University Press, 1889).
9. Quoted, from a study done by Sally Hacker and Joseph Schneider in 1972, in Casey Miller and Kate Swift, *Words and Women* (Garden City, NY: Anchor, 1976), p. 21.
10. Richard A. Wasserstrom, "On Racism and Sexism," in Richard A. Wasserstrom (ed.), *Today's Moral Problems,* 3rd ed. (New York: Macmillan, 1985), p. 7.
11. Ibid., p. 21.
12. Ibid., p. 28.
13. Elizabeth H. Wolgast, *Equality and the Rights of Women* (Ithaca, NY: Cornell University Press, 1980), pp. 33–34.
14. Charles S. Farrell, "Black Students Seen Facing 'New Racism' on Many Campuses," *The Chronicle of Higher Education,* vol. 34, no. 20 (January 27, 1988): 1.

CHAPTER 11 *Ridicule, Rudeness, and Snobbery*

1. *Newsweek,* October 11, 1976.
2. James Boswell, *The Life of Samuel Johnson* (New York: Dell, 1960), p. 121. First published in 1791.
3. Alan Dundes, *Cracking Jokes: Studies of Sick Humor Cycles and Stereotypes* (Berkeley, CA: Ten Speed Press, 1987), pp. 23, 125.
4. Ibid., p. 16.
5. Ibid., pp. 17–18.
6. Ronald de Sousa, *The Rationality of Emotion* (Cambridge, MA: MIT Press, 1987), p. 293.
7. Thomas Hobbes, *Of Human Nature,* Chapter 9, printed in L. A. Selby-Bigge (ed.), *British Moralists,* Vol. II (New York: Dover, 1965), p. 299. More recently, Roger Scruton's account of humor retains the idea of putting down (or "devaluing"), while dropping the idea of feeling superior. See his "Laughter," in John Morreall (ed.), *The Philosophy of Laughter and Humor* (Albany, NY: State University of New York Press, 1987), pp. 156–171.
8. Arthur Schopenhauer, *The World as Will and Representation,* trans. E. F. J. Payne (New York: Dover, 1969), Vol. I, pp. 58–61, Vol. II, pp. 91–101. Compare Mike W. Martin, "Humor and Aesthetic Enjoyment of Incongruities," in John Morreall, *The Philosophy of Laughter and Humor,* pp. 172–186.
9. John Rawls, *A Theory of Justice* (Cambridge, MA: Harvard University Press, 1971), pp. 337–338.
10. William M. Thackeray, *The Book of Snobs,* in W. P. Trent and J. B. Henneman (eds.), *The Complete Works of William M. Thackeray,* Vol. XIV (New York: Crowell, undated), p. 63.
11. Spiro T. Agnew, speech given on October 19, 1969, in New Orleans, Louisiana, printed in John R. Coyne, Jr., *The Impudent Snobs: Agnew vs. the Intellectual Establishment* (New Rochelle, NY: Arlington House, 1972), p. 248.
12. Quoted by John R. Coyne, Jr., ibid., p. 38.
13. Alan Dundes, *Cracking Jokes,* p. 53.
14. Ibid., p. 105.
15. Ibid., p. 74.
16. Elizabeth Mehren, "'New Sexism': Men Cry Foul at Male Jokes," *Los Angeles Times* (December 14, 1987), part V, p. 1.
17. Judith N. Shklar, "What Is Wrong with Snobbery?" In *Ordinary Vices* (Cambridge, MA: Harvard University Press, 1984), pp. 135–136.

CHAPTER 12 *Envy and Jealousy*

1. John Rawls, *A Theory of Justice* (Cambridge, MA: Harvard University Press, 1971), p. 531.
2. Friedrich Nietzsche, *Thus Spoke Zarathustra,* trans. Walter Kaufmann (New York: Penguin Books, 1978), p. 100.
3. José Ortega y Gasset, *The Revolt of the Masses* (New York: Norton, 1957), p. 65.
4. John Rawls, *A Theory of Justice,* p. 534.

5. Robert Nozick, *Anarchy, State, and Utopia* (New York: Basic Books, 1974), p. 245.

6. Max Scheler, *Ressentiment,* trans. William W. Holdheim (New York: Schocken, 1972), p. 48.

7. Immanuel Kant, "Proper Self-Respect" and "Jealousy and its Offspring—Envy and Grudge," in *Lectures on Ethics,* trans. Louis Infield (New York: Harper & Row, 1963), pp. 126–129, 215–223.

8. Friedrich Nietzsche, *The Gay Science,* trans. Walter Kaufmann (New York: Vintage, 1974), p. 233.

9. Richard Taylor, *Having Love Affairs* (Buffalo, NY: Prometheus, 1982), pp. 142–143.

10. Ibid., p. 146.

11. Jerome Neu, "Jealous Thoughts," in Amèlie Oksenberg Rorty (ed.), *Explaining Emotions* (Berkeley, CA: University of California Press, 1980), pp. 454–455.

12. John Sabini and Maury Silver, *Moralities of Everyday Life* (Oxford: Oxford University Press, 1982), p. 29.

13. Henry Fairlie, *The Seven Deadly Sins Today* (Notre Dame, IN: University of Notre Dame Press, 1979), pp. 67–68.

14. Immanuel Kant, *Lectures on Ethics,* p. 218.

PART FOUR   *Sexual Morality*

1. Michel Foucault, *The History of Sexuality,* Vol. I, trans. Robert Hurley (New York: Vintage, 1980), pp. 155–156.

CHAPTER 13   *Sex and Love*

1. Marilyn French, *The Women's Room* (New York: Summit Books, 1977), pp. 361–362.

2. Ibid., p. 407.

3. Erich Fromm, *The Art of Loving* (New York: Harper & Row, 1956), pp. 38–39.

4. Shulamith Firestone, *The Dialectic of Sex: The Case for Feminist Revolution* (New York: Morrow, 1970), p. 145.

5. Ibid., p. 149.

6. Russell Vannoy, *Sex Without Love: A Philosophical Exploration* (Buffalo, NY: Prometheus, 1980), p. 26.

7. Roger Scruton, *Sexual Desire: A Moral Philosophy of the Erotic* (New York: Free Press, 1986), p. 30.

8. Ibid., p. 251.

9. Ibid., p. 337.

10. Ibid., p. 87.

11. Robert C. Solomon, "Love and Feminism," in Robert Baker and Frederick Elliston (eds.), *Philosophy and Sex,* rev. edition (Buffalo, NY: Prometheus, 1984), p. 66.

12. Stendhal (Marie Henri Beyle), *Love,* trans. Gilbert and Suzanne Sale (New York: Penguin Books, 1975), p. 60.

CHAPTER 14   *Marriage and Adultery*

1. Shere Hite, *Women and Love: A Cultural Revolution in Progress* (New York: Knopf, 1987), p. 325.
2. Ibid.
3. John McMurtry, "Monogamy: A Critique," in Robert Baker and Frederick Elliston (eds.), *Philosophy and Sex,* rev. ed. (Buffalo, NY: Prometheus, 1984), p. 111.
4. Ibid.
5. Ibid., p. 112. Italics deleted from original.
6. Ibid., p. 113.
7. Ibid., p. 112.
8. Francesca M. Cancian, *Love in America: Gender and Self-Development* (New York: Cambridge University Press, 1987), p. 3.
9. Ibid.
10. S. I. Benn, "Individuality, Autonomy and Community," in Eugene Kamenka (ed.), *Community as a Social Ideal* (London: Edward Arnold, 1982), p. 58.
11. Larry Martz, Vern E. Smith, Daniel Pedersen, Daniel Shapiro, Mark Miller, and Ginny Carroll, "God and Money," *Newsweek,* April 6, 1987, pp. 18–19.
12. Tom Morganthau, Margaret Garrard Warner, Howard Fineman, and Erik Calonius, "The Sudden Fall of Gary Hart," *Newsweek,* May 18, 1987, p. 23.
13. Richard Taylor, *Having Love Affairs* (Buffalo, NY: Prometheus, 1982), p. 12.
14. Ibid., p. 138.
15. Ibid., p. 158.
16. Ibid., p. 59.

CHAPTER 15   *Homosexuality and Homophobia*

1. Frederick Suppe, "Curing Homosexuality," in Robert Baker and Frederick Elliston (eds.), *Philosophy and Sex,* rev. ed. (Buffalo, NY: Prometheus, 1984), pp. 394–395.
2. Malcolm Boyd, *Take Off the Masks* (Philadelphia: New Society, 1984), p. 78.
3. Ibid., p. 5.
4. Martina Navratilova and George Vecsey, *Martina* (New York: Ballantine Books, 1985), p. 154.
5. Lev. 18:22, King James version.
6. Rom. 1:26–27, King James version.
7. St. Thomas Aquinas, *On the Truth of the Catholic Faith,* Book 3: *Providence,* Part 1, trans. Vernon J. Bourke (New York: Doubleday, 1956). Quoted in Robert Baker and Frederick Elliston (eds.), *Philosophy and Sex,* rev. ed. (Buffalo, NY: Prometheus, 1984), p. 15.
8. Roger Scruton, *Sexual Desire: A Moral Philosophy of the Erotic* (New York: Free Press, 1986), pp. 307–308.
9. Adrienne Rich, "Compulsory Heterosexuality and Lesbian Existence," *SIGNS: Journal of Women in Culture and Society,* vol. 5 (1980). Reprinted in Catharine R. Stimpson and Ethel Spector (eds.), *Women: Sex and Sexuality* (Chicago: University of Chicago Press, 1980), pp. 81–82.

CHAPTER 16 *Pornography and Fantasy*

1. Helen E. Longino, "Pornography, Oppression, and Freedom: A Closer Look," in Laura Lederer (ed.), *Take Back the Night: Women on Pornography* (New York: Morrow, 1980), p. 42.
2. Robin Morgan, "Theory and Practice: Pornography and Rape," in Laura Lederer (ed.), *Take Back the Night,* pp. 134–140.
3. Beverly LaBelle, "*Snuff*—The Ultimate Woman-Hating," in Laura Lederer (ed.), *Take Back the Night,* p. 274.
4. Nancy Friday, *My Secret Garden: Women's Sexual Fantasies* (New York: Pocket Books, 1973), p. 109.
5. Matt. 5:28–29, King James version.
6. Herbert Fingarette, "Real Guilt and Neurotic Guilt," in *On Responsibility* (New York: Basic Books, 1967), pp. 91–94.
7. "Excerpts from the Minneapolis Ordinance," in Varda Burstyn (ed.), *Women Against Censorship* (Vancouver, British Columbia: Douglas & McIntyre, 1985), pp. 206–207.

PART FIVE *Caring Relationships*

1. David Hume, *An Enquiry Concerning the Principles of Morals,* edited by J. B. Schneewind (Indianapolis, IN: Hackett, 1983), pp. 16–17.

CHAPTER 17 *Parents and Children*

1. Franz Kafka, *Letter to His Father* (New York: Schocken, 1966), p. 7.
2. Ibid., p. 21.
3. Ibid., p. 89.
4. Kenneth Keniston and The Carnegie Council on Children, *All Our Children: The American Family Under Pressure* (New York: Harcourt Brace Jovanovich, 1977), pp. 17–18.
5. Natalie Abrams, "Problems in Defining Child Abuse and Neglect," in Onora O'Neill and William Ruddick (eds.), *Having Children* (New York: Oxford University Press, 1979), p. 160.
6. Jane English, "What Do Grown Children Owe Their Parents?" in Onora O'Neill and William Ruddick (eds.), *Having Children* (New York: Oxford University Press, 1979), p. 351.

CHAPTER 18 *Friendship*

1. Lillian Hellman, *Pentimento* (New York: New American Library, 1974), p. 93.
2. Ibid., p. 96.
3. Ibid., p. 95.
4. Ibid., p. 85.
5. Montaigne, "Of Friendship," in *The Complete Essays of Montaigne,* trans. Donald M. Frame (Stanford, CA: Stanford University Press, 1971), pp. 141–142.

6. E. M. Forster, "What I Believe," in *Two Cheers for Democracy* (New York: Harcourt, Brace & World, 1951), pp. 68–69.

7. James Rachels, *The Elements of Moral Philosophy* (New York: Random House, 1986), p. 11.

8. Lawrence A. Blum, *Friendship, Altruism and Morality* (Boston: Routledge & Kegan Paul, 1980), p. 76.

9. Aristotle, *Nichomachean Ethics,* trans. W. D. Ross, in Richard McKeon (ed.), *The Basic Works of Aristotle* (New York: Random House, 1941), p. 1093.

CHAPTER 19   *Work*

1. Studs Terkel, *Working* (New York: Avon Books, 1975), p. 1.

2. Ibid., pp. 1–2.

3. Ibid., p. 2.

4. Ibid.

5. Ibid., p. 390.

6. Ibid., p. 393.

7. Karl Marx, *Economic and Philosophical Manuscripts,* in Erich Fromm, *Marx's Concept of Man,* trans. T. B. Bottomore (New York: Ungar, 1966), p. 98.

8. Quoted from the writings of the Reverend Richard Baxter by Max Weber in *The Protestant Ethic and the Spirit of Capitalism,* trans. Talcott Parsons (New York: Scribners, 1958), p. 162.

9. Gilbert C. Meilaender, "Friendship and Vocation," Chapter 5 of *Friendship* (Notre Dame, IN: University of Notre Dame Press, 1981), p. 97.

10. Craig K. Ihara, "Collegiality as a Professional Virtue," in Albert Flores (ed.), *Professional Ideals* (Belmont, CA: Wadsworth, 1988), p. 60.

11. Josiah Royce, *The Philosophy of Loyalty,* excerpts in John K. Roth (ed.), *The Philosophy of Josiah Royce* (Indianapolis, IN: Hackett, 1982), p. 279.

12. Ibid., p. 281.

13. John Ladd, "Loyalty," in Paul Edwards (ed.), *The Encyclopedia of Philosophy,* Vol. 5 (New York: Macmillan, 1967), p. 98.

14. Cf. Ronald Duska, *Whistleblowing and Employee Loyalty,* excerpts in Joshua Halberstam (ed.), *Virtues and Values* (Englewood Cliffs, NJ: Prentice-Hall, 1988), pp. 246–251.

15. From Dan Applegate's memo, quoted by Paul Eddy, Elaine Potter, and Bruce Page, *Destination Disaster* (New York: New York Times Book Co., 1976), p. 185.

16. Norman S. Care, "Career Choice," *Ethics,* 94 (1984):298.

17. Hastings Rashdall, "Vocation," Chapter 4 of *The Theory of Good and Evil,* Vol. 2 (Oxford: Clarendon Press, 1907), pp. 123–124.

18. Cf. Peter A. French, *Ethics in Government* (Englewood Cliffs, NJ: Prentice-Hall, 1983), pp. 5–6.

CHAPTER 20 *Community*

1. Brian O'Connell, "What Colleges Ought to Do to Instill a Voluntary Spirit in Young Adults," *The Chronicle of Higher Education* (April 15, 1987):104.
2. Jane Addams, *Twenty Years at Hull-House* (New York: New American Library, 1981), p. 92.
3. Ibid.
4. Robert N. Bellah, Richard Madsen, William M. Sullivan, Ann Swidler, and Steven M. Tipton, *Habits of the Heart: Individualism and Commitment in American Life* (Berkeley, CA: University of California, 1985), p. 162.
5. Peter Singer, "Famine, Affluence, and Morality," in William Aiken and Hugh La Follette (eds.), *World Hunger and Moral Obligation* (Englewood Cliffs, NJ: Prentice-Hall, 1977), p. 24.
6. Ibid., p. 26.
7. Immanuel Kant, *The Doctrine of Virtue,* trans. Mary J. Gregor (Philadelphia: University of Pennsylvania Press, 1964), p. 21.
8. David Heyd, *Supererogation* (Cambridge: Cambridge University Press, 1982), p. 115.
9. James D. Wallace, *Virtues and Vices* (Ithaca, NY: Cornell University Press, 1978), p. 135.
10. Mark 12:41–44, King James version.
11. Brian O'Connell, "What Colleges Ought to Do," p. 104.
12. Ralph Waldo Emerson, "Self-Reliance," in Robert Bellah et al. (eds.), *Individualism and Commitment in American Life* (New York: Harper & Row, 1987), p. 59.
13. John O'Connor, "Philanthropy and Selfishness," in Ellen Frankel Paul et al. (eds.), *Beneficence, Philanthropy, and the Public Good* (New York: Basil Blackwell, 1987), p. 114.

CHAPTER 21 *Animals*

1. John Steinbeck, *Travels with Charley* (New York: Bantam Books, 1963), p. 8.
2. Ibid., p. 163.
3. Ibid., p. 33.
4. Ibid., p. 9.
5. René Descartes, *Discourse on Method,* excerpts printed in Tom Regan and Peter Singer (eds.), *Animal Rights and Human Obligations* (Englewood Cliffs, NJ: Prentice-Hall, 1976), p. 62.
6. Benedict de Spinoza, *The Ethics,* trans. R. H. M. Elwes (New York: Dover, 1955), Proposition 37, note 1.
7. Jeremy Bentham, *Introduction to the Principles of Morals and Legislation,* Chapter 17 (New York: Hafner, 1948), p. 311n. First published in 1789.
8. Immanuel Kant, "Duties Towards Animals and Spirits," in *Lectures on Ethics,* trans. Louis Infield (New York: Harper & Row, 1963), pp. 239–240.
9. Peter Singer, *Animal Liberation* (New York: Avon Books, 1977), p. 7.
10. Ibid., p. ix.

11. Mary Midgley, *Animals and Why They Matter* (Athens, GA: University of Georgia Press, 1984), p. 31.
12. II Sam. xii:3, King James version. Discussed in Mary Midgley, *Animals,* p. 116.
13. R. Gordon Cummings, *Five Years of a Hunter's Life in the Far Interior of South Africa* (1850). Quoted in Richard Carrington, *Elephants* (Chatto & Windus, 1958), p. 154; in Mary Midgley, *Animals,* pp. 14–15.
14. Jeremy Bentham, *Introduction to the Principles of Morals and Legislation,* Chapter 17. Quoted in Peter Singer, *Animal Liberation,* pp. 218–219.
15. Peter Singer, *Animal Liberation,* pp. 121–128.
16. Ibid., pp. 47–48.

Index

A

Abortion, 28, 33
Abraham and Isaac, 15–16, 33
Abrams, Natalie, 245
Absolute duties, 57, 59, 68
Adam and Eve, 115–16
Addams, Jane, 276–78
Adler, Alfred, 83
Adultery, 117, 205–8, 230
Agape, 22
Agnew, Spiro, 169
AIDS (Acquired Immune Deficiency
     Syndrome)
   and homosexuality, 217, 221
   lies about, 70
   and sexual morality, 188, 198
Alcohol and drug abuse
   children reporting parents for, 33, 252
   and rape, 149
   and self-deception, 3, 95–96
   types of, 87–88, 90
   and weakness of will, 110, 117
Altruism. *See* Benevolence
Amadeus, 174–75, 179
American Psychiatric Association, 217
Animals, 4, 287–98
   attitudes toward, 289–91
   as caring and reasoning, 44
   as companions, 287–89, 294–95
   rights of, 291–93
   speciesism, 293–94
Apartheid, 122–23, 130. *See also* Mandela,
     Nelson and Winnie; South Africa
Aquinas, St. Thomas, 45–46, 215

Aristotle
   and contextual reasoning, 60
   on courage, 124
   on friendship, 254, 261
   theory of virtue, 37, 40–45, 50
   on weakness of will, 110
Austin, J. L., 299n.6
Authenticity, 6–7, 14, 48, 93
Autonomy
   and authenticity, 6–7
   and children, 245–46
   Kant's view of, 57–59, 139
   moral, 4, 18, 30–32, 48, 148
   personal, 139–41, 148

B

Bacon, Francis, 155
Baier, Annette C., 300n.7
Bakker, Jim and Tammy, 205–6
Bayles, Michael, 147
Bellah, Robert, 278–79
Benevolence
   and career choice, 270–72
   and community service, 276–85
   and friendship, 256–58, 260–61
   in giving, 36
   Hume's view of, 46–47
   as justification for lying, 60
   King's view of, 22
Benn, S. I., 204–5
Bentham, Jeremy, 290, 295–97
Blum, Lawrence, 260–61
Boswell, James, 164

Boyd, Malcolm, 213–14
Brandt, Richard B., 66–69
Brownmiller, Susan, 144–45
Butler, Joseph, 98–99, 103
Butz, Earl, 163–64, 170

C

Cancian, Francesca M., 204
Care, Norman, 271–73
Caring relationships
  animals and people, 287–97
  in communities, 276–85
  defined, 239
  friendship, 254–61
  vs. justice, 24–30
  parents and children, 241–52
  at work, 263–74
Carter, Jimmy, 274
Categorical vs. hypothetical imperatives, 58–59
Challenger, 273
Character
  giving style to one's, 114
  moral substance of people, 10
  relation to conduct, 56
  and theories of virtue, 35–54
  as topic for ethics, 4
Charity
  and community, 276–85
  Jesus on, 23–24
  and motives, 36
Cheating, 33
Child abuse, 241–46
Children. *See* Parents and children
Choosing moralities, 9
Coercion, 58, 139–41. *See also* Rape; Sexual Harassment
Collegiality, 267–68
Community, 276–85
  amount owed to, 279–89
  individualism and, 278–79
  Jane Addams on, 277
  moral, 63
  Robert Bellah on, 278–79
Compromise, 131
Conflict, psychological, 38–39, 113–15, 118
Counselors, moral, 8, 31
Courage, 122–32
  acts vs. patterns of, 122–24
  Aquinas on, 45
  Aristotle on, 40–42

  definition of, 125–27
  good of, 127–29
  MacIntyre on, 49
  physical vs. intellectual, 123
  Pincoffs on, 50–51
  Plato on, 38
  Sartre on, 7
  and self-deception, 99
Creativity, moral, 7, 18–32, 179–80
Cruelty, 141–49
Customs, 11, 16, 25–27, 47

D

DC-10 crash, 269–70
De Sousa, Ronald, 165
Dean, John, 164
Deception, 56–57, 94. *See also* Lying; Self-deception
Declaration of Independence, 23, 61–62
Descartes, René, 289–90, 292
Development, moral, 24–33
Dilemmas, moral
  defined, 5
  Heinz's, 25–26, 28
  in professions, 269–70, 273–74
  resolution of, 8
Divorce, 23, 210. *See also* Marriage
Doctrine of the Mean, 40–45, 129–30
Donnerstein, Edward, 233
Dostoevsky, Fyodor, 7, 71, 81, 100–101
Drug abuse. *See* Alcohol and drug abuse
Durant, Will, 108–9, 113
Duties
  absolute, 57, 59
  childrens', 247–50
  not to harm oneself, 79–90
  parents', 243–47
  perfect vs. imperfect, 279–80
  prima facie, 59–61
  universal, 58
Duty ethics
  and autonomy, 141
  defined, 56
  and harming oneself, 80–81
  Kant's, 57–59
  Ross's, 59–61
Dworkin, Andrea, 232–33
Dziech, Billie, 148

E

Education, 30–32, 48
Ellison, Ralph, 153–54

Emerson, Ralph Waldo, 284–85
English, Jane, 249, 251
Envy, 173–80
   creative responses to, 179–80
   defined, 173–74, 182
   particular vs. general, 174–77
   self-deceiving, 177–78
   undermining respect, 3–4
Equal Rights Amendment, 157
Equality in relationships, 197–98, 204–5
Ethics
   aims in studying, 30–32
   applied vs. general, 13–14, 47, 67–69
   defined, 4, 12
   everyday vs. social, 13–14
   goals of, 13
   of justice vs. of care, 24–30
Etiquette, 167–68
Euthyphro (in Plato's dialogue), 20, 33
Excuses, 115–18
   blame-lessening, 116
   justifying-intended
      consensus-raising, 116
      consistency-lowering, 117
   See also Rationalization; Weakness of will

F

Fairlie, Henry, 183
Faithfulness, 208
Falk, W. D., 128
Fanaticism, 129–30
Fantasies, 3, 227–31
Feelings, 6, 167
Fingarette, Herbert, 97–98, 229–30, 234–35
Finn, Huck (Mark Twain character), 120
Firestone, Shulamith, 190–91, 196–97
Forgiving, 22, 91
Forster, E. M., 258–59
Foucault, Michel, 187
French, Marilyn, 189
Freud, Sigmund
   compared to Plato, 39–40, 53–54
   on religious beliefs, 105
   on self-deception, 97
Friday, Nancy, 228–30, 234–35
Friendliness, 41–42, 261
Friendship, 254–61
   definition, 256–57
   example of, 254–56
   moral limits on, 258–59
   value of, 257–58

Fromm, Erich, 190, 196
Frye, Marilyn, 154–55

G

Gandhi, Mohandas, 22
Gauguin, Paul, 15
Gender roles, 157–60, 217
Generosity, 4, 23–24, 281–82
Genovese, Kitty, 119, 131
Gilligan, Carol
   on autonomy, 28–30, 131
   on caring vs. justice, 24–26
   and contextual reasoning, 26, 44, 60
   and Hume, 46, 54
   and nurture-nature dispute, 25, 161
   and rights, 25, 71
   and theory of moral development, 26–32
God
   Abraham-Isaac story, 15–16
   Adam and Eve story, 115–16
   belief in, 21–22, 45–46, 54
   and envy, 175
   and male pronouns, 156
   and moral reasons, 11–12
   and religious guilt, 85
   skepticism about, 7, 46
   and work ethics, 266
Good will, 58
Goods
   external and internal, 48
   intrinsic vs. instrumental, 58, 64, 141, 265–66
Gratitude
   of children toward parents, 8, 247–50
   defined, 248
   duty of, 3–4, 60, 247–50
Greek ethics, difficulties with, 44. *See also* Aristotle; Plato; Socrates
Griffin, Susan, 143
Growth, moral, 18, 24–33
Guilt
   for fantasies, 228–31
   and forgiveness, 22, 91
   irrational, 84–87

H

Happiness
   Aristotle on, 40
   Freud on, 39
   Mill's definition of, 64–65
   Plato on, 39

Hare, R. M., 110–11
Harming oneself, 79–91
  drug abuse, 87–89
  duties against, 79–80
  irrational shame and guilt, 84–87
  masochism, 81–82
  servility, 83–84
Hart, Gary, 205–6
Haworth, Lawrence, 140–41
Hawthorne, Nathaniel, 86–87
Health, moral, 37–40
Heinz's Dilemma, 25–26, 28
Hellman, Lillian, 254–56, 259–60
Heyd, David, 281–82
Hite, Shere, 201
Hitler, Adolf, 5, 18, 94–95, 120, 269
Hobbes, Thomas, 166
Homophobia, 212, 219–21
Homosexuality, 212–22
  defined, 212
  and homophobia, 219–21
  and promiscuity, 218–19
  and relations with parents, 252
  and unnaturalness, 214–16
Honesty
  and authenticity, 7–8
  and categorical imperatives, 59
  MacIntyre on, 49
  and moral education, 31
  with oneself, 77
  Pincoffs on, 50–51
  and self-deception, 93–105
  and Socrates, 19–21
  See also Deception; Lying; Stealing
Hughes, John, 147–48
Human nature, 37, 47, 53
Hume, David, 46–47, 54, 239, 277
Humility
  Christian, 45
  Kant on, 75–76
  vs. servility, 83
  Socrates as a model of, 19–21
Humor, ethics of, 3, 161–67, 170–71
Huxley, Aldous, 88
Hypocrisy
  and integrity, 129–30
  and self-deception, 98–99
  and snobbery, 169

I

Ideals of love, 195–96, 247, 251
Incest, 243–44, 246–47

Integrity, 129–30, 194

J

Jealousy, 174, 180–84, 207
Jefferson, Thomas, 61
Jesus, 23–24, 215, 228–29, 234–35, 282
Johnson, Samuel, 99–100
Johnson, Sonia, 101–2
Jokes, 3, 161–67, 170–71
Justice
  Gilligan and Kohlberg on, 24–30
  King on, 21–22
  MacIntyre on, 49
  Plato on, 38–39
  Ross on, 60

K

Kafka, Franz, 241–42, 244, 249–50
Kant, Immanuel
  absolute duties, 57, 68, 70–71
  on animals, 290–92, 294–95
  on duties to oneself, 75–76, 79–80
  duty ethics of, 57–59, 68–69
  on envy, 183
  on impartiality and friendship, 257, 260
  and kingdom of ends, 276
  on perfect vs. imperfect duties, 279–80
  and supererogation, 281
Kennedy, John F., 131
Kierkegaard, Søren, 15–16, 119
King, Martin Luther, 18, 21–23, 32–33, 35–36, 45, 135–36, 161
Kohlberg, Lawrence, 24–33, 43, 71, 131

L

LaBelle, Beverly, 227
Ladd, John, 268–70
Language and prejudice, 155–57, 161–67
Laws, 11, 25–27
Libertarians, 62, 69
Liberty rights, 62
Locke, John, 61–62, 68–69
Love
  humanitarian, 190
  ideals of, 195–96, 247, 251
  King on, 21–22
  parents and children, 241, 250
  romantic, 190
  sexual, 189–99

Love (*continued*)
  true, 190, 195–96, 198, 209
Loyalties, 9, 268–70
Lying
  defined, 56–57
  discussion cases, 70
  as failure to respect people, 57–59
  to oneself, 95–96, 100–101
  to parents, 68
  to prevent bad consequences, 64, 70–71
  prima facie duty against, 59
  to protect privacy, 62
  and rule-utilitarianism, 66

M

MacIntyre, Alasdair, 47–59
MacKinnon, Catharine, 232–33
McMurtry, John, 201–6, 208
Malamuth, Neil, 233
Mandela, Nelson and Winnie, 122–23, 127
Marriage, 200–211
  criticisms of, 201–5
  and extramarital affairs, 205–8
  as moral issue, 200–201
  open, 209
  traditional, 200
Marx, Karl, 105, 265–66
Masochism, 81–82
Masturbation, 108, 113
May, Larry, 147–48
Mean, Doctrine of, 40–45, 129–30
Meilaender, Gilbert, 266
Meiland, Jack, 104–5
Melden, A. I., 62–63, 68–69
Mele, Alfred, 112
Midgley, Mary, 33–34, 293–95
Mill, John Stuart, 64–66, 68–69, 140–41
Montaigne, Michel de, 258–59
Morality
  character vs. conduct, 4
  characterized, 10
  complexity of, 5, 15
  creativity in, 18–24
  everyday vs. social, 3
  relative, 11, 16
  and religion, 11–12
  and rules, 10
Morgan, Robin, 224
Mozart, Wolfgang Amadeus, 174–75, 179
Murdoch, Iris, 3

N

Narrative quest, 48–49
Navratilova, Martina, 214
Nazis
  Albert Speer, 94–95
  cruelty of, 150
  Field Marshal Rommel, 125–26, 130
  and Lillian Hellman, 255–56
  loyalty to, 269
  lying to, 59, 68
  and Sartre's example, 5–6, 8, 11
  and Simone Weil, 82
  See also Hitler
New, Jerome, 181–82
New Testament
  on fantasies, 228–29, 234–35
  on giving, 23, 282
  on homosexuality, 215
Newman, Jay, 129
Niebuhr, Reinhold, 105
Nietzsche, Friedrich, 114, 175–76, 179
Nonviolence, 22. *See also* Violence
Nozick, Robert, 176–77

O

Obscenity, 231–34
O'Connell, Brian, 284
Ortega y Gasset, José, 176
Orwell, George, 259

P

Paradoxes
  of self-deception, 95–97
  of weakness of will, 109–15
Parents and children, 241–52
  abuse and violence, 243–47
  Carnegie Council Report, 242–43
  duties of, 243–50
  Euthyphro case, 20
  Franz Kafka case, 241–42
  Sartre's case, 5–9, 15
Parks, Rosa, 21
Persons, choices among, 49–52
Philanthropy, 276–85
Plato, 11, 19–20, 35, 37–40, 53–54, 107–8
Pleasure
  and happiness, 64–65
  quality vs. quantity of, 65–66
  rational vs. irrational, 66

Pornography, 223–36
  Attorney General's Commission on, 224
  definition, 224–25
  examples of use of, 225–27
  and fantasies, 227–31
  obscenity, 231–33
  President's Commission on, 223
Practices, social, 48–49
Prejudice
  covert vs. overt, 152–53, 161–62
  education as liberating from, 30
  gender roles, 157–60
  and humor, 163–67
  and language, 155–57
  speciesism, 292–93
  stereotypes, 153–55
Pride
  Aquinas on, 45
  Aristotle on, 41
  Kant on, 75–76
Prima facie duties, 59–61
Procrastination, 119
Prudence
  Aristotle on, 43–44
  vs. courage, 128
  and morality, 79–80
Pryor, Richard, 165
Put-downs
  of oneself, 81–87, 101
  of others, 163–71

R

Rape, 139, 141–45
  date, 143–45
  immorality of, 11, 57, 143, 149
  irrational pleasures, 66
  motivations for, 142
Rashdall, Hastings, 271–73
Rationalization, 9, 94, 115
Rawls, John, 76, 135–37, 168, 176–77
Reasons, moral, 9–10
Regan, Tom, 292–93
Relativism, 11, 16
Religion
  commandment to honor parents, 247
  Freud's view of, 105
  and guilt, 85
  and homosexuality, 214–15
  and marriage, 200, 203
  and moral reasons, 11–12
  patriarchal, 101
  and virtues, 45–46

See also Bakker, Jim and Tammy; Jesus;
  King, Martin Luther; *New Testament*;
  Weil, Simone
Respect for persons, 4, 135–84
  character- vs. minimal-, 135, 148, 150
  collegiality, 267–68
  Kant on, 57–59
  parents and children, 243–47
  prejudice, 152–61
  rape, 141–45
  ridicule, 163–67
  rudeness, 167–68
  sexual harassment, 145–50
  snobbery, 168–71
Responsibility
  and authenticity, 7
  of children, 247–52
  for drug use, 87–89
  for lies, 70–71
  of parents, 243–47
  for self-deception, 97–99
Ressentiment, 177–78
Rich, Adrienne, 219
Ridicule, 163–67
Right action, theories of
  assessment of, 67–69
  duty ethics
    Kant's, 57–59
    Ross's, 59–61
  rights ethics
    Locke's, 61–62
    Melden's, 62–63
  utilitarianism
    Brandt on, 66–67
    Mill on, 63–66
Rights
  of animals, 291–93
  of children, 244–48
  Declaration of Independence, 23, 61–62
  human, 61
  liberty (negative), 62
  and self-respect, 80
  welfare (positive), 63
Rights ethics
  and autonomy, 141
  and harming oneself, 80
  Locke's, 61–62
  Melden's, 62–63
  and world hunger, 280–81
Rommel, Field Marshal, 125–26, 130
Ross, David, 59–61, 68–69
Royce, Josiah, 268
Rubin, Theodore Isaac, 83–84

Rudeness, 167–68
Russell, Bertrand, 188

S

Salieri (character in *Amadeus*), 174–75,
    179, 183
Sanders, William B., 144, 149
Sartre, Jean-Paul
    on authenticity, 6–7, 93, 192
    on choosing moralities, 9
    example of student, 5–7, 15
    MacIntyre's disagreement with, 48
    on moral creativity, 7, 18
    on nonobjectivity of moral reasons, 7, 12
    on self-deception, 7, 102
    "The Wall," 71
Scheler, Max, 178
Schopenhauer, Arthur, 166
Scruton, Roger, 193–95, 218, 220,
    305 n.7
Self-acceptance, 114, 179
Self-control, 107–9
Self-deception, 91–106
    and authenticity, 7
    as beneficial, 102
    and character, 4
    definition and tactics, 94–95
    and harming oneself, 82
    lying to oneself, 95–96, 100–101
    paradoxes of, 95–97
    and prejudice, 154–55
    repression vs. suppression, 97
    responsibility for, 97–99, 142
    and self-respect, 93, 99–103
    and weakness of will, 114–15
Self-esteem, 75–76, 99–102
Self-fulfillment
    and inner harmony, 39–40
    and marriage, 204
    and sexual love, 194–96
    and virtues, 37, 49
    and work, 30, 265–66, 271
Self-interest
    and caring, 26–30
    and love, 191–92, 204–5
    vs. selfishness, 10, 79–80, 239
    vs. selflessness, 83–84, 278
Self-respect
    and courage, 122, 127–30
    vs. harming oneself, 4, 77, 79–91
    Kant on, 58, 75–76
    and self-deception, 93, 99–103

    vs. self-esteem, 75–76, 89
    vs. servility, 83–84
    and weakness of will, 107, 113–15
Self-understanding, 39, 47–49
Servility, 83–84
Seven Deadly Sins, 46, 141, 174
Sexism, 3, 152, 154–57. *See also* Women
Sexual harassment, 139, 145–50
Sexual morality, 187–235
    adultery, 205–10
    fantasies, 227–31, 234–35
    homophobia, 212, 219–21
    homosexuality, 212–19
    marriage, 200–205
    pornography, 223–27, 231–35
    promiscuity, 218–19
    sex and love, 189–99
    traditional views of, 187
    See also Rape; Sexual harassment; Women
Shaffer, Peter, 174–75
Shame, 84–87
Shklar, Judith N., 171
Singer, Peter, 280, 291–93, 297
Slote, Michael, 303 n.13
Snobbery, 168–71, 175
Snyder, C. R., 115
Snyder, Jimmy, 161
Sociopaths, 136
Socrates
    equated knowledge and virtue, 110
    and MacIntyre's ethics, 48
    as morally creative, 18–21, 32–33
    on religion and morality, 11–12
Solomon, Robert, 91
South Africa, 11, 61, 122–23
Speciesism, 292–93
Speer, Albert, 94–96, 98, 103
Spinoza, Benedict de, 289–90, 292,
    294–95
Stanton, Elizabeth Cady, 18, 22–24, 30,
    32, 35–36, 61
Stealing, 25
Steinbeck, John, 287–89
Stendhal, 198
Stereotypes, 153–55
Supererogatory acts, 281–82
Sympathy, 46–47

T

Taylor, Richard
    on extramarital affairs, 206–10
    on jealousy, 181–82, 207–9

Temperance
  Aquinas on, 45
  Aristotle on, 41
  Plato on, 38
  See also Weakness of will
Terkel, Studs, 263–65
Terrorists, 129–30
Thackeray, William, 169
Thoreau, Henry David, 22
Tolerance, 31–32
Tools, concepts as, 14

U

Utilitarianism
  act-, 64
  and animals, 290–92
  and autonomy, 141–42
  and career choice, 271–72
  defined, 63
  and drug use, 89
  and harming oneself, 80
  and lies, 64
  rule-, 67, 247
  and world hunger, 280

V

Vannoy, Russell, 192–97
Violence
  family, 241–47
  male, 119, 131, 150
  and pornography, 223, 226–34
  and racism, 152–53
  rape, 141–45
  terrorism, 129–30
Virtue ethics, 35–53
  Aquinas's, 45–46
  Aristotle's, 37, 40–45, 50
  and community service, 281–83
  and harming oneself, 80
  and human nature, 37, 47, 53
  Hume's, 46–47
  MacIntyre's, 47–49
  Pincoffs's, 47, 49–52
  Plato's, 37–40, 44
Virtues
  artificial vs. natural, 47
  defined, 4, 35–36, 52
  dependent, 120
  Doctrine of the Unity of, 39, 53
  instrumental vs. noninstrumental, 50–51
  as involving habits, 40–41

  moral vs. intellectual, 40–41
  moral vs. nonmoral, 50–52
Volunteerism, 276–85

W

Wallace, James, 125–27, 131
Walton, Douglas, 126–28
Wasserstrom, Richard, 158–61
Weakness of will, 4, 107–21
  definition, 107–8
  excuses for, 115–18
  inner conflict, 113–15
  and integrity, 129–30
  occasional vs. habitual, 107–9
  paradoxes of, 109–15
  responses to, 113–15
  skilled vs. brute resistance to, 112
Weber, Max, 266
Weil, Simone, 82
Weiner, Linda, 148
Weitzman, Lenore, 210
Welfare rights, 63
Whistleblowing, 273
Wisdom
  Aquinas on, 45
  Aristotle on, 43–44
  Plato on, 38
Wittgenstein, Ludwig, 155, 299 n.6
Wolgast, Elizabeth, 159–61
Wollstonecraft, Mary, 23
Women
  abortion decisions, 28
  caring, ethics of, 24–32
  gender roles, 157–60
  lesbian, 212, 214
  and masochism, 81–82
  and pornography, 223–35
  and rape, 139, 141–45, 149
  rights movement, 22–23
  sexism, 3, 152, 154–57
  and sexual harassment, 139, 145–51
  See also Addams, Jane; Genovese, Kitty;
    Johnson, Sonia; Mandela, Nelson and
    Winnie; Stanton, Elizabeth Cady;
    Parks, Rosa; Weil, Simone; Woolf,
    Virginia
Woolf, Virginia, 85
Work, 263–74
  alienation, 265–66
  career choice, 270–72
  collegiality, 267–68

Work (*continued*)
   contribution to self-fulfillment, 30,
      265–66, 271
   ethics of, 265–67
   professional dilemmas, 273–74

Y

Ysais, Gregory, 123–24, 127, 131